ALSO BY MICHAEL T. KLARE

*Blood and Oil: The Dangers and Consequences of
America's Growing Dependency on Imported Petroleum*

Resource Wars: The New Landscape of Global Conflict

*Light Weapons and Civil Conflict: Controlling
the Tools of Violence*

World Security: Challenges for a New Century

*Rogue States and Nuclear Outlaws: America's
Search for a New Foreign Policy*

*Low Intensity Warfare: Counterinsurgency, Proinsurgency,
and Antiterrorism in the Eighties*

American Arms Supermarket

Supplying Repression: U.S. Support for Authoritarian Regimes Abroad

War Without End: American Planning for the Next Vietnams

RISING POWERS, SHRINKING PLANET

RISING POWERS, SHRINKING PLANET

THE NEW GEOPOLITICS OF ENERGY

MICHAEL T. KLARE

Metropolitan Books

Henry Holt and Company   New York

Metropolitan Books
Henry Holt and Company, LLC
Publishers since 1866
175 Fifth Avenue
New York, New York 10010
www.henryholt.com

Metropolitan Books® and ® are registered trademarks of
Henry Holt and Company, LLC.

Library of Congress Cataloging-in-Publication Data

Klare, Michael T., 1942–
    Rising powers, shrinking planet: the new geopolitics of energy / Michael T. Klare.—
1st ed.
        p.   cm.
    Includes bibliographical references and index.
    ISBN-13: 978-0-8050-8064-3
    ISBN-10: 0-8050-8064-3
    1. Power resources—Political aspects.   2. Energy industries—Political aspects.   3. Energy
policy.   4. Natural resources—Management.   I. Title.
HD9502. A2K524 2008
333. 79—dc22   2007047174

Henry Holt books are available for special promotions
and premiums. For details contact: Director, Special Markets.

First Edition 2008
Designed by Jo Anne Metsch
Maps by Glenn Ruga of Visual Communications

Printed in the United States of America
1   3   5   7   9   10   8   6   4   2

This book is dedicated to my students, past, present, and future, at Hampshire College and the other members of the Five College consortium—Amherst, Mount Holyoke, and Smith Colleges and the University of Massachusetts at Amherst. I am eternally grateful for your energy, enthusiasm, and inspiration.

CONTENTS

RISING POWERS,
SHRINKING PLANET

PROLOGUE:

THE UNOCAL AFFAIR

Nothing like it had ever occurred before. On June 22, 2005, a state-controlled Chinese oil company, CNOOC Limited, announced an $18.5 billion bid for the Unocal Corporation, a 115-year-old American energy firm with substantial oil and natural gas reserves in North America and Asia. The unsolicited offer—the largest ever made by a Chinese company for a foreign enterprise—sent shock waves through the international business community. It overshadowed all previous Chinese takeover bids by several billion dollars, represented China's first attempt to acquire a major American energy producer, and put CNOOC Ltd. in head-to-head competition with the Chevron Corporation—America's second biggest oil company—which had also put in a bid for Unocal. Although both sides trumpeted the financial advantages of their respective offers, in the end it was geopolitics, not superior price, that determined the outcome. Fearing the loss of valuable energy reserves to a state-backed Chinese firm, Republicans in Congress mounted a successful legislative drive to block China's acquisition of Unocal.

In the past, foreign businesses had been allowed to purchase major American energy properties—most notably in 1990, when Venezuela's state-owned oil company, Petróleos de Venezuela S.A., acquired Cities Service (now CITGO), along with its refineries and service stations.

But CNOOC's bid came at a moment when Americans were becoming increasingly anxious about China's growing economic might and the rising price of gasoline. These issues fused in the popular imagination because China had recently arrived on the scene as a major oil consumer and was already being linked to global increases in energy costs.

The battle over Unocal also coincided with the emergence of widespread American unease over the adequacy of worldwide oil supplies. Throughout the twentieth century, petroleum output had largely kept pace with rising international demand, as worldwide energy stocks remained plentiful—and affordable. Cheap oil had, in fact, fueled the global ascendancy of the United States, which seemed to reach its apogee in 1991 with the disappearance of the one other superpower of that epoch, the Soviet Union. Barely a decade later, however, America began to see its dominance challenged—not by a new Great Power rising to match it, but because of an entirely new phenomenon. Though still confident of its military superiority, the United States was faced with an imminent shrinkage in global oil supplies at the same time it was growing more reliant on imported energy—a development that forced it to depend on unfriendly (or unreliable) foreign suppliers and drove it into cutthroat competition with other oil-deficient nations like China. According to numerous energy experts, the global oil industry was no longer able to increase output in tandem with rising demand; some were even predicting an imminent downturn in production. "The world will soon start to run out of conventionally produced, cheap oil," warned Professor David L. Goodstein, a physicist at the California Institute of Technology and author of *Out of Gas*.[1] Though other analysts disputed this pessimistic outlook, Goodstein's point of view was taken up by enough experts to add urgency to the debate over Unocal's fate.

By 2005, Unocal, the object of all this agitation, was no longer a major player in America's domestic oil market, having long before sold its distinctive "Union 76" chain of service stations to ConocoPhillips. However, it still possessed large untapped oil and gas deposits in Asia and North America, making it an appealing takeover target for any company (or country) seeking additional hydrocarbon reserves as a hedge against future scarcity. With relatively few untapped fields available for exploitation, a major avenue of expansion for the energy giants lay in the acquisition of the oil and gas assets of smaller firms.[2] Claiming ownership of some 1.7 billion barrels of "oil equivalent" in proven reserves—about two-fifths actual petroleum, three-fifths natural gas—Unocal was being eyed by several energy-hungry firms in the United States and abroad. That its largest deposits were located in Asia, the fastest-growing segment of the global energy market, only added to its appeal.[3]

The bid from CNOOC Ltd. came as Unocal's future seemed decided. In April 2005, Chevron had entered the game with a $16.5 billion offer, outbidding all previous contenders, and few analysts doubted that the deal would sail through to completion. Some even hinted that Chevron was paying more than Unocal was worth, so desperate were its officers to acquire new hydrocarbon assets at a time when the company was extracting more oil and gas from its existing reserves each year than was being replenished through new discoveries.[4] In a February 2005 speech widely viewed as a turning point in the history of the U.S. oil industry, Chevron CEO David O'Reilly told senior associates it was no longer possible to assume that global hydrocarbon reserves would keep growing indefinitely and that Chevron's aging fields would be adequately replaced with newfound deposits. Seen in this light, Chevron's inflated offer for Unocal's untapped supplies seemed entirely logical.[5]

As expected, Chevron's bid quickly received U.S. government approval. Then, with the final vote on the merger by Unocal's shareholders only six weeks away, CNOOC entered the picture. Many at Chevron's San Ramon, California, headquarters and in government offices in Washington were understandably shocked. "Capital Nearly Speechless on Big China Bid," read a *New York Times* headline. "Administration officials and many lawmakers were almost tongue-tied about the implications of the sale," the article continued. While American officials had long spoken in general terms of the benefits of increased Sino-American trade, the *Times* noted, none of them had remotely considered that a Chinese firm would seek ownership of U.S. energy assets considered vital to the economy.[6]

For its part, CNOOC Ltd. emphasized the purely commercial aspects of the transaction. An offshoot of the government-controlled China National Offshore Oil Corporation—both the parent and subsidiary are known as CNOOC—it had long sought to establish collaborative ties with foreign energy firms and prided itself on its Western-style management approach.[7] Its chairman, Fu Chengyu, stressed this philosophy in a letter to Unocal executives, pointing out that his company's "friendly, all-cash proposal is a superior offer for Unocal shareholders."[8] Fu also promised to retain all of Unocal's U.S.-based employees, and to make other concessions to Unocal shareholders.[9]

Suddenly enmeshed in a high-stakes bidding war with a dollar-rich foreign company, Chevron immediately tried to derail the Chinese offer. Rather than outmatch it, as market rules would seem to dictate, Chevron launched a political counteroffensive. First, it requested that the federal government carefully weigh the geopolitical implications of the sale to a Chinese government-owned firm, which ensured a lengthy assessment process; second, it informed Unocal stockholders that such a review—which would commence only if Unocal accepted the Chinese offer—would surely drag on for months and could result in CNOOC's disqualification and the possible devaluation of Unocal's stocks.

To press its case in Washington, Chevron put together a formidable team of lobbyists and public relations operatives. Among them were Wayne L. Berman, a key figure in the Federalist Group, a Republican lobbying organization with close ties to the Bush administration, and Drew Maloney, a top Republican lobbyist and former legislative director for Rep. Tom DeLay, the once-powerful Texas lawmaker who resigned his post after being charged with improper fundraising activities.[10] The company also relied on sympathetic members of Congress, especially Rep. Richard W. Pombo (R-Calif.), then chairman of the House Natural Resources Committee and a favored recipient of Chevron political donations.[11]

As the Unocal drama unfolded, it rapidly became apparent that this was to be a corporate battle unlike any in American history. Even though the CNOOC bid was among the largest ever offered by a foreign firm for an American company, it was the political rather than the financial aspects of the contest that dominated the headlines. In an environment in which CNOOC's offer could be characterized as a dangerous expression of Chinese determination to become a major world economic power at America's expense, it proved relatively easy to re-cast the corporate struggle as a matter of *national security,* an issue bearing on the safety and survival of the nation. Since ensuring a copi-ous supply of energy was essential for the American economy, it was argued, any action that might constrain that flow would automatically pose a threat to the country's vital security interests.[12]

This "national security" dimension was first raised in the House of Representatives on June 28, six days after CNOOC announced its bid. Republican Congressman Joe Barton of Texas, chairman of the Energy and Commerce Committee, sent a letter to President Bush calling on him to block the sale. "We urge you," the letter read, "to protect Amer-ican national security by ensuring that vital U.S. energy assets are never sold to the Chinese government."[13] Two days later, a number of Democrats joined the fray along with a sizable majority of Republi-cans. They endorsed House Resolution 344, a nonbinding measure calling on the president to conduct a thorough review of the economic and security implications of the Chinese offer. Noting that oil and nat-ural gas resources were "strategic assets," and that the global demand for energy was "at the highest levels in history," the resolution asserted that CNOOC was likely to channel Unocal's critical energy assets to the Chinese regime, jeopardizing "the national security of the United States."[14]

Opponents of the deal then sought to wield a more potent and binding instrument: the little-known Exon-Florio amendment of 1988, which authorized the executive branch to review any foreign invest-ments in this country that might have potential national security impli-cations and block those considered injurious to national interests.[15] To set the stage for such government intervention, Republican opponents of the merger organized a July 13 hearing before the House Armed Services Committee. Many of the themes that have since dominated public discussion of U.S. energy policy were raised at that meeting: that oil and natural gas resources are finite and possibly inadequate to satisfy both rising American and international needs; that China was emerging as America's most significant rival in the struggle to secure the world's untapped oil and gas reserves; and that this struggle could someday lead to violent conflict. "In a world in which [energy] resources are certainly finite, and possibly contracting," Pentagon consultant Frank J. Gaffney Jr. testified, "we will inevitably find ourselves on a collision course with Communist China, particularly if worldwide demand for oil approaches anything like the projected 60 percent growth over the next two decades."[16]

In the face of such inflammatory rhetoric, lonely voices calling for adherence to the free-trade principles that the Bush administration otherwise vociferously championed were drowned out.[17] By the end of July, a slew of bills were pending in Congress that would put every imaginable obstacle in the way of the Chinese bid, and public opinion, inflamed by sensationalist media coverage, was tilting strongly against the transaction.[18] "I didn't expect so many people would be so sensitive to this," a worried Fu Chengyu said in an interview. After all, he noted, his company was "following a system that was set up by leading Western countries, especially the U.S."[19] Fu directed his own lobbyists in Washington to redouble their efforts on the company's behalf—to little effect.

On July 26, 2005, Congressman Pombo pushed through an amendment to the Energy Policy Act, one of the Bush administration's high-priority legislative initiatives, requiring the Department of Energy and other government agencies to conduct a four-month review of China's energy policies before even commencing the review mandated by the Exon-Florio provision. Given that Unocal's shareholders were due to vote on Chevron's competing offer in just two weeks, this essentially scuttled CNOOC's bid. Recognizing that it no longer stood a chance of prevailing in what had become a savage geopolitical contest, CNOOC threw in the towel: On August 2, it announced that it was withdrawing its bid.[20] Eight days later, Unocal's shareholders voted to accept Chevron's offer.

American and Chinese analysts still refer to the Unocal Affair as a critical watershed in U.S.-China relations, establishing the limits of American tolerance of Beijing's economic aspirations—but it was far more than that. The contest offered the first window into the global fear of resource scarcity and the new geopolitics of energy that will likely accompany it. In the emerging international power system, we can expect the struggle over energy to override all other considerations, national leaders to go to extreme lengths to ensure energy sufficiency for their countries, and state authority over both domestic and foreign energy affairs to expand. Oil will cease to be primarily a trade commodity, to be bought and sold on the international market, becoming instead the preeminent strategic resource on the planet, whose acquisition, production, and distribution will increasingly absorb the time, effort, and focus of senior government and military officials.

This new system—think of it as a new international energy order—was already forming when the Unocal fight began. The players in this new order had taken on their twenty-first-century roles: Russia—once the bruised, battered, poverty-stricken loser of the Cold War—had emerged as an imperious power broker of Eurasian energy supplies; the United States—not long ago billed as the world's unchallenged superpower—had become distressingly dependent on foreign oil suppliers who, in President Bush's words, "do not share our interests";[21] rising powers China and India, with the world's fastest-growing economies, were aggressively challenging older powers in the global hunt for vital energy reserves. But CNOOC's defeat on national security grounds confirmed that a new chapter in the history of international politics had begun, one in which the pursuit and control of energy resources would be the central dynamic of world affairs, and governments—rather than private corporations and interests—would assume commanding roles.

The prospects are worrying. A world of rising powers and shrinking resources is destined to produce intense competition among an expanding group of energy-consuming nations for control over the planet's remaining reserves of hydrocarbons and other key industrial materials. To enhance their competitive stances vis-à-vis one another, energy-deficient countries may forge strategic partnerships with friendly energy-rich states, often cementing these arrangements with massive arms transfers, new or revived military alliances, and troop deployments to unstable energy-producing regions. Such moves, which are already visible on the political landscape, are a recipe for all sorts of conflicts, any of which might someday spin out of control.

The intensifying competition for energy is also changing the way policymakers are looking at our resource-stressed world. Regions that once held abundant raw materials, but have been depleted of their original natural wealth, are losing much of their geopolitical significance, while regions with untapped energy and mineral reserves have acquired sudden global significance. Central Asia, once off-limits to all but Soviet central planners, is now the site of a frenzied international hunt for oil and natural gas; Africa, at one time prized for its rubber and copper ore, then largely abandoned and forgotten, is being pursued again with a vengeance by the major energy producers.

Global climate change, closely connected to the soaring use of hydrocarbon energy supplies, was barely on policymakers' radar when the Unocal Affair erupted. But it, too, has now entered the equation. While the public is conscious of the dangers to the planet posed by rising sea levels, growing desertification, and increasingly powerful storms, there is less awareness of the perils climate change holds for the procurement of energy supplies: Greater hurricane and typhoon activity will endanger oil and gas drilling in exposed offshore areas; diminished rainfall and the loss of glacier-fed rivers will reduce water flow into many hydroelectric dams; violent storms will destroy refineries and electrical grids; and higher temperatures will boost the demand for air-conditioning. All this will ultimately add to the mounting pressure on national leaders to satisfy their countries' energy needs at whatever financial or military price.

Clearly, the United States and Chevron were the victors in the 2005 tussle over Unocal. American and Chinese leaders fully recognized, however, that this was but one battle among many in the emerging world order of the twenty-first century. If anything, senior officials of both countries saw the Unocal Affair as the opening encounter in a long, potentially brutal fight over vital sources of energy. Some of these engagements, it was understood in both capitals, would be won by the Americans and some by the Chinese, but the competition itself would be relentless—especially since other energy-hungry states, including India, Japan, and the European powers, were already entering the fray. The resulting power struggle, in every sense of the word, will surely prove to be the defining characteristic of the new century.

1

ALTERED STATES

t was not supposed to turn out this way. When the Cold War ended in 1990, American policymakers generally assumed that the United States would henceforth enjoy a position of unchallenged preponderance. It would be secure in its "sole superpower" status by virtue of its unquestioned military superiority and the absence of credible competitors. Military prowess had always proved the determining factor in anointing global champions in the past and would—so the thinking went—continue to do so in the future. "For America, this is a time of unrivaled military power, economic promise, and cultural influence," then Texas governor George W. Bush declared in September 1999. Given our overpowering strength, he asserted, the United States had an extraordinary opportunity to extend its dominant position "into the far realm of the future."[1] But once he assumed the mantle of the presidency and sought to employ this great strength in extending American power around the world, he discovered that military superiority does not constitute the decisive, or even necessarily the leading, determinant of global paramountcy in this troubled new era. Other factors have come to rival military power in importance, and one—energy—has acquired unexpectedly vast significance.

In this new, challenging political landscape, the possession of potent military arsenals can be upstaged by the ownership of mammoth reserves of oil, natural gas, and other sources of primary energy. Hence, Russia, which escaped from the Cold War era in a shattered, demoralized condition, has reemerged as a major actor in the international arena by virtue of its colossal energy resources. For all its military might, the United States has, in contrast, sometimes found itself reduced to cajoling its foreign oil suppliers—including long-term allies such as Saudi Arabia—to increase their petroleum output in order to slow the upward spiral in energy prices.[2] The "sole superpower" has, in short, found itself scrambling—on the battlefield, on global trading floors, and in diplomatic back rooms—to somehow come to terms with what Sen. Richard G. Lugar (R-Ind.) has termed "petro-superpowers"— nations that wield disproportionate power in the international system by virtue of their superior energy reserves.[3]

Other major energy-consuming nations have also been forced to adjust to this changing landscape. China, which enjoys enormous economic clout because of its enviable balance-of-payments position—in late 2007 its foreign currency reserves stood at a staggering $1.4 trillion—is nonetheless becoming ever more dependent on imported petroleum and so must scour the world for available supplies. Japan, with the world's second largest economy—yet even more dependent on imported energy supplies than China—has found itself locked in fierce competition with Beijing for access to some of the same overseas reserves.

On the other side of the ledger, energy-rich states like Kazakhstan and Nigeria have come to enjoy greater leverage in world affairs, attracting a constant stream of high-level visitors from energy-consuming nations—often bearing promises of investment financing, military aid, and other forms of largess. Nursultan Nazarbayev, the autocratic president of Kazakhstan, has been a much-lauded guest in Beijing, Moscow, and Washington, while his country has been showered with arms and other military equipment by all three—surely a rare feat in the annals of military diplomacy. Equally telling, the outspoken president of Venezuela, Hugo Chávez, has appeared immune to U.S. retaliation despite his frequent verbal attacks on the Bush administration and his close association with the leaders of "pariah" states such as Cuba, Iran, and Syria. (For all the invective hurled between the two countries, Venezuela continues to supply the United States with about 10 percent of its imported oil, some 1.4 million barrels per day.[4])

Why has energy come to play such a pivotal role in world affairs? To begin with, its continued availability—in great profusion—has never been as critical to the healthy operation of the global economy. Energy is required to keep the factories humming, power the cities and suburbs that house the world's rising population, and produce the crops that feed the planet. Most important, petroleum products are utterly essential to sustain the international sinews of globalization—the planes, trains, trucks, and ships that carry goods and people from one region of the planet to another. According to the U.S. Department of Energy (DoE), world energy output must increase by 57 percent over the next quarter century—from approximately 450 to 700 quadrillion British thermal units—in order to satisfy anticipated international demand.[5] Without this additional energy, the world economy will fall into recession or depression, the globalization project will fail, and the planet could descend into chaos.

But the wheels of industry are not the only ones to slow without an abundant supply of energy; military forces are equally dependent on a copious infusion of critical fuels. For major powers like the United States that rely on airpower and mechanized ground forces to prevail in conflict, the need for petroleum products multiplies with each new advance in weapons technology. During World War II, the American military consumed one gallon of petroleum per soldier per day; during the first Gulf War of 1990–91, the rate rose to four gallons per soldier per day; in the Bush administration's wars in Iraq and Afghanistan, it leapt to sixteen gallons per soldier per day.[6] Because the Pentagon is sure to increase its reliance on high-tech weaponry, and because other major powers, including China, Japan, Russia, and India, seek to emulate it in this regard, the already voracious military component of global energy demand can only grow.

At the same time, the competition for energy has never been so intense. Since World War II, the major industrialized powers—the United States, Japan, and the Western European countries—have jointly consumed the lion's share of the global energy supply. Because the energy industry was generally successful in boosting supplies to satisfy rising demand, the world was spared the cutthroat competition that had characterized the Eurasian energy race prior to World War II and helped launch the war in the Pacific in 1941. In the past few decades, however, a new class of contenders has entered the fray—rising economic dynamos like China, India, and Brazil—and it is not at all apparent, looking into the future, that the energy industry can satisfy both the surging needs of these new consumers *and* the already elevated requirements of the mature industrial powers. "Energy developments in China and India are transforming the global energy system by dint of their sheer size and their growing weight in international fossil-fuel trade," the International Energy Agency (IEA) reported in its *World Energy Outlook* for 2007. Despite huge investment in new oil-production capacity additions, "it is very uncertain whether they will be sufficient to compensate for the decline in output at existing fields and keep pace with the projected increase in demand."[7] Hence, an intense and sometimes brutal competition for untapped supplies has erupted.

Every nation with a significant need for imported energy is contributing to the intensity of this struggle, but there can be no ignoring the dramatic impact of China's soaring growth rates. As recently as 1990, China accounted for a mere 8 percent of global energy consumption while the United States was absorbing 24 percent of the available supply and the Western European nations 20 percent. But China's growth in the past decade and a half has been so vigorous that, by 2006, its net energy use had jumped to 16 percent of total world consumption. If its growth continues at this torrid pace, China will hit the 21 percent mark by 2030—exceeding all other countries, including the United States.[8] The challenge for China, of course, will be to procure all that additional energy. To succeed, the Chinese leadership will have to oversee a substantial increase in the yield of its domestic energy production while obtaining staggering quantities of imported fuels, especially oil. By the nature of things, this can only happen at the expense of other energy-starved nations. No wonder the rise of China has produced such alarm among older industrial powers.

What makes all this even more anxiety provoking is another worrisome factor in the energy-squeeze equation: intimations of future scarcities of vital fuels, especially petroleum. An increasing body of evidence suggests that the era of "easy oil" is over and that we have entered a new period of "tough oil." Each new barrel added to global reserves, experts suggest, will prove harder and more costly to extract than the one before; it will be buried deeper underground, farther offshore, in more hazardous environments, or in more conflict-prone, hostile regions of the planet. A similar scenario is likely to play out when it comes to most other existing fuels, including coal, natural gas, and uranium. Given this, the future adequacy of global energy stocks is in serious doubt.[9]

Ever since the onset of the Industrial Revolution, humans have succeeded in developing new sources of energy to supplement those already in use—first coal, then oil, and later natural gas and atomic fuel. The development of these fuels has made possible a stunning expansion of the global economy over the past century and a half, as well as a quadrupling of the human population. But all of these materials are finite in quantity, and the supply of most, if not all, is likely to be exhausted by the end of this century. Many experts believe that when it comes to petroleum, this process of exhaustion is already well under way.

Scientists are avidly seeking ways to develop a new spectrum of fuels to replace those now at risk of depletion while releasing far fewer or zero climate-altering "greenhouse gases" into the atmosphere. But no major energy-consuming nation has yet devoted sufficient resources to this problem to ensure that these alternatives will be available on a large enough scale to replace existing energy sources in the foreseeable future. As a result, government and corporate officials alike continue to view fossil fuels (oil, coal, and natural gas) as the world's principal energy source for some time to come. According to the DoE, these fuels will still be satisfying an estimated 87 percent of global energy needs in 2030.[10] With both old and new consumers reliant on these traditional fuels—and no practical, plentiful alternatives in sight—the struggle over them is certain to be fierce.

In this context, anxiety extends to the net supply of basic energy in general: the sum of all primary fuels, including oil, natural gas, coal, nuclear power, hydropower, renewables like wind and solar, and traditional fuels such as wood and charcoal. When pondering the adequacy

of future reserves, however, the greatest dread is usually reserved for petroleum, which, for the last half century, has been—and remains—the
world's most important source of energy. While oil accounted for approximately 40 percent of world energy use in 2006 (natural gas, the
number two fuel, supplied only 25 percent) and is expected to remain
number one in 2030, it is the energy source most likely to dwindle in the
decades ahead. Although there is considerable controversy over the size
of the remaining petroleum reserves, enough is known to conclude that
global oil output will, at some not-too-distant moment, reach a maximum, or "peak," level and then commence an irreversible decline. The
gradual disappearance of conventional liquid oil may, for a time, be
offset by the development of synthetic fuels derived from "nonconventional" petroleum substances—Canadian tar sands, Venezuelan
extra-heavy crude, Rocky Mountain oil shale—but the financial and
environmental costs of using these materials are huge, and they are
unlikely to rescue us, even briefly, from a dramatic and painful contraction in primary energy supplies.[11]

As a result, the problem of "energy security"—as it is widely
termed—has climbed toward the top rung of the international ladder
of unease and concern.[12] Not surprisingly, this has fundamentally
changed the perception of what constitutes "power" and "influence" in
a dramatically altered international system, forcing policymakers to
view the global power equation in entirely new ways.

The New International Energy Order

In the planet's new international energy order, countries can be divided into energy-surplus and energy-deficit nations. Under the old
order, a nation's ranking in the global hierarchy was measured by
such criteria as its stockpile of nuclear warheads, its warships at sea,
and the number of men it had under arms; superpowers had, above
all, super-allotments of the power to destroy. In the new order, a nation's rank will increasingly be determined by the vastness of its oil
and gas reserves or its ability to mobilize other sources of wealth in
order to purchase (or otherwise acquire) the resources of the energy-
rich countries.[13]

The realignment of the global power lineup into energy-surplus and energy-deficit states has obvious economic implications. After all, deficit states like China, Japan, and the United States are compelled to pay ever higher prices for imported fuels as they compete with one another for those materials the surplus states are prepared to supply. The surplus states, on the other hand, are sure to become richer as they parcel out their increasingly valuable commodities at whatever prices the market will bear. Thus, in 2006 alone, oil-exporting countries sucked up an estimated $970 billion from oil-importing states—three times more than they received in 2002[14]; with the price of crude in 2007 approximately double what it was in 2006, this amount was sure to reach much higher. Already, this shift in fortunes has delivered immense wealth to Russia, which has enjoyed remarkable growth since 2000 as a result of its lucrative oil and natural gas exports. It is also responsible for the sudden emergence of spectacularly prosperous financial centers like Abu Dhabi and Dubai in the oil-producing Middle East.

Some of these incredibly affluent petro-states have used a portion of their swelling "sovereign wealth funds" (investment funds controlled by governments) to purchase major stakes in prominent U.S. banks and corporations. In November 2007, for example, the Abu Dhabi Investment Authority acquired a $7.5 billion stake in Citigroup, America's largest bank holding company, as it sought to recover from losses incurred in the subprime mortgage market; in January 2008, Citigroup sold an even larger share, worth $12.5 billion, to the Kuwait Investment Authority and several other Middle Eastern investors, including Prince Walid bin Talal of Saudi Arabia. Abu Dhabi has also made substantial investments in Advanced Micro Devices, a major chip maker, and the Carlyle Group, a private equity giant.[15]

Of course, there are significant economic gradations among the surplus and deficit nations. Russia has become immensely wealthy during the current energy boom because it possesses vast stocks not only of oil but also of natural gas and coal. This has allowed it to provide cheap energy to its own citizens and industries while also exporting vast quantities of oil and gas at a high profit to countries on its periphery. Likewise, Saudi Arabia, with the world's largest proven reserves of untapped petroleum, will continue getting rich off oil exports for many years to come. But not all oil suppliers are this fortunate. Many—like Chad, Gabon, and Equatorial Guinea—are likely to produce modest quantities of oil for a couples of decades, generating huge fortunes for a privileged few, before running dry and returning to pre-boom impoverishment. A similar diversity prevails in the case of the deficit countries. The wealthy countries, including China, Japan, and the United States, will be able to buy their way out of scarcity, though no doubt damaging their economies in the process; poorer countries, lacking such advantages, will suffer egregiously.

Equally significant—and just as complex—are the geopolitical implications of the new power realignment. When military power was the principal determinant of a nation's global ranking, nuclear-armed behemoths like the United States and the Soviet Union occupied the top stratum and were able to influence the behavior of lower-ranked powers. Admittedly, military prowess still conveys an advantage in today's world, but it increasingly finds itself overshadowed by the clout of energy abundance. Saudi Arabia, for example, with a negligible military, commands substantial leverage in world affairs due to its possession of the world's largest known petroleum reserves. Even countries with smaller oil inheritances, such as Azerbaijan, Kazakhstan, Angola, and Sudan, are coming to enjoy influence disproportionate to their size and condition. The governing elites of these energy-surplus states have been able to exploit their privileged status to wring concessions of various sorts from their principal customers—whether in the form of political support at international institutions like the U.N. Security Council, the transfer of arms and military assistance, or even a disinclination by their clients to probe conspicuous human rights abuses. Sudan, for instance, has long been able to impede effective international intervention in the ongoing conflict and carnage in Darfur through the diplomatic patronage of its leading oil consumer, the People's Republic of China.[16]

Here, too, there are gradations of power and influence. Russia has come to enjoy great influence as an energy-surplus state, in large part because it is a leading supplier of oil and natural gas to Europe. But it also retains a nuclear arsenal left over from its superpower heyday and is using its newfound energy profits to modernize its decrepit military forces. Saudi Arabia may field a relatively small military force, but it

possesses some of the world's most sophisticated arms—mostly purchased from the United States and Great Britain with a small fraction
of its immense oil wealth. Other surplus states, lacking strong armies
or powerful friends in the international system, remain vulnerable to
invasion by powerful energy-importing states.

Whatever their ranking in this new alignment of power, both surplus and deficit nations are taking bold—and often risky—steps to enhance their competitive positions. In many cases, this entails the
formation of opportunistic associations of one sort or another: energy
suppliers' groups, like a proposed "natural gas OPEC" modeled on the
original Organization of Petroleum Exporting Countries; consumers'
organizations, like the International Energy Agency (IEA); and even
new proto-alliances or power blocs among selected exporters and importers, such as the strategic energy alliance between China and Russia
(aimed in part at undercutting U.S. influence in Asia). While it is still
too early to foresee the full impact of these arrangements, there is no
doubt that a global political realignment of historic proportions—all
pivoting around the vigorous pursuit of energy—is now under way.

One dramatic expression of this realignment is the extent to which
ownership of untapped petroleum reserves is being concentrated in
the hands of national oil companies (NOCs). Noteworthy examples
include mammoth firms like Saudi Aramco, the National Iranian Oil
Company, and Petróleos de Venezuela S.A. (PdVSA) that are entirely
or principally owned by national governments. Until recently, most of
the world's petroleum reserves were controlled by large Western energy firms such as Exxon Mobil, Chevron, British Petroleum (now
BP), Royal Dutch Shell, and TotalFinaElf (now Total S.A.) of France.
Today, these companies are increasingly overshadowed by the NOCs,
which include nine of the world's top ten petroleum-reserve holders
on the planet. Together, the national oil companies (including Russian
state-controlled firms that allow some minority participation by Western energy firms) oversee an estimated 81 percent of all known petroleum reserves—an enormous source of latent power for the states that
control them.[17] And because they operate in the countries with the
most promising untapped energy fields, they are bound to retain their
dominant position for years to come.[18] (See Table 1.1.)

Table 1.1

OIL RESERVES OF TOP FIFTEEN COMPANIES

(In Rank Order by Proven Reserves; as of Jan. 1, 2006)

Rank	Company	Type	Proven Reserves (bbl)	Percent of World Total
1	Saudi Aramco	NOC	264.3	21.9
2	National Iranian Oil Co.	NOC	137.5	11.4
3	Iraq National Oil Co.	NOC	115.0	9.5
4	Kuwait Petroleum Corp.	NOC	101.5	8.4
5	Abu Dhabi National Oil Co.	NOC	92.2	7.6
6	Petróleos de Venezuela S.A.	NOC	80.0	6.6
7	National Oil Corp. of Libya	NOC	41.5	3.4
8	Nigerian National Petroleum Corp.	NOC	36.2	3.0
9	Lukoil (Russia)	IOC	16.1	1.3
10	Qatar Petroleum	NOC	15.2	1.3
11	Gazprom	NOC	13.8	1.1
12	Pemex (Mexico)	NOC	12.9	1.1
13	Petrobras (Brazil)	NOC	12.2	1.0
14	China National Petroleum Corp.	NOC	11.5	1.0
15	Chevron (USA)	IOC	8.0	0.7
	Total, Top Fifteen		957.9	79.3

Sources: *Oil & Gas Journal,* March 26, 2007; BP, *Statistical Review of World Energy, June 2007.*
bbl = billion barrels
IOC = international energy company
NOC = national oil company

In contrast to private firms, largely motivated by the lure of profits and a desire to increase shareholder value, the NOCs are often driven by what the Congressional Research Service terms "governmentally mandated objectives." These can include the redistribution of national

wealth, a key objective for President Chávez in Venezuela; the creation
of jobs, important in Saudi Arabia; or the promotion of national economic development.[19] But for many of the countries involved, the
national oil companies are also being wielded by their governments as
a tool of foreign policy. "It is no surprise," the James A. Baker III Institute
of Rice University reported, "that NOCs, with their vast access to the
world's resources, are becoming important players in global power
politics."[20] Examples of such efforts include President Chávez's use of
Venezuela's oil giant PdVSA to create an anti-American bloc in Latin
America, and Vladimir Putin's employment of Russian natural gas
monopoly Gazprom to restore Moscow's dominance over the former
Soviet republics on its periphery.[21]

Increasingly, the national oil companies are forming strategic alliances with one another to advance the foreign policy objectives of their
state owners and magnify their combined power vis-à-vis the Western
oil giants (also known as international oil companies, or IOCs). In 2006,
for example, PdVSA announced that it would team up with several
other national oil companies, including Petropars (an affiliate of the National Iranian Oil Company) and Petróleo Brasileiro S.A. (Petrobras), to
develop Venezuela's extra-heavy crude in the Orinoco River basin; previously, PdVSA had conducted most of its joint ventures with Western
IOCs.[22] Although often justified on economic grounds, these NOC-to-
NOC alliances are clearly also intended to reinforce ties between the
governments involved and diminish the influence once enjoyed by the
Western powers and the corporate oil giants in energy-rich, once under-
developed and colonized areas of the world.[23]

In yet another flexing of their prodigious muscles, the national oil
companies increasingly are moving from their historic focus on "up-
stream" operations—the production of hydrocarbons at the source—to
"downstream" activities, such as the refining, transport, and marketing
of oil, natural gas, and their derivatives. Russia's Gazprom has taken a
big lead in this, establishing joint ventures with European firms to engage in the direct sale of natural gas to Western European customers;
likewise, Saudi Aramco has partnered with the China National Petrochemical Corporation (Sinopec) to build refineries and sell petroleum
products to Chinese customers.[24] By entering such lucrative fields,

these companies both increase the income derived from their core products and supplant the Western oil giants in areas they once largely controlled. In such cases, of course, they also increase the clout of the energy-surplus states that control them.

Faced with this challenge and a ferocious struggle over diminishing sources of supply, the energy-deficit states are building or strengthening strategic ties with current (or likely future) suppliers to enhance their advantages in the competitive free-for-all to come. Needless to say, linkages of this sort have always played a role in the global energy equation. For over sixty years, the United States has maintained close ties with the Saudi royal family, while the French have long maintained bonds with the oil-producing states of Francophone Africa. But these "special relationships" with key energy providers are becoming more widespread—and more onerous. Arrangements like these have always come at a substantial cost, politically, militarily, and financially; they now come with far larger price tags attached.

The geopolitical dimensions of such relationships are especially evident in Kazakhstan and the other former Soviet republics of the Caspian Sea basin, where Washington and Beijing continue to make strenuous efforts to gain access to the region's newly developed oil and natural gas fields, and Russia—though possessing adequate supplies of its own— seeks control over the transportation of much of this energy to market.

In the early 1990s, the United States was the first to seek a foothold in the area, soon after the collapse of the USSR. In order to bind the "stans" of Central Asia and other states in the region more tightly to the West—rather than to Russia or Iran—while facilitating the flow of Caspian energy to European and American markets, the Clinton (and then Bush) administrations began to emphasize military-to-military ties with friendly regimes and the establishment of military bases or basing rights in the region. They also championed the construction of the Baku-Tbilisi-Ceyhan (BTC) pipeline, a 1,040-mile conduit connecting Azerbaijan's Caspian oil center of Baku to the Turkish port of Ceyhan on the Mediterranean Sea. Western banks and oil companies supplied most of the financing for this pipeline and the associated drilling operations, but the U.S. government also invested considerable political capital through high-level diplomatic exchanges (including lavish receptions at the White House for the region's reigning potentates) and considerable economic and military assistance.[25]

By the late 1990s, China, too, was engaged in a vigorous form of diplomacy in many of the same lands. Like the United States, it sought to tap into the energy potential of the Caspian Sea basin and, in an almost exact replica of the American game plan, the Chinese began to sponsor the construction of a pipeline that would carry Caspian crude not west, to the Mediterranean, but east, to its own consumers. It simultaneously strove to establish a constellation of friendly states in the region through lavish offerings of aid and diplomatic favors. The Chinese even spearheaded the formation of a regional political body—the Shanghai Cooperation Organization—to advance its geopolitical interests in the area.[26]

These are characteristic of the types of relationships now being forged around the world between major energy consumers and potential suppliers. In every case, these relationships, in turn, entail fresh calibrations of the power relationships among major energy-consuming nations. Already edgy and competitive, they hint at future scenarios of conflict among the so-called Great Powers of a far more dangerous sort. While still at an early stage, such often pugnacious maneuvering for energy resources is bound to have profound consequences for international peace and security; if nothing else, it will redraw the atlas of international politics in a way that has not been seen since the onset of the Cold War some sixty years ago.

The Commanding Role of the State

Because the acquisition of adequate supplies of energy has always been a national priority, government officials have long played a significant role in the procurement and distribution of vital fuels. This has been particularly true in periods of war or crisis. It was Winston Churchill, while serving as First Lord of the Admiralty on the eve of World War I, who insisted that the British government assume majority ownership of the Anglo-Persian Oil Company (APOC, the progenitor of British Petroleum) and responsibility for its protection; believing that war with Germany was inevitable, he wanted to ensure uninterrupted

British access to Iranian oil for the British warships that he recently had converted from coal to oil propulsion.[27] In World War II, Adolf Hitler, at the helm of oil-deficient Germany, ordered an invasion of the Soviet Union that was intended, in part, to obtain desperately needed petroleum from Soviet fields in the Caucasus; the Japanese government similarly ordered its petroleum-starved military to seize the oil-rich Dutch East Indies in 1941, and, as a precautionary move, attack the American fleet at Pearl Harbor, thereby igniting World War II in the Pacific.[28]

During the Cold War, the United States and other Western powers largely relied on market forces and the international oil companies, rather than state-directed efforts and outright military intervention, to ensure adequate supplies of energy. Freeing these companies to establish worldwide operations in the pursuit of corporate profit, so the argument went, was the best way to ensure the maximum production of energy and avoid crippling inefficiencies. The oil majors were also credited with developing new fields in "frontier" regions of Africa, the Middle East, and Southeast Asia.[29]

Now, the pendulum is swinging back: Lacking confidence in the capacity of private firms to overcome the many challenges on the horizon, government leaders are again taking the lead when it comes to the acquisition of energy. Certainly, as their colossal profits of the last few years indicate, private energy companies still play significant roles, but key strategic decisions are increasingly being made by government officials. It was a harbinger of things to come that President Clinton and his top aides took a commanding role in negotiating the various treaties and agreements that made possible the construction of the BTC pipeline—and it was their successors in the Bush administration who led the drive to ensure its completion. Likewise, Chinese president Hu Jintao was largely responsible for Beijing's decision to construct a trans-Kazakhstan pipeline that is now carrying Caspian oil to western China.[30]

In nations with an abundant supply of energy, a similar process is under way as government officials seek to maximize the advantages of their privileged position within the new international energy order. The most conspicuous model for this sort of behavior has been pioneered by Russian president Vladimir Putin. He has overseen the

Kremlin's drive to restore state control over Russia's most valuable oil and gas assets—many of which had been auctioned off to superrich "oligarchs" in the chaotic days following the Soviet Union's collapse. Putin was also responsible for transforming the state-controlled natural gas monopoly Gazprom into one of the world's largest, richest, and most powerful energy firms.[31] Almost as impressive has been the success of President Chávez of Venezuela in gaining control over his country's semi-privatized energy assets and then using this great wealth to advance his populist social agenda.[32]

One way to describe the growing role of senior government officials in national energy policy is to brandish the term "resource nationalism," which might be defined as the management of energy flows in accordance with vital state interests. Some analysts have tended to apply this term solely to nations with an abundance of energy that have maximized state control over domestic oil and gas deposits and sought to leverage this latent power into a source of political advantage.[33] But there is no conceptual reason to limit the term's use that way; it also applies to efforts by leaders of the deficit states to protect their national interests in a world of intense competition over the available pool of supply.[34] For example, some states with limited supplies of oil and natural gas but a robust network of rivers have sought to maximize the hydroelectric potential of these waterways by building multiple dams, even if this means impeding the flow to downstrem countries. Hence Turkey has become embroiled in a bitter dispute with Syria and Iraq over its plans to build a series of dams on the upper Tigris and Euphrates Rivers.[35]

However one applies "resource nationalism," one thing is clear: The state, itself, is acquiring greater authority over national energy sectors—as the owner of key assets and/or as a key actor in the procurement, transportation, and disposition of energy flows. The expression most widely employed to describe such a phenomenon is "statism," or, in some cases, "neo-mercantilism." Typically, Western analysts ascribe such behaviors to Chinese, Venezuelan, and Russian officials but rarely to American or other Western leaders. It is not unusual, moreover, for these analysts to characterize the actions of such foreign officials as a latent threat to Western interests while viewing similar Western behavior as ordinary diplomacy. For example, think-tank analysts Flynt Leverett and Pierre Noël asserted in 2006 that in Beijing, "a statist approach to managing external energy relationships is increasingly pitting China against the United States in a competition for influence in the Middle East, Central Asia, and oil-producing parts of Africa."[36] Mikkal E. Herberg of the National Bureau of Asian Research offered a similar view in his 2005 testimony before the Senate Foreign Relations Committee: "For China's leaders, energy security is too important to be left to the markets, and so far its approach has been decidedly neo-mercantilist and competitive."[37]

While the use of terms like "statist" and "neo-mercantilist" to describe the energy behaviors of China and other rising powers is certainly reasonable, it would be misleading to conclude that these were unique or distinctive features of non-Western countries. Quite the opposite: Virtually all major energy-importing countries, including the United States, Japan, and the major Western European countries, have been engaging in activities that could easily be characterized as "statist" or "neo-mercantilist."[38]

For example, the National Energy Policy (NEP) adopted by the Bush administration on May 17, 2001, explicitly called for a more assertive government role in helping American energy companies overcome barriers to investment in foreign oil and gas ventures. Among its prime directives, the NEP enjoined the president to "make energy security a priority of our trade and foreign policy" and to assume overall responsibility for management of the nation's energy diplomacy.[39] Ever since, senior administration officials, from the president on down, have made repeated efforts to persuade the leaders of foreign energy-producing states to increase their oil and gas exports to the United States and allow increased investment by American firms in their hydrocarbon industries. George W. Bush, for example, met on several occasions with Vladimir Putin in a tireless campaign to open more of Russia's energy industry to American investment. Vice President Dick Cheney also played a key role in these efforts, visiting Kazakhstan in May 2006, three weeks after strongman Nursultan Nazarbayev won a third six-year term as president with 91 percent of the votes in a mockery of an election. Dispatched to persuade Kazakh leaders to ship more of their oil to the West rather than funnel the bulk of it to China and Russia, the vice president famously praised Nazarbayev for the impressive "political development" his country had achieved.[40] And, of course, ever since taking control of Baghdad in April 2003, the Bush administration has vigorously sought to influence the reshaping of Iraq's national oil legislation, hoping to increase the opportunities for U.S. firms to participate in the development of that country's mammoth petroleum reserves.[41] Such efforts, on a global scale, have easily rivaled—or even overshadowed—those conducted by other energy-seeking governments, including China's.

The role of the state and government-backed companies in the procurement of foreign energy supplies has also been buttressed in other Western countries. Japan, with the largest energy deficit of all the major industrial economies, has called on national firms to assume a significantly greater role in the acquisition of overseas oil and gas reserves. This is not exactly an original policy—Tokyo has long been influenced by mercantilist thinking—but it has been accorded increased vigor in recent years. In March 2006, Tokyo adopted a "New National Energy Strategy" mandating that an ever-greater proportion of Japan's oil imports be supplied by Japanese energy firms. According to a government press release, "[T]he oil volume in exploration and development by Japanese companies will be raised to around 40 percent by 2030"; it was then at 15 percent.[42] To help achieve this objective, the all-powerful Ministry of Economy, Trade, and Industry oversaw a 2005 merging of the Inpex Corporation (once part of the government-owned Japan National Oil Company) with the Teikoku Oil Company.[43] Officials of the new enterprise indicated that the move was intended to enhance the combined firm's ability to compete with "countries such as China and India" in the acquisition of overseas oil and gas reserves.[44]

Other Western governments, including France and Italy, have similarly engaged in "statist" endeavors—especially in Africa, where they have long maintained a paternalistic relationship with former colonial possessions.[45] As the United States did in Iraq, so France has intervened in a number of these possessions, including Chad, the Congo Republic (Congo-Brazzaville), and Gabon.

In other words, the resurgence of "statist" energy behavior is not the product of a singular economic system. It is not even an indication of where a country stands in the new international energy order. It is, instead, a consequence of the fundamental characteristics of energy in this demanding new era.

An Edge of Desperation

In assuming a greater role in the management of their country's energy policies, national leaders appear driven not only by hard-headed calculations about global energy supplies, but also by what can only be viewed as a degree of hysteria over the future adequacy of reserves and outsized fears about the possibility of losing out to more aggressive procurement tactics by rivals. It was this underlying edge of desperation that cemented CNOOC's fate in the Unocal struggle and that has stirred an increasingly inflamed debate over "energy security" in the United States.

Perhaps no one has better articulated this anxiety than Sen. Lugar, who first bemoaned the rise of "petro-superpowers." Describing energy as the "albatross" of U.S. national security, his warning on the risks posed by excessive American reliance on imported oil have become ever more strident. "In the absence of a major reorientation in the way we get our energy, life in America is going to be much more difficult in the coming decades," he warned in March 2006. "U.S. dependence on fossil fuels and their growing scarcity worldwide have already created conditions that are threatening our security and prosperity and undermining international stability. In the absence of revolutionary changes in energy policy, we are risking multiple disasters for our country that will constrain living standards, undermine our foreign policy goals, and leave us highly vulnerable to the machinations of rogue states."[46]

Such pessimistic scenarios have, in recent years, spread widely in Congress. Many legislators are especially troubled by America's expanding dependency on petroleum imports from that perennial site of conflict and terrorism, the Middle East—already the source of over one-fifth of the nation's oil imports. Others worry about the emergence of powerful energy suppliers like Russia and Venezuela, ready to impose their own political agenda on the United States and its allies. Two themes, however, predominate: fear that global energy supplies will fall short of anticipated demand and that the rising industrial powers of the developing world—with their booming economies, surging middle classes, and new automotive cultures—will trigger a brutal struggle for whatever energy there is. "We are near an energy crisis," Congressman Richard Pombo declared at the height of the debate over Unocal. "We are almost equal in terms of supply and demand, and that is why the price of oil has gone up dramatically. The U.S. economy is growing. The Chinese economy is growing. The Indian economy is growing. The Brazilian economy is growing. All of these different economies are growing and they all are competing for the same source of energy."[47]

In addition to U.S. legislators, American military officials and defense consultants have begun to express alarm over the future availability of energy supplies. Perhaps no one has been more articulate in this regard than James R. Schlesinger, the only American official who has served both as secretary of defense (1973–75) and secretary of energy (1977–79). Now a consultant to the Department of Defense and a member of the Defense Policy Board, he told the Senate Foreign Relations Committee in 2005 that while the United States may be the world's "preponderant military power," the defense establishment "is heavily dependent on oil" and so will face a growing array of perils in the future. Not only will future oil shortages and the resulting high prices place a heavier burden on the Pentagon budget, but the day may come when the U.S. military will be unable "to obtain the supply of oil products necessary for maintaining our military preponderance."[48] That these concerns are shared by officials within the military hierarchy was confirmed by a 2007 study commissioned by the Defense Department on its future energy requirements. Noting that the armed forces' reliance on energy-intensive, high-tech weaponry is likely to collide with the reality of ever-diminishing worldwide oil supplies, the study warned that the current Pentagon strategy of global military engagement "may be unsustainable in the long-term."[49]

The leaders of other energy-deficit nations are usually more reticent when it comes to sensitive matters of this sort—particularly in a country like China, where government statements are carefully scripted—but there is no doubt that many share the same anxieties.

Indeed, it is hard to imagine that President Hu Jintao would have dedicated as much time as he has to traveling through Central Asia and Africa, currying favor with prospective oil producers, if he did not feel immense pressure to line up as many additional reserves as possible while supplies last. The same can be said of Japanese leaders, who have devoted equally outsized attention to these producers. An edge of desperation—however well disguised—is just as apparent in the behavior of officials in Beijing, Tokyo, New Delhi, and elsewhere as it is of those in Washington.

This concern, however expressed, has led some American officials to call for a radical change in energy behavior, usually entailing an emphasis on the use of domestic sources of energy, the rapid development of alternative fuel sources, and other measures aimed at "energy independence." In his 2006 State of the Union address, President Bush himself acknowledged that this country is "addicted" to oil, and urged accelerated efforts to develop alternatives—though his actual policy suggestions were hardly designed to make a significant dent in the problem.[50] In a sense, such suggestions represent a desire—conscious or otherwise—to disengage from the new international energy order and somehow forge a self-sufficient energy system. It is hard not to see the appeal of such a strategy, especially given the intense competitive pressures of the new environment. Most policymakers recognize, however, that disengagement of any sort—no less of a major sort—is just not likely to be an option, as no modern industrial economy can function in isolation from the global commerce in energy.

The dilemma facing American policymakers has been made even more formidable by a growing recognition that global warming poses a substantial threat to America's future well-being and that the principal source of heat-trapping "greenhouse" gases is carbon dioxide released during the burning of fossil fuels. To address this unprecedented danger in time to avert its most catastrophic effects would require investing mammoth sums in the development of fossil-fuel alternatives while imposing strict constraints on the oil consumption of automobiles and other petroleum-fueled devices—acts no politician, of either major party, is yet prepared to undertake. Instead, leaders of both Congress and the executive branch urge largely cosmetic changes while providing inadequate funds for the development of alternatives and acquiescing to a glacial rate of progress by Detroit.

Under such circumstances, there can be no talk of even the most partial sort of "energy independence," but only its opposite: increased reliance on imported energy. "Until such time as new technologies, barely on the horizon, can wean us from our dependence on oil and gas, we shall continue to be plagued by energy insecurity," former Secretary Schlesinger bluntly testified in 2005. "We shall not end dependence on imported oil nor, what is the hope of some, end dependence on the volatile Middle East."[51] Indeed, the anxieties expressed by Lugar, Schlesinger, and their compatriots have, in the real world, led American leaders to plunge into the new international energy order with renewed vigor and a determination to prevail. For all their talk of increasing U.S. reliance on domestic sources of energy, President Bush and his associates accelerated U.S. military efforts to dominate the Persian Gulf area and worked tirelessly to persuade the leaders of such key supplier states as Saudi Arabia and Kuwait to boost their oil exports to the United States.[52]

China's leaders are no less determined. Rather than lick their wounds after the Unocal debacle, Chinese firms simply redoubled their efforts elsewhere. Just three weeks after CNOOC withdrew its offer, the China National Petroleum Corporation (CNPC), another state-controlled firm, made a $4.2 billion bid for PetroKazakhstan, a Canadian-owned firm with substantial oil and gas assets in Kazakhstan;[53] a month later, CNPC and Sinopec jointly acquired the Ecuadorian oil and pipeline assets of Calgary-based EnCana Corporation.[54]

China's avid pursuit of oil and gas reserves has, in turn, been a source of acute concern for other rapidly developing nations with mounting energy requirements. "I find China ahead of us in planning for the future in the field of energy security," Indian prime minister Manmohan Singh declared in early 2005. "We can no longer be complacent and must learn to think strategically, to think ahead, and to act swiftly and decisively."[55] Impelled by these words, India's principal state-owned energy firm, the Oil and Natural Gas Corporation, soon began bidding against Chinese firms for the purchase of promising exploration blocks in Africa and the Caspian Sea basin.[56]

Singh's comments could have been uttered by leaders of any of the major energy-seeking nations, and his chosen riposte—to instruct state-owned or home-based firms to accelerate their pursuit of foreign reserves—has been emulated by virtually all of them. The result has been the energy equivalent of an arms race to secure control over whatever remaining deposits of oil and natural gas are up for sale on the planet, along with reserves of other vital materials. This resource race is already one of the most conspicuous features of the contemporary political landscape and, in our lifetimes, may become *the* most conspicuous one—a voracious, zero-sum contest that, if allowed to continue along present paths, can only lead to conflict among the major powers.

For the time being, leaders of those nations are attempting to limit their competitive endeavors to conventional channels of diplomacy and commerce: state visits and ambassadorial contacts, development grants and loans, economic and military aid, joint ventures, trade agreements, and so on. As the desperation level mounts, however, they are demonstrating an ever-increasing inclination to supplement such traditional measures with more unconventional and illicit means. Indeed, the use of irregular tactics has increased on both sides of the energy equation.

In perhaps the most striking recent example on the surplus side of the ledger, Russian leaders employed previously neglected environmental regulations to force Royal Dutch Shell and its Japanese partners to surrender majority ownership of the Sakhalin-2 oil and gas project to Gazprom in 2006—at a net loss to the original investors of several billion dollars.[57] Russia's autocratic style is now being copied by Kazakhstan, which has also cited long-ignored environmental regulations in a drive to coerce Western firms into paying huge punitive fees and dilute their control of major oil fields in its territory.[58] On the deficit side of the ledger, China has allegedly armed and provided military support to a Sudanese government accused of the wholesale slaughter of civilians in Darfur and the non-Muslim south in return for privileged access to Sudanese oil.[59]

That such actions will produce friction and antagonisms is obvious. Thus, when Moscow forced Shell and its partners to abandon work on the Sakhalin-2 project, Japan's chief cabinet secretary (later prime minister) Shinzo Abe told reporters, "I am concerned that major delays might have a negative influence on overall Japanese-Russian relations."[60] The comments, though mild sounding, represented an unusually strong reproach of a powerful neighbor. Episodes like this leave enduring residues of resentment—and not just in Tokyo. Over the past few years, Russia's Gazprom has cut off the gas flow to Ukraine and threatened similar action against other former Soviet republics on its periphery in a relentless drive for higher prices and greater influence, causing widespread anger and bitterness. As such maneuvers increase and national humiliations build—while global energy stockpiles dwindle—even minor disagreements, disputes, and disparities anywhere on the planet could provide the spark for serious conflagrations. Add in elements of national pride, irrationality, and simple miscalculation in tough or contested times, and you have the makings of a potentially fatal brew.

2

SEEKING MORE,
FINDING LESS

The sudden arrival of aggressive new contenders on the global resource playing field, coupled with the emergence of powerful energy brokers like Russia, was bound to alarm the United States, Japan,
and major European energy-consuming nations, prompting them to
accelerate their own efforts to secure abundant reserves of critical materials. The global resource race is, however, being propelled by something else, no less powerful: a perception that the world's stockpiles of
essential commodities—oil in particular—are shrinking. While the
potential arrival of the "peak oil" moment has captured most of the resource headlines, international concern also extends to natural gas and
uranium, as well as copper, cobalt, chromium, titanium, and other industrial minerals.

Such times of panic clutter the historical record. In the nineteenth
century, the earliest industrial powers engaged in a scramble for control over promising sources of coal and iron, then the most sought-
after resources; after World War I, the major European powers took
part in a desperate search for foreign sources of petroleum, fearing the
depletion of their own meager supplies. In the past, such bouts of anxiety over scarce resources were invariably extinguished when new
sources came on line: Shortages of coal became less important when
petroleum began to flood the market, and feared shortages of oil evap-

orated after World War II when the seemingly limitless fields of the Middle East were discovered.

It is easy enough to conclude, then, that the "peak oil" theorists are but so many boys once again crying wolf—that the current upsurge of concern over energy scarcity is destined to prove a passing phenomenon, either because colossal new reservoirs will be discovered or alternative fuel sources will come on line. Considerable evidence suggests, however, that the situation today is qualitatively different. Not only is the consumption of, and demand for, energy and other vital resources reaching unprecedented heights, but many existing reserves are visibly being drained faster than new reserves can be brought on line. While scientists do speak optimistically of promising substitutes on the (unfortunately distant) horizon, none are being developed fast enough— or on a large enough scale—to replace the ones now facing depletion. This is the case not just for one or two key commodities, but for many.

Obviously, this is particularly true of global energy supplies. The worldwide requirement for primary energy is expected to rise by 57 percent between 2004 and 2030—an extraordinary jump in energy use over such a short time span. All regions of the planet are expected to play a part in driving this massive surge, but the developing nations of Asia will play an especially conspicuous role. According to the U.S. Department of Energy, their combined energy demand will grow by 128 percent over this same period, far more than any other region.[1] If these projections prove even close to accurate, their fulfillment would require a substantial boost in the output of *every* source of energy, including oil, natural gas, coal, nuclear power, hydropower, biofuels, traditional fuels, and renewable sources like solar and wind power.

If renewable sources of energy and some of the new fuels now under development were to become available on a large scale in the years just ahead, we might have some confidence that this mammoth increase in demand could somehow be met. At present, however, there is no reason to believe that this will occur. According to the latest DoE projections, renewables, including old-style hydropower, will account for a mere 8 percent of world energy consumption in 2030— an insignificant increase over their current share. On the other hand, nonrenewable fossil fuels—oil, coal, and natural gas—are still projected to jointly satisfy a whopping 87 percent of world energy requirements, about the same proportion as today.[2] But because worldwide energy demand in 2030 will be so much greater, the supply of all three will have to be correspondingly larger to retain this combined share: Oil production will have to rise by an estimated 42 percent, natural gas by 65 percent, and coal by 74 percent.[3] And this is where the problem lies: In the view of many energy analysts, increases of this magnitude are almost inconceivable in a world where a peak in oil and gas production may be in the cards, possibly followed by a contraction in the overall global supply; even coal, the most abundant of the three, may not satisfy future expectations.

Unlike that of renewable resources, the exploitation of nonrenewable materials is governed by a natural extraction cycle. Typically, when a natural resource is harnessed for human use, production ramps up quickly and then grows less rapidly until a maximum level of output is reached—"peak oil," in the case of petroleum. Once this peak is attained, output remains at a plateau for some period of time before beginning a downward slide that continues until little remains of the original planetary supply. Of course, each individual resource follows its own production curve, depending on the size of the original reserve base and the average rate of extraction. Hence some materials, like petroleum, have moved closer to their peak level of output than others. Nevertheless, a growing number of critical materials, including natural gas, coal, uranium, and several key minerals, also appear to be approaching their maximum levels of sustainable output. As suggested by scientists at the Army Engineer Research and Development Center of the U.S. Army Corps of Engineers, "The earth's endowment of natural resources are being depleting at an alarming rate—exponentially faster than the biosphere's ability to replenish them."[4]

There is a second, even more important, aspect of the extraction curve when it comes to distinguishing the current era from those of the past. When a major resource is first exploited for human use, developers naturally go after the easy-to-excavate deposits: those that lie close to the surface, are concentrated in large and rich deposits, are located close at hand, or are found in welcoming countries. This is the "easy oil," "easy coal," and "easy natural gas" that companies prefer to exploit. Typically, most of these "easy" deposits are exhausted by the time a resource approaches its peak moment, as now appears to be the case for oil, and soon will be so for natural gas, coal, uranium, and a number of other vital substances. This means we are largely left with "tough oil": deposits buried deep underground or far offshore, scattered in small, hard-to-reach pockets that often contain significant impurities, or located in unfriendly, corrupt countries or hazardous locations. Even if the resources exist, investors may be disinclined to risk the vast sums that will be needed to develop these unappetizing deposits, or extraction and transportation difficulties of all kinds will cut into future supplies.[5]

This is largely why the leaders of the major energy-consuming nations express alarm about the future resource equation. It is becoming increasingly evident that new discoveries are failing to keep pace with the exhaustion of existing reserves, and that new deposits are almost invariably of the "tough oil" variety. To fully appreciate the depth of their concern, it is necessary to look at the global supply of critical materials, their projected rates of depletion, and the discouraging prospects for finding new reserves to replace those now being exhausted.

Global Oil Availability: Approaching the Summit

Petroleum was once ridiculously abundant. In 1950, when the great post–World War II American economic expansion initially took off, the world possessed approximately two trillion barrels of the stuff—the rough equivalent of 84 trillion gallons of gasoline, or enough fuel to drive a vehicle getting 28 miles to the gallon (the current average for American cars) completely around the planet 95 billion times. The regular discovery of giant new fields, combined with the relatively cheap cost of extracting petroleum, fueled a colossal increase in global energy consumption and helped spark the emergence of new industries, markets, and materials—highway construction, suburban housing, malls, air travel, petrochemicals, plastics, synthetic fibers, agribusiness, and tourism, to mention but a few.

The relative plenitude of petroleum, along with its liquid character and high energy yield per unit of weight, also spurred the creation of the automobile culture that is perhaps the defining feature of American civilization—and is now being embraced by rising economic powers like China and India. Today, approximately 95 percent of the world's transportation fuel is provided by petroleum, propelling virtually all the cars, trucks, buses, trains, planes, and ships in use around the globe. Because the international exchange of goods is largely performed via these means of transport, low-cost petroleum has also fueled the onrush of globalization and a vast explosion in international trade. "Oil is the lifeblood of modern civilization," notes energy analyst Robert L. Hirsch. "It fuels most transportation worldwide and is a feedstock for pharmaceuticals, agriculture, plastics, and a myriad of other products used in everyday life."[6]

To keep this petro-civilization running smoothly, the global energy industry has pumped more and more oil from the ground. Worldwide petroleum consumption jumped from 10 million barrels per day in 1950 to 25 million in 1962, 50 million in 1971, and 75 million by the end of the century.[7] These huge leaps were made possible by relentless exploration efforts and the steady accretion of new reserves. The 1950s, '60s, and '70s were particularly propitious in this regard, with the discovery of many giant fields—"elephants," in the lexicon of petroleum geologists—and the development of whole new producing areas, including the North Slope of Alaska, the North Sea area between Britain and Norway, and Africa's Gulf of Guinea.[8] Although the 1980s and '90s witnessed a drop-off in new oil-field discovery, the world entered the twenty-first century with proven reserves of over one trillion barrels of oil.[9]

At the dawn of the new century, most energy experts assumed that output would continue to rise in tandem with a steady increase in demand. In 2003, for example, the Department of Energy projected that total world consumption would grow by 55 percent between 2001 and 2025, jumping from 77 to 119 million barrels per day. It confidently predicted that global *output* would expand by an even greater amount, reaching 125 million barrels per day in 2025—6 million barrels above projected demand.[10]

Since then, however, the expert community has come to doubt the ability of the energy industry to sustain production increases of this magnitude. Some geologists believe that peak oil output has already been reached, or will soon arrive, and that a decline in productivity will follow; others claim that output will continue to rise for another decade or so before reaching that peak, but without achieving the elevated numbers projected by the DoE; still others contend that the department's higher figures are attainable, but only through the accelerated development of "nonconventional" liquids like Canadian tar sands and Venezuelan extra-heavy crude. While controversy in this matter persists, the optimism that prevailed early in the century is essentially gone.[11]

Three critical factors account for this turnaround in outlook: a more rapid than expected decline in the output of existing fields; a disappointing record when it comes to the discovery of new fields; and the closing of the era of "easy oil."

A surprisingly large share of the world's current oil production—nearly 50 percent—comes from just 116 giant fields, each of which produces more than 100,000 barrels per day. Of these, all but four were discovered more than a quarter of a century ago, and many of them are showing signs of diminished capacity. Among those that are now in decline (or are soon expected to be) are some of the world's most prolific, including Ghawar in Saudi Arabia, Cantarell in Mexico, and Burgan in Kuwait—three mammoth fields with a combined yield (in 2006) of 8.2 million barrels per day, or approximately one-tenth of total worldwide output.[12] The decline of these older fields matters greatly because every lost barrel from an existing reservoir must be replaced by an added barrel from some new deposit just to stabilize world production at existing levels; if the net rate of decline exceeds the rate of increase in newer fields, there can be no hope of meeting higher levels of demand. The fact that so many major fields appear to be undergoing rapid decline simultaneously is thus a major source of concern.[13]

When considering the problem of mature oil-field decline, no country matters more to the supply equation than Saudi Arabia. For worldwide production to meet global needs in the decades ahead, Saudi Arabia must provide no less than 14 percent of total world oil supplies in 2030, according to the DoE's latest projections.[14] But this assumes that the kingdom's major fields, including Ghawar, will produce greater, not diminished, yields in the years ahead—a heroic feat that many energy specialists consider well beyond their capacity.

The most pessimistic assessment of future Saudi output has come from Matthew R. Simmons, a prominent oil-industry investment banker and the author of a much-cited study on the subject. Saudi Arabian crude production "is at or very near its *peak sustainable volume*," he wrote in 2005, "and is likely to go *into decline* in the very foreseeable future."[15] (Emphasis in the original.) Initially, Simmons's conclusions were dismissed by DoE experts, who cited assurances by senior Saudi officials of their confidence "in their ability to sustain significantly higher levels of production capacity well into the middle of this century."[16] As Simmons's research began to circulate more widely, however, the department began to backtrack. Between the 2004 and the 2005 editions of its *International Energy Outlook,* the DoE downgraded its projected 2025 Saudi output from 22.5 to 16.3 million barrels per day, a 28 percent reduction; in the 2006 edition, it reduced its 2025 estimate again to 15.1 million barrels per day.[17] Even this lower number is now considered wildly optimistic by many analysts. The Saudis themselves say they prefer to maintain output in the 10–12 million barrel range, supposedly to maintain prices at an even keel but largely, in the view of outside experts, to prevent the wholesale deterioration of older fields through the use of risky and destructive methods of increasing yields, such as pumping large amounts of seawater into the petroleum reservoir in order to force oil upward.[18]

Even if the world's older fields were to continue their decline, major consumers would still have enough petroleum in the decades ahead—but only if new fields now coming on line were ample enough to both supplant those now being exhausted *and* provide the added oil needed to satisfy rising international demand. But that is not happening. Although the major oil companies are spending more and more money each year on exploration, they are finding fewer new fields, and those they find tend to be smaller on average than those discovered in previous years.[19] According to the U.S. Army Corps of Engineers, the largest volume of new reserves was discovered in the 1950–60 period, when reservoirs holding approximately 480 billion barrels of oil were identified. Since then, the rate of discovery has dropped in every decade, yielding only 150 billion additional barrels in the 1990s. Meanwhile, net extraction overtook reserve additions for the first time in the 1980s, and consumption now exceeds the discovery rate by a ratio of two to one.[20] We are seeking more, but finding less.

Both of these problems—declining rates of output in older fields and a disappointing record of discovery in previously undeveloped areas—could be mitigated to some degree if private and public energy investors were prepared to undertake a massive program of investment in promising but problematic fields in Africa, the Caspian Sea basin, the Middle East, and Siberia. According to an estimate offered by the International Energy Agency, the amount of fresh investment needed to ensure adequate supplies of petroleum in 2030 is no less than $5.4 *trillion*.[21] This is where the third and possibly most formidable impediment to increased oil output comes in: the reluctance of major investors to risk their capital in the development of "tough oil" reserves in remote, hazardous, and unfriendly environments.

Oil exploration and extraction was once an attractive field for investment—when the reserves involved were relatively easy to develop and the ruling governments placed no obstacles in the way of repatriating energy profits. But few such opportunities exist today. As Chevron chief executive David O'Reilly made clear in a widely placed 2005 advertisement, "the era of easy oil is over." Not only are many existing fields in decline, his ad noted, but "new energy discoveries are mainly occurring in places where resources are difficult to extract, physically, economically, and even politically."[22] O'Reilly pledged to increase Chevron's investment outlays in order to overcome these challenges, but it is highly doubtful that his company—or others around the world—are prepared to spend enough to substantially boost production under these daunting circumstances.

That global energy experts are becoming increasingly pessimistic about this prospect was suggested in a pair of high-level reports issued in July 2007. The first, the International Energy Agency's *Medium-Term Oil Market Report*, predicted that world economic activity would grow by an average of 4.5 percent per year between 2008 and 2012, driven by unbridled growth in China, India, and other Asian dynamos.

On this basis, the IEA calculated that oil demand would rise by about 2.2 percent per year, pushing world oil consumption from 84 million barrels per day in 2007 to an estimated 96 million barrels in 2012. With luck and a fresh burst of investment, the study concluded, the oil industry would be able to increase output sufficiently to meet this higher level of demand—just barely. Beyond 2012, however, it sees virtually zero likelihood of the industry sustaining further increases. "Oil looks extremely tight in five years' time," the IEA warned.[23] This is so, it suggested, not just due to a decline in mature producing fields but also to the likelihood that investment levels will not rise fast enough to boost production in more problematic resource zones.[24]

A strikingly similar prognosis was offered in *Facing the Hard Truths About Energy*. Prepared for the U.S. Department of Energy by the National Petroleum Council (NPC), an industry-backed organization, the report opened with a deceptively optimistic assessment of global energy stocks. "Fortunately, the world is not running out of energy resources," it bravely asserted.[25] But deeper in the study, the "hard truths" of the title begin to stand out: Although the promised resources may exist somewhere, most are of the "tough oil" variety and could only be coaxed out of the ground with massive doses of fresh investment that may not be forthcoming.

"Many of the expected [geopolitical] changes could heighten risks to U.S. energy security in a world where U.S. influence is likely to decline as economic power shifts to other nations," the NPC report notes. "In years to come, security threats to the world's main sources of oil and natural gas may worsen."[26] Under such circumstances, investors are hardly likely to risk vast sums to develop trouble-prone reserves—no matter how urgent the need for additional energy supplies.

If "tough oil" investments fail to beckon, only one other possible source of new liquid fuels exists: the conversion of nonliquid oil-bearing materials such as Canadian tar sands and Rocky Mountain oil shale into synthetic petroleum fuels. The world harbors considerable reservoirs of nonconventional resources, approximately equal to the remaining supply of conventional petroleum. But right now, with existing technologies, considerable energy must be invested just to extract these materials and convert them into usable liquids. Moreover, the net energy return is not particularly impressive. For example, it takes about one billion cubic feet of natural gas to produce one million barrels of synthetic oil from tar sands.[27] Furthermore, the extraction and conversion of these materials into synthetic liquids entails significant environmental risks, making them highly unattractive at a time of growing ecological consciousness. While nonconventional petroleum materials may eventually contribute several million barrels of liquids per day to the global oil supply, they will not compensate for the impending decline in major conventional oil fields.[28]

Add all this together, and it becomes distressingly evident that the more optimistic scenarios are not likely to pan out. If the IEA's July 2007 medium-term assessment proves accurate, global oil output will climb to approximately 96 million barrels per day in 2012—and not rise much beyond that in the years that follow. The CEO of Total, Christophe de Margerie, provided a very similar assessment at a London energy conference in October 2007. "One hundred million barrels [per day] . . . is now in my view an optimistic case." He then added, "It is not my view: it is the industry view, or the view of those who like to speak clearly, honestly, and [are] not just trying to please people."[29] Given that the DoE expects worldwide petroleum demand to reach 104 million barrels in 2020 and then climb considerably higher, it is obvious that the world faces an increasingly wide gap between supply and demand; it follows that severe shortages are inevitable—unless, perhaps, a great and disastrous global depression comes first, severely lowering energy demand worldwide.

In their desperate efforts to set aside adequate stocks of energy for the years of scarcity that such studies predict, the top officials of many states are seeking new reserves and sources of supply, often in distant, hazardous, hard-to-reach fields, whether in Central Asia, sub-Saharan Africa, or environmental frontiers like the now-melting Arctic region. Lacking more attractive options, the major energy-consuming nations are proceeding to, or planning to, exploit all these sites, seeking drilling rights wherever oil reservoirs may be found.[30]

By and large, however, they are concentrating their efforts on the acquisition of drilling rights or coproduction agreements with a handful

Table 2.1
THE WORLD'S LEADING OIL PRODUCERS, ACTUAL (2005)
AND PROJECTED (2030)
(In rank order at end of 2005; countries in italics show rising production.)

Rank	Country	Production			
		Actual (2005)		Projected (2030)	
		mbd	Percent of World Total	mbd	Percent of World Total
1	*Saudi Arabia*	10.7	13.1	16.4	15.3
2	*Russia*	9.5	11.6	11.5	10.7
3	*United States**	8.0	9.8	9.1	8.5
4	*Iran*	4.2	5.1	5.0	4.7
5	China	3.8	4.6	3.3	3.1
6	Mexico	3.8	4.6	3.5	3.3
7	Norway	3.0	3.7	1.4	1.3
8	*United Arab Emirates*	2.8	3.4	4.9	4.6
9	Venezuela**	2.8	3.4	1.7	1.6
10	*Nigeria*	2.8	3.4	5.2	4.9
11	*Kuwait*	2.7	3.3	4.1	3.8
12	*Algeria*	2.1	2.6	3.9	3.6
13	Canada**	2.0	2.4	1.5	1.4
14	*Iraq*	1.9	2.3	5.3	4.9
15	United Kingdom	1.9	2.3	0.5	0.5
16	*Libya*	1.7	2.0	1.9	1.8
17	*Brazil*	1.7	2.0	3.9	3.6
18	*Kazakhstan*	1.3	1.6	3.7	3.5
19	*Angola*	1.3	1.6	4.0	3.7
20	*Qatar*	1.1	1.3	1.8	1.7

Source: U.S. Department of Energy, *International Energy Outlook 2007*, Table G2, pp. 188–89.

mbd = million barrels per day

*Includes natural gas liquids

**Does not include extra-heavy oil or liquids derived from tar sands of oil-producing countries that exhibit a capacity for higher yields in the future. Although many countries still produce *some* oil, very few produce a lot, and fewer still are perched on the rising curve of production. If those countries that have already reached (or are approaching) peak production are eliminated from the list of major producers, only fifteen are left with significant potential to boost output: Algeria, Angola, Azerbaijan, Brazil, Iran, Iraq, Kazakhstan, Kuwait, Libya, Nigeria, Qatar, Russia, Saudi Arabia, the United Arab Emirates, and Venezuela. This privileged group may be joined by a couple of others as a result of intensified exploration, but is unlikely to grow substantially. From now on, these fifteen countries will constitute the main pivots of global energy geopolitics and so are the focus of close attention in the chapters that follow. (See Table 2.1.)

Natural Gas: How Much of a Panacea?

Concern over the future adequacy of global oil supplies is driving a push for greater reliance on other sources of energy. Natural gas is an especially attractive alternative because its use releases less carbon dioxide into the atmosphere than oil or coal per unit of energy—a significant factor, given climate change fears—and because it can be converted into a wide range of other products, including liquid fuels, artificial fertilizers, and hydrogen for use in fuel cells. Natural gas is also at an earlier stage in the extraction life cycle than petroleum, and so its net output should continue to rise after the production of oil goes into decline. For all these reasons, the Department of Energy indicated in 2005 that "natural gas is projected to be the fastest growing component of world primary energy consumption" during the first few decades of the twenty-first century.[31]

At present, the United States is the world's leading consumer of natural gas, using 21.8 trillion cubic feet of it in 2005, or 22 percent of all gas expended worldwide.[32] (It takes some 5,600 cubic feet of natural gas to achieve the energy output of one barrel of oil, so the 21.8 trillion cubic feet consumed by this country in 2006 is the rough equivalent of 4 billion barrels of oil.) Unlike petroleum, natural gas is not widely used as a source of energy for transportation, but rather to generate electricity, heat homes and businesses, and for a variety of industrial and agricultural purposes.[33] Because gas releases less CO_2 than coal, it is expected to find ever-widening use in the generation of electricity, especially as American utilities come under stronger pressure to reduce their emissions of climate-altering greenhouse gases. With this in mind, the DoE predicted in 2007 that natural gas consumption in the United States would rise by 17 percent between 2004 and 2030, reaching 26.1 trillion cubic feet per year at the end of that period.[34]

The real growth in natural gas usage, however, is expected to occur in Europe and Asia. The European Union countries and Japan are already seeking more gas to replace coal in electricity generation, thereby complying with their obligations under the Kyoto Protocol to substantially reduce greenhouse gas emissions. The developing nations of Asia plan to use more gas in part for this reason, but also to compensate for potential shortages of petroleum and to manufacture fertilizers and other materials.[35] According to the Department of Energy, annual gas consumption in most of Europe will grow by 43 percent between 2004 and 2030, rising from 18.8 to 26.9 trillion cubic feet, while in developing Asia it will rise by 222 percent, from 8.5 to 27.4 trillion cubic feet. A large increase, estimated at 46 percent, is also projected for Eastern Europe and the former Soviet Union as these nations experience stronger economic growth.[36]

Although many countries are expected to contribute to the rising demand for natural gas, China and India stand out because of their exceptionally high rates of growth. Natural gas consumption in China is expected to increase by 6.5 percent per year between 2004 and 2030, the highest rate of any large economy; India is projected to come in second, at 5 percent per year. Rapid growth in demand is also expected from other developing countries, especially Mexico and Brazil. All told, worldwide natural gas consumption is expected to expand by 64 percent over the next quarter century, reaching 163 trillion cubic feet (or the equivalent of 29 billion barrels of oil) in 2030.[37]

Energy analysts generally believe that the world's producers are indeed capable of keeping pace with this staggering increase in demand—at least for the next few decades. But gas, like petroleum, is a finite substance, subject to the same life-cycle dynamics of discovery, extraction, and depletion. A peak in natural gas *will* occur, though it may follow that of petroleum by a decade or so. In the meantime, delivery bottlenecks could prove the equivalent of scarcity, given the inherent difficulties of moving a gaseous substance over great distances.

The remaining supply of natural gas cannot be plotted with the same precision as petroleum for a variety of reasons, including the fact that gas deposits are often amalgamated with oil reserves. As in the case of petroleum, there are also nonconventional sources of gas that eventually may be added to the tally of proven reserves: gas in remote or hard-to-reach locations (sometimes termed "stranded" gas), methane trapped in coal beds, and methane hydrates (frozen crystals of gas buried in frigid regions or lying on the bottom of northern seas).[38] Nevertheless, the oil giant BP has used the best information available to estimate that the world currently possesses 6,405 trillion cubic feet of conventional gas reserves[39]—enough to satisfy world demand for sixty-four years at the current rate of consumption, or forty years at the higher rates projected by the DoE for 2010 and beyond.

Many natural gas enthusiasts contend that with additional exploration, new reserves will be discovered, thereby extending its extraction life cycle. However, these optimistic scenarios are all belied by the fact that, as with oil, the discovery rate for gas has been falling in recent years. According to French geologist Jean Laherrère, the discovery of new gas deposits peaked in the early 1980s and has been in sharp decline since.[40] A peak in production must inevitably follow. Indeed, a group of energy experts at Texas A&M University has predicted the peak for conventional natural gas will occur in 2019.[41] Another study that included nonconventional sources as well places the planetary gas peak in the 2025–30 time frame.[42] Either way, it will evidently trail that for oil by a mere decade or two.[43]

Then, of course, there is that problem of transporting gas— especially from one continent to another. Oil, being a liquid, is relatively easy to carry by a wide variety of means, including pipes, ships, trains, and trucks; natural gas, being a gas—and therefore far more voluminous than oil—is difficult to move by any of these means except pipelines in its natural state. Major energy-consuming nations separated from their sources of supply by large oceans must import it by sea in liquefied form—a far more difficult and costly method.

To fully appreciate the nature of this dilemma, it is necessary to pinpoint the world's remaining reservoirs of natural gas. Even more than petroleum, gas supplies are highly concentrated in a small number of well-endowed nations. According to BP, just three countries— Iran, Qatar, and Russia—possess an astonishing 56 percent of the world's proven reserves; another eight countries—Algeria, Kazakhstan, Nigeria, Saudi Arabia, Turkmenistan, the United Arab Emirates, the United States, and Venezuela—jointly share an additional 21 percent.[44] (See Table 2.2.) Except for Venezuela and the United States (which together possess a mere 5.7 percent of world reserves), all of these countries, along with most other significant producers, are located in Africa, the Persian Gulf region, and the former Soviet Union. This poses a significant dilemma for consumers in China, Japan, South Korea, Taiwan, and the United States in particular, which must either construct technologically challenging pipelines or import their supplies by ship in the form of liquefied natural gas (LNG).

A few words about liquefied natural gas. At normal surface temperatures, natural gas occupies about 600 times as much space as an equivalent quantity of petroleum. Only when made more compact through conversion into a liquid—a task that entails cooling it to minus 260 degrees Fahrenheit—can it be transported by ship on specially designed LNG carriers to distant locations, where it must then be transformed back into a gas, a process called "regasification." This is an extraordinarily costly and difficult process: a complete LNG "train," comprising a gas liquefaction facility and its associated LNG carriers, can cost several billion dollars. Delivery in the form of LNG is also far less energy efficient than delivery by pipeline, as it takes considerable energy to cool the gas, transport it long distances in a super-cooled state, and then restore it to its original gaseous condition.[45]

The mammoth costs associated with the construction of a complete LNG train and the necessary regasification plants in receiving countries, coupled with the fact that all these facilities must remain in operation for several decades for the original financiers to recoup their investment, makes it unlikely that enough will be built to satisfy

Table 2.2
THE WORLD'S TOP HOLDERS OF NATURAL GAS RESERVES
(In rank order by reserves as of end of 2006)

Rank	Country	Reserves		Production	
		tcf	*Percent of World Total*	*bcf*	*Percent of World Total*
1	Russia	1,682.1	26.3	21,607.1	21.3
2	Iran	993.0	15.5	3,706.5	3.7
3	Qatar	895.2	14.0	1,747.4	1.7
4	Saudi Arabia	249.7	3.9	2,601.6	2.6
5	United Arab Emirates	214.0	3.3	1,673.2	1.6
6	United States	209.2	3.3	18,500.7	18.5
7	Nigeria	189.9	2.9	995.5	1.0
8	Algeria	159.0	2.5	2,982.9	2.9
9	Venezuela	152.3	2.4	1,013.1	1.0
10	Iraq	111.9	1.7	#	#
11	Kazakhstan	105.9	1.7	843.7	0.8
12	Norway	102.1	1.6	3,092.3	3.0
13	Turkmenistan	101.0	1.6	2,195.7	2.2
14	Indonesia	92.9	1.5	2,612.2	2.6
15	Australia	92.0	1.4	1,373.2	1.4
	Total, Top 15	5,350.2	83.5	64,045.1	64.2

Source of data: BP, *Statistical Review of World Energy June 2007*, pp. 22, 24. Note: Totals may not correspond due to rounding.

tcf = trillion cubic feet

bcf = billion cubic feet

= negligible

anticipated demand in the Western Hemisphere and East Asia after 2015, when most of the gas reserves in areas outside Africa, the Persian Gulf, and the former Soviet Union will have been substantially depleted.[46] Hence, even as countries in Europe, Africa, and the Russian periphery continue to enjoy abundant supplies, the news for the United States, China, and Japan could be decidedly gloomy. In the United States, for example, imported LNG is expected to jump from 2 percent of the nation's gas supply in 2003 to 20 percent in 2025 as production at home and in Canada (a major supplier) goes into decline. For this to happen, however, dozens of new LNG trains would have to be established in producing countries and an equivalent number of regasification plants built in American ports, despite enormous financial and regulatory hurdles. Many harbor communities also worry that these huge, potentially explosive facilities—and the ships themselves—will become targets for terrorists.[47]

A growing reliance on LNG imports also requires that the receiving nations contemplate increased dependence on distant partners whose reliability must be assured over decades. Inescapably, the construction of LNG offloading plants will create vested interests in the continued "stability" and "friendship" of overseas supplying nations. Given the history of imperial domination, this is sure to have significant political and military consequences, especially when one considers that the principal suppliers of LNG in the years to come are likely to be Iran, Nigeria, Qatar, Saudi Arabia, and Venezuela—countries whose future stability and political orientation can hardly be taken for granted.[48]

Heavy dependence on natural gas delivered by pipeline can present similar challenges. While such conduits may not be as expensive as LNG facilities, they still represent major investments and cannot easily be replaced with other means of energy delivery. The potential for economic blackmail—of a kind Russia imposed on its natural gas customers Ukraine, Belarus, and Georgia in 2006—is consequently enormous. Hardly surprising, then, that these countries bowed to Russian demands rather than endure a prolonged cutoff in essential energy supplies.[49] Pipelines of this sort (at least those installed aboveground) also present almost irresistible targets to saboteurs, terrorists, and criminals of every stripe.

Yet another challenge to the gas-consuming nations could be posed by the formation of a "natural gas OPEC." Although no formal decision has yet been made to form such an entity, the fourteen members of the Gas Exporting Countries Forum—including industry leaders Russia, Iran, Qatar, Algeria, and Libya—agreed in 2007 to form a commission to explore the creation of a natural gas cartel.[50] "In the long run, yes, we are moving toward a gas OPEC," said Chakib Khelil, Algeria's oil minister.[51] Once established, it is likely to lead to higher prices or constraints on the construction of new pipelines and LNG facilities (to keep prices at elevated levels), thus restricting global availability.[52]

As a result, even though there may not be an absolute shortage of natural gas in the years just ahead, the leading gas-consuming nations may face periodic shortages as a result of political upheavals, supplier restraints, or inadequate connectivity to their major foreign sources of supply. With this in mind, leaders of the gas-importing countries are trying to strengthen their relationships with their principal suppliers ahead of time and hasten the construction of gas pipelines and LNG trains. As in the case of oil, they are also seeking control over promising sources of gas in formerly neglected areas of Asia and Africa, and in ecological frontiers such as Siberia and northern Alaska—efforts that are likely to prove as contentious as the global struggle over untapped supplies of oil.

Coal and Uranium

Government officials speak of their desire to develop novel sources of energy—biofuels, hydrogen, tidal power, and so on—but their actions suggest a deeply ingrained preference for more familiar fuels. In the United States, modest sums are being allocated for the development of fossil-fuel alternatives, while some of the biggest subsidies and tax breaks have been reserved for two of the most prominent old-energy systems: coal-fired electric power plants and nuclear reactors. Other major energy consumers, especially China and India, are following suit. As a result, the worldwide demand for coal and uranium—like that for oil and natural gas—is soon likely to encroach upon the planet's natural limits.

The instinctive preference American leaders have for old-energy systems like coal plants and nuclear reactors was evident in the Bush administration's National Energy Policy of 2001 and the Energy Policy Act passed by Congress in 2005—both of which propose numerous incentives for the construction of additional facilities of these types. Coal-fired power plants are, of course, a major source of carbon dioxide and other greenhouse gases, as well as of the poisonous emissions responsible for "acid rain"; nuclear reactors raise the specter of accidents like those at Three Mile Island (1979) and Chernobyl (1986), along with the problem of long-lasting radioactive wastes that cannot safely be disposed of. To allay such concerns, the White House sought to emphasize the promise of what it called "clean coal" and "safe," "environmentally friendly" nuclear reactors. "[O]ur plan funds research into new, clean coal technologies," Bush proclaimed when releasing the NEP in 2001. He further claimed that "[n]ew reactor designs are even safer and more economical than the reactors we possess today. And my energy plan directs the Department of Energy and the Environmental Protection Agency to use the best science to move expeditiously to find a safe and permanent repository for nuclear waste."[53] These assurances were then incorporated into the 2005 energy bill, which provides billions of dollars in subsidies and tax breaks for the measures envisioned by Bush.[54]

Chinese leaders have demonstrated similarly strong preferences for coal and nuclear power. China possesses the world's third largest reserves of coal (after the United States and Russia) and relatively little oil and natural gas, and so has favored the exploitation of this one abundant domestic source of energy. According to the latest projections from the U.S. Department of Energy, coal use in China will rise by about 130 percent between 2004 and 2030, at which point China alone will account for nearly half of the world's coal consumption.[55] Because coal use on this scale will wreak havoc on China's environment and make it the world's leading CO_2 emitter, Beijing no doubt will come under enormous domestic and international pressure to reduce its coal usage. Indeed, senior Chinese officials have begun to acknowledge the urgency of addressing the environmental risks posed by the country's excessive reliance on coal; at present, however, there is no indication that they are prepared to take any of the dramatic steps necessary to do so.[56] In their haste to increase the country's electricity supply, moreover, Chinese leaders have also approved construction of dozens of additional nuclear reactors.[57]

There are nonetheless many environmentalists and others in both China and the United States who fiercely oppose increased reliance on these sources of energy. They stress that subsidies lavished on these "old energy" systems represent funds that would be better spent on "new energy" options like biofuels, renewables (especially solar and wind power), hydrogen-powered fuel cells, and even more daring approaches, including tidal and geothermal energy.[58] Advocates of these alternatives typically stress their environmental attractions, but there is another reason for according them higher priority: coal and uranium (the fuel source for most nuclear reactors)—no less than oil and natural gas—are finite materials and so face eventual depletion.

Of the two, coal is the more abundant. According to BP, the world possesses proven reserves of 909 billion metric tons of coal, about half in the form of anthracite and bituminous coal, the other half in less desirable subbituminous coal and lignite. The countries with the largest combined reserves are the United States (246.6 billion metric tons), Russia (157.0 billion), China (114.5 billion), India (92.4 billion), and Australia (78.5 billion); smaller but still important reserves are held by South Africa, Kazakhstan, and Ukraine.[59] If these figures prove accurate, there are sufficient coal reserves to satisfy anticipated demand—now running at about 5 billion metric tons per year—for a long time to come. The fact that coal is thought to be so plentiful has led many energy experts to view it not only as a primary fuel for use in generating heat and electricity, but also as a feedstock for chemical conversion into synthetic liquids and gas—generally termed "coal-to-liquids" and "syngas," respectively. If coal's boosters have their way, the United States could, in fact, witness a huge increase in coal production for these alternative energy applications.[60]

At present, the leading users of coal are China (accounting for 38.6 percent of world consumption), the United States (18.4 percent), India (7.7 percent), Japan (3.9 percent), and Russia (3.6 percent).[61] These countries use coal to produce electricity, provide power and heat for some industries, and manufacture coke (a solid material produced by burning coal at high temperatures and then employed in the manufacture of steel). In the coming years, coal demand is expected to remain relatively stable in Russia and Japan and to grow in the United States, India, and China—which, in particular, is expected to consume ever-increasing quantities as it struggles to keep up with rising demand for electrical power. As many as a thousand new coal-fired power plants are expected to come on line in China over the next twenty-five years. India, too, is expected to build many more coal-fired plants in order to satisfy its growing need for electricity.[62]

For most of these countries, a pronounced reliance on coal can be explained by its presumed abundance and relatively low cost. However, a number of experts have come to doubt the horn-of-plenty claims for coal's plenitude. They point out that many reserve estimates are decades old and that the few recent surveys conducted have almost always resulted in substantial reductions in proven reserves. "The conventional wisdom has it that globally there is an abundance of coal which allows for an increasing coal consumption far into the future," a report prepared by Energy Watch Group (EWG) for the German parliament affirmed in March 2007. However, if results from most recent surveys are representative of coal reserves as a whole, "there is probably much less coal left to be burnt than most people think."[63] The EWG has estimated that world coal production will reach a plateau in the 2025–30 period before beginning a downturn sometime after 2040.[64]

Additional hints of a less sanguine assessment of the global coal equation were provided by two disturbing events in the United States in August 2007. An accident at the Crandall Canyon Mine in Huntington, Utah, in which six miners and three rescuers perished, revealed that the miners were practicing an inherently risky technique known as "retreat mining," involving the gradual narrowing of the few underground pillars that remain to hold up the mountains that lie above after most of the underground coal has been extracted—inviting seismic jolts or tremors as the earth settles.[65] The use of such techniques is inevitable, coal experts explained, because older, more prolific seams of coal have long since been exhausted. "The days of easy, shallow coal are gone," observed James Kohler of the federal Bureau of Land Management in Utah.[66]

As if to confirm this prognosis, the Bush administration approved a controversial regulation just a few weeks later, making it easier for mining companies to literally blast apart the tops of mountains in Appalachia—while dumping the wastes into streams below—in order to gain access to deeply buried coal seams. Though fought by environmentalists and Appalachian residents, the move was defended by the administration on the grounds that it would make it easier to extract deeply buried coal at a time when the United States seeks to diminish its reliance on imported petroleum.[67]

Nuclear power, too, poses a problem of future fuel supply. Global uranium supplies are considered adequate to meet civilian reactor needs at present, largely because massive stockpiles are left over from the bomb-building endeavors of the two superpowers during the Cold War era; once this backlog is expended, however, supplies could become scarcer. Indeed, many of the most prolific mines in the United States, the former Soviet Union, and their respective allies were exhausted during the Cold War, and only less productive mines remain in operation today.[68]

According to the U.S. Department of Energy, the 440 civilian power reactors now in operation around the world require between 165 and 185 million pounds of uranium per year. At these rates of consumption, the available supply—mostly concentrated in mines and stockpiles in Australia, Canada, Namibia, Niger, South Africa, the United States, and the former Soviet Union—is considered adequate for another forty years.[69] However, many analysts believe that numerous additional reactors will be built in the years ahead as fears grow of oil and natural gas exhaustion and of the environmental consequences of burning coal.[70] If so, the available supply is likely to dwindle.

In the United States, the biggest push for what has been termed a "renaissance" of nuclear energy has come from the George W. Bush administration. As a result of incessant White House lobbying, the Energy Policy Act of 2005 provides various incentives for the construction of new reactors, including a $1 billion tax credit spread over eight years for the first five new reactors brought on line.[71] As a result, eager utilities are rushing to file applications for permits to begin construction of the first new reactors to be built in the United States since the 1970s. According to one report, as many as thirty such applications were expected by the end of 2007, mostly for sites in the South; if all these proposed reactors come on line, they would boost the nation's electricity supply by more than 30,000 megawatts.[72] (A megawatt is enough electricity to power 500 homes.)

In addition to the United States and a number of European countries—Great Britain announced in January 2008 that it would build a new generation of nuclear power plants—the push for nuclear power is strongest in China, India, and other newly industrialized nations of Asia. According to a January 2006 report from Deutsche Bank, "[M]uch of the new demand [for nuclear power] will come from developing countries, where 130 new nuclear reactors are planned over the next 15 years,"[73] many of them in Asia. As a result, "[t]he uranium market has been attracting an increasing amount of attention in the global community and energy markets," the bank notes. The new reactors being built in Asia "represent the potential areas of growth, and players in the market will clearly profit from securing uranium provision to these regions."[74]

In perhaps the most dramatic expression of concern over the future supply of uranium, Premier Wen Jiabao of China signed an agreement with Australian officials on April 3, 2006, for the eventual delivery of up to 20,000 tons per year to China—double Australia's current exports to *all* foreign customers.[75] According to newspaper accounts, the deal followed months of intensive diplomacy and, because of the sensitive national-security nature of anything nuclear, entailed a decision by Australian leaders to overcome long-standing suspicions of China. Chinese mining firms have also sought uranium in Niger, despite attacks on company operations by rebel groups opposed to the present government (with which Beijing maintains close ties).[76]

Russia is also seeking additional sources of uranium. Despite the catastrophic 1986 nuclear accident at its reactor in Chernobyl—then part of the USSR, now part of Ukraine—Russia continues to rely on nuclear power for approximately 15 percent of its electricity supply and has announced plans to build many more reactors over the next twenty-five years.[77] Indeed, Sergei Kiriyenko, the head of Rosatom, the Russian

Federal Atomic Energy Agency, told American officials in May 2006 that Moscow intended to build up to forty new reactors between then and 2030. Because many of Russia's existing uranium mines are reaching exhaustion, Rosatom plans both exploration for new mines at home and an increase in imports from Kazakhstan, Kyrgyzstan, and Uzbekistan—all once key components in the Soviet nuclear establishment.[78]

As yet, this incipient global competition for uranium lacks the intensity of the search for petroleum and natural gas—but it will surely accelerate.[79] Some countries may try to minimize their future need for uranium by constructing "breeder" reactors, which manufacture as well as consume nuclear fuel. But the processes involved remain experimental and are fraught with danger. It is unclear, then, whether such reactors will ever prove practical on a commercial basis. More worrisome yet, the fuel produced by breeder reactors is plutonium—an exceedingly lethal substance with a 24,000-year half-life that is used in the manufacture of nuclear weapons.[80] Most nations, then, will spurn the breeder option—but this only leads them back to a growing reliance on uranium.

And Minerals, Too

As with energy supplies, so, too, the world's most valuable minerals are being extracted and consumed at a breakneck pace. Between 1995 and 2005, for example, worldwide production of aluminum jumped by 64 percent, from 19.4 to 31.9 million metric tons; iron production by 50 percent, from 1.0 to 1.5 billion tons; and copper output by 42 percent, from 11.7 to 16.6 million tons.[81] The consumption of these and other key minerals is expected to continue growing by these amounts for decades to come.[82] As noted by Deutsche Bank in its *Commodities Outlook for 2006*, the surge in world demand "has contributed to one of the most durable and powerful rallies in industrial metals prices in history."[83]

To satisfy this explosion in demand, mineral producers are accelerating extraction at older mines, commencing production at new ones, and building additional smelters and refining facilities. Needless to say, many of the world's existing deposits of key industrial minerals are being depleted at an unprecedented rate. These materials, too, are finite resources created by powerful geological forces many eons ago and, once consumed, will not be replenished in historical time. Fortunately, the earth still possesses plentiful supplies of many vital minerals, including iron ore and bauxite (the raw material for aluminum). However, copper, cobalt, lead, nickel, platinum, tin, titanium, and zinc are considerably less abundant, and concern is rising over their future availability.[84]

Like the energy giants, the major mining companies are searching for new reserves, but they, too, are looking harder and finding less. "Like oil, most of the easy-to-reach deposits of basic materials like copper, nickel, and gold have already been found and exploited," the *Wall Street Journal* reported in July 2006. "That has left lower-grade deposits in remote, politically volatile countries that will cost more to develop than the mother lodes of yesteryear."[85]

Of the minerals with less-than-abundant reserves, copper is by far the most important. The first metal produced by humans—some ancient smelters have been dated as far back as 12000 BC[86]—copper continues to be widely used today. Because it is an excellent conductor of electricity and is highly corrosion-resistant, it is widely used for electrical wiring, plumbing, and other household purposes. Until recently, most of the world's copper was consumed by the mature industrial powers; since 2000, however, there has been a sharp upswing in demand from China and other newly industrialized countries.[87] According to Deutsche Bank, the world demand for refined copper is expected to grow by about 60 percent over the next ten years, from approximately 14 to 22 million metric tons per year.[88]

In the past, the world's mining companies have satisfied rising copper demand by increasing production at known ore concentrations, especially in Chile, Indonesia, and Zambia. Chile, in particular, has played a key role in satisfying demand, boosting its net output from approximately 1.5 million metric tons per year in 1990 to 5.5 million tons in 2005, when it provided 36 percent of total world supply.[89] But some experts believe that the Chilean mines have reached their peak level and may soon go into decline.[90] Indonesia is also showing signs of slowing output.[91]

Mining officials insist that the development of new mines—notably in Mongolia and the Democratic Republic of Congo—will eventually compensate. In Mongolia, for example, Ivanhoe Mines Ltd. of Canada is developing a huge copper and gold deposit in the remote South Gobi region; in Congo, Phelps Dodge hopes to develop the Tenke Fungurume project, if security conditions improve in that war-wracked, utterly devastated country that, at this point, lacks just about anything that would pass for an infrastructure.[92] It is not at all clear, however, that even if these new sources come on line, they would compensate for the decline in older mines and provide for a significant increase in global demand. Deutsche Bank, in its 2006 assessment of long-term requirements, predicted the emergence by 2010 of a large gap between worldwide demand and output.[93]

Similar future shortfalls are expected for chromium, cobalt, columbium, lead, nickel, platinum, tantalum, titanium, and zinc. Although not as important as iron and copper, all of these minerals play a critical role in the manufacture of various key products. Cobalt, for instance, is used to make rechargeable batteries and high-temperature steel alloys (especially for military and aerospace applications); chromium and nickel help produce high-strength alloys and stainless steel; columbium and tantalum are used to make specialty steels for aerospace applications, as well as microcircuits for cell phones and other handheld electronic devices; platinum is employed both in jewelry and as a catalyst in the growing market for automobile exhaust systems and electric fuel cells; titanium is a lightweight, high-strength substitute for steel and aluminum in many military and aerospace applications; and zinc, used as an alloy, is also a protective coating for steel and other metals.[94]

Like copper, these minerals come from mines around the world, many in production for decades and showing signs of near-term exhaustion. In most cases, alternative sources of supply are known to exist, but often—and this, by now, is becoming a familiar tune—in more remote and hazardous locations, where the ores involved are often of lower grades. It is impossible to predict just which of these materials will experience significant shortages in the near-term future, but, to take one example, the known supply of cobalt is expected to prove inadequate to meet expected world demand as early as 2012.[95]

As a result, key officials of major resource-consuming nations have begun to play a direct role in the pursuit of overseas supplies of some of these vital minerals. The Japanese government, for example, has established a special program to finance the development of new ore deposits by Japanese companies and their overseas partners.[96] As part of this effort, the Japan Oil, Gas, and Metals National Corporation, an offshoot of the powerful Ministry of Economy, Trade, and Industry, launched a Joint Basic Exploration Scheme in 2003 to underwrite new mining ventures in the developing world. As of 2004, the project was supporting two projects in Argentina exploring for copper; two in Brazil, for copper and nickel; two in Chile, for copper; two in Indonesia, for copper and zinc; and two in Mongolia, for copper.[97]

The Chinese government has moved in this direction as well. In June 2006, for instance, the state-controlled China Machine-Building International Corporation agreed to build three coal-fired power plants in Zimbabwe in return for chromium ore and other minerals.[98] Beijing announced an even more sweeping initiative in September 2007: In return for a $5 billion reconstruction and development loan to the Democratic Republic of Congo, China will gain exclusive access to vast hoards of Congo's copper, cobalt, and nickel. This will make China the leading investor in Congo and, eventually, a major producer of African minerals. Some private mining firms have complained about the deal, saying it would freeze them out of the country, but Chinese and Congolese officials insist that Congo's vast resources would remain essentially inaccessible without China's help in building roads, railroads, and other infrastructure.[99]

Scarcely had the dust settled on China's disclosure of its $5 billion loan for mining operations in the Congo when Beijing announced an even more audacious undertaking: a $3 billion plan to develop the world's largest copper mine at Aynak, some 20 miles east of Kabul in war-torn Afghanistan. "This is the biggest investment in Afghanistan's history and 10,000 people will be employed to work there," said Ibrahim Adel, Afghanistan's mining minister.[100] Conditions in the area are so primitive that the Chinese will first have to build a coal-fired electrical plant to supply power to the mine along with a new railroad—Afghanistan's first—to haul the required coal (and later the copper ore) before the mine can be brought into full operation. A state-owned firm, China Metallurgical Group, will be responsible for oversight of the entire project.[101]

Of one thing we can be certain: The planet's natural stocks of many vital resources are shrinking, endowing the relatively few untapped reservoirs that remain with vast geopolitical significance.

The Ultimate Squeeze: Global Climate Change

And we mustn't forget that national leaders desperately seeking vital resources will soon be confronted with a set of even greater challenges: the severe effects of global warming. Some of these, like a projected two-to-three-foot rise in the global sea level, may or may not be fully realized in this century; others, like more frequent droughts in generally arid areas and more intense hurricanes and typhoons, are already being observed.[102] These and other potentially dire impacts of climate change will affect all aspects of human life but have a particularly direct and significant impact on the global quest for energy and resource security. In addition, as the catastrophic effects of climate change multiply, vast amounts of energy will no doubt be diverted into such onerous tasks as constructing dikes and seawalls, rebuilding flooded towns and cities, and relocating hundreds of millions of refugees, among other tasks.

Of global warming's many consequences, an increase in severe storm events is likely to be among the first to have a dramatic impact. According to the 2007 report of the Intergovernmental Panel on Climate Change (IPCC), widely considered the most authoritative scientific assessment of the problem, "it is *likely* that future tropical cyclones (typhoons and hurricanes) will become more intense, with larger peak wind speeds and more heavy precipitation associated with ongoing increases of tropical sea surface temperatures."[103] (Emphasis in the original.) This is especially worrisome news for oil and gas producers in the United States, because a large share of domestic production, processing, and distribution of both fuels is concentrated in the Gulf of Mexico and adjacent states—precisely the area where recent killer hurricanes, including 2005's Katrina and Rita, delivered their maximum damage. Just how vulnerable oil and gas facilities are to such storms was demonstrated by Katrina's fury, which destroyed or damaged dozens of multimillion-dollar rigs and forced the suspension of one-third of domestic U.S. oil production.[104] Many other key offshore producing areas, including those in Southeast Asia and the Persian Gulf, will also suffer from increased storm activity.

Climate change will affect the global energy equation in other significant ways. For example, countries in tropical and temperate areas that rely on hydropower for a significant share of their electricity generation could experience a sharp decline in power output due to a decline in annual rainfall. Many developing nations that have built large dams in recent years to harness the power-generating potential of large rivers, such as the Nile, the Ganges, and the Mekong, may find these costly investments sitting idle for long stretches of time as the channels that feed them run dry.

Some experts have nonetheless predicted that global warming could actually facilitate the future procurement of energy by melting (or substantially shrinking) the Arctic ice cap and thereby allowing year-round drilling for what are believed to be substantial oil and gas reserves buried beneath the Arctic Sea.[105] But even if one overlooks the fact that a climate warm enough to melt the Arctic ice cap could well threaten to turn lower latitudes into uninhabitable wastelands, it is likely that accompanying severe storm events would make drilling operations in the cold waters of the northern latitudes exceedingly hazardous and costly.

The greatest effect of global warming on the energy equation, however, probably will be to force leaders to place greater emphasis on the development of alternative fuels, which is guaranteed to raise numerous problems and perils as yet largely unconsidered. Which alternatives should be given preference, and how should they be manufactured? At this point, there is no consensus, as each option currently being considered poses its own set of problems.

This is not the place to review this matter in great depth, but, to take just one example, in the United States—where petroleum is expected to provide about two-fifths of the nation's total energy supply through 2030—the preferred non-CO_2-emitting liquid fuel is ethanol derived from corn. But a substantial increase in ethanol use will raise a number of significant issues. At present, most of the ethanol consumed in the United States is made by cooking corn kernels and fermenting the resulting mash—a method that consumes considerable energy as the corn is grown, harvested, and transformed into fuel. If ethanol really catches on—and this is hardly a given—it would involve the use of a sizable fraction of America's prime farmland. It might, in other words, contribute relatively little to the nation's net energy balance while appropriating land needed to grow basic food crops—driving up food prices worldwide and potentially causing widespread hunger and starvation.[106] Government officials are attempting to overcome these hurdles by fostering the development of new modes of production, such as the use of chemical enzymes to break apart plant cellulose ("cellulosic ethanol") and the substitution of switchgrass, wood chips, and other biomass for corn as the original feedstock for the fuel. At the present rate of development, however, it will be decades before cellulosic ethanol is available on a large enough scale to replace petroleum liquids in a meaningful way.[107]

In the meantime, the United States—and China as well—can expect to come under enormous pressure in the years ahead to reduce their use of coal as a fuel in generating energy. Environmentalists in both countries will no doubt advocate much greater reliance on renewable sources of energy, especially wind and solar power, but these options have never received the attention they deserve, and so are not near ready to replace coal and oil in the planet's fuel diet. As a result, government officials will probably turn at first to more familiar sources, notably natural gas and nuclear power, with all their attendant problems. This, of course, brings us right back to the original dilemma faced by these leaders: the accelerated depletion of natural gas and uranium and the likelihood of an intensified struggle over their dwindling planetary reserves in the decade ahead. In other words, no matter how they attempt to solve the energy dilemma in the face of the increasingly severe effects of climate change, these officials will have an accumulating array of economic, geopolitical, and environmental challenges to handle (or mishandle).

Needless to say, climate change will also affect the global struggle over other vital resources, especially water and arable land. Rising planetary temperatures and changing weather patterns will increase rainfall in some parts of the world, especially in more northerly latitudes, but reduce it in others, including many prime growing areas in the tropics and temperate zones. Large interior areas of North and South America, North Africa, and East, South, and Central Asia could become deserts or precarious dust bowls, barely capable of supporting human life. Rising sea levels will also wipe away valuable croplands in low-lying coastal regions, particularly rice-growing areas of Southeast Asia, the Philippines, and Indonesia.[108] All of this is likely to produce tens or even hundreds of millions of environmental refugees who will need to be rescued, fed, housed, and relocated in new communities—a colossal task that itself will entail the consumption of massive amounts of energy.

Never before in history have national leaders been confronted with so many challenges related to the acquisition, allocation, and use of vital natural resources. For some, simply obtaining enough materials to keep pace with runaway economic growth will seem an all-consuming task; for others, the real task will be to perpetuate accustomed standards of living in the face of intense competition from aggressive new challengers. In the end, however, every one of them (or their successors) will face the dilemmas posed by shrinking planetary resources stocks and the increasingly harsh effects of global climate change.

3

THE "CHINDIA" CHALLENGE

O f all the distinguishing features of the new international energy order, none is more striking or momentous than the emergence of "Chindia"—the shorthand name for the combined economic powerhouses of China and India—and other developing nations as major consumers. Until recently, the global hunt for vital resources had been dominated almost entirely by the mature industrialized powers. Three centers of economic might—the United States, Japan, and Europe—devoured the vast majority of the oil, natural gas, coal, uranium, and other primary sources of energy used worldwide, along with disproportionate amounts of other industrial commodities such as iron ore, copper, aluminum, and tin. In the past decade or so, however, brash young competitors have been muscling their way onto the scene with roaring economies that devour mammoth quantities of raw materials just to sustain their explosive rates of growth. The emergence of these assertive new consumers has completely altered the resource playing field.

It's no mystery which country is far out in the lead among these new contenders: the People's Republic of China. Only a minor player in the global resource rivalry as recently as the 1980s, China's rise has been nothing short of astonishing. Take oil: In 1980, it consumed a relatively modest 1.7 million barrels a day. By 1990, its oil consumption had jumped to 2.3 million barrels per day, putting it in fifth place after

Germany, Japan, Russia, and the United States; by 2006, at a prodigious 7.4 million barrels per day, it outpaced every other nation but the United States. By that time, when it came to iron ore, copper, aluminum, and many other industrial minerals, China had actually *surpassed* the United States in total consumption. Every indicator suggests that, with its energy and mineral demands surging, China will draw ever closer to this country in terms of gross resource consumption.

Less far along the resource curve—but gaining quickly—is India. After decades of relatively slow growth, it is forging ahead in industrial output and, in the process, generating a voracious demand for energy and other basic materials. In 1990, it was the twelfth leading consumer of petroleum; by 2005, it had moved into sixth place, poised to overtake number five, Russia, and number four, Germany. If India, like China, follows anything like its present growth curve, it will be in search of ever-increasing supplies of energy and other raw materials.

Together, China and India are expect to account for nearly half of the entire increase in global energy demand over the next quarter century, thoroughly transforming the international energy equation. "The staggering pace of Chinese and Indian economic growth in the past few years, outstripping that of all other major countries, has pushed up sharply their energy needs, a growing share of which has to be imported," the International Energy Agency observed in 2007. Although a potential source of economic opportunity for some, the agency noted, this spurt in demand is likely to place enormous strain on the world's energy infrastructure. With new sources of supply not expected to satisfy rising demand, a global "supply-side crunch" in the years ahead "cannot be ruled out."[1]

To ensure that their countries do not lag behind the older powers in the inevitable struggle over resources they deem necessary, the leaders of China and India have been crisscrossing the planet, hunting for new investment opportunities and putting down bids on whatever promising assets appear on the market. The formal aspects of these acquisition agreements are then typically delegated to state-owned or controlled enterprises like CNOOC and Sinopec in China or the Oil and Natural Gas Corporation in India. Leaders of both countries have also sought to establish strategic alliances between their national energy firms and those of major energy-producing states in Africa, Latin America, Central Asia, and the Middle East.

In their global hunt for resources, China and India have often viewed each other as competitors but have also begun seeking ways to collaborate in order to avert debilitating bidding wars. Some preliminary agreements have been signed, fueling talk of, if not the reality of, "Chindia"—an economic amalgamation of the two. While such cooperation is fraught with uncertainties, any association of such dynamic economies, however informal, would prove formidable indeed.

From the Red Guards to the "Four Modernizations"

When the Chinese Communist Party (CCP) established effective control over the mainland in October 1949 at the end of a grueling civil war, China was a ravaged, backward, impoverished nation. Despite its immense population and potential wealth, its gross domestic product (GDP) was less than 3 percent that of the United States. In response to a nationwide longing for stability and growth, the CCP, led by its chairman, Mao Zedong, devoted itself to economic expansion and the reconstruction of the country's damaged infrastructure. As Song Qingling, the widow of Sun Yat-sen (who had founded the Chinese republic in 1911) declared at a May 1950 party celebration in Shanghai, "We are going to bring prosperity to our city and to China, the likes of which our long history has never recorded."[2] Propelled by this sort of nationalistic zeal, the country did indeed achieve considerable economic growth in the 1950s and early 1960s.

Having presided over this relatively impressive bout of economic expansion (accompanied, however, by a number of significant setbacks, including the disastrous "Great Leap Forward" collectivization drive of 1958–60), Mao began having second thoughts about the value of unrestricted growth. Fearing that ongoing industrialization and agricultural reform would result in the perpetuation, even accentuation, of class distinctions, with factory managers, intellectuals, and Communist Party bureaucrats forming a privileged new stratum that would simply take the place of China's old mandarin rulers, Mao unleashed the "Great Proletarian Cultural Revolution" in 1966. Youthful, idealistic legions of Red Guards—for the most part, secondary school and college students brandishing the works of Mao—stormed factories, schools, and government institutions, demanding the removal of senior officials and their "reeducation" through hard manual labor in the countryside. The result, predictably, was nationwide social and economic chaos, in which industrial and agricultural output was severely degraded and enormous numbers of Chinese died. Mao finally sought to halt the slide into mayhem and disaster by calling in the Chinese military—the People's Liberation Army—to restore order, but by then the damage inflicted on the economy had been staggering.[3]

In the mid-1970s, as Mao's health began to decline, the Communist Party leadership was torn apart by a vicious power struggle between radicals who sought to institutionalize the utopian ideals of the Cultural Revolution and a more moderate faction who wanted to put economic growth ahead of class warfare. For a time, it was unclear which group would prevail: the radical wing, led by Zhang Chunqiao (a Shanghai ideologue) and Jiang Qing (Mao's fourth wife), or the moderate faction, led by Hua Guofeng (a party stalwart named premier in early 1976) and Deng Xiaoping (a former party secretary who had been driven from office during the Cultural Revolution and was only rehabilitated in 1973).

The matter was not settled until after Mao's death in September 1976, when Zhang and Jiang were driven from power and the moderate wing consolidated its control over the party—and so the nation. As the new head of government and party chairman, Hua promulgated what came to be celebrated as the "Four Modernizations": the vigorous and depoliticized expansion of agriculture, industry, defense, and science (combined with technology). Many of the industrial initiatives set back by the Cultural Revolution were resumed, and China was launched on a period of renewed economic growth.[4]

In these years, power increasingly gravitated toward the chief architect of reform, Deng Xiaoping. Declaring that economic growth should trump social reconstruction as the party's highest priority, Deng oversaw the privatization of agriculture and the introduction of market reforms in industry. "During the 'Cultural Revolution' there was a view that poor Communism was preferable to rich capitalism," he later explained, but, he insisted, "[t]he main task of socialism is to develop the productive forces, steadily improve the life of the people, and keep increasing the material wealth of society. Therefore, there can be no Communism with pauperism. . . . So to get rich is no sin."[5] Galvanized by this new, un-Mao-like approach to economic growth, the Chinese mustered remarkable entrepreneurial talent and, under the banner "To get rich is glorious," threw themselves into productive endeavor.

By 1986, China's economy had clearly undergone a fundamental transformation.[6] In place of a Soviet-style, centralized economic system, most industrial firms and agricultural units were now empowered to make their own investment decisions, reward productive and creative workers with material benefits, and engage in other market-driven practices. "[W]ith agriculture effectively privatized and the profit motive now accepted as the dominant force throughout the economy," British journalist John Gittings wrote in *The Changing Face of China,* "the scene by 1989 . . . was unimaginable at the start of the decade." By then, "material incentives, autonomy for enterprises, [and] the encouragement of competition" had become the norm.[7] Freed to attract foreign capital and develop new products for export to welcoming markets abroad, Chinese firms posted record gains in output and sales. The net result was a gravity-defying surge in economic growth, boosting China's GDP to $1.1 trillion in 2000—ten times the level for 1970.[8]

Plunging full speed ahead into the twenty-first century, China's economic expansion has shown no signs of slowing down. Annual growth rates during the first six years of the new century have hovered at around 10 percent, and most economists contend that this lofty rate will persist for the remainder of this decade and beyond. In 2004, with a GDP estimated at $1.9 trillion, China moved into sixth place among the world's largest economies; in 2005, it jumped ahead of Britain and France to become the fourth largest; and many analysts predict that by 2008 it will overtake Germany for the number three slot. Indeed, some economists believe that if China's economic results were recalibrated to reflect the artificially low value of its currency, it would already be closing in on Japan as the globe's number two economic power.[9]

Given such growth rates, any government would be justified in resting on its laurels. But for the Chinese Communist Party, which still rules an economically "free" but politically shackled nation, rapid growth of this sort has become its very raison d'etre. At one time, the party could claim that its right to govern derived from its unswerving commitment to the establishment of an egalitarian, classless society, but that objective has long since been tossed overboard. Today, the party's mandate to rule largely stems from its success in raising living standards. "Common prosperity is not an unreachable goal," CCP general secretary Hu Jintao explained in 2005; rather, it has become "the basic principle and pursuit of socialism."[10] Obviously reluctant to grant political rights to its citizens, the party must continue to deliver on its economic promises if it hopes to retain the loyalty of its subjects.

Crowding the Shanghai Skyline

One way to measure China's extraordinary record of growth is in the steady accumulation of dollars, yen, euros, and other foreign currencies in its banks and investment accounts; another, more concrete form, is in a mind-boggling countrywide epidemic of industrial expansion, infrastructure development, and personal accumulation. New factories, refineries, power plants, highways, bridges, dams, ports, airports, rail lines, shopping malls, schools, hospitals, hotels, stadiums, and housing estates have sprung up almost overnight. Small villages have been transformed into cities, cities into giant metropolises. Within these cities, moreover, the material goods owned by ordinary Chinese have grown in size and value. China's output of refrigerators jumped from 5.9 million units in 1993 to 15.9 million in 2002; of washing machines, from 8.9 million to 15.9 million; of passenger cars, from 240,000 to over 1 million[11]—and the ownership of such basic consumer goods has only accelerated since. Not everyone, of course, has benefitted from this explosion of personal wealth—tens of millions of impoverished peasants have actually lost ground in these years—but even greater numbers of citizens have done well; they add up to the largest cohort of human beings *ever* to rise from poverty to middle-class comfort in the space of a single generation.[12]

One way to appreciate this extraordinary boom is to gaze over central Shanghai, the country's great southern seaport and commercial hub, where some 4,000 new skyscrapers—almost double the number found in New York City—now occupy a crowded horizon. And the future promises more of the same: Another 1,000 skyscrapers, along with gargantuan apartment and shopping complexes, are slated to be built by the end of the first decade of the twenty-first century. Most of these buildings are cooled in summer by air-conditioning; most house computers and other advanced electronic devices as well as a wide variety of modern appliances, all powered by a vast electrical grid. To transport Shanghai's estimated 13 million people to and from work, moreover, the city is constructing highways at a dizzying pace and adding new lines to its 310-mile subway system, already one of the world's largest.[13] Traffic congestion is an around-the-clock phenomenon, and subway cars are almost always packed, yet the population continues to grow, swelled by eager or desperate transplants from the countryside, some simply seeking better-paying jobs in the metropolis, others forced off their land and into a world of eternal low-wage employment.[14]

Another impression of this high-speed development can be gleaned by visiting China's automobile showrooms, where newly affluent consumers are buying motor vehicles in unprecedented numbers. Until the late 1990s, private automobiles were the exclusive prerogative of party functionaries and senior managers; now, ordinary middle-class citizens are lining up to buy cars of their own. "Our living standard has improved to the point where we think it's time to buy a nice car," said Sang Guodong, the owner of a small clothing factory, while examining new models at a Beijing dealership.[15] In 2005, customers like Sang purchased a record 5.9 million private vehicles, pushing China ahead of Germany and Japan as the world's second largest automobile market after the United States. If auto sales continue at their current breakneck pace, China will surpass the United States as the number one market by 2020, when there will be an estimated 130 million cars and trucks on Chinese roads; by 2030, the Chinese vehicle fleet is expected to reach 270 million units.[16]

The rapid growth in Chinese automobile ownership is partly a reflection of pent-up demand: With China's average income, when measured in purchasing parity (the ability to buy a bundle of basic goods with local currency) approaching $6,000 per year—the level at which consumers in other developing countries have begun turning in their bicycles and scooters for private cars—hundreds of millions of citizens are poised to join the ranks of automobile owners for the very first time. But an auto-ownership society also reflects a strategic decision by China's leaders in the 1990s to spur industrialization and urban employment by promoting the development of a large domestic auto-manufacturing industry. Prompted by lavish government subsidies and tax breaks, private and state-backed firms—along with local government agencies—have poured billions of dollars into the development of automobile plants and ancillary industries over the past decade or so. As a result, the motor-vehicle industry now employs about 1.7 million workers, making it a key factor in the Chinese economy.[17]

To accommodate all these new private vehicles, China has been building new highways at a frenetic pace. Under current plans, it is adding approximately 2,000 miles of expressway a year to an existing national grid of about 20,000 miles—a project that will eventually endow China with a superhighway network larger than the existing U.S. interstate highway system. Local governments in all major cities are also adding highways, bridges, tunnels, parking lots, and garages. Despite this, the country's streets, roads, and highways are becoming more congested all the time, contributing to an already severe problem of smog and greenhouse-gas emissions. In Beijing, for example, levels of nitrogen oxide—a pollutant released by gas-powered motor vehicles—currently exceed the World Health Organization's clean-air guidelines by 78 percent, even as an estimated 1,000 new cars hit the city's streets every day.[18]

All of these objects—the skyscrapers, highways, railways, subways, bridges, airports, planes, automobiles, and appliances—have one thing in common: They rely on a colossal hoard of raw materials and massive infusions of energy for their construction, operation, and upkeep. Every large building requires many tons of steel and concrete, along with plywood (to hold concrete in place when poured), glass, and copper (for electrical wiring); every highway needs mammoth supplies of concrete and asphalt; every car needs steel, chromium, aluminum, and glass, plus oil for propulsion; every computer and appliance needs a regular, reliable flow of electricity. The expansion of China's infrastructure has been made possible, in other words, by a staggering increase in the production and procurement of basic resources, especially oil, coal, natural gas, iron ore, copper, aluminum, lead, tin, cement, and timber. Without that, none of the impressive gains could have been achieved.

To fully appreciate the scope and magnitude of China's use of non-renewable resources, consider the data. The production of raw steel in China rose from 66.1 million metric tons in 1990 to 349.4 million tons in 2005—an increase unmatched anywhere. At the start of this extraordinary surge, China trailed Japan, the United States, and the former Soviet Union in steel production; now, it towers above them all. The same pattern is evident for copper and aluminum. In 1993, Chinese plants produced 736,000 metric tons of copper; by 2005, they were supplying 2.8 million tons; over the same period, China's production of aluminum rose from 1.2 to 7.8 million metric tons. In each case, China's 2005 production topped that of all other countries by a significant margin.[19]

Supplying power to all the new factories, homes, malls, and office buildings constructed over the past quarter century and propelling the millions of new cars, trucks, and buses on China's expanding system of roads has involved a staggering increase in electricity output as well as fuel production and importation. In 1990, China consumed approximately 27.0 quadrillion British thermal units of energy, representing 7.8 percent of world energy consumption; by 2006, its net consumption had jumped to 68.6 quadrillion BTUs, or 15.6 percent of world usage.[20] In that period, it increased its consumption of all major sources of energy, especially coal, which accounted for the largest share of its energy supply, and petroleum, the second leading source. Soaring from 2.3 million barrels per day in 1990 to 7.4 million barrels in 2006, petroleum consumption growth was particularly striking—an increase of over 200 percent.[21]

All such figures pale, however, compared to estimates of China's *future* energy demand. According to the most recent projections by the U.S. Department of Energy, its net energy consumption will climb from 59.6 quadrillion BTUs in 2004 to 145.5 quadrillion in 2030, an increase of 144 percent. If these projections prove accurate, China's share of world energy consumption will jump from 13.3 percent to 20.7 percent, an extraordinary gain in such a short period of time. To obtain this additional energy, China will have to increase its supply from *all* potential sources, including coal, oil, nuclear, hydropower, biofuels, and natural gas. But its projected increase in oil consumption has attracted the greatest notice. According to the DoE, its requirement will jump from 6.4 million barrels per day in 2004 to 15.7 million in 2030, an amount equivalent to projected oil use by Latin America and the Middle East combined.[22]

Historically, Chinese officials have relied as much as possible on domestic energy sources, an approach adopted in the early years of Communist rule to immunize the country as much as possible from the effects of economic and trade sanctions (such as those imposed by the United States on Cuba after the rise of Fidel Castro) and, in an impoverished land, to minimize expenditures on imported commodities. Thanks to the presence of large domestic deposits of oil, coal, and other key materials, this approach succeeded for a time. But no longer. Domestic oil, for example, will provide only about one-quarter of the country's anticipated requirement by 2030, with the rest being imported; an even larger share of its natural gas will have to be imported by that time, along with vital supplies of uranium. And while China boasts enormous reserves of coal, many of its deposits are of low quality or located far from coastal urban and industrial centers, and so Beijing has already begun importing even this standard-bearer of energy self-sufficiency.[23]

Obtaining so much additional energy will prove a formidable challenge requiring an estimated investment of $3.7 trillion over the next twenty-five years, according to the International Energy Agency.[24] And yet, every gain in farm and factory output, home and office construction, and consumer lifestyle enhancement will require the use of additional electricity and fuel. To put this in perspective: The added 86 quadrillion BTUs needed to reach China's projected 2030 energy use is equivalent to Europe's *entire* energy consumption in 2007— representing the combined output of every power plant, refinery, reactor, hydroelectric dam, natural gas field, and wind farm in Britain, France, Germany, Italy, Spain, and a dozen other countries. To acquire this is a Herculean task guaranteed to make or break the Chinese economic miracle. (See Table 3.1.)

Managing the Procurement of Resources

Theoretically, direct responsibility for decisions regarding the acquisition and use of energy and other raw materials does not rest with central planners in Beijing, as in the Maoist era, but with individual firms and enterprises. Nonetheless, senior party and government officials continue to exercise considerable control over such endeavors. At the

Table 3.1

CHINA'S ENERGY OUTLOOK

Category	Actual (2006)		Projected (2030)	
	Amount	Percent of World Total	Amount	Percent of World Total
Total energy consumption, quadrillion BTUs	68.6	15.6	145.4	20.1
Petroleum production, mbd	3.9	4.7	4.9	4.2
Petroleum consumption, mbd	7.4	9.0	15.7	13.4
Natural gas production, tcf	2.1	2.0	n.a.	n.a.
Natural gas consumption, tcf	2.0	1.9	7.0	4.3
Coal consumption, quadrillion BTUs	48.1	38.6	95.2	47.8
Nuclear energy consumption, billion kilowatt-hours	48*	1.8	329	9.1
Carbon dioxide emissions, million metric tons	4,707*	17.5	11,239	26.2

Sources: For 2006 data: BP, *Statistical Review of World Energy June 2007.* For 2004 data and 2030 projections: U.S. Department of Energy, *International Energy Outlook 2007.*
*Data for 2004
BTU=British thermal unit
mbd=million barrels per day
tcf=trillion cubic feet

pinnacle of political and economic power in Beijing is the senior leadership of the Chinese Communist Party, largely concentrated in its Political Bureau (Politburo) and its executive arm, the Politburo Standing Committee. The most powerful figure in China, CCP general secretary Hu Jintao, also serves as China's president and chairman of the Central Military Commission, the body charged with oversight of the country's armed forces. Day-to-day management of government operations is the responsibility of the premier (prime minister), Wen Jiabao, but basic policies are drawn up by Hu Jintao and his Politburo colleagues.

Born in 1942, Hu Jintao was originally trained as a hydraulic engineer but has spent most of his professional life as a Communist Party functionary. After serving as party chief in Guizhou Province and the Tibet Autonomous Region, he was brought to Beijing in 1992 to serve on the Politburo Standing Committee and fill various high-level posts in the party hierarchy. In 1998, Hu was named vice president of China, and, in 2002, the party's general secretary. Since then, he has consolidated power by assuming the presidency in 2003 and chairmanship of the military commission, a crucial power center, in 2004.

Hu gave no hint of a special interest in energy issues prior to his selection as party chief but, since 2002, has devoted enormous attention to China's energy needs. In what must have been a surprise to many Western diplomats, on his very first trip abroad as president, in June 2003, he chose to visit Kazakhstan, one of China's major new suppliers of energy. Hu used this symbolically weighted occasion to revitalize Beijing's then-dormant plan to construct an oil pipeline from Chinese-owned oil fields in western Kazakhstan to Chinese territory.[25] He has also played a direct and vigorous role in Beijing's efforts to increase oil and gas imports from Africa, the Caspian Sea basin, and the Middle East.

Clearly, Hu's unstinting effort reflects the strategic outlook of the entire Chinese leadership. Premier Wen has played a similar role in the procurement of foreign energy assets (including Russian oil and Australian uranium), as has Ma Kai, the chief minister of the National Development and Reform Commission, a sort of superministry for economic affairs.[26]

These officials, and their senior associates, appear to work from a common script when crafting the nation's energy policies, including a continued preference for domestically generated energy. This is especially evident in Beijing's continued emphasis on the one energy source that China possesses in great abundance: coal. In this, they have been undeterred by the disastrous environmental consequences of excessive coal use. The Chinese are also building dams to generate hydropower on whatever free-flowing rivers remain in the country and are going to extreme lengths to develop whatever oil and gas deposits remain within their extended territory, including hydrocarbon reserves in the far-western Xinjiang autonomous region and undeveloped natural gas fields in the East China Sea.[27]

But despite their earnest desire to rely on local sources of energy, top officials know that domestic supplies alone will not begin to meet the country's mounting needs, especially when it comes to oil. Even under the best scenarios it will not be possible to raise domestic production much above 4 million barrels per day, when, by 2030, 15 million barrels may be needed.[28] In tackling the mammoth problem of finding those missing 11 million barrels over the coming decades, the Chinese leadership has adopted a strategic approach that is clearly evident in their diplomatic initiatives and the activities of state-controlled Chinese energy firms, even if not always articulated in public statements and documents.

Chinese leaders appear to have had three key priorities since China first began importing oil in the early 1990s: first, to diversify the country's sources of imported energy; second, to rely as much as possible on suppliers with overland, not maritime, connections to China; and third, to entrust the procurement of foreign energy supplies to state-controlled firms.[29]

Diversification as policy is evident in the countries supplying China with petroleum. As recently as 1996, China obtained over two-thirds of its imported oil from just three countries: Indonesia, Oman, and Yemen. By 2007, its pool of producers expanded to include Saudi Arabia (already supplying 16.8 percent of its imports in 2003), Iran (13.8 percent), Angola (11.2 percent), and Sudan (4.7 percent).[30] In 2006, China also began to import considerable oil from Kazakhstan through a newly constructed pipeline. Further diversification is on the horizon, given new supply arrangements with such producers as Algeria, Chad, Equatorial Guinea, Libya, Nigeria, and Venezuela. Wherever possible, however,

China has favored ties with producers on its periphery that are capable of delivering oil by overland pipelines. This is a reflection, no doubt, of Beijing's long-standing desire to minimize its vulnerability to naval blockades or embargoes—say, an oil blockade imposed by the United States in response to some future military move by China against Taiwan.[31]

To a striking extent, Beijing has relied on the power of its considerable purse to acquire the resources it seeks. It has devoted many billions of dollars annually to procuring imported oil and natural gas, helping to boost the global market price for these commodities. Chinese officials have also invested billions more in gaining access to promising reserves of foreign oil and gas. In undertaking this global campaign, Beijing has largely relied on the country's three major state-controlled energy firms: the China National Petroleum Corporation (CNPC); the China National Petrochemical Corporation (Sinopec); and the much-discussed China National Offshore Oil Corporation (CNOOC). Each of them has established partially privatized subsidiaries and supposedly enjoys a free hand in seeking out investments wherever promising opportunities arise, but the central government clearly sets their overarching objectives and oversees their efforts to acquire foreign assets. It does so by setting the broad political and economic parameters in which all state-controlled firms must operate, selecting their chief operating officers, vetting their major acquisitions, and providing low-cost loans from state-owned banks to help finance such purchases.[32]

President Hu and Premier Wen have also traveled the world in pursuit of promising energy assets, acting as advance men for the executives of Chinese companies. They routinely extol the virtues of ties with China—especially when addressing the leaders of developing nations—and dole out favors and financial incentives; in addition, they invite their counterparts from such countries to elaborate state visits and summit meetings in Beijing. These encounters have led to the signing of numerous supply agreements and associated protocols over the past few years.[33]

In seeking such ties, Chinese leaders have exhibited a distinct preference for forging alliances between their own state-controlled firms and the national oil companies of major supplying countries, such as Saudi Aramco, the Nigerian National Petroleum Corporation, Russia's Gazprom, and Venezuela's PdVSA. Such alliances establish political bonds between the two countries and allow for maximum participation by government officials in setting the guidelines for future deals. In 1999, for example, China established a "strategic oil partnership" with the Saudis, under which Sinopec would cooperate with Aramco in developing oil and gas fields in Saudi Arabia while Aramco would invest in refineries and petrochemical plants in China.[34] Under a similar accord signed by Presidents Hu and Putin in Beijing on March 21, 2006, CNPC and Gazprom will cooperate in supplying 80 billion cubic meters of Russian gas annually to China, beginning around 2012.[35] CNPC is also slated to cooperate with PdVSA in developing the vast heavy-oil reserves in Venezuela's Orinoco belt.[36] In every case, the signing of these accords was accompanied by a flurry of diplomatic activity and promises of cooperation on a wide range of other endeavors.

Measured by the time devoted to these various undertakings, the acquisition of adequate supplies of energy is clearly at the top of Chinese economic priorities. In just the past few years, however, high-ranking officials have also begun to focus on a different, if related, aspect of the energy equation: the devastating environmental consequences of China's reliance on coal and fossil fuels to produce electricity and power the country's transportation systems. By dint of its massive coal use, China is poised to become the world's number one emitter of carbon dioxide, the principal component of climate-changing greenhouse gases. Excessive coal consumption is also the major cause of acid rain and other pollution hazards, producing widespread respiratory illness in the country's heavily industrialized northeast. Because widespread environmental degradation is beginning to act as a major drag on the economy and tarnish the nation's image abroad, belated steps are being taken to close especially heavily polluting factories and power plants; at this point, however, the leadership's impulse to expand national energy supplies far outweighs any newfound concern for the environment.[37]

Along Comes India

China may be the toughest new player in the global resource race, but another aggressive contender has run out onto the field. Although India commenced its own economic reform process a decade or so after China embraced the "Four Modernizations," it has already begun to rival China in terms of sustained economic growth. Since it, too, lacks sufficient domestic supplies of energy and other key materials to sustain this momentum, India finds itself competing with both older energy-consuming nations, such as the United States and Japan, as well as China for access to critical resources.

With its vigorous democratic traditions and vast, rambunctious civil society, India looks very different from Communist-ruled China. From a raw materials perspective, however, the two are remarkably comparable. Like China, India entered the post–World War II era with a largely agricultural economy, scant industry, and a relatively primitive infrastructure (except for its railroads, which were well developed under British rule). The first great leaders of both countries—Mao Zedong and Jawaharlal Nehru—favored self-sufficiency in key economic areas, along with the establishment of giant state-owned enterprises. While central planning was far more extensive in China, the Indian government did extend state control over huge swaths of the nonagricultural economy; foreign investment in key industries was prohibited, and imports largely discouraged.

India's economic growth was relatively sluggish from the 1950s through the 1970s, but then, like China before it, India experienced an economic awakening. A grandson of Nehru, Rajiv Gandhi, began the process, after succeeding his mother, Indira Gandhi, as prime minister in 1984. A decade after the Chinese, he began reducing state control over the economy, allowing greater space for a burst of private entrepreneurship. In the early 1990s, Rajiv Gandhi's party, the Indian National Congress—Gandhi himself had by then been assassinated by a Sri Lankan Tamil separatist—accelerated the pace of reform, opening the way to substantial foreign investment.

India's once-sluggish economy began to boil. From independence in 1947 to 1980, gross domestic product grew at a tepid rate of about 3.5 percent annually. From 1980 to 2000, that rate jumped to 5.6 percent, and in recent years, to nearly 7.0 percent. This steady climb helped foster the emergence, as in China, of a substantial middle class, even while hundreds of millions of Indians—mostly living in small villages and rural areas—continued to exist in dire poverty. The rise of a well-educated middle class with the usual consumer appetites proved to be a transformative economic development.[38]

The Congress Party lost public favor in the late 1990s as the benefits of growth failed to penetrate to the masses of rural poor. As a result, the Hindu nationalist Bharatiya Janata Party (BJP) emerged as the dominant parliamentary bloc following the elections of 1999. Despite his differences with the Congress Party, the new prime minister, Atal Bihari Vajpayee, accelerated the process of reform, privatizing more state-owned firms and quickening the pace of foreign investment. This, in turn, stimulated the rise of the urban middle class, producing significant pockets of affluence in large cities like Mumbai (formerly Bombay), New Delhi, Bangalore, and Chennai (formerly Madras). But then, the uneven distribution of India's newfound wealth began to undermine the BJP, and in 2004 Congress returned to power under Prime Minister Manmohan Singh, who, as finance minister in the early 1990s, had been among the earliest promoters of economic reform.[39]

The results, whether under the BJP or the Congress Party, were impressive. By 2004, with a GDP of $691 billion, India had moved into eighth place among the world's economies. When measured in terms of purchasing parity, it had already taken fourth place behind Japan, China, and the United States.[40] More to the point, India had a growing mass of affluent consumers ready to buy a full suite of desired consumer goods, ranging from refrigerators and air conditioners to cars and computers.[41]

Many economists predict that India will actually gain ground on China in the coming decades as its manufacturing base expands and it exploits its formidable lead in computer know-how.[42] According to India's Finance Ministry, the country's manufacturing sector is growing by 9.4 percent per year[43]—one of the highest rates in Asia—due, in part, to the size of its well-educated workforce and the relatively low cost of labor. Indian factory workers often start at a mere $2 per day, whereas comparable Chinese wages are two or three times that. With salaries continuing to rise in China, many large industrial firms—including GM, IBM, BMW, and Intel—are now setting up shop in India as well.[44] "Increasingly, what we're seeing is that multinational manufacturers have a lot more interest in India," notes Ng Buck Seng, head of Asia research at Manufacturing Insights, a consultancy that advises international manufacturers.[45]

As in China, India's newly affluent wage earners have splurged on basic consumer goods, and there, too, one sees a special reverence for automobiles. Until very recently, car ownership was extremely rare in India; in the past few years, however, India has become one of the world's fastest-growing car markets, with 1 million vehicles sold every year. "Car showrooms, the bigger the better, are the new temples here, and cars the icons of a new individualism taking root," observed Amy Waldman of the *New York Times*.[46] To serve this burgeoning market, automobile makers from around the world—among them, Toyota, Renault, Nissan, Volkswagen, Suzuki, and Hyundai—are rushing to set up plants in India, some designed to sell small cars sporting price tags of only $2,500. With prices like these and seemingly unquenchable demand, India's vehicle fleet is expected to increase tenfold between 2006 and 2030, from 11 million to 115 million units.[47]

To make room for all these new cars, India is building its first nationwide four-lane highway system. The 3,625-mile "Golden Quadrilateral" superhighway will connect India's four largest cities, New Delhi, Mumbai, Chennai, and Calcutta; another 40,000 miles of narrow two-lane roads will be substantially improved and modernized. This massive undertaking—just the first phase of it is projected to cost $6.25 billion—represents India's biggest infrastructure project since independence.[48] Many other huge projects aimed at enhancing the nation's transportation infrastructure, including new airports, rail links, and container ports, are also under way.

Not surprisingly, these endeavors—combined with the growth in personal income—are significantly increasing India's hunger for basic raw materials. According to the U.S. Department of Energy, India's net energy consumption will rise by an estimated 2.8 percent per year between 2004 and 2030—nearly three times the rate of the United States and seven times the rate for the wealthy nations of Europe. In 2030, India will still follow the United States, China, and Russia in net energy consumption, but lead all other countries, including Japan.[49] This will, of course, require an increase in all forms of energy. Domestic coal supplies will remain a major energy source, but petroleum use is projected to grow by 76 percent in those years, from 2.5 to 4.4 million barrels per day; natural gas will rise by 255 percent, from 1.1 to 3.9 trillion cubic feet.[50] Because India can only supply a fraction of this from domestic reserves, it has already begun to follow the well-trodden Chinese path abroad. (See Table 3.2.)

India is also experiencing a strong growth in demand for iron ore, copper, aluminum, nickel, tin, and other industrial minerals. Its production of raw steel, for example, jumped from 18.2 million metric tons in 1993 to 34.0 million tons in 2005, an increase of 87 percent; its output of copper soared by over 1,000 percent in the same period.[51] All told, according to the projections of investment bankers Goldman Sachs, Indian and foreign companies are gearing up to invest $86 billion in India's metals sector over the next few years.[52]

Energy self-sufficiency was long a major objective of both the Congress Party and India's Hindu nationalist parties, including the BJP. But, again like their Chinese counterparts, India's leaders have had no choice but to look abroad for vital raw materials. Only recently, however, have officials in New Delhi begun to grasp the magnitude of this challenge and taken steps to address it. Prime Minister Singh has been particularly forthright on the subject. "[We] must learn to think strategically, to think ahead, and to act swiftly and decisively," he told Indian energy company officials in 2005.[53]

In response to this prodding, India's major state-owned energy firms—Oil and Natural Gas Corporation (ONGC), Indian Oil Corporation (Indian Oil), and Hindustan Petroleum Corporation—have stepped up their hunt for investment opportunities in foreign producing areas. "The entire country is looking the world over for oil, wherever assets are available," said P. Sugavanam, director of finance at Indian Oil.[54] This search has already led to the acquisition of oil and gas properties in Algeria, Indonesia, Kazakhstan, Libya, Russia, Sudan, Syria, and Vietnam. ONGC and Indian Oil are pursuing additional assets in Africa, Latin America, and Central Asia.[55] Like the Chinese, the Indians have sought to gain every advantage they could by promoting alliances between their state-owned firms and the national oil companies of friendly countries. Hence, ONGC is partnered with Venezuela's PdVSA in the development of the Orinoco heavy-oil belt, and with a subsidiary of the National

Table 3.2

INDIA'S ENERGY OUTLOOK

Category	Actual (2006)		Projected (2030)	
	Amount	Percent of World Total	Amount	Percent of World Total
Total energy consumption, quadrillion BTUs	17.1	3.9	31.9	4.5
Petroleum production, mbd	0.8	1.0	1.3	1.1
Petroleum consumption, mbd	2.6	3.1	4.4	3.7
Natural gas production, tcf	1.1	1.1	n.a.	n.a.
Natural gas consumption, tcf	1.4	1.4	3.9	2.4
Coal consumption, quadrillion BTUs	8.5	6.8	15.2	7.6
Nuclear energy consumption, billion kilowatt-hours	15*	0.1	144	4.0
Carbon dioxide emissions, million metric tons	1,111*	4.1	2,156	5.0

Sources: For 2006 data: BP, *Statistical Review of World Energy June 2007*. For 2004 data and 2030 projections: U.S. Department of Energy, *International Energy Outlook 2007*.
*Data for 2004
BTU=British thermal unit
mbd=million barrels per day
tcf=trillion cubic feet

Iranian Oil Company in the exploitation of Iran's offshore South Pars gas deposit.[56]

The "Chindia" Prospect

India has an additional problem not faced by Beijing in its early forays into the world of foreign energy reserves—China itself. India must compete not only with the major Western and Japanese firms, but with already powerful, state-backed Chinese firms that got into the hunt first and have a formidable stash of hard currencies to draw upon. On several occasions, Indian firms on the verge of securing promising foreign assets have been trumped when a Chinese company stepped in and made a bigger offer. In August 2005, for example, India's ONGC lost out to China's CNPC in a high-stakes bidding war for PetroKazakhstan, the Canadian firm with large oil and gas fields in Kazakhstan.[57]

In responding to the China challenge, Indian officials have adopted several strategies. They have, in some cases, stepped up the competitive pressure by trying to outbid Chinese firms or by searching more aggressively in less-desirable producing areas, like Myanmar (formerly Burma) and Ecuador. But New Delhi has also pioneered another approach— *joining* China, rather than fighting it. Since early 2005, Indian energy officials have been meeting regularly with their Chinese counterparts to promote cooperation in the pursuit of overseas energy assets and the development of large infrastructure projects like oil and natural gas pipelines. Executives in the state-owned energy firms of both countries have participated in these meetings, leading to a number of company-to-company agreements. "We see this in the long term as a strategic partnership," said Talmiz Ahmad, a senior official of India's Ministry of Petroleum and Natural Gas, following a five-day visit to Beijing in August 2005. He added, "I could imagine a company like CNOOC submitting a joint offer [for an energy asset] along with an Indian company."[58]

Ahmad's vision of future partnership first became reality in late December 2005, when CNPC and ONGC did indeed make a successful joint offer for a minority stake in Syria's Al Furat Petroleum Company (owned by the Syrian Petroleum Company and several Western firms).[59] Three weeks later, on January 12, 2006, Chinese and Indian officials signed a mutual cooperation pact in Beijing, establishing a mechanism by which each country's energy firms would notify the other's in advance when preparing a bid for an overseas oil or gas deposit, thus opening the way to a plethora of possible joint offers. The pact also envisioned Sino-Indian collaboration in areas like marketing and exploration. Further consultation and additional protocols will be needed before the pact is fully operational, but the stage has been set for closer cooperation in the pursuit of foreign energy assets.[60]

Given the powerful competitive impulses that seem to govern every major power when it comes to energy, forging a close partnership between China and India will take far more cooperative effort and determination than has yet been demonstrated.[61] Nevertheless, leaders on both sides of the Himalayas see the advantage of heightened collaboration—of pursuing the "Chindia" project—and are making gestures in this direction. In April 2005, Prime Minister Wen used the occasion of a four-day state visit to India to lay some of the groundwork. The visit began with a trip to Bangalore, epicenter of India's booming software industry, where Wen touted the attractions of Sino-Indian collaboration in computer electronics. He then traveled to New Delhi, where he called for greater cooperation in the energy field.[62]

Eighteen months later, in November 2006, President Hu arrived in India for a four-day state visit of his own, during which he signed a ten-point joint resolution with Prime Minister Singh that further advanced the Chindia project.[63] "As two large Asian states and as two of the fastest-growing economies of the world, cooperation between India and China transcends the bilateral [level] and has global significance," Singh told reporters after the signing.[64] Of particular note was an agreement to double the volume of bilateral trade from the current $20 billion per year to $40 billion by 2010, and another to collaborate in the field of civilian nuclear energy. The two leaders also agreed to seek a speedy and peaceful resolution to an outstanding border dispute—the cause of a bitter 1962 war in the Himalayas.[65]

The high-level exchanges continued in January 2008 with a state visit to Beijing by Prime Minister Singh. Before arriving in the Chinese capital, Mr. Singh insisted that India had no intention of trying to contain China's rise, but that the two countries should cooperate for mutual benefit. He returned to this theme once in Beijing: "There is enough space for both India and China to grow and prosper while strengthening our cooperative engagement," he declared.[66] Singh's accommodating remarks were echoed by Chinese officials, and the two sides agreed to a number of joint initiatives, including a plan to commence negotiations on a regional trade agreement. They also raised their goal for two-way trade to $60 billion by 2010—a 50 percent increase over the target set only two years earlier at the previous Indo-Chinese summit.

Although many in the Indian elite still resent China's aggressive and successful drive to win their 1962 border war, the two countries have reopened a direct land trade route through the Himalayas that traverses the

15,000-foot Nathu La pass—now the site of the world's highest customs post.[67] Despite India's March 2006 decision to conclude a nuclear trade agreement with the United States (viewed both in Washington and New Delhi as part of a mutual effort to contain Chinese influence in the region),[68] China and India continue to pursue collaboration in many fields and in June 2007 announced that they would hold their first-ever joint army maneuvers—a combined counterterrorism exercise in China.[69]

Sounding the Alarm . . . and Striking Back

The emergence of China and India as aggressive contenders on the global resource playing field has hardly gone unnoticed by analysts and policymakers in the older energy-consuming nations. The Western media have been full of reports about and commentaries on the rise of China and India and the energy challenge this poses. "The World Begins to Feel the Dragon's Breath on Its Back," was the headline of a typical commentary of this sort in the *Financial Times*.[70] "Asian Rivals Put Pressure on Western Energy Giants," was the headline for another such report in the *Wall Street Journal*, which noted, in characteristic prose, that "major Western oil companies, already feeling squeezed as easy-to-exploit oil and natural gas fields become scarcer, have brash new rivals to contend with in Asia."[71]

American intelligence analysts have chimed in with their own contributions. Particularly revealing was *Mapping the Global Future*, a 2004 report by the National Intelligence Council, a U.S. government agency, on the prospective world security environment of 2020. "The likely emergence of China and India, as well as others, as new major global players—similar to the advent of a united Germany in the 19th century and a powerful United States in the early 20th century—will transform the geopolitical landscape, with impacts potentially as dramatic as those in the previous two centuries." Energy will be central to this transformation, according to the council's analysts: "China and India, which lack adequate domestic energy resources, will have to ensure continued access to outside suppliers; thus, the need for energy will be a major factor in shaping their foreign and defense policies, including expanding naval power."[72]

Such assessments almost invariably betray a degree of anxiety about the growing prominence of Asia's new powerhouse economies—

especially among those who fear the loss of American primacy. Ordinarily, senior U.S. officials would prefer to confine such fears to private conversation or unattributed comments in the press. By the spring of 2005, however, gas prices at the pump had risen so sharply that the Bush administration felt compelled to affix blame for the nation's misery—and the oil-seeking efforts of China and India fit the bill perfectly. On the eve of an April 2005 presidential meeting with Crown Prince (now King) Abdullah of Saudi Arabia at the president's ranch in Crawford, Texas, Secretary of State Condoleezza Rice told reporters that American consumers should blame their pain on the emergence of new "large-scale consumers" abroad.[73] "Obviously, with the states like China, India, and others coming on line, there is a concern about supply and demand."[74] Then, Bush himself jumped in. "The price of crude is driving the price of gasoline," he explained, "[and] the price of crude is up because not only is our economy growing, but economies such as India and China's economies are growing."[75]

To deal with this challenge, Bush said that he would press the Saudi prince to boost Saudi exports, thereby increasing crude supplies and reducing gas prices at the pump. "The Crown Prince understands that it's very important for there to be—[to] make sure that the price is reasonable," he said. "A high oil price will damage markets, and he knows that. I look forward to talking to him about that."[76] The president famously sought to demonstrate his close rapport with Abdullah by walking hand in hand with him around his ranch—an image captured by news cameras and beamed around the world, producing unflattering comments about America's close embrace of the Saudi royal family.[77]

Reportedly, the hand-holding proved effective: National Security Adviser Stephen J. Hadley announced after the meeting that Abdullah had promised Bush that he would take immediate steps to increase Saudi oil output.[78] Though oil-industry analysts have since questioned the value of Abdullah's pledge,[79] what makes this episode so striking in retrospect (aside from the scapegoating of China and India and the pandering to a Saudi prince) was the degree to which the president of the United States assumed a central role in negotiating with a foreign provider over its oil production rates—a task that, in the past, might have been delegated to executives of the major oil companies.

And the president, like his Chinese and Indian counterparts, continued to play a significant role in international energy negotiations, meeting in subsequent years with the leaders of major oil-producing nations in an effort to ensure that the United States was not left behind in the global race to secure new or expanded sources of supply. In January 2008, for instance, Bush again met with Abdullah (now king) during a swing through the Middle East, and reiterated his pleas for increased Saudi oil output on behalf of beleaguered American families. "My point to His Majesty is going to be," he told reporters before the meeting, "when consumers have less purchasing power because of the high prices of gasoline" the U.S. economy will slacken, and so "there will be less barrels of [Saudi] oil purchased."[80] And when the president was not available for missions of this sort, he sent his top aides, including Vice President Cheney and Secretary of State Rice. Cheney, for example, has played a key role in Bush administration efforts to woo the authoritarian leaders of the oil-producing states of the Caspian Sea basin.

No less concerned by the efforts undertaken by China and India to secure new sources of energy, government officials in Japan have copied the Americans in mounting counterefforts of their own. China and Japan have already squared off over the development of undersea gas reserves in the disputed waters of the East China Sea, and both are competing furiously for future Russian oil and gas exports from eastern Siberia and Sakhalin Island. The Japanese have also redoubled their efforts to acquire new drilling rights in North Africa and the Middle East. In 2004, China overtook Japan as the world's second biggest consumer of petroleum, raising the level of anxiety in Japan and prompting an intensified search for foreign sources of energy—a search that will only become more frantic with time.

In the meantime, the struggle for control over key deposits of vital raw materials has gained participants almost by the month as Brazil, Indonesia, Malaysia, South Korea, Turkey, and other rapidly developing nations joined the fray. The resulting "Great Game" over energy, with all its potential for rivalries, alliances, conflicts, schisms, betrayals, and flash points, will surely be a pivotal if not the central—feature of world affairs for the remainder of this century.

4

AN ENERGY JUGGERNAUT

Nothing better exemplifies the altered power relationships of the new international energy order than the emergence of Russia as an energy superpower, capable of leveraging its extraordinary resource abundance into immense geopolitical influence. Not so very long ago the battered, forlorn loser of the Cold War, with seemingly scant prospects of renewal, Russia now enjoys a booming economy and a prominent role in world affairs—especially as a supplier of oil and natural gas to energy-starved nations in Europe and Asia. Russia already provides more than a quarter of the natural gas consumed in Western Europe—a share that will only grow—and is poised to become a major supplier of oil and gas to China, Japan, and other booming East Asian economies. Using its growing clout as an energy provider, its leaders have demanded a greater say in the management of international relations. "We are aware that old impressions fade slowly," Energy Minister Viktor Khristenko observed in May 2006, "but it is time for the West to recognize the maturing role and state of progress that Russia has achieved."[1]

What a reversal of fortune in the blink of an historical eye. Admittedly, Russia had been a significant energy producer during the Soviet era, but the breakup of the USSR in 1991, the ensuing economic chaos, and the wholesale liquidation of state assets led to a sharp decline in its energy output. According to BP's *Statistical Review of World Energy,* Russian oil production plunged from 11.1 million barrels per day in 1989 to a dismal 6.1 million barrels in 1996; its natural gas and coal production underwent similar descents.[2] Only when global oil prices began their dramatic rise and modern production technologies were introduced did a significant turnaround begin. By the end of 2006, the Russians were producing 9.8 million barrels per day (of far more lucrative) oil,[3] and, according to the U.S. Department of Energy, the country was on track to reach 10.3 million barrels by 2015 and 11.2 million by 2025.[4]

This dramatic comeback almost reversed the post-Soviet decline in Russian industrial output by itself, while fueling a remarkable surge in overall economic growth. The country's gross domestic product began to climb again in 2000, the year Vladimir Putin was elected president, and in 2006 grew by approximately 6.7 percent—more than that of any other member of the G-8 club of major industrialized nations. In the same period, Russia's per-capita GDP quadrupled, to nearly $7,000 annually, while about 20 million people were lifted out of poverty.[5] Leading this tide of new wealth were Russian energy giants Gazprom, the state-controlled natural gas monopoly; Rosneft, the leading state-owned oil firm; and Lukoil, Russia's largest privately owned oil company. "The value of Gazprom in 2000 was $9 billion. Today, it is between $250 and $300 billion," boasted board chairman Dmitry A. Medvedev in December 2006.[6]

None of this would have been possible without the impressive raw material inheritance of the Russian Federation. Stretching across eleven time zones and encompassing 6.5 million square miles—more than any other nation—the country harbors some of the world's largest reserves of oil, gas, coal, uranium, and other vital materials. "Russia is exceptionally well-endowed with energy resources and the energy sector plays an increasingly central role in the Russian economy," the International Energy Agency reported in 2004. "Russia holds the world's largest proven natural gas reserves, the second-largest coal reserves, and the seventh-largest oil reserves. It is the world's biggest producer and exporter of natural gas, providing close to a quarter of [Western] Europe's gas needs. It is also the second-largest oil producer and a major exporter of oil to Europe and increasingly to Asia."[7] With vast

Table 4.1

RUSSIA'S ENERGY PROFILE

(As of end of 2006)

Category	Proven Reserves		Production	
	Amount	Percent of World Total	Actual	Percent of World Total
Petroleum, bbl	79.5	6.6	3.6	12.3
Natural gas, tcf	1682.1	26.3	21.6	21.3
Coal	157.0 bt	17.3	144.5 mtoe	4.7
Nuclear energy output, trillion BTUs	n.a.	n.a.	2,117.0	5.6

Source of data: BP, *Statistical Review of World Energy June 2007.*

n.a. = not applicable

bt = billion metric tons

bbl = billion barrels

mtoe = million metric tones of oil equivalent

tcf = trillion cubic feet

stockpiles of as-yet-untapped supplies to draw upon, Russia can continue to propel its economic growth through energy production and exports for decades to come.[8] (See Table 4.1.)

Aside from Russia's impressive economic growth, the revitalized energy landscape had its most dramatic effect on Moscow's geopolitical clout, largely because the Russian Federation—alone of the Great Powers—produces far more energy than it consumes. That allows it to export a significant share of its total output to its energy-deficient neighbors. In 2006, for example, Russia produced 9.8 million barrels of oil per day and consumed only 2.7 million barrels, leaving 7.1 million for export—an amount only Saudi Arabia topped.[9] It likewise consumed only 432 of the 612 billion cubic meters of natural gas produced that year, leaving 180 billion for export, making it the world's number one supplier of that commodity.[10] Adding to its national energy wealth, Russia also produces significantly more coal than it consumes and can export surplus energy from its electrical power system.

From a political perspective, no Russian export is more significant, however, than its sales of natural gas to Western Europe and the former

Eastern European satellites of the USSR. By the 1970s, these regions were connected to Russia's mammoth natural gas reservoirs in western Siberia by the world's largest network of pipelines. Today, these conduits (almost entirely owned by Gazprom) provide a substantial share of Europe's natural gas consumption—96 percent for Greece, 70 percent for Austria, 47 percent for Poland, 43 percent for Germany, 30 percent for Italy, and 26 percent for France.[11] These countries, which are expected to use even more natural gas in the future, have little choice—however strong their desire for diversification—but to rely on Russian gas. No gas producer in Africa or the Middle East possesses such colossal volumes, no less than the extensive pipeline system (or, in the case of liquefied gas, LNG facilities), needed to satisfy the expanding European market.

These key factors invest Russia with singular importance in the new international energy order. Together, they ensure that Russia would be an energy juggernaught even if it had a weak central government and its energy resources were largely controlled by private firms like those that dominate oil and gas extraction in the West. Indeed, it appeared that Russia was headed in this very direction in the aftermath of the USSR's demise, when Russian president Boris Yeltsin presided over the systemic privatization of the country's most valuable energy assets. With the Putin succession, however, this process was radically reversed, leaving the central government once again in substantial control of critical elements of Russia's vast—and now vastly more profitable—energy infrastructure. As a result, senior government officials, determined to exploit the nation's energy reserves to restore Moscow's commanding role in world affairs, have been able to harness natural resource power for geopolitical advantage.

Putin in Command

In Russia's rise to energy superpowerdom, the decisive role of Vladimir Putin cannot be overestimated. At every pivotal moment, he intervened directly (if often behind the scenes) to ensure the triumph of the state over powerful private interests—most notably, the super-rich "oligarchs" who gained control over Russia's most highly prized energy assets after the breakup of the Soviet Union.[12] He also shaped

the overarching strategy governing the Kremlin's struggle to central-
ize its energy authority. Like a commanding general in time of war, he
first mapped out an overall plan of attack and then supervised its
implementation—skirmish by skirmish, battle by battle.[13]

Putin began his career as a field agent in the KGB, the Soviet secret
intelligence service. After fifteen years in intelligence work, much of it
spent in East Germany, he returned to his birthplace, St. Petersburg,
and assumed various positions in the municipal government. In 1998,
he was picked by President Yeltsin to head the Federal Security Service,
the Russian Federation's successor to the KGB; a year later, Yeltsin
chose him to be prime minister. When Yeltsin resigned unexpectedly
on December 31, 1999, Putin became acting president and served in
that capacity until winning his first full term as president, on March
27, 2000; four years later, he was reelected with an even larger share of
the vote.

While serving as a functionary in the St. Petersburg municipal administration in the mid-1990s, Putin managed to complete a doctor-
ate at the St. Petersburg Mining Institute, a historic school with ties to
Russia's governing elites. (It should be noted that geologists commonly
view oil, coal, and natural gas as "mineral" resources.) Here, evidently,
he developed or refined his belief in the crucial role of the state in the
management of the country's natural resource endowment and first
expressed his thoughts on how energy production could contribute to
the reemergence of Russia as a Great Power. In contrast to a widely
held view among Russian economists that privatization and reduced
state control would best spur economic growth, Putin concluded that,
in the natural resource sector at least, state ownership and oversight
was needed to power the economy and prevent the reckless exploitation of Russia's raw materials by foreign investors or unscrupulous
private interests.[14]

When, exactly, he reached these conclusions is not known, but in
1999 he published a summary of his dissertation, "Mineral Raw Materials in the Strategy for the Development of the Russian Economy," in
the journal of his alma mater. This text, according to Martha Brill Olcott of the Carnegie Endowment for International Peace, probably
constitutes the best indication of Putin's views on the subject. "In the

article," Olcott observed, "Putin argues that Russia's natural resource base will not only secure the country's economic development but will also serve as the guarantor of the country's international position." She further notes that "he argues this quite strongly, in a language that should have served as ample warning for the owners and managers of Russia's privately held oil companies, that the state would set the priorities in the oil industry."[15]

"The stable development of the Russian economy in the coming years," Putin wrote in the summary, "needs to be based on the planned growth of its component parts, including in first place, the potential of its mineral resources . . . which will serve as a guarantee of the country's economic security. . . . [T]he development of the raw material sector helps form a strong industrial base which is capable of satisfying the needs of both industry and agriculture; it makes an important contribution to the income of the country as its products remain the basic source of foreign currency. . . . The structural reconfiguration of the national economy on the basis of the country's existing raw materials will be a *strategic factor* of Russia's economic growth in the near term."[16] (Emphasis added.)

From portraying the development of the nation's raw materials as a "strategic factor" to calling for state oversight of this process proved but a short leap once Putin had power in his hands—especially in the Russian context, where the Kremlin (whether in czarist or Soviet times) had always exercised a commanding role in key sectors of the economy. In the summary of his dissertation, Putin did not preclude a significant rule for private interests, including foreign investors—who, he noted, could provide valuable expertise and capital. But it was essential, he argued, that private interests be subordinated to the guiding hand of the state, acting on behalf of the collective interests of the Russian people. "The state," he asserted, "has the right to regulate the process of the acquisition and the use of natural resources, and particularly mineral resources, independent of on whose property they are located."

This extraordinary power should be the state's, Putin claimed, "because it acts in the interests of society as a whole."[17] Nor, he argued, should the state's role be confined to oversight functions alone. In a transitional economy like Russia's, it must also play a decisive role as the *owner* of critical resources and their means of delivery. As noted by Olcott, Putin's stated views and political behavior suggest that he did "not believe in the sanctity of property awarded in the first years following the collapse of the Soviet Union. He view[ed] the ceding of control of this strategic sector to private hands as a costly mistake that must be reversed."[18]

Although his 1999 paper did not explicitly call for the renationalization of properties in private hands, he made no secret of his inclinations on this question: "At the beginning of the market reforms in Russia, the state let go of the natural resource complex for a time. This led to a stagnation of the potential of the nation's natural resources . . . as well as having a number of other negative consequences. . . . [T]he modern strategy of rational resource use cannot be based exclusively on the possibilities of the market as such. This is particularly true in conditions of transitional [economies]."[19]

As president, Putin found himself in an exceptional position to implement these views and quickly began to do so. His first objective was to break the power of the oligarchs and restore state control over the assets they had acquired in the chaos and corruption that had accompanied the USSR's collapse in 1991. As his first target, he chose a formidable adversary indeed—Mikhail Khodorkovsky, the wealthiest man in Russia at that time and the CEO of Yukos, then one of Russia's leading oil producers.

Khodorkovsky, like Putin, had risen from relative obscurity to great prominence in those heady days following the USSR's demise. But whereas Putin sought power and influence in the political sphere, Khodorkovsky sought to accumulate vast wealth in the newly established corporate world. In 1986, at age twenty-three, Khodorkovsky took advantage of Communist Party leader Mikhail Gorbachev's glasnost ("openness") and perestroika (economic "restructuring") policies to open a café that also served as a front for computer and alcohol sales. Three years later, he and a number of business partners founded one of Russia's first private banks, Bank Menatep. Through a series of banking transactions that many now consider illicit, Khodorkovsky accumulated sufficient capital to acquire ownership of Yukos in 1995.

In one of the great coups—or steals—of the century, he paid only $350 million for an enterprise whose market capitalization was then estimated at $31 billion. Once at its helm, Khodorkovsky made further investments in the energy field and rapidly transformed the company into a giant oil and gas conglomerate.[20]

By the fall of 2003, Putin and Khodorkovsky—then the most powerful figures in Russia—were on a seemingly inescapable collision course. Two critical developments brought matters to a head: Khodorkovsky signaled his intention to enter Russian politics, notably by bankrolling parliamentary candidates opposed to Putin's state-centric energy policies, and Yukos became involved in discussions with American firms, including Exxon and Chevron, about the possibility of their acquiring a substantial stake in the company. Either of these initiatives would have been viewed by Putin as constituting a fundamental challenge to his energy strategy and his own power; the combination must have seemed an intolerable threat.[21]

On October 25, 2003, while visiting Yukos facilities in Siberia, Khodorkovsky was arrested by Russian security agents on multiple tax-evasion and fraud charges and flown back to Moscow. While Putin has strenuously denied playing a role in the arrest, most observers believe that the seizure of such a high-profile figure could not have occurred without his connivance.[22] Khodorkovsky was held without bail in a Moscow jail and eventually placed on trial. On May 31, 2005, he was found guilty and sentenced to nine years in prison.

Putin had now done more than simply eliminate a powerful obstacle to his energy strategy: He had also opened the door to the renationalization of Yukos's oil assets. In August 2004, while Khodorkovsky and other top Yukos officials were in jail awaiting trial, the Moscow Arbitration Court seized control of Yuganskneftegas—the company's most productive oil subsidiary—for failure to pay $3.4 billion in back taxes.[23] What happened next reads like a Hollywood-style stock swindle scenario. On December 19, 2004, the Russian government auctioned off the shares of Yuganskneftegas to a previously unknown bidder, the Baikal Finans Group (BFG), for the equivalent of $9.35 billion—just over half of what the company was then thought to be worth. Giving its address as a cell phone store in Tver', a medium-sized city northwest of Moscow, BFG offered no indication of its backers or the source of its funds.[24] Business analysts were still trying to figure out exactly who was behind the BFG acquisition when managers of state-controlled Rosneft announced on December 31 that they had assumed ownership of the mysterious firm and were now in possession of the former Yukos subsidiary—which meant, of course, that the whole operation was now in the hands of Vladimir Putin and his associates.[25]

The Making of Gazprom

Putin next set his sights on an even bigger prize: Gazprom, the world's largest natural gas producer. It alone claims ownership of 16 percent of the world's natural gas reserves—more than that possessed by all the countries in North America, South America, and Asia combined. It also controls the world's largest pipeline network, extending from gas-producing fields in Siberia and Central Asia to markets throughout Western and Southern Europe. The company is Russia's biggest earner of hard currency and provides about one-quarter of federal tax revenues. It also enjoys a monopoly on the export of Russian gas, which makes it the country's most important economic link to its neighbors—especially the former Soviet republics on its periphery that depend on Gazprom for much of their energy supply.[26]

The company came into existence in the final days of the USSR when Mikhail Gorbachev, then president, combined the gas ministry's far-flung operations into one unified enterprise. This giant entity, dubbed Gazprom (for gas industry), was partially privatized in 1993, though the Russian state retained 39.4 percent of its shares and appointed a majority of its board members. During the Yeltsin era, charges of corruption were regularly brought against its directors, and the company failed to provide the sort of stimulus to economic growth envisioned by Putin in his 1999 essay. So, when assuming office in 2000, Putin chose two close allies, Alexei Miller and Dmitry Medvedev, to serve as Gazprom's CEO and chairman of the board and took other steps to improve the company's performance. His key goal, however, was to restore full state control over the company. In June 2005, with its board now dominated by Putin loyalists, Gazprom agreed to sell an additional 10.7 percent of its shares to the Russian state, giving the government majority ownership.[27] (In December 2007, Putin chose Medvedev as his favored candidate for president in the March 2008 elections, almost assuring his selection. Putin, under this scenario, will be chosen prime minister by Medvedev.)

Since 2005, by all accounts, Putin has assumed personal responsibility for Gazprom's continued growth. "Putin effectively controls the company and makes all key decisions about its strategy and displays a surprising acquaintance—for a politician of his rank—with the minute details of its operations," Vladimir Milov, director of the Institute for Energy Policy, a Moscow think tank, observed in 2006.[28] From the beginning, his intentions were clear: to turn Gazprom into an energy powerhouse that would help propel Russia into the front ranks of major world powers. "Under Mr. Putin," noted Gregory L. White of the *Wall Street Journal*, "Gazprom has emerged as the flagship of the Kremlin's drive to build an energy behemoth able to compete with such international titans as Exxon Mobil Corp. and to use Russia's vast reserves of gas and oil to rebuild some of the geopolitical heft that vanished with the collapse of the Soviet Union in 1991."[29]

One of Putin's primary goals was to diversify Gazprom's holdings into the petroleum sector. At one point, its top officers announced plans to merge with Rosneft, the state-controlled oil company, but this effort was abandoned after that firm acquired Yuganskneftegas in early 2005 and became a major energy actor in its own right. Instead, Gazprom set out to acquire Sibneft, a privately held oil firm with substantial holdings in Siberia. In October 2005, Sibneft's principal owner, billionaire Roman Abramovich, an oligarch from the glory days of privatization then living safely in London, agreed to sell a controlling share to Gazprom for a hard-to-resist $13 billion. With this one transaction, the company became the owner of Russia's fifth largest oil producer while the Russian state—through its ownership of both Sibneft and Rosneft—assumed control of one-third of the country's total oil production.[30]

As it happened, this was just the start of Putin's plans for Gazprom. He soon began eyeing oil and gas assets acquired by foreign companies during Yeltsin's tenure, when Russia's bargaining power in such negotiations had been far weaker. Although the Russian government had signed long-term production contracts with giant multinationals like BP, Royal Dutch Shell, and Exxon Mobil, Putin launched a search for ways to invalidate the Yeltsin-era agreements and allow Gazprom to assume a dominant role in the exploitation of these valuable reserves. His game plan first came to light in 2006, when he initiated a no-holds-barred struggle to force the foreign owners of the Sakhalin-2 consortium to sell off a majority stake of their venture.

Sakhalin is a long, narrow island situated off the eastern coast of Russia, just north of Japan's Hokkaidō Island. According to the U.S. Department of Energy, its offshore seabed constitutes one of the most promising new sources of energy in the region, with estimated petroleum reserves of 12 billion barrels and natural gas reserves of 90 trillion cubic feet (the energy equivalent of 16 billion barrels of oil).[31] An immense prize by any reckoning, it was the target of prominent Western companies in the early 1990s, when Russia was still reeling from the breakup of the Soviet Union; a number of these firms were awarded multibillion-dollar "production-sharing agreements" (PSAs) by Yeltsin's government to develop Sakhalin's hydrocarbon riches. (PSAs are complex arrangements whereby a government retains ultimate ownership of an energy reservoir but grants a leasehold over it to a private entity or entities for a specified period of time in return for a share of the future resources extracted.) The first of these ventures, Sakhalin-1, was awarded to a consortium headed by Exxon, while the biggest and most elaborate, Sakhalin-2, was granted to a consortium led by Royal Dutch Shell and backed by the Japanese combines Mitsui and Mitsubishi. Together, the three members of the second project committed $20 billion for development of the field, making this the biggest single foreign investment in Russia.[32]

When completed, Sakhalin-2 is expected to be the world's largest combined oil and natural gas enterprise, encompassing multiple offshore drilling rigs, 500 miles of oil and gas pipelines, an oil terminal, and a multibillion-dollar plant for converting gas into LNG for overseas transport. Toward the end of this decade, when all of these facilities are up and running, it is believed that Sakhalin-2 will produce some 180,000 barrels of oil per day and 9.6 million tons per year of LNG for customers in Japan, South Korea, and the United States (via an LNG regasification plant being constructed in Baja California near the U.S.-Mexico border).[33]

For years, environmental activists in Russia, Japan, and elsewhere had complained that construction of these facilities, already damaging the island's fragile environment, was risking the survival of endangered species, including the Western Pacific gray whale.[34] Predictably, given Russia's historically poor record of environmental protection and the government's disdain for nongovernmental organizations, these complaints had little impact. Then a strange thing happened: On September 6, 2006, the Federal Service for the Supervision of Natural Resources, known by the vaguely reptilian acronym of Rosprirodnadzor, suddenly filed suit to withdraw the environmental permit for all work on Sakhalin-2, citing multiple environmental violations by the Shell-led consortium.[35] Two weeks later, the Ministry of Natural Resources (MNR), acting on Rosprirodnadzor's complaint, annulled the consortium's operating permit, effectively halting work on the project until it complied with a set of costly environmental modifications suddenly demanded by Russian regulators.[36] At the time, Russian officials insisted that protection of the environment was their sole concern, but most observers saw in this Putin's desire to compel Shell and the other Sakhalin-2 investors to make room for Gazprom.[37]

For three months, the consortium tried to resist the Russian regulators. "Specific issues referred to by Rosprirodnadzor and MNR are immaterial," the partners argued. "All concerns are being addressed expeditiously in cooperation with the relevant authorities and do not constitute any legal grounds for annulment."[38] But as soon as the consortium brought one component of the project up to standards that satisfied the regulators, something else was found to be in noncompliance. On October 25, 2006, for example, MNR's director, Yury Trutnev, told reporters, "Here we need to consider halting construction on several parts of [an offshore] pipeline. I do not think that it will be correct to halt the project entirely, but we have to demand compliance with environmental legislation."[39] Six weeks later, following yet another Rosprirodnadzor investigation, MNR suspended twelve wateruse licenses, preventing further work on the landward stretch of the pipeline.[40]

Finally, in December, the consortium threw in the towel. Concluding that they would be forced to spend billions of dollars to satisfy Russian regulators without ever seeing a cent of profit, Shell and its partners agreed to sell a majority stake in the Sakhalin-2 partnership to Gazprom at a discounted price. At a Kremlin meeting presided over by Putin himself, Gazprom announced that it would acquire 50 percent plus one share of the venture for $7.45 billion, considerably less than the estimated market value of the energy assets involved. Shell, once the majority shareholder, saw its stake drop from 55 to 27.5 percent, while the stakes held by Mitsui and Mitsubishi dropped from 25 and 20 percent to 12.5 and 10 percent, respectively.[41] And what about all those environmental problems discovered by Russian regulators? These had been "resolved," Putin assured reporters.[42]

By now, Putin had achieved two paramount objectives: He had ensured state control over the most promising new sources of oil and gas in Russia's Far East, and he had completely recast the relationship between the Russian government and foreign energy firms, turning them into junior partners in any major oil and gas enterprises. By gaining control of Sakhalin-2, moreover, he had added another 1 billion barrels of oil and 17.3 trillion cubic feet of natural gas to Gazprom's already massive proven reserves.[43] As for relations with foreign firms, it was evident that none of them could expect to be a main project operator any longer.[44]

In line with this stance, the Kremlin took several other steps to consolidate state control over vital energy assets. Most strikingly, on October 9, 2006, Gazprom announced that it would develop the supergiant Shtokman offshore natural gas field by itself, rather than form a consortium with major Western firms, as had previously been expected. Located in the Barents Sea about 340 miles from the Russian coast, the Shtokman field is considered one of the world's largest remaining untapped sources of energy, housing an estimated 3.7 trillion cubic meters of natural gas and 31 million metric tons of gas condensate, together the equivalent of 20 billion barrels of oil.[45] Originally, Gazprom had planned to convert the gas into LNG for sale to the United States in particular; in its October announcement, however, the company indicated that it would develop the field on its own and transport the gas to Europe by pipeline.[46] (Gazprom later amended its stance slightly, agreeing to invite selected foreign firms to play purely supporting roles in the project.[47])

In June 2007, in yet another assertion of Kremlin authority, Russian officials forced British oil giant BP to cede its holdings in the $20 billion Kovykta natural gas field to Gazprom for an estimated $600–$800 million. An immense deposit near Lake Baikal in Siberia, Kovykta contains an estimated 2 trillion cubic meters of natural gas and 83 million tons of gas condensate, readily convertible into liquid fuel. BP and a group of Russian private investors (incorporated as TNK), with a joint 62.7 percent stake in the field, had unveiled ambitious plans to pipe its abundant gas to China but had been blocked from building the necessary infrastructure by Russian officials, who once again wore their opponents down through lengthy court proceedings—first by issuing impossible-to-meet production demands and then by charging them with breach of contract. In the end, TNK-BP agreed to sell out rather than risk the loss of their Siberian assets; BP now hopes to participate as a joint partner with Gazprom, but prospects for that appear grim.[48]

Bush and Putin

Putin's drive to reassert state control over Russia's natural resources was accompanied by a pronounced shift in Moscow's relationships with the major Western powers. When President Yeltsin first awarded production-sharing agreements to Shell, Exxon, and other foreign firms in the early 1990s, he was forced to acquiesce to terms that were more characteristic of novice oil producers in Africa than mature oil powers like Kuwait or Saudi Arabia. By the time Putin was ready to hijack Sakhalin-2, he understood—and the rest of the world recognized—that there was little the major Western powers could do to stop him. "Times have changed in Russia," observed Oleg V. Mitvol, the Rosprirodnadzor official who spearheaded the campaign to annul the consortium's operating permit. "We want international investment, but we don't want to be made into a banana republic."[49]

A revealing expression of this shifting balance of power can be found in the shattered expectations for the "U.S.-Russian Energy Dialogue" initiated by George W. Bush early in his presidency. In the period following September 11, 2001, Bush sought Russia's aid in his Global War on Terror, and a seemingly agreeable Putin promised to help in any way he could. Initially, Bush asked for intelligence sharing and overflight rights for U.S. aircraft bound for Afghanistan, which the old USSR, of course, would never have considered granting. Later, he suggested that Russia could serve as an alternate source of energy supplies for the United States, thereby diminishing American reliance on the ever-turbulent Middle East. To further this goal, Bush proposed greater cooperation between American and Russian energy firms, entailing just the sort of American corporate investment in Russian energy projects that Putin would soon come to reject.[50]

Although many in the Bush camp continued to view Russia through the hostile lens of the Cold War, the president made an early effort to approach Putin free of such baggage. After his first meeting with the Russian leader, a one-on-one encounter in Slovenia, he famously declared, "I looked the man in the eye. I found him to be very straightforward and trustworthy."[51] He thus had every reason to believe that Putin would be open to his energy priorities when the two held their first summit meeting in Moscow, on May 24, 2002—and, at that early stage, it did appear that the Russian president was prepared to meet Bush's expectations. The two actually announced the establishment of a "new energy dialogue" between their countries. According to a White House fact sheet, that "dialogue" was intended to pave the way for a U.S. role in developing Russia's vast natural resource bounty. "We welcome the fact that the Russian Federation has confirmed its role as a major world energy provider," Bush and Putin declared at the conclusion of their Moscow encounter. They would, the two leaders agreed, work to "facilitate commercial cooperation in the energy sector, enhancing interaction between our companies in exploration, production, refining, transportation, and marketing of energy, as well as in implementation of joint projects."[52]

As the first step in this endeavor, the two countries sponsored a "U.S.-Russia Commercial Energy Summit" in Houston in October of that year, with representatives of seventy or so major U.S. and Russian energy firms in attendance. Signaling the importance it attached to this endeavor, the White House dispatched such luminaries as Secretary of Commerce Donald Evans and Secretary of Energy Spencer Abraham to address the gathering; the Russian government was represented by Minister of Energy Igor Yusufov.[53] One after the other, these dignitaries touted the advantages of marrying American technological expertise to Russian energy abundance. Still, several speakers warned of the numerous obstacles that would have to be overcome before all these benefits could be achieved—in particular, the construction of new export pipelines and loading facilities allowing for the delivery of Russian oil and gas to the United States. All agreed, however, that tackling these challenges was well worth the effort.[54] As Yusufov suggested, "We do have some undeveloped resources in the Russian Federation that can become very reliable sources of energy for the United States."[55] In the euphoria of the moment, participants in the meeting agreed to hold a commercial summit in Moscow the following year and establish a Commercial Energy Working Group to promote further collaboration among American and Russian energy companies.

The spirit of cooperation lingered into 2004, despite widespread international concern provoked by the arrest of Khodorkovsky and the absorption of Yukos's assets into state-controlled Rosneft. But few of the grand collaborative ventures envisioned at the various summits ever materialized. With this in mind, Bush tried to persuade Putin again to head down the path of cooperation (as the American president defined it) during a private meeting in Bratislava, the capital of Slovakia, on February 24, 2005. The two emerged smiling at a press conference following the meeting. "Cooperation on energy issues remains an area of great promise for U.S.-Russian relations," they affirmed in a joint statement.[56] But despite the lofty words, as the months rolled by, it became clear that Putin had no more intention of abiding by commitments made at a time of relative weakness than he had of turning Yuganskneftegas back to its imprisoned owner.

In September 2005, when Sen. Chuck Hagel (R-Neb.) convened a Senate subcommittee hearing on "Energy Supplies in Eurasia and Implications for U.S. Energy Security," senior figures in the Bush administration were openly beginning to express alarm over developments in Russia[57]—and things only went downhill from there. None of the pipelines or other projects advocated by the Bush administration for the enhanced delivery of Russian oil and gas to the United States seemed to be making the slightest headway. Worse yet, Putin seemed intent on bolstering Russia's energy ties with Europe and Asia. Gazprom's October 2006 decision to pump future gas from the Shtokman field directly to Europe rather than converting it into LNG for delivery to the United States was a particularly severe blow.[58] The White House was also troubled by Moscow's use of the natural gas spigot as a tool of political warfare, especially among the former Soviet republics on its periphery. In the cases of Ukraine and Georgia, both of which were threatened with a gas cutoff in the middle of winter, the political message had been unambiguous: Stray too far from Moscow's orbit and you will suffer the consequences.

All of this was too much to be ignored. At a much publicized pro-democracy conference in Latvia on May 4, 2006, Vice President Cheney concluded his remarks on Russia by declaring, "No legitimate interest is served when oil and gas become tools of intimidation or blackmail, either by supply manipulation or attempts to monopolize transportation."[59] President Bush did not offer equally harsh remarks on Russia's energy behavior, but he was publicly critical of the erosion of democracy and the human rights situation in Russia during Putin's watch.[60] He also approved a number of military moves—which any Russian leader would have seen as provocative—including the promised future deployment of antimissile batteries in Poland (supposedly intended to intercept missiles from Iran but widely viewed in Moscow as aimed at Russian weapons). These further soured ties between the two countries, sparking talk of a "new Cold War."[61]

The Sino-Japanese Competition for Siberian Oil

Vladimir Putin also exhibited an increasingly imperious manner as he skillfully manipulated the fierce competition between China and Japan for access to Russia's untapped oil and gas reserves in eastern Siberia. Both countries would like to reduce their energy reliance on the ever-turbulent Middle East. Russia, which shares a long common border with China and is only separated from Japan by the relatively narrow Sea of Japan, is an obvious source for such diversification. In addition, its vast reserves in eastern Siberia are far away from existing markets in Europe but comparatively close to Asian ones.

Two factors, however, give this competition for Siberian oil its particular fierceness (and Putin his leverage): It's unclear whether eastern Siberia possesses sufficient reserves to quench the future thirst of both China and Japan, and there is, at present, no pipeline to bring the oil to either country. As a result, where the next pipeline ends will determine much—and Putin remains the ultimate arbiter of this high-stakes game.

By all accounts, Chinese leaders had assumed that the oil and gas would naturally flow to China, given the increasingly close relations between the two countries and the relative proximity of the fields to the Chinese border. After all, as early as July 16, 2001, China and Russia had signed a "treaty of friendship and cooperation," pledging close collaboration in economic and security matters—a pledge many in Beijing assumed would lead to cooperation in energy affairs as well. What they did not count on was the audacity and persistence of then Japanese prime minister Junichiro Koizumi.

In early 2003, Koizumi launched a vigorous campaign to persuade Moscow to build its future Siberian pipeline with Japan, not China, in mind. During a state visit to Moscow that January, he wrung a pledge from Putin to consider a pipeline from eastern Siberia to Nakhodka on Russia's Pacific coast, directly opposite Japan. He offered, in return, a promise of substantial Japanese financing. "Both sides share the recognition that the realization of a project in the Russian Far East and the Siberian region to develop energy resources and construct a pipeline for transportation of such resources would be of mutual benefit," Putin and Koizumi declared.[62] And it is not hard to see why: Tokyo would secure a prolific new source of energy, while Moscow would gain a wealthy, potentially pliant new customer with the deep pockets necessary to help finance costly infrastructure projects in a largely undeveloped region.

The unexpected Japanese initiative undoubtedly shocked Chinese leaders, who began a fierce lobbying campaign of their own. This evidently was a major topic of discussion when Premier Wen visited Moscow in September 2004. "Cooperation in the field of petroleum and natural gas is an important area of the trade and economic cooperation between the two countries," he told reporters after meeting with senior Russian officials.[63]

But such efforts still proved no match for the allure of Koizumi's charm offensive. The Japanese prime minister repeatedly lobbied Putin and kept raising the sum Tokyo was willing to commit—to as much as $9 billion, according to some accounts.[64] He and his aides also touted the advantages of a pipeline route that would terminate on Russia's Pacific coast, permitting oil sales not only to Japan but to many potential clients, rather than one customer alone.[65] On December 31, 2004, obviously swayed by these appeals, the Kremlin announced that Japan had prevailed: the East Siberia–Pacific Ocean (ESPO) pipeline, as it was now called, would extend 2,500 miles from Taishet in Siberia to Perevoznaya Bay, just a few hundred miles across the Sea of Japan from the main Japanese islands.[66]

Officials in Tokyo were elated by the Russian decision. As *Oil & Gas*

Proposed Routes for the East Siberia Pacific Ocean Pipeline

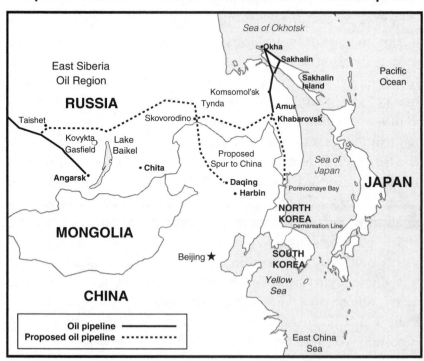

Journal noted, "Russia's decision to build the pipeline from eastern Siberia to the Pacific could be regarded as a diplomatic victory for Japan over China, both of which have lobbied hard for an oil route serving their needs."[67] But Tokyo's elation proved short-lived, as Russia and China drew ever closer in response to the growing international assertiveness of the United States. In the end, President Hu prevailed on Putin to retract his promise and adopt a more evenhanded stance on the ultimate destination of Siberian energy.

The Chinese leader had his first opportunity to persuade Putin to reverse course at a summit meeting in Moscow on July 1, 2005. Although many items were on the agenda, joint efforts to contain and push back the United States in Central Asia evidently were at the top of the list. The two signed a "Declaration on World Order in the 21st Century" calling for regional collaboration in efforts to resist the "aspirations for monopoly and dominance in international affairs" exhibited by certain unnamed countries, widely understood to be the United States.[68]

It must have been obvious to each head of state that Sino-Russian strategic cooperation would not go very far without Russian acquiescence on the Siberian pipeline issue—as Hu no doubt made clear. Certainly, when Russian officials announced plans later in the year for construction work to begin on the ESPO pipeline, there was no mention of a Pacific coast terminus. The pipeline was now to reach the railroad junction of Skovorodino, a mere thirty miles from the Chinese border—and a long haul from the Pacific. From Skovorodino, the announcement indicated, oil would be loaded onto railroad cars for delivery to either China's refinery complex in Daqing or to Perevoznaya Bay on the Pacific for transshipment to Japan and other Asian nations. Meanwhile, plans would be developed to extend the pipeline from Skovorodino one way or the other—or both ways—at some unspecified future moment.[69]

Neither the Japanese nor the Chinese were entirely satisfied. At one point, Japan threatened to withhold financing for the project,[70] but for the most part Koizumi relied on diplomacy to advance his cause. At a summit meeting in Tokyo in November 2005, he again implored Putin to extend the line all the way to the Pacific, reportedly receiving a noncommittal response.[71] In answer to probing questions from Japanese journalists, the deputy press secretary of the Japanese Ministry of Foreign Affairs provided this synopsis of the Koizumi-Putin interchange, underscoring Putin's utter control of the outcome: "The truth of the matter is, what President Putin did during the meeting with Prime Minister Koizumi was that he drew a map on a piece of paper, saying that from a place called Taishet through Skovorodino to the Pacific Ocean, this is the route that the pipeline is supposed to take." While the precise orientation of the final leg had yet to be determined, the official noted, "this line is called the Pacific Ocean line or something like that. The name tells itself. That is what President Putin said."[72]

Similar conversations, no doubt, have been held between Putin and Chinese officials—with equally vague nods in the direction of Chinese aspirations. At yet another Hu-Putin summit in Beijing on March 21, 2006, for instance, Putin agreed to substantially boost Russian deliveries of oil and gas to China. Sino-Russian energy cooperation "is entering a qualitative new level," the two affirmed at the meeting's end.[73] But nothing in this declaration or in Putin's parting comments suggested that he was committed to extending the ESPO pipeline from Skovorodino to Daqing.[74] Only much later, when Beijing sent a down payment for construction of the Daqing leg, did the Russians agree to begin drawing up engineering plans for that offshoot. Meanwhile, Moscow still insists that it will someday continue the line all the way to the Pacific coast, but no date has been set for this to happen.[75]

Gazprom Flexes Its Muscles

If Hu Jintao and Junichiro Koizumi, the leaders of two of the more powerful nations on the planet, were engaged in obsequious diplomacy with Moscow, imagine the lengths to which the leaders of weaker lands on Russia's periphery have had to go to ensure the continued delivery of essential fuel supplies from a previously humbled, now ascendant superpower in Moscow. Not surprisingly, the Kremlin, too, considered itself ready to go one step further in relation to states that had formerly been part of the Soviet Union, with control over the source of much-needed natural gas supplies as its weapon of choice.

During the Soviet era, these states had all been integrated into the highly centralized oil and gas delivery systems mandated by central authorities in Moscow. For the most part, this meant they consumed oil and natural gas pumped from fields in Russia and the Central Asian republics; while this constrained their energy choices, these regions were at least essentially energy-subsidized by Soviet central planners.

When the USSR collapsed, these republics—now independent—naturally hoped to rely on these same sources of supply. On assuming office, Putin quickly made it clear, however, that they would have to begin paying for their energy in a "marketized" environment. At first, Russia continued to provide oil and gas to its former partners at deeply discounted rates, hoping thereby to retain some degree of influence over them; as some of these countries began to stray from Moscow's orbit, however, Russian leaders began to apply energy pressure. They decided to reserve the lower rates for only their most loyal clients and began insisting on market rates for any country that was threatening to pursue an independent course. This decision, once implemented, sparked a series of clashes with the former Soviet republics.[76]

The first—and still most dramatic—occurred on January 1, 2006. In the early hours of New Year's Day, Gazprom suddenly cut off the flow of natural gas to Ukraine—in the middle of a particularly harsh cold spell, no less. Ostensibly, the cutoff was triggered by Ukraine's refusal to pay the higher prices the company was demanding. In fact, until then, the Russians had been notably lenient, providing Ukraine with gas at $50 per 1,000 cubic meters at a time when prevailing prices in Western Europe were $220 or more. This had been true even after Ukraine's "Orange Revolution" of December 2004, which had replaced a pro-Moscow president, Viktor Yanukovich, with a pro-Western candidate, Viktor Yushchenko. But when Yushchenko refused even to consider higher rates in endless negotiations with Gazprom, Moscow simply turned off the spigot.

Ukraine would have been plunged into an immediate (and possibly lethal) energy crisis except for one thing—Gazprom's main gas pipeline to Western Europe ran through its territory, and the Ukrainians promptly responded to the Russian cutoff by siphoning off gas meant for Europe to satisfy their own requirements. The result was a double public relations catastrophe for the Russians: Not only were they accused

of using energy as a political instrument to punish a former vassal that
dared to challenge their authority, but their future reliability as a supplier to more important (and panicked) customers in Western Europe
was called into question. Thus impugned, Moscow quickly worked out
an interim settlement with the Ukrainians that allowed the gas to resume flowing on January 3.[77]

In spite of the bad press it received, Gazprom was not deterred
from wielding the energy cudgel again. The next two states to face the
company's displeasure were Georgia and Belarus, both of which were
ordered to pay substantially higher prices for their imported fuel or
face a total gas cutoff—again in the deep of winter—on January 1,
2007. That Georgia, the former Soviet republic in the southern Caucasus, should be exposed to Moscow's wrath was hardly surprising, given
President Mikhail Saakashvili's close ties with Washington and a long
history of friction between the two countries. But Moscow's hard-line
stance toward Alexander Lukashenko, the obstinately Soviet-style
president of Belarus—once considered a close Putin ally—was unexpected. (Most observers concluded that Lukashenko had simply lost
his usefulness to Moscow.)[78] In any event, both countries vowed defi-
ance when threatened by a gas cutoff and appealed to the West for support; but, despite muted disapproval of Russian behavior by European
officials, the two countries were largely left on their own. Both considered their meager options and concluded that capitulation was the
wiser course of action: Georgia bowed to Gazprom's price demands on
December 22, 2006; Belarus on New Year's Eve.[79]

In yet another expression of Gazprom's expanding sway, Armenia
agreed in April 2006 to sell a crucial stretch of natural gas pipeline to
the company in return for a continued discount on Russian gas. The
stretch of pipeline involved, only twenty-four miles long, is valuable to
Moscow because it provides a direct connection between Gazprom's
vast Eurasian distribution system and Iran's natural gas fields. (Armenia and Iran share a narrow common border.) Though this conduit is
exceedingly short, it would allow Gazprom to market Iranian gas to
Europe and various former Soviet regions, if conditions someday permit. Armenia's willingness to part with the critical pipeline, thereby
further limiting its own energy-import options, underscores its con-

tinuing reliance on Russian military support in a largely unfriendly neighborhood—Armenia is an almost exclusively Christian nation surrounded by Muslim neighbors—and the undeniable attraction of deeply discounted energy supplies.[80]

It was not surprising that Moscow would choose to employ its energy clout to extract concessions from former Soviet republics; more startling was the degree to which the major European powers muffled their criticism of Moscow's overbearing treatment of these countries. True, assorted European leaders expressed dismay at the lack of finesse exhibited by their Russian counterparts, but Russia has paid no significant price for its strong-arm tactics. In fact, quite the opposite is true: Only months after Gazprom cut off the flow of gas to Ukraine, European energy officials were lining up at its door to sign new multibillion-dollar supply agreements. In June 2006, for example, Denmark's state-owned DONG Energy A/S signed a twenty-year contract with Gazprom that will bring Russian gas to the Danish market in 2011. At about the same time, the Dutch energy company NV Nederlandse Gasunie agreed to take a stake in Gazprom's planned "Nord Stream" natural gas pipeline under the Baltic Sea to Germany and beyond.[81] In November 2006, Italian energy giant Eni forged a strategic alliance with Gazprom aimed at boosting Russian gas exports to Italy.[82] Asked about Gazprom's aggressive behavior toward Ukraine, the company's chief executive, Paolo Scaroni, told reporters, "We see no blackmail at all."[83]

The only plausible explanation for all this is that the Europeans have already become too heavily reliant on Russian natural gas not to be aware of the way such tactics could someday be used on them, yet see no escape from their predicament. At present, the Western European countries rely on gas for about 23 percent of their combined energy supply, a number that is certain to rise as they cut back on their use of coal and petroleum in accordance with the Kyoto Protocol (and any successor aggreements). With local gas production—mostly concentrated in the North Sea—in decline, and alternative suppliers in Africa and the Middle East incapable of meeting Europe's rising needs, the only plausible source of increased supplies is, of course, Russia.[84] Rather than turn their backs on Moscow, European leaders have largely chosen to acquiesce in Russia's dominance in the energy field, and to encourage their national firms to eke out what profits they can from cooperation with Gazprom and other Russian enterprises.

Gazprom's Global Interests

Having restored state control over Russia's most crucial oil and gas assets, Putin turned in his final years as president (he is obliged under the country's constitution to step down in May 2008) to an even more ambitious goal: gaining control over, or part ownership of, pipelines and processing facilities in other countries—a feat that would give Russia an even more exalted status in the new international energy order. This strategy first became evident in 2006, when Gazprom acquired bits and pieces of pipeline in the former Soviet space. It has been gaining momentum ever since.

Some of Gazprom's first foreign pipeline acquisitions occurred in the context of disputes over pricing for long-standing Russian natural gas clients, starting with that strategic stretch of pipeline Gazprom pried away from Armenia in 2006. Belarus was the next to hand over pipeline control, as part of its New Year's Eve agreement with Moscow. In return for a deeply discounted rate of $100 per 1,000 cubic meters of natural gas, it agreed to allow Gazprom to acquire a 50 percent stake in the Belarus gas-transit monopoly, Beltransgaz, a major conduit for natural gas supplies to Western Europe.[85]

Russia's other acquisitions in Europe have been of a more conventional, corporatist nature, although all reflect Putin's personal lobbying and diplomacy. In March 2006, for example, Putin presided at a ceremony in Athens marking the inking of an agreement to build an oil pipeline across the Balkans from Burgas on Bulgaria's Black Sea coast to Alexandroupolis in Greece on the Aegean. The $1.3 billion pipeline will be majority-owned by a consortium of Gazprom, Rosneft, and Transneft, with minority shares held by Bulgarian and Greek firms; when completed, it will carry oil from Russia as well as the Tengiz field in Kazakhstan to the Mediterranean.[86] In another such endeavor, Putin was present in Vienna on May 23–24, 2007, when Gazprom announced the formation of a joint venture with Austria's leading gas utility, OMV, to build a major gas storage and distribution center at Baumgarten, near the Austrian capital.[87] And, in his last trip abroad as president, Putin signed an agreement with Bulgarian officials in January 2008 to facilitate construction of the "South Stream" gas pipeline from Russia under the Black Sea to Bulgaria, Greece, and Italy.[88]

The Russian president and other senior officials were also heavily involved in efforts to extend Russian participation in the development, production, and distribution of hydrocarbon assets in Central Asia and the Caspian Sea basin. In particular, Moscow has sought to ensure a dominant role for Gazprom in the transportation of Central Asia gas to Western Europe. Under a May 2007 agreement with Kazakhstan and Turkmenistan, Gazprom will be the prime mover in a complex plan to increase the flow of natural gas from these countries to European markets by way of Russia. This plan took a step closer to reality in December 2007 when President Putin presided over a Kremlin ceremony in which the leaders of Kazakhstan and Turkmenistan agreed to proceed with construction of a gas pipeline to carry Turkmen gas through Kazakhstan to Russia for onward delivery via Gazprom's extensive pipeline network to customers there and in Europe.[89] These moves, like so many others, reflected a concerted drive to acquire ownership or control over an ever-expanding network of energy-delivery systems reaching from one end of Eurasia to the other.

As if to symbolize Putin's almost unbounded ambitions, a government-backed submarine expedition planted the Russian flag on the seabed at the North Pole on August 2, 2007, in an audacious gesture to claim the area as an extension of Russian territory—and thus gain control over any hydrocarbon deposits that may be found in the earth below the Arctic Ocean.[90] Many energy experts believe that the Arctic region harbors valuable deposits of oil and gas and that, with the polar ice cap shrinking year by year due to global warming, these reserves could, in the not-too-distant future, be accessible to high-tech drilling.

With his tenure as president drawing to a close, the former KGB officer turned supreme national leader could claim a remarkable series of cold-eyed, hard-nosed successes in his drive to implement the energy strategy he first disclosed in an obscure academic journal in 1999. A large share of Russia's massive oil and gas reserves has been brought back under state control, and the systemic development and exploitation of those reserves have helped fuel impressive economic growth for eight consecutive years. In the process, Russia has become a major supplier of energy to Central, Southern, and Western Europe, and has begun to acquire ownership of critical elements of energy infrastructure in these and other areas. Putin's dreams of employing Russia's resource abundance to restore the country's status as a major world power, thereby commanding the respect—if not the affection— of all other major powers, are now a distinct reality.

But Vladimir Putin is hardly gone from the world stage, and his commanding role as the ultimate architect of Russia's energy policies is unlikely to fade. Assuming that Dmitry Medvedev is elected president in March 2008 as expected, and that he picks Putin to serve as prime minister (as he has said he would), the Russian leader would continue to dominate national affairs—though with a different job title. As prime minister, Putin would also exercise control over the various government ministries that oversee the energy industry, so his influence in this domain would remain undiluted. Medvedev is also expected to defer to his mentor on major foreign policy matters, so for all practical purposes Putin will remain in command of the Russian energy juggernaut. "I formulated tasks for the development of Russia from 2010 until 2020," Putin declared at a Kremlin press conference on February 14, 2008. "The fate is taking shape in a way that I have a possibility to participate directly in achievement of these goals."[91]

5

DRAINING THE CASPIAN

The Caspian Sea basin and Central Asia, areas once largely sub-
sumed within the Soviet Union, are now the cockpit for a
twenty-first-century energy version of the imperial "Great Game" of
the nineteenth century. The region is today divided among eight new
states—Armenia, Azerbaijan, Georgia, Kazakhstan, Kyrgyzstan, Tajikistan, Turkmenistan, and Uzbekistan—plus Russia and Iran. Although
the Caspian's untapped hydrocarbon reserves are not as voluminous as
those of the Persian Gulf area, they constitute an important new
source of energy and so exercise a powerful magnetic force. Virtually
all the major energy-consuming nations have sought a foothold in the
Caspian basin, while Russia—though not in need of oil and natural
gas itself—has worked to dominate the transportation and distribution of the region's energy riches. The result has been a dangerous vor-
tex of competitive pressures.

The greater Caspian area has emerged in recent years as a crucial
arena for investment by international energy companies, both private
and state-owned. According to a January 2007 Department of Energy
assessment, "The Caspian Sea region, including the Sea and the states
surrounding it, is important to world markets because of its potential
to become a major oil and natural gas exporter over the next decade."[1]
DoE projections of future energy output make this vague description

graphic indeed. The Caspian Sea area is expected to post a 171 percent rise in oil production between 2005 and 2030, one of the few areas of the world with the potential to achieve an increase of this magnitude. Natural gas production, predicts the DoE, will grow by at least as much, if not more.[2] Just as significant, the new nations of the Caspian region are eager to export their surplus energy to international markets and, for the most part, are willing to cooperate with foreign firms in making this possible.

Few could have foreseen this extraordinary situation just two decades ago. Until the breakup of the Soviet Union, the states of Central Asia and the Caucasus were under the tight control of Moscow, and whatever oil and gas surpluses they produced were largely consumed within the boundaries of the USSR. Foreign energy firms were not allowed to operate in this area, and most decisions regarding the design and placement of oil rigs, refineries, and pipelines were made by Soviet central planners. Moscow generally tended to favor the development of oil and gas fields in Russia proper, leaving some of the basin's most promising hydrocarbon deposits undeveloped. Because the Soviets lacked the know-how—and the inclination—to develop offshore fields in the Caspian Sea, these, too, were left largely untouched.

All this changed after 1991 with the emergence of independent Caspian basin states. Wishing to escape the iron grip of the Soviet economic system but lacking the technical and financial capacity to fully exploit their oil and gas reserves, they eagerly sought assistance from Western firms. The first company to take advantage of this unprecedented opening was Chevron, which in 1993 signed a multibillion-dollar accord with the government of Kazakhstan to develop the huge onshore Tengiz field. Since then, a host of other companies, including firms from Italy, France, Britain, Norway, China, and Japan, have acquired rights to other promising fields in the region.[3]

These firms—and the governments that have encouraged and facilitated their efforts—have joined the energy equivalent of a gold rush, a rare opportunity to gain access to assets that had previously been off-limits. For the United States and Europe, the Caspian offers an attractive alternative to the Persian Gulf and its troubles. The Chinese perception is similar, in part due to anxiety over the Gulf's chronic instability and in part because of fear that the United States might someday use its dominant position there to block China's access to its oil reserves. Many in Europe hope that the Caspian will reduce their dependence on Russia, even as the Russians seek to gain greater control over Caspian oil and gas deliveries to foreign markets. This complex interplay of motives animates an increasingly fierce struggle for the region's energy supplies.

The Caspian's Long-Term Promise

The Caspian Sea basin is not exactly an undeveloped energy-producing region. At the end of the nineteenth century, the areas around Baku (in modern-day Azerbaijan) and Grozny (in Chechnya, an embattled republic of the Russian Federation) were major petroleum producers. At that time John D. Rockefeller's Standard Oil Company was the leading producer in the world's number one oil supplier, the United States. With the demand for petroleum products growing worldwide, savvy investors saw an opportunity to challenge America's dominance by expanding output in the Caucasus. Two prominent European families—the Nobels of Sweden and the Rothschilds of France—were particularly ambitious, acquiring substantial holdings in the Baku region. Thanks in part to their daring and business acumen, by the 1880s the Baku area had nearly equaled U.S. output. Huge fortunes were made and the city became a major center of wealth and commerce. However, careless and rapid expansion damaged Baku's oil fields and production gradually slowed.[4]

Following World War I and the establishment of the Soviet Union, all foreign enterprises in Baku were nationalized and their operations reconfigured to meet the growing needs of the rapidly industrializing USSR. Oil production continued, but the Soviets developed newer fields in western Siberia, closer to the Russian industrial heartland. Still, Baku was pumping enough oil at the onset of World War II to attract a major German assault, which was finally stopped by Soviet forces in the mountains west of Grozny. Some analysts believe that Hitler's failure to capture Baku and its oil reserves represented one of the critical turning points of World War II, forcing

Germany to confront the industrially ever-stronger Allies with dwindling stocks of petroleum.[5]

Production was restored for a second time after the war, but with greater emphasis now being placed on expanding the Soviet Union's fields in western Siberia, drilling and processing facilities in the Baku region were allowed to deteriorate. While some investment was put into Central Asia's abundant natural gas and uranium resources, old oil rigs in the Baku area were not replaced and the whole area took on the look of an abandoned, environmentally ravaged wasteland. "[Baku's] landscape is littered with the detritus of past oil crazes," Guy Chazan of the *Wall Street Journal* could observe as late as 2005. "Along with faded gems like the Villa Nobel [once the family palace] are forests of Soviet derricks still standing by the Caspian, rusting amid pools of black sludge."[6] Vivid images of this nightmarish expanse can be seen in the 1999 James Bond movie *The World Is Not Enough.*

By the time of the Soviet collapse in 1991, the major Caspian producers—Azerbaijan, Kazakhstan, Turkmenistan, and Uzbekistan—were negligible factors in the international petroleum trade. That year their combined output was a mere 995,000 barrels per day; three years later, daily Caspian production had slipped to 835,000 barrels, barely 1 percent of total world output.[7] But by then, foreign energy firms were eyeing the Caspian's potential oil wealth. Acutely aware that Soviet oil geologists had identified but failed to develop promising deposits in Kazakhstan and the Caspian seabed, these companies were eager to take advantage of Moscow's historic neglect. And the new elites rising to power in the region were likewise inclined to align themselves with the West, both to demonstrate their independence from Moscow and generate new sources of wealth for themselves. Before long, the energy giants—Chevron, Exxon, BP, and Shell—were scouring the region for promising oil and gas concessions.

When this quest began, many energy analysts—giddy at the prospect of finding mammoth new oil and gas reservoirs—issued highly inflated assessments of the Caspian's ultimate energy potential. In an April 1997 report to Congress, for example, the U.S. Department of State claimed that the region harbored as much as 200 billion barrels of oil, or about ten times the amount thought to lie in the North Sea.[8]

Although not backed up by rigorous geological data, the figure of 200 billion barrels became something of a mantra, repeated whenever the region's oil prospects came up for discussion.[9] The Department of Energy was only a bit more circumspect, reporting in June 2000 that the Caspian Sea basin harbored 18–35 billion barrels of oil in "proven" reserves along with an estimated 235 billion barrels in "possible" reserves.[10] Nevertheless, that 200-billion-barrel figure continued to act as a powerful lure to investors and their government backers.

Just a few years into the new century, however, a more cautious assessment of the Caspian's potential came to prevail. "The Caspian Sea region contains proven oil reserves estimated to be between 17 and 44 billion barrels, comparable to Qatar on the low end and the United States on the high end," the DoE reported in September 2005.[11] These figures, not the 200 billion barrels bandied about in the 1990s, currently dominate commercial assessments of the basin's long-term potential. But what most interests global energy firms today are a rather different set of projections: those covering the region's day-to-day productive capacity. Because many of the Caspian's most promising oil and gas fields are still undeveloped or just entering commercial production, the region is expected to post ever-increasing output tallies at a time when so many other fields around the world are delivering less. Hence, according to the DoE, combined Caspian oil production is projected to climb from 2.1 million barrels per day in 2005 to 4.3 million barrels in 2015, 4.8 million in 2020, and 5.7 million in 2030.[12] It is to secure a piece of this *added* output that so many energy-consuming nations have been drawn to the Caspian Sea area.

And while the Caspian's oil first attracted foreign firms to the region, natural gas is likely to sustain their interest over the long term. Azerbaijan, Kazakhstan, Turkmenistan, and Uzbekistan together hold 321 trillion cubic feet in proven gas reserves—which, if combined, would make them the world's fourth largest gas provider after Russia, Iran, and Qatar.[13] All four, moreover, are believed to possess additional, "possible" gas reserves. Because these reservoirs were only partially developed by the Soviets, they possess great potential for increased output in the future. In addition, a lack of adequate pipeline capacity to deliver the fuel to foreign customers inhibits the full use of the region's reserves; with added conduits, however, they could prove a major new source of energy for Europe, the Indian subcontinent, and the Far East.[14]

Investor interest has largely focused on four countries in the region: Azerbaijan and Kazakhstan with respect to oil and natural gas; Turkmenistan and Uzbekistan with respect to natural gas alone. Some more modest oil and gas deposits are also believed to lie in the Russian and Iranian segments of the Caspian Sea.[15] Georgia, though possessing little oil and gas of its own, has come to play a significant role as a transit country for the export of Caspian oil and gas. (See Table 5.1.)

Initially, a major focus of investor interest was Azerbaijan, which, after all, had once been among the world's leading oil producers. Although the country's onshore fields had long been in decline, substantial reserves were thought to lie in its segment of the Caspian Sea. In 1994, a consortium of BP, Chevron, Exxon Mobil, and several other firms signed what some termed the "deal of the century" to develop the offshore Azeri, Chirag, and Guneshli (ACG) fields. Together, these three associated fields were believed to harbor as much as 6.5 billion

Table 5.1

CASPIAN SEA BASIN OIL AND GAS RESERVES AND PRODUCTION

Country	Petroleum			Natural Gas	
	Reserves, bbl	Production		Reserves, tcf	Production, 2006, bcf
		Actual (2006), tbd	Projected (2030), tbd		
Azerbaijan	7.0	654	1,100	47.6	222.4
Kazakhstan	39.8	1,426	3,700	105.9	843.7
Turkmenistan	0.5	163	300	101.0	2,195.7
Uzbekistan	0.6	125	600	66.0	1,955.6
Totals	47.9	2,368	5,700	320.5	5,217.4

Sources: Reserves and 2006 production from BP, *Statistical Review of World Energy June 2007*; projections for 2030 from U.S. Department of Energy, *International Energy Outlook 2007*, Table G2.

bbl = billion barrels
tbd = thousand barrels per day
tcf = trillion cubic feet
bcf = billion cubic feet

barrels of oil, promising to make the project one of the largest in the world. By 2006, they were producing approximately 400,000 barrels per day, and that figure is expected to jump to 1 million barrels by 2010, accounting for the bulk of Azerbaijani output. Another offshore field, Shah Deniz, is thought to hold large supplies of natural gas. However, no other major sources of hydrocarbons have been found in Azerbaijan's coastal waters, prompting some developers to pull out of the country.[16]

As Azerbaijan's star dimmed, Kazakhstan's grew brighter. Though not a major producer during the Soviet era, it has received considerable foreign interest and is now on the verge of significant production increases. "After years of foreign investment into the country's oil and natural gas sectors, [Kazakhstan] has recently begun to realize its enormous production potential," the DoE reported in October 2006.[17] The country's petroleum output is expected to rise from 1.3 million barrels per day in 2005 to 3.5 million barrels in 2015 and considerably more by 2025. Natural gas production is also expected to grow from about 0.57 trillion cubic feet in 2005 to 1.84 trillion in 2015.[18]

Several major onshore fields account for the bulk of Kazakhstan's current production. Tengiz, the largest, is located in swamplands bordering the northeast shore of the Caspian Sea; controlled by a consortium of Chevron, Exxon Mobil, Kazakhstan's state-owned KazMunaiGaz, and Russia's Lukoil, it was producing about 450,000 barrels per day in 2006 and is expected to deliver 700,000 barrels per day by the end of the decade.[19] Other large onshore deposits include Karachaganak, operated by Eni of Italy, BG Group (formerly British Gas), Chevron, and Lukoil; and the Aktobe field, operated by the China National Petroleum Corporation (CNPC).

Kazakhstan's greatest potential, however, lies in two big offshore fields, Kashagan and Kurmangazy. Kashagan, located in the northern Caspian near the oil hub of Atyraū, is considered the largest oil field outside the Middle East, with estimated reserves of 7–13 billion barrels of oil and natural gas liquids; a consortium of Royal Dutch Shell, Exxon Mobil, ConocoPhillips, Eni, Total of France, Inpex of Japan, and KazMunaiGaz is developing the field, with production slated to begin in 2011.[20] Despite its great promise, however, Kashagan has suffered major delays due to legal wrangling among the consortium's members and assorted geological and environmental problems.[21] (Kashagan's oil contains high concentrations of poisonous hydrogen sulfide gas and the Caspian Sea harbors threatened populations of seals and sturgeon.) Kurmangazy poses equally significant problems, including the fact that it overlaps Kazakhstan's maritime border with Russia and so its exploitation is certain to be the subject of complex bilateral negotiations. Despite all this, the two fields are expected to significantly boost the country's net energy output.[22]

While few analysts doubt Kazakhstan's potential, questions have arisen about how rapidly the government will boost production and how it will deal with a number of competing objectives, including short-term versus long-term economic gain, state control versus international participation, and the high risk of environmental damage that these projects entail. Initially, it appeared that foreign participation and rapid development rather than environmental protection and careful consideration of the long term were to be the prevailing norms, but in August 2007 the government signaled a possible change of course. It suspended a permit for operations at the Kashagan field, claiming environmental violations and unacceptable construction delays; in September, heavy environmental fines were levied against operators of the Tengiz field. After prolonged and sometimes tense negotiations, both actions resulted in higher payments to the government and a bigger role for KazMunaiGaz, the state-owned energy company—after which, as had been the case for Russia's Sakhalin-2 project, the environmental issues were miraculously resolved.[23]

Neither Turkmenistan nor Uzbekistan possess significant quantities of oil, but their vast natural gas reserves are of great interest to foreign producers. BP credits the two countries with combined proven gas reserves of 167 trillion cubic feet, roughly comparable to Algeria's known reservoirs. Both are also believed to possess "possible" reserves that might, someday, add up to roughly an equal amount.[24] Development has proceeded slowly, mainly due to difficulties in moving the gas to market. The only existing export pipelines are controlled by Russia's Gazprom, which has been in no rush to see Central Asian supplies compete with Russian gas sales in Europe. If, however, new conduits are constructed, Turkmenistan and Uzbekistan could become major suppliers to Europe, South Asia, and China.[25]

Enter the Americans

The very first foreign energy company to penetrate the region in the post-Soviet era was the Chevron Corporation (originally the Standard Oil Company of California). In 1990, it sought a piece of Kazakhstan's giant Tengiz field; though stymied by still-powerful Soviet bureaucrats, the company came to a quick agreement with Kazakhstan's new leaders shortly after the country declared independence in 1991.[26] The deal then represented the largest single investment by an American firm in the former USSR, and it continues to stand out even today.[27] To move the field's abundant oil to market, moreover, Chevron helped spearhead the formation of the Caspian Pipeline Consortium (CPC), which ultimately constructed a new export conduit from Kazakhstan along the north shore of the Caspian Sea to the Russian Black Sea port of Novorossiysk.[28] Soon enough other American firms, including Exxon Mobil and ConocoPhillips, arrived in the region, seeking Caspian assets of their own. In 1994, Exxon became a major stakeholder in the Azerbaijan International Operating Company (AIOC), established to operate the ACG fields in Azerbaijan's sector of the Caspian Sea.

Although first triggered by the commercial instincts of American oil firms, interest in the area's energy potential soon came to be seen by U.S. officials as a vital *strategic* matter. Washington promptly began working to foster the emergence of robust, economically viable states in the non-Russian space of the former Soviet Union. American policymakers saw these nations both as a bulwark against any future imperial Russian superpower and as one means to reduce U.S. dependence on oil supplies from the Middle East. By helping to launch new energy projects, these officials believed, U.S. firms could help generate fresh sources of income for the struggling young Caspian states—thus enabling them to escape the political and economic embrace of Moscow—while simultaneously funneling new oil and gas supplies into international markets. This approach was embraced with particular enthusiasm by the Clinton administration.[29] As Bill Clinton explained to President Heydar Aliyev of Azerbaijan at a White House meeting in August 1997, by supporting his country's energy ventures, "[W]e not only help Azerbaijan to prosper, we also help to diversify our energy supply and strengthen our nation's security."[30]

In accordance with this outlook, the U.S. government assumed direct responsibility for negotiations with local Caspian officials over prospective petroleum projects and helped American firms gain access to promising oil and gas deposits. President Clinton himself participated in these endeavors, often telephoning the region's leaders on behalf of U.S. firms or inviting key figures like Azerbaijan's Aliyev to the White House for red-carpet receptions.[31]

"We have been very successful in encouraging high-level visits to and from the region," Stuart Eizenstat, undersecretary of state for economic, business, and agricultural affairs, observed in unusually revealing testimony before the Senate Foreign Relations Committee in October 1997. "Georgian President Shevardnadze, Azerbaijani President Aliyev, and Kyrgyz President Akayev visited Washington this summer [and] Kazakhstani President Nazarbayev will visit Washington in November. . . . The First Lady [Hillary Clinton] will visit Kazakhstan, Kyrgyzstan, and Uzbekistan in November; our new Ambassador-at-large to the NIS [newly independent states of the former USSR] Steve Sestanovich will be traveling to Central Asia and the Caucasus next week."[32] By all accounts, this sort of direct White House engagement persisted throughout the Clinton era, boosting the American presence throughout the region. The Departments of State and Defense also played a significant role, providing substantial quantities of economic and military assistance to ever-more-friendly Caspian basin governments.[33]

Other strategic considerations—largely dictated by the distinctive geographic features of the region—also helped to shape U.S. policy in the region. To begin with, the Caspian Sea is landlocked, and so hydrocarbon exports of any sort must travel overland by pipeline to foreign markets. Most of the region's existing pipelines had been constructed by the Soviets during the Cold War era, and so pass through Russia en route to other customers. Although American officials were not opposed to some Caspian energy being transported to market by these conduits, they wanted to make sure that nowhere near all of it would travel by this path in the future. As a result, both the Clinton and Bush administrations vigorously promoted alternative export routes.

As it happens, however, the most sensible alternative route for bringing Caspian energy to market would be through pipelines crossing Iran to its well-established export facilities on the Persian Gulf coast. Even in the 1990s, of course, the notion of bolstering Iran's regional wealth and power in any way was absolutely anathema to Washington. Faced with this quandary, American officials assumed leadership in planning and overseeing the construction of the Baku-Tbilisi-Ceyhan (BTC) pipeline, a far lengthier, more complex, and more expensive conduit whose main attraction was simply that it would bypass both Russia and Iran. Under plans drawn up during the Clinton administration and completed during that of the younger Bush, the line now stretches over 1,000 miles from Baku on Azerbaijan's Caspian coast to Tbilisi in Georgia and on to Ceyhan on Turkey's Mediterranean coast, where tankers upload Caspian crude for delivery around the world.[34]

Though both administrations trumpeted the economic benefits of the BTC conduit, it was clear from the start that Washington was largely driven by a desire to diminish Russia's role in the transportation of oil and gas, exclude Iran from participation in the development of Caspian energy, and bolster the U.S. presence in the region. "This is about America's energy security, which depends on diversifying our sources of oil and gas," then Secretary of Energy Bill Richardson declared at a critical stage in the pipeline's development. "It's also about preventing strategic inroads by those who don't share our values."[35]

George W. Bush had been highly critical of Clinton's foreign policy during the 2000 presidential campaign, but he quickly embraced his predecessor's strategic endeavors in the Caspian Sea region once in office. Like Clinton, the new president placed a high premium on the completion of the BTC pipeline and on the development—with substantial American participation—of new oil and gas fields in Azerbaijan and Kazakhstan. He also endorsed the principle of U.S. officials taking a lead role in securing local government approval for such endeavors. These, and related policies, were incorporated into

Caspian Sea Basin Showing Major Pipeline Routes

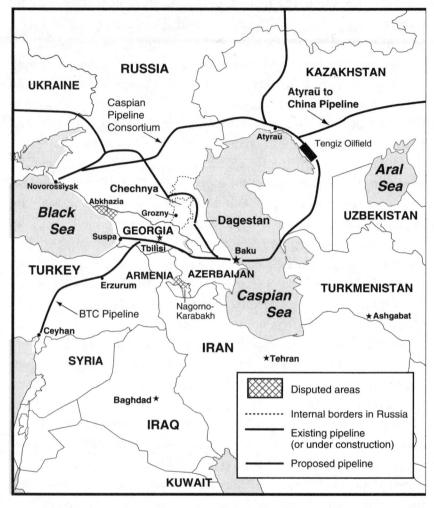

the administration's National Energy Policy in May 2001, just a few months before the terror attacks of September 11, 2001.[36]

Because the Al Qaeda networks responsible for the attacks were based in Taliban-ruled Afghanistan and maintained ties to violent Islamic groups operating in neighboring Central Asian states, U.S. relations with the Caspian nations were significantly militarized by 9/11 and the subsequent Global War on Terror. Within weeks of the attacks, Washington requested the assistance of friendly local states in conducting military operations against Al Qaeda and the Taliban in Afghani-stan.[37] For the first time, overflight rights for U.S. military aircraft were secured throughout the region, and new U.S. logistical bases were estab-lished at Manas International Airport in Kyrgyzstan and at Khanabad air base in Uzbekistan. President Bush also sought Moscow's assistance in the Afghan operations, and, suspecting that American intervention in the region would lead to increased turmoil in the Persian Gulf, asked the Russians to increase their own petroleum exports. In return, the ad-ministration gave its blessing to the pipeline built by Chevron and its CPC partners to carry Tengiz oil across Russia to the Black Sea.[38]

For a time, the White House tamped down its competitive stance on Caspian Sea energy procurement in an attempt to collaborate with Russia and the Central Asian states in suppressing Al Qaeda and other extremist organizations. But the underlying objectives of U.S. strategy, including permanently rolling back Russian influence in the region, remained fundamentally unchanged. Indeed, as the immediate shock of 9/11 began to wear off and the fighting in Afghanistan began to subside (at least for the time being), basic American objectives re-asserted themselves with a vengeance.

When, in 2002, Washington's attention began to shift from the on-going operations in Afghanistan to a possible invasion of Iraq, many in the region concluded that the United States was essentially pursuing its own national interests, not promoting Caspian basin security. Fol-lowing that invasion in March 2003, whatever post-9/11 spirit of co-operation still existed in Central Asia largely evaporated. By that point, moreover, Russia was determined to play a far more assertive role in the region, exhibiting ever-less tolerance for the presence of American military bases in the former Soviet republics of the USSR. In addition, China, which had not really figured in the Caspian's geopolitical equa-tion prior to 9/11, was now beginning to play a more conspicuous role. Suddenly, the Bush administration found itself caught up in an unexpected three-way contest for regional power and influence as well as control over the flow of oil and gas—one in which the other two players were beginning to work in something akin to partnership.[39]

American energy firms and the Bush administration remained determined to seize the decisive role in this contest. Giant U.S. companies had already become major partners in the three biggest fields in the region—the Kashagan and Tengiz fields in Kazakhstan and the ACG complex in Azerbaijan—and played a key role in many other projects. The White House, meanwhile, launched a campaign to promote the construction of new energy conduits beneath the Caspian Sea itself that would send oil and natural gas from Kazakhstan and Turkmenistan westward via the BTC pipeline or parallel natural gas lines.[40] In 2005, Karen Harbert, assistant secretary of energy for policy and international relations, said, "The administration has consistently supported the development of new pipeline projects, especially an East-West transport corridor that would stretch from Kazakhstan through Azerbaijan, Georgia, and Turkey to the Mediterranean."[41] In addition, following the death of Turkmenistan's president-for-life Saparmurat Niyazov in December 2006, the administration put a diplomatic full-court press on his successor, Gurbanguly Berdymukhammedov, to build a natural gas conduit beneath the Caspian to Azerbaijan that would connect to a new gas pipeline being built alongside the BTC oil line.[42]

The increasing resistance from Moscow, however, caused no end of heartache for the Bush administration, which had come to view a newly risen Russia as an unexpectedly serious impediment. In one of the most dramatic expressions of White House determination to counter Russian inroads in the region, Vice President Cheney flew to Kazakhstan in May 2006 to urge President Nazarbayev to export Kashagan oil via a trans-Caspian conduit and the BTC pipeline, rather than pipelines traversing Russia.[43] President Bush also hosted the leaders of Azerbaijan and Kazakhstan at the White House in a further attempt to enhance America's leverage in the region.[44] But this is the sort of game that Putin proved capable of playing with great skill and undeniable advantages in the former Soviet republics.[45]

The Pull from the North

Soon after Chevron and other U.S.-based companies began to seek access to Caspian oil and gas reserves, Moscow began to take a significant interest in the region. At first, Russian authorities seemed most concerned about the conspicuous presence of American firms—and their government backers—in an area that had been an integral part of the former Soviet Union and was still viewed in Moscow as lying within Russia's sphere of influence. "It hasn't been left unnoticed in Russia that certain outside forces are trying to weaken our position in the Caspian basin, to drive a wedge between us and other Caspian states," observed Andrei Y. Urnov, the head of the Caspian Sea working group in the Russian Ministry of Foreign Affairs.[46] Aggressive Russian efforts to frustrate U.S. objectives—some overt, some hidden—followed.[47] In time, however, this stance gave way to a more pragmatic approach, aimed at maximizing Russian participation in the extraction of Caspian oil and gas and its transportation to markets in Europe and elsewhere.

In 1994, Moscow suspended its opposition to the trans-Caucasus pipelines being developed by the AIOC to export Azerbaijani crude oil via Georgia after a Russian company, Lukoil, was granted a 10 percent share in the consortium. Moscow also softened its criticism of Chevron's participation in Kazakhstan's Tengiz field once Russian companies gained a significant role in the transportation of its oil via the Caspian Pipeline Consortium, and a Russian-American joint venture, LukArco, was given a 5 percent stake in the field itself. At this time Lukoil was also awarded a share of the giant Karachaganak field and several smaller reservoirs in Kazakhstan.[48]

As Russian leaders grasped the economic and geopolitical benefits of participation in Caspian energy ventures, they worked to increase opportunities for Russian firms. One notable consequence was a sharp reversal in Moscow's stance on the demarcation of the Caspian Sea's offshore boundaries—the legal basis for any undersea drilling endeavors. Prior to the breakup of the USSR, exploitation of the sea's undersea resources was governed by a 1921 treaty between Iran and the Soviet Union. But with the emergence in 1991 of three new littoral states, Azerbaijan, Kazakhstan, and Turkmenistan, an alternative legal framework had to be established.

Once negotiations commenced on a new Caspian treaty, Moscow initially favored a modified version of the 1921 accord, giving each of the five littoral states an exclusive coastal zone but leaving most of the deep water under shared jurisdiction—an approach that would have given Russia veto power over any U.S.-backed plans to extract oil and gas in deep waters off Azerbaijan.[49] But when Russian firms began eyeing promising exploration zones in waters abutting Russia's own Caspian shoreline, Moscow changed its tune. It instead embraced the approach favored by Azerbaijan and Kazakhstan, giving each littoral state control over all coastal waters extending out to the median line separating them. In May 2003, Russia signed an agreement with those two states dividing the northern Caspian Sea into three exclusive economic zones, with each signatory gaining a slice roughly proportional to the length of its coastline.[50]

Russia then moved aggressively to develop energy prospects in its own coastal waters and set the stage for joint development of hydrocarbon reserves straddling the Russian-Kazakh maritime boundary. In January 2006, Lukoil, which won the right to explore Russia's coastal zone in 1995, announced the discovery of a major oil and gas field. Called Filanovsky, the field is estimated to hold 600 million barrels of oil and 1.2 trillion cubic feet of natural gas.[51]

In addition, in a series of well-timed moves, the government (in conjunction with Gazprom, Rosneft, and other state-controlled firms) concluded multibillion-dollar deals with key Caspian producers or transit states for the purchase, transport, and reexport of their energy output to well-heeled customers in Europe and beyond. The first of these agreements was reached in April 2006 with President Nazarbayev of Kazakhstan. It allowed for a substantial increase in the capacity of the CPC pipeline to carry Tengiz oil to the Russian Black Sea port of Novorossiysk. When fully modified, this conduit will be able to carry about 67 million tons per year, a hefty increase over the 28 million tons it carried in 2006.[52]

The Russians next turned their attention to the transportation of Central Asian gas. In September 2006, Gazprom CEO Alexei Miller signed an agreement with Turkmenistan for the purchase of 50 billion cubic meters of natural gas per year through 2009, at $100 per thousand cubic meters. Although considerably more than the $65 that Gazprom had been paying Turkmenistan previously, the rate was still far lower than the $235 or more that Gazprom was charging its customers in Western Europe. The deal also provided the company with an assured source of supply for the domestic Russian and Ukrainian market, freeing up more Russian gas for export to Europe at the higher price and boosting the company's profits (along with Russian state revenues).[53]

An even more ambitious Russian push commenced in 2007. In its first stage, Presidents Putin and Nazarbayev agreed to establish a joint venture to transport natural gas from the giant Karachaganak field to Gazprom's processing plant at Orenburg in Russia for export via the Gazprom pipeline network to customers in Europe.[54] Putin and Nazarbayev next joined with President Berdymukhammedov of Turkmenistan to announce the construction of a new natural gas pipeline that would carry Turkmen gas via Kazakhstan to Russia. To be built along the east coast of the Caspian Sea, it will initially deliver 20 billion cubic meters per year (later to be upgraded to 30 billion cubic meters).[55] Immediately afterward, the three heads of state indicated that a fourth, President Islam Karimov of Uzbekistan, had joined them in pledging to modernize and expand the old Soviet-era Turkmenistan-Uzbekistan-Kazakhstan-Russia pipeline (also known as the Central Asia–Center line) to allow for increased gas exports from Turkmenistan and Uzbekistan to Russia.[56]

This trio of agreements, if brought to fruition, will give Russia substantial control over the allocation of Central Asian natural gas for some time to come. Other plans for its transportation via other routes and to other destinations remain in play, including proposed pipelines traveling eastward to China and westward beneath the Caspian Sea to Azerbaijan, Georgia, and Europe, but these were still largely paper projects at the start of 2008.[57]

In its pursuit of energy-juggernaut status, Russia has also sought to extract more uranium from the region to feed its growing array of nuclear power plants. With many of its own mines substantially depleted, Rosatom, the Federal Atomic Energy Agency, has developed plans to increase its uranium imports from Kazakhstan, Kyrgyzstan, and Uzbekistan.[58] Kazakhstan, with an estimated 20 percent of the world's uranium reserves, is a major target of the Russian import drive. In May 2007, officials from Russia and Kazakhstan agreed to set up joint ventures to accelerate the extraction of Kazakh uranium and establish an international uranium-enrichment facility at Angarsk in Russia.[59]

The country also possesses Central Asia's largest coal reserves—and these, too, are being extracted at an accelerated pace for export to Russia.[60]

As Russia's energy and economic interests have grown, so, too, has its political involvement in the Caspian Sea basin. Under the umbrella of the Commonwealth of Independent States (CIS) and its military spin-off, the Collective Security Treaty Organization (CSTO), President Putin and other top Russian officials engage in a regular whirlwind of diplomacy in the region, meeting frequently with their Central Asian counterparts and engaging them in assorted joint endeavors. Rarely a week goes by without news reports of an encounter between Putin (or one of his top deputies) and assorted Caspian potentates. Some of these interchanges are mere photo opportunities; others entail hard bargaining—and, no doubt, serious arm-twisting—over trade deals, pipeline routes, votes at the United Nations, and so forth.[61]

In jockeying for geopolitical advantage on this critical playing field, Moscow and Washington have brought to bear a military dimension to this contest that cannot be ignored. Both countries have forged significant military ties with the Caspian states, and both have established (or retained) bases there: the United States in Afghanistan, Kyrgyzstan, and (for a time) Uzbekistan; Russia in Armenia, Azerbaijan, Georgia (under protest), Kyrgyzstan, and Tajikistan. Leaders of both countries claim that these undertakings represent a prudent response to specific security threats, notably from Al Qaeda, the Taliban, and other extremist movements. But they clearly serve as important tokens of presence in the region, as do the requisite arms transfers, military exercises, and alliance systems.

China's "Go West" Strategy

When the struggle for geopolitical advantage in the Caspian basin first got under way in the 1990s, it looked like a two-way contest between the United States and Russia. Recently, however, another major player—the People's Republic of China—has begun pursuing its own strategic interests in the region. Often, Beijing has seemed to side with Moscow, giving rise in Washington to ominous talk of a Sino-Russian axis in Central Asia. The closer you get to where the action is, however, the more complex this potentially lethal three-way dance appears, with China generally following a course aimed at maximizing its own energy security.[62]

China first sought a significant presence in Central Asia after the breakup of the Soviet Union in 1991. With the sudden emergence of five untested states on its periphery—many harboring ethnic groups with kinfolk living in China—Beijing became concerned about the prospect of regional instability. Initially, it sought to eliminate the possibility that any of these countries might serve as a sanctuary for Uighur separatists fighting to establish an independent Muslim state ("East Turkestan") in China's remote Xinjiang autonomous region. So Chinese officials began promoting regional cooperation on matters of border protection and antiterrorism—a drive that led in 1996 to the establishment of the "Shanghai Five," a consortium that included China, Kazakhstan, Kyrgyzstan, Russia, and Tajikistan, with an initial mandate of combating extremism and separatism.[63] In 2001, this entity was upgraded into a full-scale regional body, the Shanghai Cooperation Organization (SCO), and Uzbekistan was added to its membership roster.[64]

But while border and internal security considerations dominated China's early relations with the new Central Asian republics, energy inevitably came to the fore. Ever since China became partially dependent on imported petroleum in 1993, it has been eyeing the oil and gas reserves of the Caspian Sea basin and seeking to construct pipelines from that region to its own territory. Indeed, Hu Jintao has made the increased procurement of Caspian energy a major government priority ever since becoming president in 2003 and has assumed personal responsibility for expanding his country's ties with the region.

China's "Go West" strategy has been driven, above all, by sheer need. The region's vast reserves of untapped oil and gas were bound to attract Beijing's attention.[65] Aside from that need, though, two additional energy motives drive China. The first is geography. Because the Central Asian states are situated on China's periphery, their oil and gas supplies can be pumped directly to Chinese territory and then carried by domestic pipelines to urban and industrial areas throughout the country. While the distances involved are considerable, there is still an obvious attraction in relative proximity. In addition, China's leaders hope Caspian energy will help spur economic development in Xinjiang and other western provinces, which have largely failed to benefit from spectacular growth elsewhere in the country, leading to social and political discontent.[66]

Another Caspian-specific motive is energy security. "China's leaders are uncomfortable with the fact that the United States is the preeminent power in the Middle East, the region that provides China with the bulk of its oil imports," explains Erica Downs of the RAND Corporation. "China currently does not possess the naval capabilities necessary to defend its sea shipments of oil and, consequently, regards their

Western China and Central Asia

passage through waters dominated by the U.S. Navy . . . as a key strategic vulnerability."[67] This vulnerability can be somewhat minimized, Chinese strategists believe, by increasing energy shipments by land, notably from Russia and the Caspian region.[68]

Much of the Chinese effort has been focused on Kazakhstan, which has received unflagging attention from Chinese leaders.[69] China's avid courtship of Kazakhstan began in 1997, when Beijing offered $4.3 billion for a significant stake in the Aktobe oil field and pledged another $3.5 billion to build a 1,900-mile pipeline (one of the world's longest) from it to the Chinese border. Although the state-controlled CNPC acquired an 88 percent stake in the Aktobe field, the pipeline plan languished because of its high cost. However, soon after assuming the presidency, Hu Jintao visited Kazakhstan and reaffirmed Beijing's commitment to the pipeline—"an important sign," he told reporters at the time, "that China places great attention and importance on developing friendly relations with Kazakhstan."[70] Construction of the first leg of the conduit, connecting the Aktobe field with the oil hub at Atyraū near the Caspian coast, was completed in 2003; the second segment, a 615-mile stretch from Atasu in central Kazakhstan to Alashankou on the Sino-Kazakh border, was finished in December 2005. The third and final segment, which will join the other two, is scheduled to be completed in 2011.[71]

To fill this new pipeline with crude, China has been buying up oil fields across Kazakhstan. In 2003, CNPC acquired a 50 percent share of the North Buzachi field, believed to possess between 1.0 and 1.5 billion barrels of oil. CNPC then joined with Sinopec to bid for the 16.67 percent share of the giant Kashagan reservoir held by British Gas (now BG Group) when that firm decided to sell its holdings; however, the two companies were blocked by other members of the Kashagan consortium, who used their contractual rights to acquire BG's share themselves.[72] Thwarted, CNPC went on to purchase PetroKazakhstan, the Canadian-based company with substantial assets in Kazakhstan, for $4.2 billion in August 2005, gaining control of the South Kumkol field and part ownership of the North Kumkol and Kazgermunai fields.[73] (To satisfy Kazakh authorities, CNPC was compelled to resell part of its new holdings to the Kazakh state-owned company,

KazMunaiGaz.[74]) While none of these reservoirs compares in size to Kazakhstan's two largest fields, Tengiz and Kashagan, they provide China with a constellation of reserves that together will one day represent a significant source of energy.

Though CNPC and Sinopec spearheaded the Chinese drive, the central government played a critical role in the pursuit of Kazakh reserves. President Hu himself took an active part in negotiations, meeting on several occasions with his Kazakh counterpart, Nursultan Nazarbayev, to ensure favored treatment for Chinese firms. In July 2005, Hu and Nazarbayev even declared a "strategic partnership" between the two countries, with a special focus on increased energy ties.[75] Though scant in public particulars, the arrangement is thought to entail the acquisition of additional Kazakh fields by Chinese companies and the expansion of the burgeoning Sino-Kazakh pipeline system.[76]

Beijing has also been on the lookout for oil and gas from the other Central Asian republics. In Uzbekistan, for example, Chinese energy firms have scoured the country for possible acquisitions while Chinese leaders have courted the country's autocratic ruler, President Karimov. After widespread Western condemnation of Karimov's brutal suppression of a civil uprising in the town of Andizhan in May 2005, leaving several hundred unarmed protestors dead,[77] China invited the Uzbeki president for a gala state visit. While in Beijing, Karimov signed a $600 million deal for the joint development of oil fields around Bukhara by CNPC and Uzbekistan's state-owned company, Uzbekneftegaz. "We support efforts by the Uzbekistan government to stabilize their domestic situation and their commitment to the country's peaceful development," a Chinese Foreign Ministry official said at the time—a powerful signal, however blandly put.[78]

The Chinese have even put considerable effort into wooing the leaders of Turkmenistan, a country that currently sells most of its natural gas to Russia. Beijing hopes to be able to tap into that country's ample reserves, too, once a planned gas pipeline is actually built across the breadth of Central Asia to China. During a state visit to Beijing in April 2006, Turkmenistan's authoritarian president, Saparmurat Niyazov, signed an agreement with Hu Jintao pledging to speed work on its construction.[79] When Niyazov died in December 2006, his successor, Gurbanguly Berdymukhammedov, quickly promised to honor the commitments of his predecessor. But given the huge costs of the project and Gazprom's prior claims on Turkmenistan's gas, it is doubtful that the pipeline will materialize anytime soon.[80]

Not all of the projects the Chinese leadership is pursuing are likely to reach fruition, but eventually the entire region will probably be crisscrossed by pipelines carrying Caspian oil and gas to China. In time, other types of energy are likely to flow in the same direction. There are reports, for example, that Beijing plans to build a $4 billion power plant in Kazakhstan to convert that country's abundant coal reserves into electricity for China's western provinces.[81] In fact, virtually every conceivable source of power—including the region's undeveloped river systems—are being eyed by Beijing as possible sources of electricity.[82]

No less than the Americans and the Russians, the Chinese have endeavored to protect their energy investments in the region by establishing military ties with local powers. Rather than be perceived as overly aggressive, Beijing has preferred to extend its power through the SCO. The Russians clearly hope that Beijing's geopolitical aspirations can be channeled through the six-country consortium, but both Moscow and Washington fear that Beijing will eventually dispense with this artifice and pursue its interests in a far more direct fashion. Far sooner than once predicted, China is likely to emerge as a major actor in the Caspian Sea basin, and the results are bound to be dramatic.[83]

Other Foreign Hunters

As if the extraction-driven, multipronged campaigns of China, Russia, and the United States were not enough, the Caspian's resources are also being pursued by a host of other nations, including India, Japan, South Korea, Turkey, and various European countries—all of which are contributing to the systematic exploitation of the region's energy reserves. All, moreover, support international efforts to develop

Table 5.2

INTERNATIONAL PARTICIPATION IN MAJOR OIL AND NATURAL GAS PROJECTS IN AZERBAIJAN AND KAZAKHSTAN

Project	Company	Home Country of Company	Percent Stake in Project	Status of Project
Azerbaijan: Azeri, Chirag, and Deepwater Guneshli (Azerbaijan International Operating Company, AIOC)	BP*	UK	34.1	Signed September 20, 1994; exports began late 1997. Chirag field producing 158 tbd as of May 2006; Azeri field producing 238 tbd as of April 2006. Most of this oil is exported via the Baku-Tbilisi-Ceyhan (BTC) pipeline.
	Chevron	USA	10.3	
	Inpex	Japan	10.0	
	SOCAR	Azerbaijan	10.0	
	Statoil	Norway	8.6	
	Exxon Mobil	USA	8.0	
	TPAO	Turkey	6.8	
	Devon Energy	USA	5.6	
	Itochu	Japan	3.9	
	Amerada Hess	USA	2.7	
Azerbaijan: Shah Deniz	BP*	UK	25.5	Signed June 4, 1996. Production has been under way since December 2006 but with intermittent shutdowns. A new natural gas pipeline, the South Caucasus Pipeline (also named the Baku-Tbilisi-Erzurum pipeline) is being built to deliver this gas to Turkey.
	Statoil	Norway	25.5	
	SOCAR	Azerbaijan	10.0	
	LukAgip	Russia/Italy	10.0	
	Total	France	10.0	
	OIEC	Iran	10.0	
Kazakhstan: Karachaganak (Karachaganak Integrated Organization, KIO)	Eni*	Italy	32.5	Producing 203 tbd as of October 2006; 70 percent of oil exported via CPC.
	BG Group	UK	32.5	
	Chevron	USA	20.0	
	Lukoil	Russia	15.0	

Table 5.2 (*Continued*)

Project	Company	Home Country of Company	Percent Stake in Project	Status of Project
Kazakhstan: Kashagan (Agip Kashagan North Caspian Operating Company, Agip KCO)	Eni*	Italy	18.52	Production slated to begin in 2011, with target output of 1.2 mbd by 2013. Ultimate development costs could reach $135 billion. In January 2008, the consortium's foreign members agreed to give KazMunaiGaz another 8.5 percent stake and to reduce their own shares by 1.71 percent each to compensate.
	Total	France	18.52	
	Exxon Mobil	USA	18.52	
	Royal Dutch Shell	UK/Holland	18.52	
	ConocoPhillips	USA	9.26	
	KazMunaiGaz	Kazakhstan	8.33	
	Inpex	Japan	8.33	
Kazakhstan: Tengiz	Chevron*	USA	50.0	Agreement signed in 1993. Producing 271 tbd in 2005. Most of this oil is exported via the CPC pipeline.
	Exxon Mobil	USA	25.0	
	KazMunaiGaz	Kazakhstan	20.0	
	LukArco	Russia/UK	5.0	

Sources: U.S. Department of Energy, "Azerbaijan: Production-Sharing Agreements," June 2006; "Kazakhstan: Major Oil and Natural Gas Projects," October 2006, electronic documents accessed at www.eia.doe.gov.
*Indicates lead operator
CPC=Caspian Pipeline Consortium
mbd=million barrels per day
tbd=thousand barrels per day

additional energy transportation networks to facilitate the extraction and export of Caspian Sea oil and gas supplies. (See Table 5.2.)

European and Japanese companies quickly followed the Americans into the Caspian basin in the early 1990s. British Petroleum (now BP) conspicuously acquired the lead role in the Azerbaijan International Operating Company, the developer of the Azeri-Chirag-Guneshli reservoir, as well as a substantial interest in the Shah Deniz natural gas field, also located in Azerbaijan's sector of the Caspian Sea. To transport the oil and gas extracted from these fields to market in the West, BP spearheaded construction of the BTC oil pipeline and helped form the consortium that is now building a natural gas pipeline from Baku to Turkey, following the route of the BTC conduit. Several European and Japanese firms have partnered with BP in these ventures, including Statoil of Norway, Total of France, and Inpex and Itochu of Japan.[84]

The Europeans and Japanese have also secured a substantial presence in some of Kazakhstan's major reservoirs, including Karachaganak and Kashagan. Eni-Agip of Italy (now Eni) and British Gas (now BG Group) hold a significant stake in the Karachaganak field; Eni, Total, Royal Dutch Shell, and Inpex are key players (along with Exxon Mobil and ConocoPhillips) in the Kashagan consortium.[85] South Korea, with growing energy needs of its own, has also been active in the Caspian region; in November 2006, a state-owned firm, Korea National Oil Corporation, acquired a 25 percent stake in Kazakhstan's Egizkara oil field and a smaller share of other blocks.[86]

The Europeans are also interested in the construction of additional pipelines to transport Caspian oil to their doorstep, preferably without crossing Russia. At present, oil from the Tengiz field in Kazakhstan, for example, is carried by the CPC pipeline to the Russian port of Novorossiysk and then shipped by tanker across the Black Sea and through the narrow, congested Bosporus (dividing European Istanbul from its Asian side) before reaching the Mediterranean. To avoid this, several European consortia are developing plans for pipelines that would originate on the western coast of the Black Sea and traverse southeastern Europe to ports on the Aegean or Adriatic.[87] A consortium of eastern European and Baltic nations has also been formed to extend an existing pipeline through Ukraine (the Odessa-Brody line) to Gdansk in Poland and eventually onward to Lithuania in order to carry oil supplied by Azerbaijan.[88]

Even more ambitious plans are being developed for the eventual shipment of Caspian natural gas to Europe without traversing Russia. Several multinational consortia have been established for this purpose. One of them, Nabucco, enjoys strong support from the European Union and would carry gas from BP's Shah Deniz field in offshore Azerbaijan through Georgia, Turkey, Bulgaria, Romania, and Hungary, terminating in Baumgarten, Austria. Partners in this multibillion-dollar enterprise include Turkey's pipeline company Botas, Bulgaria's pipeline operator Bulgargaz, Romania's Romgaz, Hungary's MOL, and Austria's OMV.[89] Another, White Stream, is an even bolder undertaking. It would absorb gas from the later stages of the Shah Deniz project and carry it by an extended seabed pipeline under the Black Sea to Ukraine or Romania for onward delivery to customers throughout Europe.[90] Given the high cost of these endeavors and the complex negotiations involved, it is unclear when, and if, they will reach fruition; there is no doubt, however, of Europe's desire to both increase its supplies of natural gas and reduce its dependence on Russia.

All of the existing and proposed oil and gas pipelines from the Caspian currently travel northward (to Russia), westward (to the Black Sea and the Mediterranean), or eastward (to China). But the leaders of India and Pakistan aim to change that by building pipelines heading south, to their own energy-seeking countries. Both New Delhi and Islamabad would like to tap into the natural gas reserves of nearby Turkmenistan by constructing a pipeline across Afghanistan to Pakistan and then onward to India—an endeavor long precluded by unending civil war and ethnic strife in Afghanistan as well as the historic animosity between the two great powers of South Asia. However, with the 2001 ouster of the Taliban regime in Afghanistan and the establishment of friendlier relations between India and Pakistan, negotiations have commenced among all interested parties over the route and financing of the proposed conduit—though until Afghanistan is less convulsed with violence, this remains but a dream of a project.[91]

For the time being, India is a minor player in the pursuit of Caspian energy, but New Delhi is certainly eager to tap into this relatively convenient source. In 2005, India's state-owned Oil and Natural Gas Corporation (ONGC) reportedly made a substantial offer for PetroKazakhstan, only to be outbid by China's CNPC.[92] ONGC and Gas Authority of India Limited have also sought participation in the Shah Deniz gas project in Azerbaijan's sector of the Caspian Sea.[93] No doubt these and other Indian firms will seek similar acquisitions in the years ahead as India's thirst for energy grows.

A Desolate Prospect

What will all these efforts to exploit the Caspian basin's energy reserves mean for the region itself? In the short run, oil and natural gas
output will rise, exports will increase, and vast fortunes will flow into
the bank accounts of the companies involved and the local officials
who control the allocation of energy revenues. According to one estimate, Azerbaijan's income from oil revenues in 2010 alone will be
twice its entire gross domestic product in 2005.[94] If this money were
prudently invested in education, infrastructure, and job creation, the
citizens of these countries could hope to see considerable benefits, but
most analysts express little confidence that the Caspian's elites and
their cronies will prove any more interested in distributing energy
revenues widely than those of most other "petro-states" around the
world—with predictable results. Edward Chow of the Carnegie Endowment for International Peace summed up the typical situation in
testimony before Congress: "Increased oil income has coincided with
more autocratic rule, enhanced the ruler's ability to temporarily pay
off parts of the elite by sharing some of this wealth, and allowed defer-
ral of desperately needed fundamental economic and political reforms."[95]

Predictably enough, the stench of corruption is already pervasive in
Azerbaijan, where President Ilham Aliyev exercises ultimate control
over the economy. Before succeeding his father, Heydar Aliyev, as chief
executive in 2003—in elections widely viewed as tainted—Ilham ran
the state oil company, SOCAR, and he retains strong ties to the nation's
energy industry.[96] According to Guy Chazan of the *Wall Street Journal*,
energy and other key industries are "dominated by murky state monopolies run by the president's cronies."[97] A new round of parliamentary
elections in November 2005 was advertised as fulfilling a commitment
to greater governmental accountability, but opposition parties were
marginalized by heavy-handed government tactics, and the president's
party claimed most of the available seats.[98] "This parliament will not be
able to control the oil revenues," Ali Kerimli, a leader of the opposition
Azadlik (Freedom) bloc, told Chazan bluntly. "The president will decide
everything."[99]

The situation is not much different in Kazakhstan, where another dynasty, headed by Nursultan Nazarbayev, effectively monopolizes state power. As in Azerbaijan, key segments of the economy—and especially the energy industry—are dominated by state monopolies, which in turn are controlled by Nazarbayev's friends and relatives.[100] "Widespread allegations of bribery, corruption, diversion of funds, as well as increasing ownership and policy influence of the President, members of his family, and close associates continue to be made," two experts on Kazakhstan's oil industry, Mark J. Kaiser and Allan G. Pulsipher, wrote in *Oil & Gas Journal*. State-owned companies, such as KazMunaiGaz, reportedly are held to much less stringent standards of accounting transparency than are international energy firms, which, of course, makes the diversion of funds to Nazarbayev's family and cronies that much easier.[101]

The big losers, of course, are ordinary citizens—who, if history is any guide, will continue to be excluded from most of the benefits of instant energy wealth. This kind of exclusion, in turn, fuels the rise of antigovernment movements and, in some areas, radical Islamic organizations. So far, the ruling elites of the Central Asian and Caspian states have been able to muzzle the most potent expressions of popular discontent through systematic repression and, when necessary, brutal application of lethal force—but this is an inherently risky strategy.[102] As demonstrated in so many other areas where the rapid accumulation of oil wealth has been concentrated in a few hands, failure to satisfy the rising aspirations of impoverished masses can lead to civic unrest, separatism, or armed rebellion.[103]

Perhaps the greatest danger in this Muslim-majority region is that opponents of the prevailing Caspian regimes will be drawn to extremist Islamic movements as a means of expressing their rage toward the corrupt and self-perpetuating elites that appear, so far, to be the almost exclusive beneficiaries of the Caspian energy boom. With the electoral process viewed as little more than a farce, and most established religious institutions subject to tight state control, the sole challenge to government authority in many of these countries is coming from banned or underground religious movements such as the Islamic Jihad Group of Uzbekistan (IJG) and the Hizb ut-Tahrir (Party of Liberation), a militant pan-Islamic organization with branches in forty countries, including Great Britain. Members of these and similar groups have been accused of planning or conducting antigovernment assaults in Kazakhstan, Kyrgyzstan, and Uzbekistan, and are believed to maintain links with Al Qaeda and other extremist organizations operating in the region.[104] Although the IJG and Hizb ut-Tahrir are not yet a threat to existing governments, they—or other movements like them—could grow in numbers and potency as the promised benefits of oil wealth fail to improve the lot of the masses.

Another energy-related peril linked to internal instability in the Caspian states is the possibility that the major external powers will take opposing sides in local or regional disputes to protect their investments, and then collide with one another militarily. This is not far-fetched, given the American and Russian forces deployed throughout the region. China, too, could someday join the fray. The fact that all three powers are pouring arms and military equipment into the area in the pursuit of geopolitical advantage only adds to the risk of future conflagrations.

All these risks—corruption, authoritarianism, instability, and outside intervention—are short- and medium-term dangers. But what of the long term? What do the people of the region have to look forward to decades down the pike? The answer is likely to be environmental degradation and, for the most part, unrelieved poverty.

True, the U.S. Department of Energy claims that the Caspian Sea basin harbors many oil and gas deposits yet to be discovered or fully mapped, suggesting that the region will remain productive for decades. But most industry analysts are far more pessimistic, indicating that the Caspian's energy fecundity will probably last not much more than a quarter of a century.[105] According to an assessment by Julia Nanay of PFC Energy, a Washington consultancy, Azerbaijan's major fields will reach peak production of about 1.2 million barrels per day in 2009, remain at this level for perhaps a decade, and then plunge to a mere 200,000 barrels per day by 2021—barely enough to satisfy the country's domestic requirements.[106] The picture for Kazakhstan is only somewhat more promising, with oil output in 2020 potentially still exceeding several million barrels per day but a sharp drop-off expected well before the middle of the century.[107] The Caspian's natural gas output will probably peak later than its oil output, but it, too, will eventually reach maximum levels and then subside.

At present, one can walk the streets of Baku or Astana or Almaty and marvel at the soaring profiles of new luxury hotels and corporate headquarters. Caspian energy centers are all enjoying a temporary upsurge of economic activity as money flows into the region and oil-company executives arrive daily for meetings with high government officials. It is a moment eerily reminiscent of the 1890s, when the Nobels and Rothschilds built their mansions in Baku and sparked a similar petroleum-fed boom. Those older mansions—mostly long since abandoned—complement the oil rigs left from that earlier period, which are today nothing but twisted hulks. Several decades from now, when most of the Caspian's remaining oil and gas reserves have been sucked from the earth, the new facilities now under construction will join them. Once again, as Guy Chazan said of the pre-boom landscape, the Caspian will be ringed with oil derricks rusting amid pools of black sludge.

6

THE GLOBAL ASSAULT
ON AFRICA'S VITAL
RESOURCES

Long before the current international hunt for energy got under way, European powers scoured Africa for critical raw materials. From the colonial era until well after World War II, Africa provided Europe with much of its copper, iron, diamonds, rubber, timber, cotton, coffee, tea, and other basic commodities. In what was once termed "the scramble for Africa," Britain, France, Spain, Italy, Germany, Belgium, and Portugal divided up the continent into a patchwork of colonies to systematize the extraction of these materials. With decolonization in the 1960s and the rise of the Middle Eastern oil producers, the "scramble" took off elsewhere, and Africa lost some of its resource importance. But all that is again changing: As every barrel of oil has come to matter and the major energy-consuming powers growing leery of excessive reliance on the Middle East, Africa is reemerging as a potential source of critical materials. In the past few years, a new "scramble" has commenced on that continent, with energy supplies as its primary target and some new players—including formerly Third World nations like China, India, Indonesia, and Malaysia—joining in.[1]

What makes Africa so enticing today is precisely what made it so attractive to foreign predators in previous centuries: a vast abundance of vital raw materials contained in a deeply divided, politically weakened continent, remarkably open to international exploitation. Africa holds some of the world's largest untapped deposits of petroleum and natural gas, along with major reserves of bauxite, chromium, cobalt, copper, platinum, titanium, and uranium. A number of the world's largest remaining tropical forests are located in sub-Saharan Africa, along with some of its most prolific sources of gold and diamonds. Gold, copper, and exotic timber have, of course, been in great demand since ancient times; on the other hand, substances like uranium, titanium, and tantalum have only recently become crucial ingredients in planetary life—and death.

Because of its tortured history, Africa lacks the sorts of defenses against foreign resource exploitation that other previously colonized regions have established over time. Decolonization occurred relatively recently in the region—Portuguese colonies, for example, were only granted independence in 1975—and many African societies have been so enfeebled by colonization, the slave trade, economic exploitation, and post-colonial struggles for power that robust, fully functioning states have never been established. With few trained professionals, these countries have no choice but to rely on foreign corporations for technical support if they want the mammoth oil and gas projects that have sprung up in recent years to function. As elsewhere, but possibly more so here, the revenues (or "rents") derived from such projects typically line the pockets of well-connected government officials—often with no "trickle-down" effect whatsoever. Not surprisingly, foreign companies find it far more appealing to do business in Africa than in the Middle East, Venezuela, or even the Caspian region, where state-owned firms like Saudi Aramco, PdVSA, and KazMunaiGaz operate under tight government supervision, constricting opportunities for profitable deal making.[2]

As the global thirst for energy has increased, Africa has been the site of some of the fiercest competition among the major international companies and energy-hungry countries. The older, established firms from Europe, Japan, and the United States are, of course, very much on the scene, but so are vigorous new competitors from the developing world and the former Soviet Union. All are participating in the new race to carve up Africa's hydrocarbon deposits. When, for instance, economic sanctions were lifted on Libya, companies from Australia,

Brazil, Canada, China, Great Britain, India, Indonesia, Italy, Japan, Norway, Russia, Turkey, and the United States promptly sought the rights to promising hydrocarbon development blocks (geographic areas in which the owner has the right to explore for and extract oil and gas).[3] A similar struggle to gain entry to prized fields is under way in offshore areas of Angola, Nigeria, and Equatorial Guinea.[4]

All of this has certainly raised Africa's profile in the new international energy order, even though the continent does not possess hydrocarbon reserves of the magnitude of those found in the Persian Gulf region. What they lack in size, however, they more than make up for in vigor: Because many of Africa's oil and gas fields are only now being developed, they hold the promise of greater output in the future, when many deposits in other parts of the world are sure to be in decline. "It is unlikely that Africa or West Africa will ever take the place of the Middle East in its importance to the world's oil and gas markets," Deputy Assistant Secretary of Energy John R. Brodman told a Senate subcommittee in 2004, "but it will nevertheless continue to be an important source of additional supplies to the United States and the world market."[5]

It follows that Africa has come to be viewed with greater geopolitical significance by the major oil-importing powers, especially the United States and China.[6] Africa now provides about 20 percent of America's imported oil, and its share is expected to rise to 25 percent by 2015, as new offshore fields in Angola and Nigeria come on line. "African oil is of strategic national interest to us," Walter Kansteiner, assistant secretary of state for African affairs, affirmed as early as 2002, and "it will increase and become more important as we go forward."[7] The U.S. military, in particular, has been devoting special attention to Africa—often under the guise of the Global War on Terror, but with an eye to the safety of offshore oil platforms in the Gulf of Guinea and the sea lanes that connect these rigs with the eastern United States.[8] In May 2003, for example, the head of the U.S. European Command, General James Jones, indicated that the carrier battle groups under his command would shorten their visits to the Mediterranean and "spend half the time going down the west coast of Africa."[9]

Until 2007, the American military had managed to exercise control over its globally dispersed forces from five Unified Combatant Commands, one for each major region of the world save for Africa (which was divided up between the European, Central, and Pacific Commands), with an additional, Northern, command devoted to defense of the American homeland. That February, however, President George W. Bush announced the formation of the U.S. Africa Command (AFRICOM), America's first foreign command to be established since President Carter created the nucleus of the Central Command—with responsibility for protecting the Persian Gulf oil flow—in 1980.[10] And while oil is only one of the concerns that figured in the Bush administration's decision to establish AFRICOM, its belief that "African oil is of strategic national interest to us" was undoubtedly a critical factor.[11]

China has similarly elevated the importance of Africa in its geopolitical calculations as its reliance on African oil and minerals has grown. Though lacking the military power projection capabilities available to the United States, Beijing has employed other means at its disposal to bolster China's presence on the continent.[12] Senior government officials have made repeated trips to Africa in recent years, and most of Africa's reigning leaders eagerly traveled to Beijing in November 2006 for the high-profile "summit" of the Forum on China-Africa Cooperation.[13] Three months later, in February 2007, President Hu left on his longest and most elaborate visit to the continent—a twelve-day safari that took him to eight of Africa's most important economic and political powers.[14] China has also become a major supplier of arms to African nations and has increased the tempo of military exercises and exchanges in the region.[15]

As in the nineteenth and twentieth centuries, the driving force behind the current geopolitical competition is intense craving for Africa's untapped resources. The fact that today's predators include nations like China and India—once themselves the victims of colonial exploitation—alters the picture in some respects, but the fundamental dynamic remains the same. As in previous centuries, resource-consuming nations will extract as much of Africa's wealth—in this case, oil, gas, and minerals—as they can, often jostling with one another for access to the most prolific sources of supply. In doing so, they will repeatedly proclaim their deep interest in African development, insisting that the exploitation of raw materials will contribute to the improvement of living conditions for the masses of ordinary citizens. If past experience is any guide, however, few of those living in Africa's resource-producing countries will see any significant benefit from the depletion of their continent's natural bounty.[16]

The Allure of Africa Today

Of all of Africa's resources in demand today, oil has the greatest appeal. According to BP, the African continent harbors an estimated 117 billion barrels in proven oil reserves, representing approximately 10 percent of the total world supply. Most of these reserves are concentrated in a handful of countries—Algeria, Angola, Libya, Nigeria, and Sudan—which together possess about 105 billion barrels, or 90 percent of the continent's proven reserves. A number of other countries, including Chad, the Congo Republic (Congo-Brazzaville), Egypt, Equatorial Guinea, and Gabon, possess smaller amounts. BP further reports that Africa holds approximately 8 percent of the world's proven natural gas reserves, with the largest deposits again concentrated in a handful of countries: Algeria, Egypt, Libya, and Nigeria.[17] (See Table 6.1.)

Although these oil and gas deposits are not, for the most part, as large as those found in the Persian Gulf area, they possess several notable attractions for foreign energy consumers. To begin with, African producers consume very little oil and gas on their own, and so most of what they are capable of producing will be available for export. Second, several of Africa's key producing regions have yet to be fully explored, which means that additional reserves undoubtedly remain to be discovered. Third, much of the oil being procured from West Africa is of the "light, sweet" variety (that is, highly fluid and low in sulfur) greatly prized by American, European, and Chinese refiners. Most important, Africa is experiencing a marked increase in the daily output of its growing population of wells: According to the U.S. Department of Energy, Africa's combined oil output of 10 million barrels per day in 2005 is projected to reach 18 million barrels in 2030, a potentially unrivaled surge in production.[18]

The race for drilling rights in Africa has largely been concentrated

Table 6.1
OIL AND GAS RESERVES AND PRODUCTION OF
MAJOR AFRICAN PRODUCERS
(As of end of 2006)

Country	Petroleum			Natural Gas	
	Reserves, bbl	Production, mbd		Reserves, tcf	Production, bcf
		Actual (2006)	Projected (2030)		
Algeria	12.3	2.0	3.1	159.0	2,982.9
Angola	9.0	1.4	4.0	#	#
Libya	41.5	1.8	1.9	46.5	522.4
Nigeria	36.2	2.5	5.2	183.9	995.5
Chad	0.9	0.2		#	#
Congo-Brazzaville	1.9	0.3		#	#
Egypt	3.7	0.7		68.5	1,581.4
Equatorial Guinea	1.8	0.4	3.7	#	#
Gabon	2.1	0.2		#	#
Sudan	6.4	0.4		#	#
Other Africa	1.3	0.1		42.8	289.5
Total	117.2	10.0	17.9	500.7	6,371.7

Sources: 2006 data: BP, *Statistical Review of World Energy June 2007*; pp. 6, 8, 22, 24; projected 2030 data: U.S. Department of Energy, *International Energy Outlook 2007*, Table G1, p. 187.
bbl = billion barrels
mbd = million barrels per day
tcf = trillion cubic feet
bcf = billion cubic feet
# = included in "Other Africa"

in two major oil-producing regions, each with a distinctive history: North Africa, comprising Algeria, Libya, and Sudan; and West Africa, comprising Angola, Chad, Congo-Brazzaville, Equatorial Guinea, Gabon, and Nigeria.

Of the North African producers, Algeria and Libya have been

producing oil and gas since the 1950s and still harbor substantial reserves; Sudan only began pumping oil in 1999 and is believed to possess far smaller reserves. Algeria, a former French colony, nationalized its abundant oil and gas reserves in 1972 and placed them under the control of Sonatrach, the state-owned energy company. Recently, however, Sonatrach has turned to foreign firms for assistance in operating some of its older fields and has invited international participation in the development of new hydrocarbon deposits.[19] Libya, a former Italian colony, has been ruled since 1969 by Muammar al-Qaddafi and his close associates. The country was subjected to strict U.N. sanctions in 1988 when the Qaddafi regime was found to be complicit in the downing of Pan American Flight 103, but sanctions were suspended in 1999 when he agreed to turn over two Libyan suspects for prosecution in the case and pay compensation to the families of those killed in the crash. Libya, too, has sought increased foreign participation in the development of new oil and gas fields.[20]

Sudan has been torn apart by ethnic and religious strife since gaining independence from Great Britain in 1956. A bitter civil war between the northern government based in Khartoum and the rebellious Sudan People's Liberation Army (SPLA) in the south ended with a cease-fire in December 2004; scarcely had peace been announced, however, when the world became aware of a brutal struggle in the western province of Darfur, pitting government-backed Janjaweed militias against various rebel movements. In both contests, government forces were accused of using aircraft and heavy weapons against unarmed civilians, exacting a heavy toll in human life and producing hundreds of thousands of desperate refugees.[21] Although considerable oil is believed to lie in Sudan's embattled southern and western provinces, including Darfur, few Western firms wish to operate there; China has taken advantage of this situation to become the country's major producer.[22]

The countries of the West African oil-producing region are strung along the Gulf of Guinea from Nigeria in the north to Angola in the south, with Equatorial Guinea, Gabon, and Congo-Brazzaville tucked in between; Chad, the only other significant producer in this group, is separated from the Gulf of Guinea by Cameroon. The fields originally developed in this region were located on land, usually relatively close to the coast; in recent years, however, the biggest discoveries have been in the Gulf of Guinea and the Atlantic Ocean. These offshore fields have attracted particular interest from foreign investors, in part because they are physically removed from the civil strife so often encountered on the mainland and in part because the host nations generally lack the technical expertise to develop them and so are predisposed to offer attractive terms to foreign partners who can. Nigeria

West Africa and the Gulf of Guinea

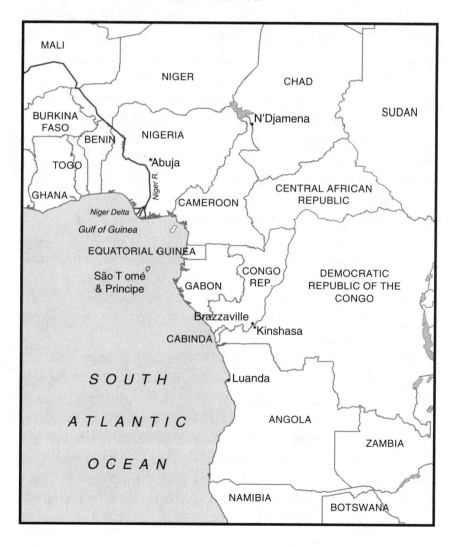

and Angola, with the longest coastlines, have benefitted the most from this trend.[23]

Nigeria, with Africa's largest reserves of petroleum and natural gas, deserves special attention. A British colony until 1960, it has struggled since independence to maintain unity in the face of powerful centrifugal forces. The Biafran war of 1967–70, a struggle for independence by the Igbo people, left an estimated one million dead. Subsequent outbreaks of ethnic and religious strife have produced widespread death and suffering. Despite Nigeria's valiant efforts to resolve these internecine pressures by legislative and judicial means, the military has repeatedly intervened in national politics, monopolizing power from 1966 to 1970 and again from 1983 to 1999. Oil money, which has meant conspicuous wealth for military elites and their cronies, delivers few benefits to the minority peoples who occupy the oil-producing areas of the Niger Delta. This, not surprisingly, has generated widespread antigovernment hostility—channeled in recent years into an armed insurgency led by the Movement for the Emancipation of the Niger Delta (MEND).[24] The organization has often sabotaged oil installations and regularly kidnaps expatriate oil-industry employees—a tactic that, in June 2007, led Royal Dutch Shell and other foreign firms to suspend production of about 710,000 barrels of oil per day.[25] Under President Olusegun Obasanjo and his hand-picked successor, Umaru Yar'Adua (chosen in a 2007 election widely considered fraudulent), the federal government has employed both sticks and carrots in efforts to quell the insurgency—flooding the Delta with troops but also funneling a slightly larger share of the country's oil revenues its way—but with limited success.[26]

Angola also deserves a close look. In 2006, already the sixth leading oil supplier to the United States, it overtook Saudi Arabia to become the number one foreign supplier for China. Because many of Angola's deep offshore wells are just coming on line, its output is sure to rise for years to come, generating billions of dollars in fresh oil revenues.[27] This is good news for the ruling elites of the Popular Movement for the Liberation of Angola (MPLA), in power since the defeat of their last remaining challenger, Jonas Savimbi of the National Union for the Total Independence of Angola (UNITA), in 2002. As yet, next to none of this money has offered any comfort to the country's impoverished masses, who, on average, live on less than $2 a day. Despite repeated promises of reform and considerable pressure from international lending agencies, the MPLA leadership has, for the most part, successfully resisted efforts to increase its transparency regarding the allocation of oil revenues, distributing these mainly to senior government officials and their close associates.[28]

Despite the continuing violence in Nigeria and seemingly intractable problems in other parts of Africa, the allure of untapped oil and gas fields is too enticing to deter the onrush of foreign energy firms. Nigeria, for all its woes in the Delta, is developing new, insurgency-proof offshore oil fields and gas-processing facilities in the Gulf of Guinea.[29] Even Sudan, despite all the violence in Darfur, continues to expand production in its southern fields.[30] You can lay a safe bet on this: Investment by international oil companies in Africa's offshore oil fields will continue to soar in the years ahead.[31]

Still a European Preserve

Given the historical, if often sordid, ties between Europe and Africa, it's no surprise that European companies continue to play a conspicuous role in the exploitation of African energy reserves. For Europeans, Africa's reserves are attractively close at hand. Eager to reduce their reliance on Russian energy—and so the potential for geopolitical blackmail—many of Europe's leaders have encouraged home-based energy firms to invest in Africa; such firms have recently accounted for 60 percent of new investment in West African oil and gas enterprises, according to David L. Goldwyn of Goldwyn International Strategies.[32] As might be expected, French firms like Total S.A. are especially visible in former French colonies such as Gabon, while British companies like BP are especially active in former British colonies such as Nigeria.

Total, the leading French oil and gas company, owes its existence, in part, to government efforts to stimulate oil production in France's African colonies, and still obtains much of its crude petroleum from the region.[33] According to company literature, Total is currently producing oil in seven African states: Algeria, Angola, Cameroon, Congo-Brazzaville, Gabon, Libya, and Nigeria. Of these, it is the leading foreign investor in both Congo-Brazzaville and Gabon and, in 2005, was securing approximately 185,000 barrels of oil per day from the two countries.[34] The company has enjoyed particularly close relations with Congo-Brazzaville's president Denis Sassou-Nguesso—having helped install him in power during a civil war in 1997—and expects to boost production there in coming years.[35] It also holds a majority or minority interest in several large exploration and production blocks in the waters off Angola and Nigeria.[36]

With roots in both Britain and the Netherlands, Royal Dutch Shell is the leading foreign producer in Nigeria and, by 2005, was churning out 1.1 million barrels per day there (before unrest in the Niger Delta forced it to shut down some of its onshore facilities). As the country's leading oil producer, Shell has been the principal target of armed attacks by angry Delta residents who have seen few benefits—and experienced grievous environmental damage—from the drilling in their midst. After a series of sabotage strikes on its pipelines and pumping stations and the kidnapping of company personnel, Shell declared a state of "force majeure" (irresistible force) in the area in January 2006, proclaiming that it would not be able to honor contracts for future oil deliveries due to circumstances beyond its control. While the sabotaged pipelines were later repaired and some production did resume, continuing violence—and the threat of more of the same—has frustrated efforts by Shell and other foreign firms to boost production in the Delta.[37] But Shell is also the lead operator of the offshore Bonga field, Nigeria's first major deepwater energy project and a major source of its crude output.

BP, which got its start in the Middle East, now holds significant interests in several African countries. In Algeria, it is cooperating with state-owned Sonatrach to increase production at Rhourde El Baguel, the country's second largest oil field, and is working with both Sonatrach and Norway's Statoil to develop promising natural gas reserves in other areas.[38] Following a meeting between Libyan strongman Muammar al-Qaddafi and British prime minister Tony Blair in May 2007, BP announced a $900 million joint venture with Libya's National Oil Company to explore for and extract oil and natural gas from the Ghadames basin and offshore parts of the Sirte basin.[39] In Angola, BP is involved in several major offshore oil projects.[40]

Aside from these French and British companies, the most prominent European firm operating in Africa is Italy's Eni (originally the Enti Nazionale Idrocarburi, a state-owned entity that was largely privatized between 1995 and 1998). Eni is an aggressive world player, with significant interests in Africa, the Middle East, and Kazakhstan. Its African holdings are particularly substantial, with major investments in Algeria, Angola, Congo-Brazzaville, Egypt, Libya, and Nigeria. As a former Italian colony, Libya has been well staked out by Eni. It operates a number of major oil fields, including one called "Elephant," and is developing several large natural gas fields in conjunction with the National Oil Company (NOC). Eni and NOC are fifty-fifty joint partners in the massive Western Libya Gas Project, while Eni is 75 percent owner of the "Greenstream" pipeline built beneath the Mediterranean to carry gas from this project to Italy and France.[41] In West Africa, Eni is a major partner in the development of several deepwater fields off the coast of Angola and a significant producer in Nigeria.[42]

Numerous other, less-familiar European energy firms have been operating in the region for several decades and enjoy close links to local elites and bureaucrats; they have also become adept at participating in complicated international consortia established under arcane governing rules guaranteed to exclude the majority of Africans from any conspicuous benefits. The Europeans clearly intend to remain major players in Africa's extractive industries for a long time to come. Nevertheless, in the past decade, their privileged position has come under assault—first from the United States and its giant energy corporations, then from China, India, and others.

The American Invasion

American oil companies have long pursued investment opportunities in Africa, but have made the continent a priority only in the past fifteen or twenty years. Today, giants like Exxon Mobil and Chevron view West Africa as one of their most important future sources of crude oil. In addition, many smaller firms have also swarmed into Africa, seeking opportunities to capture some of the exploration blocks now being auctioned off.

American firms are especially attracted to West Africa's far offshore production sites. "The terms and conditions for investment [in West Africa] are very competitive," J. Robinson West of PFC Energy, a Washington consultancy, told Congress in 2003. "The growth in oil production in the region has occurred offshore. Investors consider this safer because they are not located near or among local communities, and as a result, these companies seem confident that they will avoid the problems encountered in onshore areas such as the Niger Delta area of Nigeria."[43] As has been the case in the Caspian basin, moreover, American firms seeking new energy assets in Africa have been spurred on and assisted by successive U.S. administrations.

In addition to the by-now-familiar desire to escape the Persian Gulf's recurring turmoil and a craving for fresh sources of supply, Washington's motives for increased access to African energy include one particular to the continent. Tanker routes linking West Africa to America's East Coast refineries encounter no congested choke points like the Bosporus in Turkey or the Strait of Hormuz in the Persian Gulf and pass through Atlantic waters largely dominated by the U.S. Navy. From a geopolitical perspective, then, West Africa is an ideal energy source for the United States—an assessment often advanced by American strategists.[44]

The importance of "diversifying" U.S. energy supplies beyond the Persian Gulf was initially articulated by President Clinton in the late 1990s, with particular reference to the Caspian, but George W. Bush's administration first highlighted the importance of securing more oil from Africa. "West Africa is expected to be one of the fastest-growing sources of oil and gas for the American market," the administration affirmed in its National Energy Policy of 2001. Angola and Nigeria were projected to be the main sub-Saharan sources, but Chad, Gabon, and Congo-Brazzaville were also mentioned. To promote increased involvement by American firms in the development of these countries' energy sectors, the NEP called on the president to direct the secretaries of State, Energy, and Commerce to "deepen bilateral and multilateral engagement to promote a more receptive environment for U.S. oil and gas trade, investment, and operations" in the region.[45]

It was a message that American leaders, civilian and military, took to heart. As in the Caspian region, senior government officials have made repeated trips to Africa to implement the NEP's directives. In June 2002, for example, Secretary of Energy Spencer Abraham traveled to Casablanca, Morocco, to attend a meeting of African energy ministers. "We met with [representatives of] government and industry to discuss ways to improve energy trade and improve energy sector development to better serve U.S. and African economic growth and development," he later testified.[46] American ambassadors and trade officials play a key role in such efforts. "Our ambassadors throughout West Africa are extremely active on commercial advocacy as well as investment climate advocacy with host governments," Deputy Assistant Secretary Brodman told a Senate subcommittee in 2004. "Having served in Africa myself, I . . . recognize the importance of having folks on the ground who have a feel for how far local governments can go, how far you can steer them, how you can get deals done, how to get investment regimes shaped properly."[47]

The principal goal of American diplomatic endeavors has been to clear the way for U.S. energy firms by persuading local governments to eliminate unfavorable tax codes, prohibitions against overseas ownership of natural resources, and other barriers to foreign investment. American officials have also devoted considerable effort to unheralded but intensive lobbying for energy sector "reform" in various African nations. As a senior State Department official later noted, when Angolan president Jose Eduardo dos Santos met with President Bush in Washington in May 2004, the White House typically took the opportunity to reaffirm "our message of the importance of transparency and accountability" in major energy transactions.[48]

At the same time, American officials are deeply concerned about the potential for violent social and political unrest due to the endemic corruption, economic inequity, and misallocation of petroleum wealth in the region that will, in turn, lead to violence that could endanger the steady outflow of oil and natural gas. Such fears have spurred the Bush administration to initiate or expand a host of military aid and training programs aimed at improving the "security environment" in energy-producing areas of West Africa. "Conflicts [in Africa] produce risks that have a destabilizing impact . . . on our energy security," Brodman told Congress. "Finding affordable and effective ways to help these countries overcome these barriers is one of the new challenges to our energy security aspirations."[49] Some of these efforts are preventive in nature, aimed at reducing the likelihood of conflict by promoting accountability, good governance, and respect for human rights; however, the administration has also stepped up arms aid and counterinsurgency training—often under the rubric of the Global War on Terror—aiming to bolster these states' capacity to suppress rebellion and strife when violence does occur.[50]

To support all of these initiatives, the Department of Defense (DoD) has substantially increased its presence in Africa, usually in the guise of training missions and liaison activities. In 2002, however, it established its first semipermanent combat mission in the region, the Combined Joint Task Force–Horn of Africa at Camp Lemonier in Djibouti, under the auspices of U.S. Central Command. Since then, the DoD has used a number of "bare bones" facilities—typically, an airstrip and associated communications facilities—for training, surveillance, and support operations in Africa; the U.S. Navy, under European Command auspices, has expanded its maritime presence in the Gulf of Guinea. It is to ensure enhanced, centralized oversight over these, and projected future endeavors like them, that President Bush established AFRICOM in 2007.[51] Ordinarily, Pentagon officials dismiss any link between these efforts and America's growing reliance on African oil, yet, when speaking off the record, they are often quick to do so. "[A] key mission for U.S. forces [in Africa] would be to ensure that Nigeria's oil fields, which could in the future account for as much as 25 percent of all U.S. oil imports, are secure," a senior DoD official told Greg Jaffe of the *Wall Street Journal* in 2003.[52]

With strong Pentagon backing and driven by their own profit motives, the major American energy firms have flocked to Africa. Exxon Mobil and Chevron have been especially aggressive, snapping up promising assets throughout West Africa. Typically, these acquisitions take the form of production-sharing agreements (PSAs) between the government and a private company or consortium. In Angola, for example, Exxon is the lead operator in exploiting offshore Block 15, the country's most productive deepwater tract and the source of 9 percent of all the crude oil Exxon is producing worldwide.[53] To extract oil from this massive deposit, located in waters over half a mile deep, the company is employing a novel technology: rather than pump the crude to land for further processing, the oil is sucked up and stored on a mammoth vessel—a "floating production, storage, and offloading" unit, or FPSO—then loaded directly onto waiting tankers.[54] "Every four days," observed Jeffrey Ball of the *Wall Street Journal,* "a super-tanker sails into the area like a car pulling into a gas station, fills up and heads off to a refinery somewhere around the globe."[55] Legally speaking, all this activity is taking place in Angolan territory, but you would never know it: Except for an occasional R&R visit to mainland resorts, the foreign workers on these mammoth rigs have no contact with the country or its people.[56] (See Table 6.2.)

Exxon is also a leading producer in Nigeria—again concentrating on offshore production, the safest kind in Africa. In 2006, it extracted about 750,000 barrels of oil per day, second only to Shell's 1.1 million barrels. Reportedly, the company plans to invest as much as $11 billion in its Nigerian holdings through 2011, aiming to boost its net output there to 1.2 million barrels per day. Much of the additional oil will come from the offshore Erha tracts where, once again, Exxon will employ an FPSO system. Exxon also operates two smaller fields in Nigeria, Yoho and Bosi, with a projected combined output of 260,000 barrels per day.[57]

Exxon Mobil has sought additional opportunities in other countries in the region. In Equatorial Guinea, it is the lead operator of the Zafiro field, the country's largest,[58] as it is of the Doba field, the major producing deposit in Chad. To bring the Doba oil to market, Exxon supervised the construction of a 670-mile pipeline from southern Chad to the Cameroonian coast and then, by an undersea extension, to an FPSO in the Gulf of Guinea.[59] Much about the Chad undertaking has been the subject of international controversy, given the authoritarian nature of the Chadian regime and widely voiced fears—since confirmed by events—that revenues from the operation would be channeled into arms spending and governmental corruption.[60] The company has nonetheless repeatedly stated that it intends to expand output in Chad.[61]

Chevron, like Exxon, was one of the first foreign firms to operate in

Table 6.2
PARTICIPANTS IN ANGOLA'S MAJOR OFFSHORE BLOCKS

Block	Current (or Estimated Peak) Production, tbd	Lead Operator	Secondary Partners
Block 0	370	Chevron/CABGOC	Sonangol, Total, Eni
Block 4	n.a.	Sonangol	Norsk Hydro, ACR, SPA
Block 14	(300)	Chevron/CABGOC	Eni, Sonangol, Total, Petrogal
Block 15	570	Exxon Mobil	BP, Eni, Statoil
Block 17	(850)	Total	Sonangol, Exxon Mobil, BP, Statoil, Norsk Hydro
Block 18	(240)	BP	Sinopec
Block 24	n.a.	Devon Energy	Exxon Mobil, Sonangol, Petronas
Block 31	(260)	BP	Exxon Mobil, Sonangol, Statoil, Marathon, Total
Block 32	(130)	Total	Marathon, Sonangol, Exxon Mobil, Petrogal

Source: U.S. Department of Energy, "Angola," Country Analysis Brief, January 2007.
tbd = thousand barrels per day
ACR = Angola Consulting Resources
CABGOC = Cabinda Gulf Oil Company
Sonangol = Sociedade Nacional de Combustíveis de Angola
SPA = Sociedade Petrofina Angolana

Angola's offshore areas, helping to establish the Cabinda Gulf Oil Company (CABGOC) in 1955. CABGOC now operates Block Zero in waters off Cabinda province, the small sliver of Angola tucked between Congo-Brazzaville and the Democratic Republic of the Congo. The company also controls Block 14 and in 2007 announced plans to spend $7 billion on new drilling facilities to exploit the block's ample reserves of oil and natural gas and on a plant to liquefy the gas into LNG for export abroad.[62] In Nigeria, Chevron has holdings in the Niger Delta region and a number of offshore blocks. In 2006 and 2007 it was forced, due to insurgent activity, to cease production at its onshore fields in the Delta, but it intends to boost production at its off-shore locations.[63]

Smaller, so-called independents like Amerada Hess, Anadarko Petroleum, Devon Energy, Marathon Oil, and Occidental Petroleum have also joined the rush to Africa. Devon Energy and Marathon, for example, are both represented in Angola's offshore fields. In Equatorial Guinea, Amerada Hess is the lead operator of the Ceiba field, and Marathon runs the Alba field.[64]

While largely focusing their attention on West Africa in recent years, American firms have also gained a foothold in North Africa, which has become more hospitable to U.S. investment. Some American independents, including Anadarko Petroleum and Amerada Hess, have, for example, taken advantage of an Algerian willingness to open its energy sector to foreign participation since the election of President Abdelaziz Bouteflika in 1999. In fact, Anadarko is now the largest foreign operator in that country, with responsibility for the Hassi Berkine South and Ourhound fields in eastern Algeria; together, the two fields produced some 450,000 barrels of oil per day in 2006, or about one-quarter of the country's total output. Hess, already operating a number of smaller fields, added to its holdings during a licensing auction in December 2004.[65]

Libya presents a more complicated picture. Several U.S. firms, including Hess, ConocoPhillips, Occidental, and Marathon, once operated major concessions in the country. They were forced to suspend these operations in 1986 when Washington imposed economic sanctions on Libya as punishment for its support of international terrorism and its suspected pursuit of nuclear weapons. While the American companies withdrew their personnel and ceased cooperation with Libya's state-owned National Oil Company, they never actually renounced their concessions or abandoned hope of someday reclaiming them.[66]

This certainly must have seemed a forlorn hope after Libya was accused of masterminding the 1988 attack on Pan American Flight 103 and U.N. sanctions were imposed on the country. But the suspension of those sanctions in 1999 (they were lifted altogether in 2003) prompted a gradual warming in U.S.-Libyan relations. The final impediment to renewed American participation in Libya's energy sector was removed in February 2004 when Muammar al-Qaddafi announced that his country would terminate its nuclear weapons program and abide by the Non-Proliferation Treaty; seven months later, President Bush lifted all remaining U.S. sanctions on Libya, paving the way for American energy firms to sign new contracts with the Libyan government (or to revive old agreements). Most of the companies present in Libya before 1986 have since returned and are once again producing there.[67]

After years of isolation from the international community, Libya is eager to rebuild its ties with foreign energy firms and acquire modern production technology, which would lead to a substantial increase in its oil and gas output. To achieve these goals, the government is auctioning off large swaths of unexplored territory (both onshore and offshore) for development by foreign firms, usually in conjunction with the National Oil Company.[68] In the first auctions held in 2005, after Washington lifted sanctions, four American companies—Chevron, Exxon, Hess, and Occidental—won rights to develop one or more blocks.[69] Since then, Exxon has launched an all-out drive to expand its presence in Libya; following a 2007 meeting between CEO Rex Tillerson and Colonel Qaddafi, the company signed a major deal to explore for oil and natural gas in an area of the Mediterranean Sea some 110 miles off the Libyan coast.[70]

Along Came the Chinese

When American oil firms first arrived in Africa several decades ago, their major competitors were long-entrenched European companies. In the past few years, however, both the Americans and the Europeans have faced stiff competition from an unexpected quarter: major Chinese energy firms, vigorously backed by all the resources their government could bring to bear.

Beijing's interest in African energy is essentially identical to Washington's: Just as the United States plans to rely on African producers like Algeria, Angola, Chad, Libya, and Nigeria for an ever-increasing share of its imported energy, so does China; and, much as giant major American companies like Exxon Mobil and Chevron have been attracted to Africa by its relative openness to foreign investment, so, too, have the major Chinese energy firms. Like their American counterparts, CNOOC, CNPC, and Sinopec have bid for the right to develop exploration blocks in Angola, Chad, Equatorial Guinea, Libya, and Nigeria; they have also acquired a substantial stake in Sudan (where CNPC is the lead producer). The Chinese have gradually assembled a significant portfolio of African energy assets—and they clearly intend to expand these in the future.[71]

The Chinese appear drawn to Africa by the same impulse that sparked their interest in the Caspian Sea basin: a desire to reduce their reliance on oil imports from the Persian Gulf.[72] It is evident, in fact, that Beijing has placed a particularly high priority on the quest for African energy assets—sensing, perhaps, that it enjoys a comparative advantage in this region. The Chinese already had far closer relations than the Americans with a number of African governments because of China's conspicuous support for their liberation movements during the colonial era. Whereas Europe is inextricably tied to the abuses of colonialism and the United States to the manipulative politics of the Cold War era, China is unencumbered by these legacies and so can claim to offer a "fresh start" in Great Power relationships with the nations of Africa. In addition, the Chinese have promised to help African states emulate their success in rising quickly from Third World backwardness to relative affluence—a trajectory that many African leaders would dearly love to replicate.[73]

In the first years of the new century, the Chinese leadership launched the diplomatic equivalent of a full-court press to establish a significant presence in Africa's prime resource-producing areas.[74] President Hu Jintao has, since 2003, made three visits to Africa, while Premier Wen Jiabao toured seven African countries during the summer of 2006; of the nine members of China's Politburo Standing Committee, six have paid extensive visits to Africa since 2004.[75] Capping all of these efforts was Beijing's Summit of the Forum on China-Africa Cooperation in November 2006, which drew the top political leaders of forty-eight African states to the Chinese capital for a lavish celebration hosted by Hu and Wen.[76]

In their approach to African leaders and opinion makers, Chinese officials have consistently stressed China's sympathetic and helpful status as a previously colonized, now "developing" nation that—unlike the European countries and the United States—seeks to facilitate Africa's advancement rather than merely exploit its resources. "China is the largest developing country, and Africa is home to the largest number of developing countries," Hu told the Beijing Summit in 2006. "Building strong ties between China and Africa will not only promote development of each side, but also help cement unity and cooperation among developing countries and contribute to establishing a just and equitable new international political and economic order."[77] To sweeten this appeal, the Chinese have given their African partners substantial development assistance, including low-cost or interest-free loans and debt forgiveness, as well as other forms of preferential treatment.[78] Nevertheless, some African critics complain that Beijing's ultimate intention—no less than that of the Europeans and Americans—is simply to grab as much of Africa's raw materials as it can to sustain its high-powered economic growth.[79]

China's African initiative first got under way in the mid-1990s in Sudan, when the China National Petroleum Corporation acquired a controlling share in the Greater Nile Petroleum Operating Company (GNPOC), Sudan's leading oil producer. Since then, CNPC has expanded its presence, obtaining a substantial interest in pipelines, a refinery in Khartoum, and other energy assets. The Chinese ostensibly acquired these holdings through normal commercial channels, by buying up or outbidding other firms; they did, however, benefit from the reluctance of many Western firms to do business with the notorious Khartoum regime, controlled since 1989 by President Omar Ahmed al-Bashir—an autocratic ruler widely held responsible for promoting mass killings in both southern Sudan and the western Sudanese province of Darfur.[80]

Although CNPC has acquired many assets in Sudan, its principal holding remains the oil reserves controlled by GNPOC. Ironically, these deposits—particularly the Heglig and Unity fields in southern Sudan—were first developed in the 1960s and 1970s by Chevron. At one time the Americans had high hopes for these deposits but chose to abandon them in 1990 when fighting between the Khartoum regime and the Sudan People's Liberation Army in the south put the lives of company personnel at risk. At that point, a Canadian firm, Arakis Energy, took over the concession; but Arakis lacked the capital to develop the fields and so sought partners with the cash needed to finance the required infrastructure improvements. With few Western firms willing to participate in this enterprise, Arakis formed GNPOC in 1996 and sold a controlling interest, 40 percent, to CNPC; it retained a 25 percent share for itself, sold another 30 percent to Malaysia's state oil firm, Petronas, and a final 5 percent to the Sudanese national company, Sudapet.[81] A 930-mile pipeline to Port Sudan on the Red Sea coast was completed with substantial Chinese participation in 1999, and now the consortium is producing some 285,000 barrels per day—most of it going to China.[82] (Arakis later sold its stake in the GNPOC to another Canadian firm, Talisman Energy, which in 2002 sold that 25 percent share to India's state-owned Oil and Natural Gas Corporation.)

The Chinese have clearly expended a great deal of effort in wooing Sudan and building up their presence in the country. At the April 2005 Asia-Africa Summit in Jakarta, President Hu met privately with Bashir and, according to an official release, "reiterated that the Chinese government attaches importance to developing relations with Sudan and expects to work with Sudan to constantly push forward the friendly cooperative relations between the two countries."[83] Beijing has also shown its support for the Khartoum regime in more critical ways: by resisting efforts by members of the U.N. Security Council to impose sanctions on Sudan to force the government to cease aiding militias responsible for the slaughter of civilians in Darfur, and by supplying arms and military aid to Sudan's military.[84] These arms have been used, according to human rights observers, in a brutal campaign to drive southerners loyal to the SPLA away from the oil fields being operated by GNPOC.[85] "From the beginning," Professor Eric Reeves of Smith College told the U.S.-China Economic and Security Review Commission in August 2006, "China's behavior in oil exploration . . . [has] been marked by deep complicity in gross human rights violations, scorched-earth clearances of the indigenous populations in the oil regions, and direct assistance to Khartoum's regular military forces."[86]

Although Chinese leaders have gone to great lengths to protect their extensive investments in Sudan—even to the point of risking international approbation for their close association with Khartoum—it is not apparent that these assets can be safeguarded forever. As the desperate plight of the refugees in Darfur became widely known, China found itself under immense international pressure to sever its ties with the Bashir regime or at least support efforts to impose sanctions on Khartoum at the U.N. Security Council—either of which would endanger its access to Sudanese oil. Meanwhile, a peace agreement signed in December 2004 between the Khartoum regime and the southern rebels allows for the eventual secession of southern Sudan, which (if it were to occur) could involve the forfeiture of some of the most productive fields the Chinese are now operating. Meanwhile, the rebels in Darfur—who are not a party to the cease-fire between Khartoum and the southerners—have threatened to attack GNPOC facilities in the Darfur region, insisting that Chinese companies cease their collaboration with the Sudanese government.[87] It is entirely possible, then, that China's Sudanese investments may not prove as durable or attractive as they once appeared.

Undoubtedly aware of these risks, China has worked to expand its presence into other African oil-producing countries, especially Angola, Nigeria, and Libya. The Chinese made their first significant foray into Angola in 2004, when Sinopec acquired a 50 percent stake in offshore Block 18 from BP, the principal field operator. BP had originally planned to sell the stake to ONGC Videsh, the overseas arm of India's Oil and Natural Gas Corporation. However, Angola's national oil company, Sonangol, steered the prize to Sinopec after Beijing awarded the Angolan government a virtually interest-free $2 billion development loan.[88] (This was one of several instances in which the Chinese outmaneuvered the Indians, prompting those high-level talks in 2005 and 2006 between New Delhi and Beijing aimed at averting future cutthroat competition.) Since acquiring its stake in Block 18, Sinopec has also procured a part interest in another offshore block and has discussed joint prospecting and refining projects with Sonangol.[89]

Sinopec also obtained its first stake in Nigeria's energy sector in 2004, when it secured the right to develop two blocks in the Niger

Delta in conjunction with the Nigerian National Petroleum Corporation.[90] It soon became clear that Beijing viewed this as but an initial incursion. Increased energy cooperation between the two countries was reportedly a major topic between Presidents Hu and Obasanjo during high-level meetings in Beijing in April 2005 and then in the Nigerian capital of Abuja one year later.[91] At the Abuja meeting, Hu reportedly told Obasanjo of his desire to establish a "strategic partnership" between the two countries, which he termed "a top priority for China's foreign relations."[92]

Hu's 2006 visit coincided with the announcement of several new Chinese investments—most significantly, the acquisition by CNOOC of a 45 percent stake in the offshore Akpo field, of which France's Total was the lead operator, for an estimated $2.4 billion.[93] The stake had previously been controlled by South Atlantic Petroleum of Nigeria, a privately owned firm linked to former Defense Minister Theophilus Danjuma and other prominent Nigerian insiders, suggesting strong government backing for the sale.[94] (This was CNOOC's first major foreign purchase after losing its bid for Unocal, and was touted by company officials as a sign of the company's determination to remain a major world player.[95]) As 2007 drew to a close, CNOOC was also said to be interested in acquiring part ownership of some of Shell's Nigerian holdings.[96]

CNOOC, Sinopec, and CNPC have all bid ferociously for new exploration blocks elsewhere in Africa. In Algeria, Sinopec owns a stake in the Zarzaitine oil field, while CNOOC holds the right to develop several promising exploration blocks. In Libya, CNPC has also been active, winning the right to develop a major exploration block in October 2005; in Chad, a CNPC subsidiary has acquired EnCana Corporation's exploration rights, and another subsidiary is building a refinery; in Equatorial Guinea, CNOOC is preparing to develop an offshore block in the Gulf of Guinea.[97]

As demonstrated in their relationship with Sudan, Chinese leaders have regularly sought to cultivate close ties with governments in power, however corrupt or disreputable, assuming that this will give state-backed companies a leg up when it comes to the allocation of PSAs and exploration rights. In Angola, Ethiopia, Nigeria, Sudan, and

Zimbabwe, among other countries, this strategy has proved effective, at least in the short term. But it has not endeared the Chinese to out-of-power groups, minorities, or separatist movements that view the prevailing governments as corrupt, oppressive, or parasitical—as something that must be expunged. In this sense, the Chinese position in Africa is only as strong as the governments it has backed.

During Hu's 2006 visit to Nigeria, for example, the rebel group MEND declared, "We wish to warn the Chinese government and its oil companies to steer clear of the Niger Delta. . . . The Chinese government, by investing in stolen crude, places its citizens in our line of fire."[98] No attacks on Chinese facilities in Nigeria are known to have occurred yet, but the picture in the troubled Ogaden region of Ethiopia—where Sinopec operates a small oil field—may be a sign of the future elsewhere. On April 24, 2007, forces of the separatist Ogaden National Liberation Front overran a Chinese-operated oil field, killing nine Chinese oil workers and abducting six (later released).[99] More recently, Darfur rebels of the Justice and Equality Movement attacked oil facilities in south Kordofan, specifically targeting fields run by Chinese firms. The rebel group's leader, Abdel Aziz Nur al-Ashr, said the attacks would continue until China ended its operations in Sudan altogether.[100] Incidents like this are bound to multiply as Chinese energy firms come to be seen as complicit with governments deemed oppressive and illegitimate by groups seeking radical change.

China shares with Europe and the United States a strong interest in Africa's other raw materials, including uranium, copper, cobalt, and basic industrial minerals. For example, it obtains 90 percent of its cobalt from the Democratic Republic of the Congo, much of its chromium from Zimbabwe, considerable copper from Zambia, and nearly all of its platinum from South Africa. And Chinese mining firms, such as China Nuclear International Uranium Corporation (Sino-U), have been exploring for new uranium deposits in northern Niger, which holds about one-tenth of the world's uranium reserves.[101]

In recognition of the country's insatiable thirst for raw materials of all types, the Chinese government has often assumed a leading role in the pursuit of African minerals, just as it has in the search for oil. Many of the carefully choreographed state visits by President Hu and

Premier Wen to African countries in recent years have been to major minerals producers such as South Africa, Zambia, and Zimbabwe, where talk of mining concessions and giant ore purchases has often headed the agenda. But few such deals can compare with the September 2007 announcement of a $5 billion Chinese loan to the Democratic Republic of the Congo for infrastructure repair and development, to be repaid in copper and cobalt. According to press accounts, the loan exceeded even what the World Bank and International Monetary Fund were prepared to offer the Congo for this purpose. Reportedly, the Chinese will also receive repayment in concessions to gold and nickel deposits, and tolls on roads and railways yet to be built.[102]

As in its eager hunt for oil, China's rush to procure African minerals and timber has sometimes sparked hostility or criticism. In Niger, for instance, Sino-U has come under attack from rebels of the Niger Movement for Justice who claim the company is providing military aid to the central government; in July 2007, a company official was kidnapped by the rebels, though later released.[103] In Zimbabwe, the Chinese have sought to cement their close ties with the autocratic regime of Robert Mugabe by providing his government with lavish development aid and a wide array of modern weapons—prompting widespread criticism from Western governments.[104] In Zambia, Chinese firms have been accused of employing unsafe labor practices at the copper mines they run, thereby contributing to a 2005 explosion in which forty-six Zambian workers were killed.[105] Chinese firms have also been accused of contributing to the wholesale decimation of Africa's remaining tropical forests, in some cases engaging in illegal practices to secure ancient hardwoods that are fast disappearing from the planet.[106]

The "China Threat" in Africa

These complaints aside, China's oil and mineral acquisitions in Africa are still relatively modest compared to those of the European powers and the United States. The major oil and gas producers in Africa remain Exxon, Chevron, Shell, BP, and Total—not Sinopec, CNPC, or CNOOC. Only in Sudan can China claim a dominant interest in a major oil enterprise, but then Sudan is fifth in line among Africa's top oil producers. Nevertheless, some American policymakers regularly portray China's energy endeavors on the continent as a significant threat to U.S. strategic interests, requiring a forceful riposte.

At a public hearing on "China's Influence in Africa" convened by the Africa Subcommittee of the House International Relations Committee in July 2005—in the midst of the Unocal ruckus—Rep. Christopher H. Smith of New Jersey, a Republican and then the subcommittee's chair, echoed the general mood of hostility: "Amidst all of this hoopla over China's rapidly growing economy, there is a dark side to [its] economic expansion that is being largely ignored. . . . [T]here is concern that the Chinese intend to aid and abet African dictators, gain a stranglehold on precious African natural resources, and undo much of the progress that has been made on democracy and governance in the last fifteen years in African nations."[107]

To sustain his claim that China sought a "stranglehold" on African resources, Smith asked Commissioner Carolyn Bartholomew of the U.S.-China Economic and Security Review Commission (USCC), a Congressionally chartered body, to testify on China's business practices. The Chinese, she claimed, were threatening world energy security by buying up African oil fields and then shipping whatever crude they produce directly to China, rather than selling it on the international market. "China's energy strategy in general is a concern for United States energy security because of the Chinese government's interest in controlling oil and other natural resource production *at the source*, rather than making investments to ensure that there is a greater supply on the world market."[108] (Emphasis added.)

This claim that China seeks to control African oil "at the source" has acquired the status of self-evident truth. Yet very little hard data has been produced to substantiate it. Indeed, a study conducted by the Department of Energy to assess this danger concluded that China's acquisition of African oil and gas assets did not entail a threat to global energy availability. Whatever petroleum China gained in this manner, the report concluded, was crude that would otherwise have to be procured from other, market-based sources and so would have a "neutral" effect on world energy supplies.[109]

This assessment has not, however, quieted the concern in Washington. In its 2006 report to Congress, the USCC asserted that "China's strategy of securing ownership and control of oil and natural gas assets abroad could substantially affect U.S. energy security—reducing the ability of the global petroleum market to ameliorate temporary and limited petroleum supply disruptions in the United States and elsewhere." Pointing to China's support for authoritarian regimes in Africa and elsewhere, the commission charged that "China's energy policies, taken as a whole, are not consistent with the economic or geopolitical behavior of a reliable stakeholder [in the international system]; they distort markets and destabilize volatile regions."[110]

The Department of Defense has also fueled the anxiety over China's pursuit of African energy. "Securing adequate supplies of resources and materials has become a major driver of Chinese foreign policy," it observed in its 2006 report *Military Power of the People's Republic of China*. In particular, it claimed, the Chinese had sought "long-term resource supply agreements" with Angola, Sudan, and Zimbabwe, and was attempting to lubricate these arrangements with significant deliveries of arms and military technology—thus posing a potential threat to U.S. security interests.[111]

Of course, the Pentagon report did not mention that the United States has long provided military aid to many key African states and is now significantly expanding its involvement on the continent with the formation of AFRICOM and the search for new basing facilities. As noted, these initiatives are usually justified under the rubric of antiterrorism or as preventive measures intended to enhance the governance credentials of corrupt and unrepresentative African states—not as a response to the increased presence of the Chinese. Yet, when pressed, Pentagon officials will not deny, off the record, that senior American strategists are troubled by China's "rising influence" in Africa.[112] Indeed, the fact that AFRICOM's formation was announced on the very day Hu Jintao arrived in South Africa to begin his much-ballyhooed February 2007 visit to eight African nations was not lost on commentators in the region.[113]

Given the high stakes involved, and unmistakable evidence of a growing U.S. resolve to repulse Chinese advances in the Caspian basin and other strategically important areas, it is hard to imagine that senior officials are not equally determined to counter Chinese advances in Africa. The February 2007 announcement of AFRICOM's formation must be taken as an expression of this resolve, as must be the increased deployment of U.S. naval vessels in African waters and intensified planning for American military bases on the continent.[114] The Department of Defense has quickened the pace of arms transfers and military aid in a struggle—which the Chinese have joined—to win the loyalty of major energy producers. The Great Power geopolitical competition has returned in a major way to Africa.

A Continent of Empty Holes

And what do the Africans get out of all this? Except for thousands of holes in the ground, various large-scale environmental catastrophes, and a scattering of heavily guarded villas and Swiss bank accounts for well-connected elites, not very much. Despite the claim that large extractive projects like oil pipelines and copper mines will generate jobs and income for Africa's impoverished masses and wealth for nations, most ordinary Africans have yet to see—and may *never* see—any tangible benefit from all of the foreign investment in hydrocarbon and mineral production. After all, the real "benefits" begin to "trickle down" only once African crude is converted into refined products and its raw ores into manufactured goods elsewhere, most of which are then sold to consumers in the industrialized and newly developed countries.[115]

Take Angola, one of the leading suppliers of petroleum in West Africa. In 2006, it exported approximately 1.3 million barrels of oil per day, generating billions of dollars in foreign sales. Signs of this newfound wealth can be seen in the affluent gated communities that have sprouted up around Luanda, Angola's capital city, yet agriculture sustains two-thirds of all Angolans, who continue to live in abysmal conditions on an average of less than $2 per day.[116] Meanwhile, the International Monetary Fund and other watchdog groups report that as much as $1 billion per year is disappearing from Angola's national treasury, presumably flowing into the pockets (and foreign bank accounts) of officials close to President Jose Eduardo Dos Santos.[117] "Angola's petroleum revenues, as they are currently used, are widely viewed as a curse," a confidential report written for Royal Dutch Shell observed. "Those ordinary Angolans who are aware of Angola's oil riches have grown to realize in recent years that this resource is managed for the immense profit of a very few, and the increasing misery of the many."[118]

The situation is hardly different in Nigeria and other oil-producing countries of West Africa. Nigeria has exported more than 200 billion dollars' worth of oil during the past fifteen years, but 70 percent of its population still lives on less than a dollar a day. Here, too, there is a stark disparity between the privileged, who have benefitted enormously from this influx of oil wealth, and the vast majority of Nigerians, who have not. Despite the growth of offshore fields, most of the country's petroleum is still derived from the Niger Delta—a dismally poor, swampy area far removed from the capital of Abuja with its modern high-rises and gleaming government buildings. For decades, the elites in Abuja monopolized the nation's oil wealth while the Delta was exposed to multiple environmental hazards from oil production.[119] "The world depends on their oil," observed Anyakwee Nsirimovu of the Institute of Human Rights and Humanitarian Law in the Niger Delta, "but for the people of the Niger Delta oil is more of a curse than a blessing."[120]

The same distorted allocation of the costs and benefits occurs throughout the continent, where unrelenting poverty for the majority remains the norm. The one notable instance in which a serious attempt was made to reverse this pattern—with oil production in southern Chad and the construction of the Chad-Cameroon pipeline—is instructive. In 2000, Exxon Mobil and its partners in the Chadian oil project—Chevron and Petronas of Malaysia—turned to the World Bank to secure additional funding for the construction of that 670-mile pipeline meant to allow export to world markets. Under pressure from nongovernmental organizations in Africa, the Bank demanded that the Chadian government agree to channel most of the project's "trickle down" revenues into social and economic development.

Furthermore, to ensure compliance with this plan, independent monitors would supervise the entire process under a regime of strict transparency. No sooner had the government signed the deal, however, than it siphoned the first $4 million—an initial "signing fee"—into the procurement of foreign arms.[121] Since then, the government has repeatedly frustrated all efforts to force a full and transparent accounting of its oil-revenue expenditures, and there has been scant evidence of any genuine move toward the alleviation of poverty in the country.[122]

If poverty alleviation is not a likely outcome of major foreign resource projects, the prospects are no better for the alleviation of internal violence. By increasing the flow of illicit wealth to elites that collect the "rents" from oil, gas, and mineral production, such projects inevitably fuel resentment—and, in many cases, rebellion or violent attack—from those who feel unjustly deprived of any benefits. Adding to the prospective flames, the leading energy-consuming nations have tried to protect access to vital materials by providing arms and military training to the armed forces of their primary suppliers, thereby encouraging the rulers of these countries to rely on brute force rather than compromise and inclusion when dealing with any group that seeks a greater share of oil or mineral revenues. More often than not, this guarantees an endless succession of coups at the top and revolts, ethnic upheavals, and gang wars below.

Such is the pattern throughout much of Africa. Some local workers may get menial jobs at oil fields and mines, but most of the high-paying engineering and managerial positions are reserved for foreigners or people who are well connected to the powerful. When resource-related wars and insurgencies break out, as they often do, it is the civilian population that suffers. And when, at last, the oil or copper or cobalt is depleted, the energy and mining companies will just pick up their stakes and move elsewhere, leaving behind massive unemployment, broken promises, and large, empty holes.

7

ENCROACHING ON AN "AMERICAN LAKE"

In Africa and the Caspian Sea region, the United States remains on the offensive in the global struggle over valuable energy deposits, but in one critical region—the Persian Gulf basin—it finds itself on the defensive, trying to preserve its dominant position and restrict access to competing powers. It has long been America's intention to exercise ultimate control over this vital region, the repository of two-thirds of the world's known petroleum reserves. So extensive is the U.S. economic and military presence in the Gulf that some observers have described it as an "American lake."[1] Even so, the magnetic pull of Persian Gulf energy is far too powerful for other major consuming nations to resist its lure—and many of them, including China, India, and Japan, are seeking ways to expand their presence there. Russia also aims to expand its political and economic influence in the Gulf, adding a whole new set of challenges for American policymakers.

These other nations could, of course, avoid confrontation with the United States simply by purchasing the energy they need on the open market, and leaving it at that. Many do just this. But the Gulf exerts a powerful attraction. Because *so much* of the world's oil and gas originates there, some countries have tried to exercise a degree of control over the production and export of the area's oil supplies. Although most local Gulf governments have been unwilling to surrender ownership of their resources—having generally nationalized them in the 1970s—they are nevertheless eager to tap into the technical and financial capabilities of international companies and so have, to one degree or another, been prepared to allow foreigners to participate in the extraction of untapped reserves.

Ironically, it was to escape the Gulf's chronic instability that so many nations set out to "diversify" their sources of crude oil in the 1990s by increasing their reliance on supplies from the Caspian Sea basin and Africa. When all is said and done, however, no other oil-producing region can compensate for the sheer abundance of Persian Gulf reserves, and so every diversifying consumer has, in the end, been drawn back to the Gulf in pursuit of long-term supply arrangements. It's obvious, moreover, that the Gulf area will be even more critical to global energy supplies in the future, as other producing regions reach peak sustainable output and fall into decline.

According to the most recent data from BP, the Persian Gulf as a whole possesses an estimated 737 billion barrels of proven oil reserves, representing approximately 61 percent of the known world supply. This compares to about 12 percent for Europe and the former Soviet Union, 10 percent for Africa, 9 percent for South and Central America, 5 percent for North America, and 3 percent for East and Southeast Asia—reason enough to explain the Gulf's enduring geopolitical significance.[2]

Within this confined area, moreover, the Gulf's hydrocarbon reserves are even further concentrated in a handful of extraordinarily privileged nations. As shown by Table 7.1, five countries—Iran, Iraq, Kuwait, Saudi Arabia, and the United Arab Emirates (UAE)—possess the overwhelming bulk of the region's oil reserves, while just two—Iran and Qatar—hold the lion's share of its natural gas.

In recent years, all of these nations have been the subject of fierce efforts by China, India, Japan, and other energy-consuming nations to obtain guarantees of future supplies of oil and natural gas. The pursuing states have marshaled all the diplomatic resources at their command as well as economic incentives—and, in some cases, arms and other military hardware. Of course, similar means have long been employed by the United States (and before them, the British), so their use

Table 7.1

OIL AND NATURAL GAS RESERVES IN THE PERSIAN GULF

(As of end of 2006)

Country	Oil Reserves, bbl	Percent of World Total	Natural Gas Reserves, tcf	Percent of World Total
Bahrain	#	#	3.2	0.1
Iran	137.5	11.4	993.0	15.5
Iraq	115.0	9.5	111.9	1.7
Kuwait	101.5	8.4	62.8	1.0
Oman	5.6	0.5	34.6	0.5
Qatar	15.2	1.3	895.2	14.0
Saudi Arabia	264.3	21.9	249.7	3.9
United Arab Emirates	97.8	8.1	214.0	3.3
Total, Persian Gulf	736.9	61.1	2,564.4	40.0
Total, World	1,208.2	100.0	6,405.5	100.0

Source: BP, *Statistical Review of World Energy June 2007*, pp. 6, 22.
bbl = billion barrels
tcf = trillion cubic feet
# = negligible

by other energy-seeking states should not be surprising. But since the United States has dominated this area since 1970, Washington now views these moves as a substantial threat to core American interests.

At the very least, the key role still played by giant U.S. oil firms in the production, processing, and transportation of Persian Gulf energy is coming under increasing challenge. Although these firms were largely forced to surrender title to the Gulf's oil and gas reserves to locally owned enterprises in the 1970s, they still play a major role as service providers to the national oil companies and often participate as junior partners in building and running refineries, petrochemical complexes, and liquefied natural gas facilities. Their presence in the oil fields may be more circumspect than it once was—the logos of local companies have long since covered over American ones on oil rigs and refineries—but Exxon Mobil, Chevron, and ConocoPhillips continue to dominate many aspects of oil and gas production in the region.[3] Not only does this endow them with considerable influence over the global trade in energy—a major corporate objective since the days of John D. Rockefeller—but it also figures prominently in their annual profit calculations. Given these high stakes, it would be surprising indeed if American policymakers and oil-company executives did not view the appearance in the Gulf of vigorous national competitors like China, Japan, and Russia (and their allied national oil companies) with considerable alarm.

But market share and oil profits are not the only critical issues here. Ever since the early Cold War era, American leaders have believed that, as a matter of strategic necessity, the United States must exercise ultimate control over the flow of Persian Gulf energy, both to preserve unhindered American access to vital petroleum supplies and ensure that this country—and this country alone—had its hands on the world's principal oil spigot. Typically, this outlook has been expressed in the negative: We do not seek such control for our own economic advantage but must deny it to others lest they use it to cripple the U.S. and world economy. This was, indeed, the essence of the "Carter Doctrine," the most explicit policy expression on the subject to this day. "Let our position be absolutely clear," President Jimmy Carter told a Joint Session of Congress on January 23, 1980. "An attempt by any outside force to gain control of the Persian Gulf region would be regarded as an assault on the vital interests of the United States." Such an assault, he declared, would "be repelled by any means necessary, including military force."[4]

Again and again, senior American officials have reaffirmed this basic principle. When, in August 1990, Iraqi forces invaded Kuwait and appeared to pose a direct threat to the oil fields of Saudi Arabia, the first Bush administration quickly concluded that a U.S. military riposte was essential. In testimony before the Senate Armed Services Committee, Secretary of Defense Dick Cheney gave this explanation for President George H. W. Bush's decision to send hundreds of thousands of American troops to defend the kingdom: "Once [Saddam Hussein] acquired Kuwait and deployed an army as large as the one he possesses [adjacent to Saudi Arabia], he was clearly in a position to be able to dictate the future of worldwide energy policy, and that gave him a stranglehold on our economy."[5] For Cheney (as for President Bush and other senior officials) no more need be said: The very prospect of an Iraqi "stranglehold" on the U.S. economy was justification enough for going to war.

The first Persian Gulf War of January–February 1991 concluded with the expulsion of Iraqi forces from Kuwait. As the war drew to a close, many in Washington urged the first President Bush to send American troops all the way to Baghdad, eliminating the threat posed by Saddam Hussein once and for all. Instead, he chose to bring about "regime change" by suffocating the country through harsh economic sanctions and encouraging an internal coup d'etat by Hussein's generals.[6] This policy would later be embraced by Bill Clinton and his successor, the second President Bush, until the decision was taken to revert to military action. Throughout this period, American policymakers wrestled with the challenge of how to prevent Saddam Hussein from rearming—and again posing a threat to Saudi oil fields. Whether any set of officials favored an array of increasingly severe sanctions (backed by intermittent air strikes) or an out-and-out invasion, the basic objective was never in doubt: Hussein must not be allowed to reassemble the sort of power that could drive Iraqi armies to the Saudi Arabian border.[7]

That the Carter Doctrine in its various manifestations is the ultimate source of U.S. policy in the Gulf was confirmed by Dick Cheney— by now the vice president—in an August 2002 speech on the Bush administration's motives for a possible invasion of Iraq. "Should all [Hussein's efforts to acquire weapons of mass destruction] be realized, the implications would be enormous. Armed with an arsenal of these weapons of terror and a seat atop 10 percent of the world's oil reserves, Saddam Hussein could then be expected to seek domination of the entire Middle East, take control of a great portion of the world's energy supplies, [and] directly threaten America's friends throughout the region."[8] No doubt his listeners fully understood that the Bush administration would not allow this to occur. As many Washington insiders have since revealed, by this point the president had already given his approval to an invasion—then still eight months in the future—even though he would deny that this was the case almost to the eve of its launching in March 2003.[9]

Despite all that has happened since the U.S. invasion—despite all of the bloodshed, misery, and chaos in Iraq—there is no evidence that senior American officials have abandoned their adherence to the underlying principles of the Carter Doctrine. If anything, American elites believe it to be more important than ever that the United States exercise ultimate dominion over the region. Indeed, the possibility of a U.S. failure in Iraq—followed by regional disorder and/or the rise of a hostile hegemon like Iran—has been regularly cited as yet further reason for clinging to this view. "If we were to be driven out of Iraq," President Bush told a national television audience on September 13, 2007, "extremists of all strains would be emboldened. . . . Iran would benefit from the chaos and be encouraged in its efforts to gain nuclear weapons and dominate the region. Extremists could control a key part of the global energy supply."[10] Of all the arguments wielded by Bush to elicit support for his invasion and occupation of Iraq—the presence of WMD, links to Al Qaeda, and the promotion of democracy, among others—this is the only one that has gained traction with his critics. In fact, all of the leading Democratic candidates for president in 2007–08, including Senators Hillary Clinton and Barack Obama, have themselves insisted on the need for a robust U.S. military presence in the greater Gulf area to ensure regional stability and the uninterrupted flow of oil.[11]

The Making of an American Preserve

The Persian Gulf region first came to the attention of American policymakers during World War II, when it became apparent to President Franklin D. Roosevelt and other senior officials that the United States would eventually become dependent on imported petroleum for a significant share of its oil supply. Until that time, the United States had been largely self-sufficient in crude oil and its leaders had evinced little interest in the Gulf. The region was then under effective British imperial control, and most in Washington were inclined to leave things that way. However, when it became apparent that American self-sufficiency in petroleum would not last much beyond the war's end and that the Middle East would constitute the new center of global oil production, top officials took a fresh look at the situation and concluded that it was in America's vital interests to play a significant role in the region.[12]

The history and geopolitics of the Middle East dictated that any U.S. presence in the Gulf would initially be concentrated in the Kingdom of Saudi Arabia. At the time, Great Britain exercised direct or indirect control over Iran, Iraq, Kuwait, Oman, and the various sheikhdoms of the southern Gulf; only the Saudis remained outside London's imperial orbit. The British also controlled most of the oil concessions in the region, including producing fields in Iran, Iraq, and Kuwait. Believing that Saudi Arabia contained little or no petroleum, British officials made little effort to prevent the Standard Oil Company of California (SOCAL, later Chevron) from acquiring a substantial concession there in 1933. Thus, when the Roosevelt administration began looking for a prospective Middle Eastern oil supplier, Saudi Arabia had already emerged as the natural choice and, by war's end, was receiving substantial U.S. assistance under the Lend-Lease Act.[13]

Initially, President Roosevelt sought an economic as well as political monopoly over Saudi Arabia. Hoping to imitate the example set by the British government in 1914, when it acquired control over the Iranian concessions of the Anglo-Persian Oil Company (the predecessor of British Petroleum, later BP), Roosevelt attempted to assert government ownership over SOCAL's concession in Saudi Arabia.[14] Not surprisingly, these plans ran into fierce resistance from Congress and the American business community, forcing Roosevelt to abandon his plans for government control of SOCAL's Saudi reserves. Instead, he embraced what oil historian David S. Painter of Georgetown University has called a "public-private partnership," under which the federal government would open the doors to American investment in the Gulf and protect its oil fields while American companies would produce and transport the oil. This partnership was set in motion in the closing months of World War II, as SOCAL prepared to step up its drilling operations in the kingdom.[15]

In Roosevelt's mind, obtaining the approval of Saudi Arabia's monarch, King Abd al-Aziz ibn Saud, for this basic blueprint was the most immediate task at hand. Ibn Saud had unified the vast desert region under his exclusive control in 1932, and his word was law. To obtain his consent, an ailing Roosevelt met with him aboard the USS *Quincy* on February 14, 1945, following the Big Four conference at Yalta. According to accounts of their encounter, the two leaders agreed to a tacit alliance under which the United States would provide Saudi Arabia—and the royal family itself—with a guaranteed security umbrella in return for enduring, privileged access to Saudi oil by American companies.[16] No formal record was kept of this pivotal encounter, but senior officials repeatedly testified to its significance, and it continues to govern U.S.-Saudi relations to this day.[17]

SOCAL then commenced the full-scale development of its concession in Saudi Arabia's Eastern Province. When it became apparent that the area housed some of the largest oil fields in the world, SOCAL—by then partnered with the Texaco Company—joined forces with Standard Oil of New Jersey (later Exxon) and Standard Oil of New York (later Mobil) to establish the Arabian-American Oil Company (Aramco), soon to become the world's largest oil-producing enterprise.[18] Meanwhile, to fulfill the security aspects of the Roosevelt–Ibn Saud alliance, the Department of Defense established an air base at Dhahran, close to Aramco's major operating facilities, in 1946; the navy acquired a small base at Bahrain (then under British control) in 1948. Although its military presence was still relatively modest at this point, the United States was on its way to becoming a Persian Gulf power.[19]

For a quarter of a century, the partnership established by President Roosevelt and U.S. oil companies worked largely as envisioned. Through the technical expertise and entrepreneurial drive of American companies, Saudi Arabia overtook all other suppliers to become the world's leading oil producer, vastly increasing the world's daily energy supply and enriching Aramco's principal owners beyond anyone's wildest dreams.[20] The U.S. government also played its part, working to maintain a corporate-friendly political environment in the region— regularly entertaining the Gulf's royalty at the White House and intervening when necessary to oust any regime that moved to take control of its own oil. In 1953, for instance, the Central Intelligence Agency cooperated with British intelligence in orchestrating a coup that top-pled the elected Iranian government of Prime Minister Mohammad Mosaddeq after it had nationalized the country's oil companies.[21] Around 1970, however, the oil equation in the Gulf began to undergo a fundamental shift. The importance of U.S. and British oil companies declined as Gulf producers finally succeeded in nationalizing their oil fields and establishing state-owned firms to oversee their resources. At the same time, a phased withdrawal of British forces led to calls for greater American military involvement in the region.

American policymakers first devoted close attention to the security situation in the Gulf area in 1969–70, after the British government an-nounced that it would no longer maintain a military presence "East of Suez" beyond 1972. Until that time, the British had served as the princi-pal guardian of Western interests in the Gulf, and, for the most part, American officials had been content to leave them in that role. But with the British now departing the region and American forces fully engaged in Vietnam, President Richard Nixon chose to embark on a risky course: In place of the British, he delegated responsibility for Persian Gulf security to the U.S.-equipped forces of the shah of Iran, Moham-mad Reza Pahlavi, who had been restored to power in that 1953 coup.[22]

From 1970 to 1979, the shah would serve as the "guardian of the Gulf" on Washington's behalf, spending vast sums on imported Amer-ican arms and incurring the enmity of his own people in the process. But this "surrogate strategy" disintegrated in January 1979 when the shah—whom the Americans assumed to be invincible—was suddenly driven from power by a revolutionary movement that assumed power in the name of a radical Shiite ayatollah, Ruhollah Khomeini. Not long after, militant followers of Khomeini seized American diplomats at the U.S. embassy in Tehran and held them hostage for a humiliating 444 days. This was followed by yet another powerful challenge to U.S. in-terests: In December 1979, the USSR invaded Afghanistan, bringing Soviet troops to within several hundred miles of the Persian Gulf.

Once again, American strategists were forced to assess the security situation in the Gulf. For President Carter and his advisers, with their surrogate strategy in shreds, their diplomats held hostage, and the Sovi-ets on the move, the options had boiled down to one: The United States *itself* would have to assume overall responsibility for defense of the region. On this basis, the Carter Doctrine was born. Just a few weeks after the Soviet invasion, Carter used the occasion of his 1980 State of the Union address to enunciate the new policy. In the same speech, he announced the formation of what was to become the U.S. Central Command, given formal responsibility for protecting the flow of Persian Gulf oil, and the establishment of new American bases in the area.[23]

Security in the Gulf now came to overshadow all other aspects of the U.S. presence. While American oil companies continued to operate in the area—more often as service providers to national oil companies than as lead operators of major oil and gas fields—American troops rather than oil workers would become the most conspicuous feature of U.S. involvement in the region. This reflected the view, deeply entrenched in Washington, that the production and export of Persian Gulf oil *as a whole*, rather than the profits of individual companies, had become essential to American economic survival.[24]

Over the years, the occasions when American leaders have brought military force to bear in the Gulf came to dominate the American political landscape and so need not be recounted in great detail here, but it is essential to underscore the regularity with which they chose to apply, or threaten to apply, force. The first was the "reflagging" of Kuwaiti tankers during the Iran-Iraq war of 1980–88 and their protection by U.S. naval vessels, followed, of course, by the first Gulf War of 1990–91. Air power was intermittently used against Iraq over the next decade-plus until the invasion of Iraq commenced in March 2003.

Today, with Saddam Hussein long removed from power, American forces are still at war in Iraq. They face a kaleidoscope of threats, including a Sunni insurgency against the American occupation, a civil war among various Shiite militias, and violent criminal activity. Under present circumstances, the insurgency and civil strife are incapable of endangering the flow of oil much beyond Iraq itself. *Within* that country, of course, they have proved exceedingly capable of inflicting enormous damage: Through systemic attacks on pipelines, refineries, pumping stations, and other components of the country's vital energy infrastructure, the insurgents (and their criminal accomplices) have largely managed to keep Iraq's net petroleum output below

Major U.S.Bases in the Persian Gulf Area

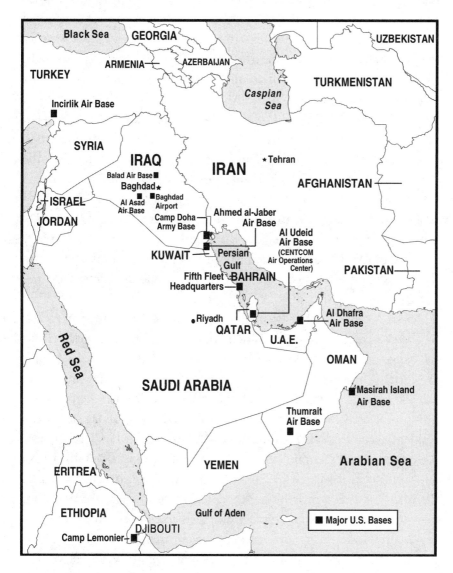

already low pre-invasion levels.[25] Even to maintain production at current, abysmally low levels, the United States and its allies in Baghdad have been forced to divert enormous sums from economic redevelopment to pipeline security, further undermining the Bush administration's political goals in Iraq.[26]

In an unambiguous signal that the United States intends to play a direct role in defending Iraq's vulnerable oil infrastructure for years to come, the navy disclosed in November 2007 that it was establishing a "command-and-control" facility atop an offshore Iraqi oil platform in the Persian Gulf to oversee the protection of vital oil-loading terminals. The navy facility is intended to guard operations at Iraq's two major terminals, Khawr Al Amaya and Al Basra—which, if fully functional, can load almost 2 million barrels per day, or approximately 2.4 percent of global demand.[27] It is also likely that the Pentagon's determination to retain at least four of its existing mega-bases in Iraq—giant facilities the size of small American cities—is likewise tied to Washington's concern for the safety of Iraq's all-important energy infrastructure.[28]

Even if the insurgents in Iraq are unable themselves to threaten U.S. interests elsewhere in the region, the ongoing conflict in that country has emboldened Islamic extremists in neighboring lands to step up their attacks on symbols of American influence and undermine regimes considered overly friendly to Washington.

Saudi Arabia—with its vast and highly exposed oil infrastructure—has been a particular target of such attacks. The first in a series of oil-related assaults occurred on May 1, 2004, when gunmen killed five Western oil-industry workers in Yanbu, the site of a major petrochemical complex.[29] A second attack took place four weeks later, when a group of armed militants (said to be allied with Al Qaeda) stormed a residential compound occupied by Western oil workers in Khobar, near the oil center of Dhahran, and killed twenty-two people.[30] Both attacks appeared to be designed to frighten expatriate oil workers and cause them to flee, thus undermining the technical proficiency of the Saudi petroleum industry. An even more ominous assault occurred on February 23, 2006, when suicide attackers broke through the outer defense perimeter of the Abqaiq oil-processing facility and detonated explosive-laden vehicles inside the kingdom's most important energy installation, potentially jeopardizing 6.8 million barrels of daily output; although the attack was foiled before the bombers could get close to the facility itself, the determination with which they carried out the assault hints at the extent to which such facilities have come to be viewed as prime targets for attack.[31]

In response to these assaults, the Saudis—no doubt in close coordination with American counterterror officials—have bolstered defenses at their major oil installations and stepped up their efforts to crush remnants of Al Qaeda; still, the risk of future terrorist assaults must be assumed to remain high. Indeed, Saudi security forces arrested 208 suspected extremists with alleged ties to Al Qaeda in a nationwide dragnet on November 28, 2007; at least some of the suspects were said to be planning attacks on vital oil facilities.[32]

The other major challenge to U.S. security interests in the Gulf is posed by the Islamic regime in Tehran, which has made no secret of its desire for a diminished American presence in the region. The Iranians have, of course, good reason to be wary of the Americans. There was, first of all, that 1953 coup that toppled Mosaddeq and replaced him with the much-despised shah, who ruled until 1979. To buttress the Shah's autocratic rule, the United States lavished arms and military hardware on his forces, while helping to train and equip his notoriously brutal secret police, SAVAK—further cause for alienation on the part of Iran's current leaders, many of whom suffered in the shah's jails and torture chambers.[33] And then there was Iran's inclusion in George W. Bush's famous "axis of evil," the trio of hostile nations (Iraq and North Korea being the others) that were put on notice of "regime change" in 2002.

Partly in self-defense and partly to advance their own regional interests, the Iranians have taken steps that have amplified the level of alarm in Washington and introduced new sources of concern. First and foremost, they are suspected of seeking the capacity to manufacture nuclear weapons under cover of a peaceful uranium-enrichment program. The Iranian leadership insists that this program is indeed intended for peaceful purposes only, while American officials contend that the only plausible explanation for an ambitious civilian nuclear program in a country awash with oil could be for the development of nuclear munitions. A partially declassified National Intelligence Estimate (NIE) released by the Bush administration in December 2007 suggested that the Iranians had pursued development of a nuclear weapons capability in the early years of the twenty-first century, but had suspended their program in 2003 in the face of intense international opposition.

Nuclear concerns aside, Iran is also a significant worry for American strategists because it has deployed numerous antiship missiles and other weapons along the northern shore of the Strait of Hormuz, the narrow waterway at the mouth of the Persian Gulf through which an estimated 17 million barrels of oil are carried by tanker every day. In case of some future crisis—perhaps a U.S. air assault on Iran's nuclear facilities—the Iranians could use the missiles to severely disrupt tanker oil traffic in the Gulf and, along with antiship mines in the Strait, provoke a major world-wide energy crisis. The Iranians are also said to be supplying arms and explosives to Shiite militias in Iraq, posing a danger to U.S. soldiers operating there, and to be aiding other militant groups in the region, including Hezbollah in Lebanon and Hamas in the Gaza Strip.[34]

Containing Iranian power and preventing its acquisition of nuclear weapons has long been a major U.S. objective and the subject of a contentious policy debate in Washington, with some officials favoring intensive diplomacy and the imposition of sanctions, and others advocating the use of force to destroy known Iranian nuclear facilities and cripple its military forces. The diplomacy-first faction, led by Secretary of Defense Robert Gates and Secretary of State Condoleezza Rice, was said to hold the upper hand as of early 2008, especially after the release of the December 2007 NIE; however, the strike-first-ask-questions-later camp, led by Vice President Cheney, retains considerable clout.[35] In a speech eerily reminiscent of the scare tactics used by the Bush administration in preparing the way for an invasion of Iraq, Cheney used the occasion of an October 2007 policy address at the Washington Institute for Near East Policy, a private research organization, to warn Tehran of the risks of noncompliance with American demands: "The Iranian regime needs to know that if it stays on its present course, the international community is prepared to impose serious consequences," he declared. "The United States joins other nations in sending a clear message: We will not allow Iran to have a nuclear weapon."[36]

Although President Bush has repeatedly stated that he favored a diplomatic resolution to the standoff with Tehran (as he did with respect to Baghdad in the months before the 2003 invasion), he has also evidently approved elaborate preparations for a range of military actions against Iran should a decision be made to employ force. According to various press reports, such action could range from limited, "surgical" strikes on nuclear installations and selected military bases in Iran—particularly those occupied by Revolutionary Guards units suspected of aiding anti-American militias in Iraq—to a sustained air campaign against a broad range of Iranian military and government facilities.[37] Whatever the scale of such an attack, the Iranians are likely to respond with retaliatory measures of their own—probably of an unconventional or "asymmetrical" nature. Such responses might include the aforementioned mining of the Strait of Hormuz and missile strikes on passing oil tankers; intensified attacks by allied Shiite militia groups on U.S. soldiers in Iraq; sabotage or missile strikes aimed at oil-producing areas of Saudi Arabia; and other steps intended to promote chaos in global oil markets.

An eerie preview of what such an encounter might look like occurred in January 2008, when five armed Iranian speedboats approached three American warships in international waters in the Strait of Hormuz, then maneuvered aggressively while radio threats were issued that the American ships would be blown up. One of these vessels, the USS *Hopper*, was on the verge of firing on the Iranian boats when they veered away, ending the engagement. Iranian officials denied any intent to cause harm, and U.S. officials later acknowledged that the source of the radio threats (which were received on an open international channel) could not be identified, but the episode was sufficiently menacing to elicit a powerful warning from President Bush. "There will be serious consequences if they attack our ships," he said at a press conference in Jerusalem, at the start of an eight-day visit to the Middle East. "And my advice to them is, don't do it."[38]

Even in the face of these myriad dangers, it is unlikely that the United States—whether governed by a Democratic or Republican administration—will abandon the basic long-term premise of U.S. policy in the Gulf: oil protection. The costs and risks of sustaining this policy have never been higher, but there is no indication that senior policymakers are prepared to contemplate any change in the

Carter Doctrine or its corollaries. Nor, for that matter, is there any sign that they are inclined to disassemble the mammoth military infrastructure established in accordance with this doctrine or abandon plans to retain at least four mega-bases in Iraq.

The Public-Private Partnership Revisited

Within the protected space provided by the U.S. security umbrella, government policy continues to favor a privileged role for American companies in the production and distribution of Persian Gulf energy. The second Bush administration, in particular, placed heavy emphasis on this aspect of the "public-private partnership," giving it special mention in the National Energy Policy of 2001. Among its principal recommendations, the NEP called for stepped-up efforts by senior government officials to persuade leaders of the Persian Gulf producers to reopen their energy industries to private—preferably American—investment.[39]

Clearly, the ultimate goal of these efforts was to remove restrictions on the foreign ownership of hydrocarbon assets and allow for the reintroduction of American companies as major producers in the region. At present, such restrictions remain the norm in most major oil-producing nations, including Iran, Iraq, Kuwait, and Saudi Arabia. Recently, however, some of these countries have shown some inclination to permit foreign firms to participate as junior partners, especially in complex offshore projects or enhanced oil-recovery operations (which entail the use of advanced technologies to reverse the decline of older, fading fields). Aware of this new opening, U.S. officials and corporate executives have been pushing for further relaxation of the curbs on outside investment in Persian Gulf oil and gas operations. "This [opening] provides an important opportunity to further encourage foreign investment in these important energy-producing countries, thereby broadening our shared commercial and strategic interests," the NEP declared.[40]

These efforts achieved their first great success—or so it seemed—in 2002, when Saudi leaders announced a "Saudi Gas Initiative" (SGI) intended to spur development of the country's vast natural gas reserves.

The original blueprint for this $20 billion enterprise called for substantial American participation, but, as negotiations proceeded, Saudi officials grew alarmed at the expanding scale of foreign involvement and so cancelled it altogether. Some components of the original SGI plan have since been resuscitated on a smaller scale—notably efforts to develop formerly untapped gas reserves in the desert wastes of the Empty Quarter (Rub al-Khali) along the border with Yemen and Oman—but the Saudis have gone out of their way to include non-American firms in the resulting partnerships.[41]

Kuwait, meanwhile, is moving forward with an initiative of its own, "Project Kuwait," intended to boost production in under-performing fields by allowing foreign participation on a junior-partner basis. Several U.S. firms, including Chevron, Exxon Mobil, ConocoPhillips, and Occidental, are expected to play significant roles, once the project is given final approval by the government.[42]

American companies have also achieved considerable success in Qatar, where the government of Sheikh Hamad bin Khalifa al-Thani has sought to invigorate the emirate's economy by attracting foreign investment for the development of mammoth natural gas reserves. Exxon Mobil is especially well represented in these ventures, having a major role in two large consortia established for the production and export of liquefied natural gas: Qatar LNG Company (Qatargas) and Ras Laffan LNG Company (Rasgas). Meanwhile, ConocoPhillips has emerged as the front-runner to partner with the Abu Dhabi National Oil Company in developing Abu Dhabi's giant Shah natural gas field. [43]

American energy firms would also like to return to both Iraq and Iran. This was evident in Iraq's case in the fall and winter of 2002–03, when senior executives of these companies met with Ahmed Chalabi and other White House–backed Iraqi expatriate leaders to discuss the reconstitution of Iraq's oil industry once Saddam Hussein was deposed and the exiles—as was widely assumed at the time—had grasped the reins of power.[44] "American companies will have a big shot at Iraqi oil" with Hussein out of the picture, Chalabi reportedly told oil-company executives at one of these encounters.[45] As things turned out, however, Chalabi and his allies failed in their bid, and other political forces—including militant Shiite groups with close ties to Iran—have assumed the paramount role in Baghdad. With the outbreak of insurgent and sectarian violence, moreover, most large U.S. firms put their plans for new energy projects in Iraq on hold, awaiting calmer conditions and the adoption of a national oil law that would guarantee the validity of long-term contracts.[46] Some of these firms, however, are likely to submit applications to Iraq's Oil Ministry in a "prequalification" process to select companies deemed eligible to bid for licenses to eventually operate in the country; as well, a number of smaller U.S. firms have chosen to invest in Kurdish Iraq, hoping that such investments will eventually be regularized by a new national oil law.[47]

American oil firms naturally look forward to a day when the existing regime in Iran is replaced by a more friendly, pro-Western one, allowing for the lifting of U.S. economic sanctions and permitting their participation in Iranian oil and gas enterprises. A number of U.S. giants enjoyed a significant presence in the country during the reign of the shah, including Chevron, Exxon, Mobil, Texaco, and Gulf, and these companies (or their merged successors) can be expected to seek a fresh opportunity to operate there if sanctions are removed.[48]

China's Growing Presence

Given the lengths to which the United States has gone to maintain its dominant status in the Gulf, it is hardly surprising that other powers have generally chosen to avoid challenging its paramount position there. Even the Soviet Union, at the peak of its strength, did not deploy any of its forces in the region. In fact, most countries have come to view the American military presence as a fact of life and have elected to take advantage of the situation by procuring oil there in the knowledge that Uncle Sam is keeping the sea lanes safe and secure. More recently, however, several countries—above all, China—have begun to establish closer ties with America's most important partners in the area, including Saudi Arabia, and forge business ties with Iran that entail significant military aspects.

China's leaders, like those of all energy-consuming nations, are all too familiar with the data in Table 7.1 (page 179). "Given China's rising economic domestic demand for oil and the location of most of the world's proven reserves in the Gulf region," China energy expert Philip Andrews-Speed observed in 2002, "the Chinese will inevitably become more dependent on oil supplies from this region, however many resources are devoted to diversifying supplies."[49] The same could be said for Japan, India, and other states that rely on imports to satisfy their petroleum requirements.

Though often forced to buy what they need from the Gulf's state-owned firms, these countries will pursue every opportunity they can to obtain production rights to valuable oil and gas assets, while simultaneously striving to forge political ties with the governments involved. As suggested by repeated visits to Riyadh by its top officials, China has invested a great deal of effort in cultivating close ties with the Saudi royal family and other elements of the Saudi leadership. No doubt Chinese leaders are fully aware that this will produce unease in Washington but have concluded that the country's energy needs trump all else.[50]

When their efforts to secure a significant beachhead in the Gulf began in the mid-1990s, the Chinese relied on local producers for only a small share of their oil imports. As recently as 1995, China obtained only about 20,000 barrels per day from Iran and 60,000 barrels from Saudi Arabia. But behind these modest numbers was a strategic decision that led to what Andrews-Speed has termed a "diplomatic offensive to secure long-term supply arrangements with key oil-exporting Gulf states."[51] Within five years, net oil flows to China had increased tenfold in the case of Iran, to 200,000 barrels per day, and sixfold in the case of Saudi Arabia, to 350,000 barrels per day.[52] By 2003, Saudi Arabia accounted for 16.8 percent of China's oil imports, Iran for 13.8 percent, Oman for 10.3 percent, and Yemen for 7.7 percent.[53]

Initially, Chinese leaders were content to secure long-term purchase agreements with major Gulf suppliers, but soon enough they began seeking opportunities to acquire exploration and production rights. China's earliest foray in this regard was a 1997 agreement to develop the al-Ahdab field in south-central Iraq, a joint venture of CNPC and the Chinese arms firm Norinco. This project was supposed to proceed only after U.N. sanctions on Iraq were lifted, but the very fact that Beijing conducted such future-oriented negotiations with Saddam Hussein's regime was considered a provocation by many in Washington.[54]

In the end, nothing came of this project while Hussein was in power or during the chaotic aftermath of the U.S. invasion. However, the Chinese maintain that the 1997 agreement remains in force and insist that they will develop the al-Ahdab field when conditions permit.[55] Although the Iraqi government has yet to adopt the final text of a law covering foreign investment in the country's oil sector, the oil minister, Hussein al-Shahristani, told the Chinese in November 2006 that they eventually will be allowed to proceed.[56]

Above all else, China has sought to establish a significant presence in Iran's energy sector. As a first venture, a consortium of Chinese firms helped construct a 240-mile pipeline from Iran's Caspian Sea port of Neka to refineries near Tehran, permitting the delivery of crude oil from Kazakhstan (where China already had substantial oil-field investments) for consumption in Iran.[57] Most petroleum supplied in this fashion is then "swapped" for crude oil exported to China or other foreign markets from southern Iranian oil fields. As that project neared completion, in August 2003, CNPC acquired an interest in the Masjed-I-Suleyman oil field, one of Iran's oldest; although output at the field had fallen far below its historic peak of 130,000 barrels per day, the Chinese hoped to halt further decline and possibly reverse it through the use of modern technology.[58]

In October 2004, China's involvement in Iran rose to a new level, when Sinopec signed an agreement with the National Iranian Oil Company (NIOC) to acquire a controlling stake in the giant Yadavaran oil field in return for a pledge to buy 10 million tons of liquefied natural gas per year for twenty-five years—a deal then thought to be worth as much as $100 billion. Under the plan, Sinopec will own 51 percent of the field while India's Oil and Natural Gas Corporation will control 29 percent and various Iranian firms another 20 percent. With production from the Yadavaran field expected to reach 300,000 barrels per day in the second decade of the twenty-first century, this could prove to be Sinopec's largest overseas undertaking; Sinopec is also slated to be involved in construction of a large refinery and an LNG export facility. Sinopec finalized its contract with NIOC for the development of Yadavaran in December 2007, but many technical obstacles remain to be overcome before this complex project can get fully under way.[59]

Saudi Arabia has also been a major target of Chinese efforts. Beijing's first great diplomatic success in the kingdom occurred in 1999 when President Jiang Zemin visited Riyadh and announced the establishment of a "strategic oil partnership" between the two countries.[60] Since then, Chinese officials have made regular return visits and invited their Saudi counterparts to Beijing; executives of Sinopec and Saudi Aramco have made similar journeys.[61] In 2003, Aramco agreed to become part owner of a $3.6 billion refinery and petrochemical complex Sinopec is building in China's Fujian Province and supply it with crude petroleum.[62] Sinopec, in turn, was awarded the right to develop natural gas in Block B of Saudi Arabia's Empty Quarter.[63]

China's crowning success occurred in January 2006, when King Abdullah agreed to visit Beijing on his first trip abroad after succeeding his brother, King Fahd, in August 2005—an honor that, in the past, most likely would have been conferred on the United States. Premier Wen made no secret of his delight when greeting Abdullah on January 24, 2006, crowing that he "appreciated King Abdullah for making China the first visiting destination country since he succeeded to the throne." Wen went on to say that "China attaches great importance to developing bilateral relations and would like to further strengthen mutual political trust, economic and trade cooperation, and cultural exchanges."[64]

This was not only a diplomatic coup for China, but an economic one as well: While hosting Abdullah in the Great Hall of the People in Beijing, President Hu presided over the signing of a "protocol on cooperation in the areas of petroleum, natural gas, and mineral resources" between the two countries, setting the stage for even greater cooperation between Chinese and Saudi energy firms.[65] Details were not made public but were thought to entail further Chinese involvement in Saudi oil and gas exploration efforts and expanded Saudi investment in Chinese refining and petrochemical enterprises.[66]

Just three months later, Hu traveled to Saudi Arabia for a follow-up meeting with Abdullah. Lending particular drama to this encounter was the fact that Hu flew to Riyadh directly from Washington, where he had engaged in what was widely considered a fruitless meeting with President Bush.[67] Not only did the Chinese president and Saudi king appear to find agreement on a wide variety of issues, but the ground was cleared for increased cooperation in the energy sphere.[68] Before leaving the Saudi capital, Hu was assured that Aramco's crude oil exports to China would jump from approximately 445,000 barrels per day to 1 million barrels by 2010, and that plans were on track for the construction of a second joint Aramco-Sinopec refinery complex in China, this one in Qingdao Province.[69]

In pursuing such ventures, the Chinese generally relied on diplomatic and commercial overtures, but arms and military technology were sometimes offered as well—a trade in which the United States and Britain had, until then, enjoyed a near monopoly. Beijing's earliest arms transfer of this sort occurred in 1987, when it sold thirty-six CSS-2 intermediate-range ballistic missiles to Saudi Arabia, which presumably sought them to balance the Israeli ballistic missile arsenal. Although considered of dubious military value, the antiquated CSS-2s were an important symbolic acquisition by Saudi Arabia. The CSS-2 sale did not, however, lead to other Chinese arms transfers to Saudi Arabia—the Saudis have continued to rely on the United States and the European powers for the bulk of their weaponry—but it did establish Beijing as a significant potential supplier of major military equipment.[70]

China gained further military visibility during the final years of the Iran-Iraq war by delivering several hundred HY-2 "Silkworm" antishipping missiles to Iran. A Chinese version of the Soviet "Styx" antiship missile, the Silkworm has a sixty-mile range and carries a 1,000-pound explosive warhead.[71] Iran's use of those Chinese-made Silkworms against Kuwaiti tankers and offshore oil platforms played a part in prodding the United States to adopt a more directly belligerent stance in that conflict. When a Silkworm missile struck the U.S.-flagged Kuwaiti tanker *Sea Island City* on October 16, 1987, blinding the American captain and wounding eighteen members of the crew, President Reagan ordered a swift U.S. military response: the destruction of an Iranian offshore oil platform reportedly used as a reconnaissance post and staging base for attacks on Persian Gulf oil shipping.[72]

After the Iran-Iraq war, China continued to supply Iran with anti-shipping missiles and other military hardware. In 1997, the commander of the U.S. Central Command, General J. H. Binford Peay, told Congress that the Chinese had sold Iran twenty patrol boats armed with the C-802 antiship cruise missile, a more advanced weapon than the Silkworm.[73] Not surprisingly, the C-802 deliveries sparked considerable alarm in Washington. "Especially troubling to us is that these cruise missiles pose new, direct threats to deployed U.S. forces [in the Gulf]," Robert Einhorn, deputy assistant secretary of state for nonproliferation, told a Congressional committee.[74] While on an official visit to Beijing in January 1998, Secretary of Defense William Cohen implored Chinese leaders to cease selling cruise missiles to Iran. Apparently unwilling to provoke the Americans on a matter of such sensitivity, the Chinese agreed.[75] However, U.S. intelligence experts believe that China had already provided Iran with upward of 150 C-802s, and that the Iranians had begun to manufacture copies using components obtained from a variety of foreign sources.[76]

Since then, the Chinese appear to have carefully avoided selling any weapons to Iran that could pose a significant threat to American security interests in the Gulf. However, U.S. intelligence sources continue to report that various Chinese companies are supplying Iran with missile know-how and components, enabling the Iranians to enhance the capability of their ballistic missiles, notably the Shahab-3 and Shahab-4.[77] In response to these findings, the Clinton and Bush administrations imposed economic sanctions on a number of Chinese companies implicated in these transactions, among them such prominent firms as the China Great Wall Industry Corporation, the North China Industries Corporation, and the China Aero-Technology Import and Export Corporation.[78] Whether these transactions are a case of the left hand not knowing what the right hand is doing, or are the product of a deliberate effort by Chinese officials to deceive Washington about the extent of their ties with Tehran, cannot be determined from afar.

What is certainly evident is that the Chinese are slowly expanding their presence in the Gulf, even while avoiding moves that could be interpreted in Washington as blatant challenges. Indeed, Beijing's assertive diplomacy and the aggressive efforts of Chinese energy firms to build collaborative ties with state-owned oil companies signal the opening moves in what is sure to be a long-term drive to increase China's influence to the point where it can compete on near-equal terms with the United States.

In this process, the Chinese are consciously attempting to benefit, however indirectly, from the widespread anti-Americanism generated by the Bush administration's invasion of Iraq and what is seen throughout the Arab world as uncritical U.S. support for Israeli mistreatment of the Palestinians. These issues were on the agenda when President Hu met King Abdullah in Riyadh in April 2006. As noted in an official Chinese account of Hu's remarks, "China advocates that all actions and proposals related to the Middle East and Gulf region should be aimed at realizing peace in this region, dialogue should be taken as the approach for realizing peace, the choices of all countries in the region and their people should be respected, and efforts should be made to hold broad consultations with all states in this region."[79] Though couched in the bland rhetoric of diplomatic discourse, these remarks were a far cry from the crusading language of President Bush, with his frequent talk of imposing Western-style democracy on Middle Eastern countries and using force to overthrow regimes considered impediments to U.S. security. It is not hard to imagine whose approach King Abdullah and his associates would have found more palatable.

Even so, the Saudis are hardly prepared to severely downgrade their ties with Washington or forge a formal alliance with Beijing. The security umbrella provided by the United States is still far too important to the Saudi royals, and China is hardly in a position to replace it. But another scenario is plausible: that the Saudi leadership, chafing at the dominant role long exercised by Washington, will see in Chinese overtures an opportunity to loosen its bonds with Washington and acquire greater maneuverability in world affairs. "We are opening new channels, we are heading East," said Prince Walid bin Talal, a wealthy Saudi investor and a member of the royal family, during Hu's 2006 visit to Riyadh. "China is a big consumer of oil. Saudi Arabia needs to open new channels beyond the West. So this is good for both of us."[80] This may not quite be the stuff of nightmares for Washington, but it is the beginning of a long-term trend whose final outcome could prove threatening indeed to the Gulf strategies embraced by one U.S. administration after another.

The Japanese and Indian Incursions

As night follows day, so Japan and India are following China to the Persian Gulf in search of promising energy assets. Both countries have long relied on the Gulf for a significant share of their petroleum imports and expect to be even more dependent on the region in the future. Indeed, Japan—with 81 percent of its total oil supply coming from the Gulf—may be the most dependent of any major power on its energy reserves.[81] Recognizing that no amount of diversification will free them from reliance on the Gulf, these countries, like China, have sought to establish a more secure position there through intensive diplomacy and the acquisition of production rights.

Of the two, Japan has been the more aggressive. For many years, Japan's Arabian Oil Company (AOC) held a concession to the offshore Khafji and Hout fields in the Kuwait–Saudi Arabia Neutral Zone, only to lose its title to the Saudi portion of the fields in 2000 and the Kuwaiti portion in 2003. AOC nonetheless continues to perform technical services for the field's Kuwaiti owners and is entitled to purchase 100,000 barrels per day of Khafji crude.[82] When its losses became apparent, Tokyo promptly turned to Iran for succor, scoring an initial success in January 2003, when Inpex—once part of the government-owned Japan National Oil Company—acquired a 20 percent stake in the offshore Soroush and Nowruz oil fields, then operated by Shell under a "buyback" contract with the National Iranian Oil Company (NIOC).[83] (Under this arrangement, the foreign operators develop a field and reap its output for a set number of years before turning production back to the national oil company.)

An even greater triumph for Inpex loomed in February 2004, when the company signed a $2 billion deal with NIOC for a 75 percent stake in the giant Azadegan field in the northwest corner of the Persian Gulf. Discovered in 1999, Azadegan is thought to hold up to 26 billion barrels of oil, making it Iran's largest petroleum find in more than three decades. Given Azadegan's massive size and its expected output of more than 250,000 barrels of oil per day, this was hailed as a mammoth coup for Inpex and a major success in Tokyo's drive to increase the oil produced by government-backed firms.[84]

It wasn't long, however, before the Azadegan project began to unravel. Recognizing that it would need help to manage such a large and complex enterprise, Inpex sought partners in Europe to provide financing and technical assistance, but European firms proved reluctant even to provide technical services for fear of retaliation from Washington, thanks to the Congressionally mandated Iran-Libya Sanctions Act of 1996, which imposes stiff penalties on foreign firms that do business with Iran. In the meantime, angry American officials began pressing the Japanese government (which holds a 29 percent share in Inpex) to cancel the project; such an endeavor, they claimed, would hinder American efforts to isolate Tehran and force it to abandon its uranium-enrichment activities. The effect on the Japanese government—which relies on the United States for its ultimate security—was quickly evident.[85] Inpex proved conspicuously slow to begin work on the field, prompting threats from Iranian officials; finally, in October 2006, NIOC cancelled Inpex's 75 percent stake in the project (leaving it only a puny 10 percent interest), claiming Inpex had failed to fulfill its contractual obligation to commence work within a reasonable period after signing the contract.[86]

Recognizing the long-term problems involved in forging closer ties with Iran while remaining tightly allied with the United States in Asia, the Japanese headed down another Chinese-pioneered path and began bolstering relations with Saudi Arabia—no doubt hoping, like the Chinese, to gain the right to develop promising oil and gas fields in the Empty Quarter. Japanese officials, late to the game, tried to make up for lost time by assiduously courting senior Saudi leaders. Just three months after King Abdullah's precedent-setting 2006 visit to Beijing, Prime Minister Junichiro Koizumi enticed the second-highest-ranking Saudi royal, Crown Prince Sultan, to embark on a gala state visit to Tokyo where he was given a privilege accorded to few foreign visitors: an imperial audience with Akihito, the emperor of Japan.[87]

Koizumi's successor, Shinzo Abe, picked up where Koizumi left off, traveling to the Gulf on an extended state visit in April 2007. Like Hu

Jintao a year earlier, Abe flew directly from a pro forma Washington meeting with George W. Bush to a much-ballyhooed encounter with Saudi officials in Riyadh. "We do not need any words to say how important the Middle East is for Japan," he told his Saudi hosts. Launching his "Look East Policy," Abe promised a "new era of Japanese relations" with the region.[88] While in Riyadh, he signed a unique agreement under which Saudi Aramco will be allowed to store vast quantities of oil on the island of Okinawa for reshipment across the Asia-Pacific region; in return, the Saudis pledged to give Japan first crack at these supplies in times of emergency. In a separate deal that Abe approved during a side visit to neighboring Abu Dhabi, the Japan Bank for International Cooperation agreed to lend $1 billion to the Abu Dhabi National Oil Company for infrastructure development in exchange for extended oil-supply contracts with Japan.[89]

The Japanese also continue to eye embattled Iraq as a future source of oil. During a visit to Tokyo in October 2006, Iraqi oil minister Hussein al-Shahristani was promised about 20 billion yen ($170 million) in loans to upgrade a refinery near Basra and additional aid for rebuilding Iraq's damaged petroleum infrastructure. In addition, two Japanese firms, the Arabian Oil Company and Japan Petroleum Exploration Company (Japex), are providing the Iraqi Oil Ministry with various forms of technological assistance.[90] "We don't want to miss a boat that leads to vast oil reserves in Iraq," Shin Hosaka, director of the oil and gas division of Japan's Trade Ministry, told reporters in October 2006.[91]

India has similarly begun using intense diplomacy to open doors to increased investment by state-owned firms in Persian Gulf oil and gas endeavors. Given their relative proximity to the Gulf, the Indians have long relied on Iran, Saudi Arabia, and other local suppliers for a substantial share of their imported petroleum; now placing greater emphasis on natural gas, they are turning to the same key producers. And, like the Chinese and Japanese, they have sought to supplement outright purchases of fuel with participation in regional production ventures.

So far, Indian firms have achieved their greatest successes in Iran. In November 2004, the state-run India Oil Corporation (Indian Oil) announced a $3 billion joint venture with Iran's Petropars, a sub-sidiary of NIOC, to develop a large block of the offshore South Pars natural gas field—one of the world's biggest—and help construct a liquefaction facility for the export of LNG to India.[92] A year later, the Indian Oil-Petropars consortium was awarded a block in the North Pars gas field, an unrelated natural gas deposit; this venture is also ex-pected to include an LNG plant and associated infrastructure.[93]

At least one aspect of this relationship has provoked considerable discomfort in Washington: an Indo-Iranian plan to construct a 1,600-mile natural gas pipeline from eastern Iran across Pakistan to India. Expected to cost $3 to $4 billion, the "Iran-Pakistan-India" (IPI) pipeline would allow the Iranians to deliver natural gas to India with-out going through the difficult and costly process of liquefaction. For this reason, it is highly favored by officials in New Delhi—even though this means overcoming their traditional hostility toward Pakistan.[94]

The IPI project has dismayed officials in the Bush administration, who have stepped up efforts to weaken India's traditionally close ties with Iran. "Our views concerning Iran are very well known," Secretary of State Rice told reporters after meeting with Indian officials in New Delhi on March 16, 2005. "We have communicated to the Indian gov-ernment our concerns about gas pipeline cooperation between Iran and India."[95] India, however, is not as beholden to Washington as is Tokyo. Indian foreign minister Natwar Singh promptly indicated that his country would proceed with the pipeline. "We have no problem of any kind with Iran," he declared.[96]

When subsequent attempts to persuade New Delhi to back down on the pipeline proved fruitless—the prospect of imposing sanctions on the Indians was unappealing in the extreme—the Bush administra-tion evidently decided to offer powerful incentives for cancelling the project instead. On March 2, 2006, President Bush traveled to New Delhi and announced a remarkable plan to provide nuclear fuel and technology for India's civilian reactor program in return for an Indian pledge to open these reactors to international inspection—and, it was widely assumed, a tacit Indian promise to drop the pipeline plan.[97] Al-though described in Washington as a strategic breakthrough, aimed largely at enhancing U.S.-Indian relations, the plan was also portrayed as a solution to India's growing energy problem. "[This] agreement addresses India's surging energy needs for its growing economy," a White House fact sheet explained.[98] Despite strong government backing in both countries, however, various objections have been raised to the nuclear accord—in the U.S. Congress because it will exempt India from nonproliferation measures imposed on other countries; in the Indian Parliament because it places some restrictions on the country's much-vaunted nuclear establishment—and so it remains unclear as to whether it will be ratified.[99]

Like the Japanese, the Indians have discovered that establishing close ties with Iran can provoke intense pressures of various sorts from an American government that is nothing short of Iranophobic. So, Indian officials, too, have followed the well-trodden path to the Saudi royals. Immediately following King Abdullah's 2006 journey to Beijing, the Indians persuaded him to return via New Delhi, where he was courted with a fervor similar to that demonstrated by senior Chinese officials. At the conclusion of his visit, Abdullah signed a "Delhi Declaration," which called for Indo-Saudi cooperation in energy matters along the same lines as those spelled out in the just inked Sino-Saudi protocol.[100]

Even more than the Chinese, the Japanese and Indians are aware of the risks of provoking the United States in the Gulf. But that doesn't change the overall picture. What Prince Walid bin Talal said of Saudi relations with China in 2006 could be applied with equal validity to India and Japan: "We are opening new channels, we are heading East."

And Russia, Too

The resource-rich Russians have not been drawn to the Gulf through a need for increased hydrocarbon imports; Vladimir Putin and his top officials have instead been attracted by a desire to increase their country's profitable trade in energy and exercise greater geopolitical influence. So Moscow, too, has been encouraging major energy firms to seek out or deepen ties with the Gulf's national oil companies, while Putin himself has presided over a substantial increase in Russian arms exports to the region.

When Saddam Hussein was still in power, Russian companies made a concerted effort to secure development and production contracts in Iraq. A consortium headed by Lukoil, for example, won the right to develop Iraq's mammoth West Qurna field, with estimated reserves of 11.3 billion barrels of oil.[101] The status of this and other Hussein-era contracts were thrown into doubt by the American invasion and remained unresolved during the early negotiations on the provisions of a new hydrocarbon law. Lukoil had every reason to believe that its claim to West Qurna would eventually be confirmed by the new regime in Baghdad when Iraqi oil minister Hussein al-Shahristani traveled to Moscow in August 2007 and encouraged Russian firms to invest in his country.[102] These hopes were soon shattered, however, when the Iraqi government—reportedly bowing to pressure from their American advisers—told Lukoil in late October that the contract was no longer valid.[103]

With its access to Iraq apparently blocked for now, Moscow has turned to the other Persian Gulf countries. In an unusually bold move, Putin reached out to Saudi Arabia and Qatar during landmark visits to both countries in February 2007. He flew to Riyadh immediately after delivering a harsh critique of American foreign policy at an international security conference in Munich. "The United States has overstepped its national borders, and in every area," he said at the conference. "They bring us to the abyss of one conflict after another," making "political solutions . . . impossible."[104] Imagine, then, the consternation in Washington when senior officials were informed that Putin had been given a red-carpet welcome by King Abdullah and accorded a twenty-one-gun salute.[105] "There is no doubt that Russia has an important role in achieving peace," Abdullah told Russia's Itar-Tass news agency at the time—no doubt adding salt to Washington's wounds.[106]

Deriding the notion that Saudi Arabia and Russia—the world's number one and two oil producers—are destined to compete in the energy field, Putin insisted that there were ample grounds for collaboration. "On the face of it, . . . it seems that we are rivals, but considering the world's growing demand for energy, that is not so," he said at a meeting of Russian and Saudi businessmen. "It is easy for us to find common ground." As evidence for this, Putin noted that Lukoil was the lead operator in developing Block A of a potentially rich natural gas field in the kingdom's Empty Quarter and that Stroitransgaz, an engineering arm of Gazprom, was serving as a contractor for Saudi Aramco.[107] He also discussed the formation of a natural gas exporters association or cartel with Saudi officials—a "gas OPEC"—along with other forms of energy cooperation. In addition, Putin reportedly broached the subject of Russian arms sales to Saudi Arabia—reportedly, a matter that had been on both countries' agendas for several years.[108]

From Riyadh, Putin traveled on to Doha, the capital of Qatar, where he met with the emirate's leader, Sheik Hamad bin Khalifa al-Thani. "We seek to develop special relations between Qatar and Russia," Sheik Hamad declared upon Putin's arrival—no doubt again startling listeners in Washington, who view Qatar as a close ally in the region.[109] (A major U.S. air base is located outside Doha.) Putin and the emir also weighed the merits of a natural gas cartel, a truly threatening development from the point of view of any major energy-consuming nation.[110] "It's important to cooperate and help each other," Putin declared after the meeting. "We also work together to defend the interests of gas exporters and coordinate our relations toward the consumers."[111]

Russia has also sought close energy ties with Iran. Gazprom has explored the establishment of direct links to Iran's gas reserves for the possible future transshipment of Iranian gas to Europe via its vast pipeline network. This may explain Gazprom's insistence on acquiring the otherwise seemingly insignificant twenty-four-mile-long gas conduit in southern Armenia, which promptly became the only existing connection between the Iranian gas pipeline network and Gazprom's system in the Caucasus and southern Russia. With this conduit in the company's hands, it should theoretically be possible for the Iranians to channel some of their surplus gas through Russia. Lending credibility to this supposition, Vladimir Putin signed an energy cooperation agreement with President Mahmoud Ahmadinejad of Iran at a meeting of Caspian Sea states in Tehran on October 16, 2007. According to press accounts, Russian and Iranian firms will seek "coordination of marketing policy in the sphere of export," a hint of coming efforts to link the two countries' gas pipeline systems. Russian companies—presumably led by Gazprom—were also invited to participate in the development of Iran's supergiant South Pars natural gas field in the Persian Gulf.[112]

Putin participated in the October 2007 meeting with yet another purpose in mind: to deter the United States from launching an attack on Iran. At the summit of regional heads of state, the Russian president presided over the signing of a five-nation declaration stating that none of the countries surrounding the Caspian Sea would allow their territory to be used as a base for military strikes on any of the others. "We should not even think of making use of force in this region," Putin avowed at the meeting.[113] While in Tehran, Putin also promised to complete work on the Russian-built nuclear reactor at Bushehr in southern Iran, further demonstrating Moscow's support. (Moscow announced the first deliveries of nuclear fuel to Bushehr two months later.) Exhibiting no sympathy for U.S. efforts to isolate Iran economically as well as politically, Putin used his visit to press forward with a wide variety of other trade deals, including the sale of Tupolev 214 and 334 airliners.[114] (It is perhaps in retaliation for these moves that the Bush administration pressured the Iraqi government into the decision, announced two weeks later, that Lukoil would be denied its claim to the West Qurna oil field.)

Battles Yet to Come

China, India, and Japan, fully cognizant of America's dominant position in the Persian Gulf region and its intolerance of overt provocation, nonetheless appear determined to circumvent America's defenses in every way they can. In this project, they appear tireless: If today's efforts prove futile, they are prepared to try again tomorrow and the day after that in the never-ending pursuit of additional oil and gas supplies. Because of the vastness of the energy resources at stake, it is hard to question the logic of such a relentless approach.

In pursuing a wider foothold in the Gulf, these countries are not necessarily deliberately choosing to confront the United States, but that may matter little. Washington is sure to view such endeavors as implicit challenges to American authority. This has been evident, for example, in Washington's hysterical reaction to the Indian gas pipeline deal with Iran—which, from New Delhi's perspective, was a commercial venture and nothing more. Given the centrality accorded to the Gulf in American grand strategy, such potential conflicts are likely to arise again and again as the struggle over dwindling oil and gas reserves intensifies.

Russia's interest in the Gulf is, of course, somewhat different and perhaps more directly intended to challenge American global power and prestige. That such a range of challengers has arisen at a time when America's own position in the Gulf is under assault from insurgents in Iraq and critics of the war at home only adds to the severity of Washington's dilemma. Although no one doubts that the Gulf remains an American lake in purely naval terms, there are growing signs of resistance to U.S. dominance—from increasingly assertive foes like Iran as well as U.S. allies. Most noteworthy, perhaps, was a startling statement in March 2007 by Saudi King Abdullah that the U.S. occupation of Iraq was "illegal," and that Arab nations should work together in solving regional problems so as to prevent the United States from determining their fate.[115] Although Abdullah's outspokenness cannot be directly attributed to the assertive diplomacy of the Chinese, Russians, and others in his world, there is no doubt that their growing presence in the area has given the Saudis and their neighbors greater maneuvering room while slowly eroding the overbearing American role in the Persian Gulf—a process that is sure to gain momentum in the years ahead.

CROSSING A THRESHOLD

While the major energy-consuming powers have engaged in resource-related conflicts with lesser powers in recent years—the United States in Iraq, Russia in Chechnya (a former hub of the Soviet oil industry)—they have so far avoided any direct clashes with one another. The leaders of these countries are well aware of the sort of devastation an all-out military encounter could produce, and none are eager to precipitate such a conflagration. Nevertheless, thanks to their policies, the barrier between peaceful and warlike activities is already breaking down. As the desire for ever-scarcer energy supplies builds, the potential to slide across this threshold into armed conflict and possibly Great Power confrontation poses one of the greatest dangers facing the planet today.

The major powers are edging up to that threshold in a variety of ways, including the delivery of arms and combat-support services to prospective oil suppliers, the practice of "gunboat diplomacy," the acquisition of bases in oil-producing areas, and the formation of military blocs to advance geopolitical objectives. In regions like the Caspian Sea and the Persian Gulf, these disparate activities appear to be feeding on one another, each military gesture weakening that firebreak further.

Few of these gestures—with the possible exception of a full U.S. carrier battle group sailing provocatively through the Strait of Hormuz for military "exercises" right off the coast of Iran—have been impressive in their own right. What matters, however, is their *accumulation*— each adding to existing levels of suspicion and hostility. Given enough time and the continuing buildup of grievances and petty acts of military contempt, even a relatively minor incident could provoke a chain reaction of actions and counteractions ending in all-out war. Such a scenario of "unintended escalation" is little acknowledged at the moment, but no less dangerous for that.

The long-term risk of escalation is growing even more potent because major energy importers and exporters regularly appeal to that most dangerous of emotions, nationalism, in making their claims for control over the management of energy flows. Nationalistic appeals, once they have gripped a populace, almost invariably promote fierce emotion and irrationality. Add to this the fact that the leaders of most countries involved in the great energy race have come to view the struggle over hydrocarbon assets as a "zero sum" contest—one in which a gain for one country almost always represents a loss for others. A zero-sum mentality leads to a loss of flexibility in crisis situations, while the lens of nationalism turns the pursuit of energy assets into a sacred obligation of senior government officials.

Efforts by leaders of rival states to pry away assets thought to belong to someone else's country naturally provoke nationalistic outcries in response, as happened in the U.S. Congress during the 2005 struggle over the ownership of Unocal—just as Beijing responded with barely suppressed fury over Tokyo's efforts to persuade Russia to send Siberian oil its way rather than to China. The preemptive acts of leaders determined to gain control over every source of energy they can get their hands on inevitably generates ill will, prodding losers in such struggles to up the ante the next time around.

Competitive Arms Transfers

There is, of course, nothing new about the connection between arms transfers and the pursuit of energy. The United States forged a relationship of this sort in 1945, when President Franklin D. Roosevelt had that fateful meeting with Ibn Saud aboard the USS *Quincy* and promised to help protect his kingdom in return for privileged access to Saudi oil. This led in time to the deployment of a U.S. military training mission in Saudi Arabia and the delivery of billions of dollars' worth of advanced munitions—an arrangement that has never ended.[1] Great Britain also supplied arms and military services to key energy providers in the Persian Gulf region, just as the French government has long offered military assistance to the oil-producing states of Francophone Africa; more recently, China has assumed a similar role in Iran and Central Asia. On the whole, however, these endeavors were largely intended to bolster ongoing relations between energy-consuming countries and the producing countries' often dominant military elites. Now, they are part of a competitive drive among the consuming nations to curry favor with prospective suppliers.[2]

African states are particularly susceptible to arms diplomacy of this sort because they usually lack the capacity to manufacture arms on their own and, in most cases, cannot afford to buy all that they seek on the open market. During the Cold War era, both superpowers took advantage of these conditions to strengthen their ties with key African states. With the end of the Cold War, the flow of weaponry (except for light arms used in internal and ethnic conflicts) diminished for a time. With Russia largely out of the picture, moreover, African states obtained most of their arms from the major Western powers.[3]

In 1996, after China acquired a major stake in Sudan's oil output, the rules of the game changed once again. At the time, Sudan faced a severe challenge from rebel forces in the south (where most of the country's oil fields are located) and desperately needed a fresh infusion of weapons for its army; when rebuffed by Western powers, the Khartoum regime turned to Beijing, which proved far more accommodating. Eager to ensure the safety of its recently acquired oil assets in southern Sudan, China provided a wide array of modern arms, which were then used to drive the rebels out of the oil-producing region in what many observers termed a "scorched-earth campaign."[4]

China's arms sales to Sudan dramatically altered the political and military environment in Africa—at least in the minds of many American policymakers.[5] For the first time since the end of the Cold War, a major non-Western government was competing for geopolitical advantage on roughly equal terms with the United States—and, to add insult to injury, was using arms transfers and military assistance, one of America's most highly developed tactics. Not surprisingly, this produced agitation and alarm in Washington, accompanied by ardent calls for counteraction of some sort—so much so that Rep. Donald M. Payne (D-N.J.) claimed to be witnessing the outbreak of a "Cold War–type dynamic in Africa."[6]

Signs of this sort of creeping "Cold Warism"—to use Payne's expression—have been especially strong in Nigeria, the continent's leading oil producer. In addition to all the usual offers of economic and development aid, medical assistance, cultural exchanges, and the like, Washington and Beijing have also been competing fiercely in the delivery of arms and military-technical services.[7]

On the American side, the rationale for military-related aid is spelled out each year in a State Department document, the *Congressional Budget Justification for Foreign Operations.* According to the 2006 edition, "Nigeria is the fifth largest source of U.S. oil imports, and disruption of supply from Nigeria would represent a major blow to U.S. oil security strategy." This is the reason, the document asserts, that the United States should help bolster Nigeria's internal security forces and protect its vital oil installations—especially "in the vulnerable oil-producing Niger Delta region."[8]

For fiscal years 2005 through 2007, this translated into a proposed allocation of $30 million in direct U.S. support to Nigerian security forces, along with $50 million in "development aid" pegged to improving the security situation in the Delta and other troubled areas. Nigeria was also slated to be the recipient of surplus American arms and equipment, including several decommissioned Coast Guard cutters for use in protecting offshore oil rigs.[9] In addition, Nigeria is a key participant in Pentagon-sponsored multinational programs that serve, under the rubric of the Global War on Terror, as additional conduits for American military aid, including the African Contingency Operations Training and Assistance Program and the Trans-Saharan Counter-Terrorism Initiative.[10]

No doubt U.S. military and diplomatic personnel would like to do even more to enhance Nigerian military capabilities (thereby further ingratiating Washington with the government in Abuja), but budgetary constraints and competition from other priorities—notably the war in Iraq—have placed some limits on such allocations. This has given China the opening it needed to curry favor with the Nigerians by providing military inducements of its own.

In 2005, when Chinese firms made their first significant bids for oil assets in Nigeria, Beijing promised to provide (probably at reduced prices and concessional lending rates) twelve F-8IIM multipurpose combat jets to the Nigerian air force, along with numerous light patrol boats for guarding the labyrinthian waterways of the Niger River Delta.[11] At the same time, Chinese munitions firm Norinco agreed to help reinvigorate Nigeria's state-owned arms company, the Defense Industries Corporation of Nigeria.[12]

Nigeria may, at present, be the epicenter of this competitive struggle, but it is hardly the only such country. The Chinese are providing modern arms to Zimbabwe—receiving valuable minerals (rather than oil) in return—as well as less-advanced weaponry to Kenya, Sierra Leone, Tanzania, and several other African states.[13] The United States, meanwhile, has been increasing its military assistance to Angola, Equatorial Guinea, Ethiopia, Kenya, Mali, and Uganda.[14] Both Washington and Beijing are also expanding their military support services in African states, including training programs, joint combat exercises, and intelligence-sharing activities.[15]

If Africa is still at an early phase in the militarization of energy competition, the Caspian Sea region provides a glimpse of what the more advanced—and more dangerous—stage looks like. Here, the major powers have moved further along the curve of military involvement in terms of the magnitude of arms deliveries and the degree to which outside forces participate in local military activities.[16]

As Nigeria is to Africa, Kazakhstan is to the Caspian basin—the epicenter of competitive arms transfers. Indeed, all three of the Caspian's major contending powers—the United States, Russia, and China—have sought access to Kazakhstan's vast energy reserves, and all three have offered a wide variety of military inducements in their competitive quest. Russia enjoys a natural advantage by virtue of its geographic proximity and the fact that Kazakhstan was once part of the USSR (which means that its armed forces, still organized along Soviet lines, retain strong historic links to the Russian military). Nevertheless, Kazakh leaders have maximized their diplomatic maneuvering room by opening the door to offers of military aid from Washington and Beijing.[17]

The United States began aiding the country's armed forces in the late 1990s, during the Clinton administration. Eager to bolster Kazakhstan's independence from Moscow and its willingness to deliver oil to the West, Secretary of Defense Cohen signed a "defense cooperation agreement" with Kazakh strongman Nursultan Nazerbayev on November 17, 1997, paving the way for various forms of American military aid.[18] This agreement, later supplemented by others, has led to a steady increase in the flow of U.S. arms and related assistance to the country as well as considerable cooperation between American and Kazakh military personnel.[19] The Department of Defense also helped establish a Kazakh "rapid reaction brigade" to protect the country's vulnerable oil facilities.[20] All told, U.S. military spending on Kazakhstan was expected to total $175 million for fiscal years 2005 through 2007.[21]

Not to be outdone, the Russians have scrambled to bolster their own military ties, already enshrined in the Collective Security Treaty Organization (CSTO), a sort of mini-NATO made up of seven former republics of the Soviet Union: Armenia, Belarus, Kazakhstan, Kyrgyzstan, Russia, Tajikistan, and Uzbekistan. As part of this mutual-defense system, Russia and Kazakhstan are joined in an integrated air-defense system, participate in joint military maneuvers, and consult regularly on common security matters.[22] All of this has been leveraged by Moscow to tighten military-to-military relations and accelerate the flow of Russian arms to Kazakh forces.[23]

Kyrgyzstan and Uzbekistan are triply blessed with militarized attention. Both are members of the Chinese-backed Shanghai Cooperation Organization (SCO); both are integrated into the CSTO air-defense system and participate in joint military exercises with Russian forces; and both also receive Russian arms and military equipment. In 2001, for example, Russia agreed to provide the Uzbeks with a major arms package consisting of advanced artillery systems, helicopters, and anti-aircraft guns.[24] Recently, China has joined the arms game, providing internal-security gear in accordance with the antiterrorism provisions of the SCO charter.[25]

But no matter how close their ties to Moscow and Beijing, the leaders of Kyrgyzstan and Uzbekistan—like those of Kazakhstan—have used the eagerness of American administrations to put down roots (and bases) in energy-rich Central Asia as a way to acquire some breathing space. Washington first took advantage of this desire during the Clinton administration, when military cooperation agreements were signed with both countries—ties accorded greater importance after 9/11, when the autocratic leaders of each agreed to house logistical bases for American forces committed to operations against the Taliban and Al Qaeda in Afghanistan.[26] In response, the Bush administration provided Kyrgyzstan and Uzbekistan with considerable arms and security-related assistance: $305 million combined for fiscal years 2004 through 2006.[27]

Faced with this American largess, the Russians and Chinese have not faltered, using periodic summits of CSTO and the SCO, annual meetings of the defense ministers of the two organizations, and combined training exercises to advance their own militarized interests. As for Uzbekistan, their greatest opportunity arose in May–June 2005, when Uzbek strongman Islam Karimov crushed a popular uprising in the eastern city of Andizhan, leaving hundreds dead or wounded. The United States and other Western nations condemned the regime's brutal use of force, while Beijing and Moscow had nothing but praise for Karimov's resolve to maintain internal order—prompting him to reaffirm his ties with CSTO and the SCO and demand the withdrawal of all U.S. forces from Khanabad air base in southern Uzbekistan. That November, Russia and Uzbekistan signed a Treaty of Allied Relations, calling for mutual defense consultations in the event of a threat to either party; this was followed a year later by joint Russian-Uzbek counterterror exercises.[28]

In a more modest way, the same pattern has been repeated in Kyrgyzstan. In October 2006, a detachment of Russian special forces joined with Kyrgyz troops in a counterterrorism exercise in southern Kyrgyzstan—a demonstration, according to Russian defense minister Sergei Ivanov, that CSTO member states "can effectively join forces in countering terrorism and extremism."[29] Ivanov also used the occasion to pledge increased Russian military aid to Kyrgyzstan.[30]

Faced with the loss of a military base and the decline of its influence in Uzbekistan, the Bush administration scrambled to strengthen its ties with Azerbaijan, providing increased security assistance to its armed forces—an estimated $147 million for fiscal years 2005 through 2007.[31] Washington also began using that country as a springboard for a broader presence in the region through the "Caspian Guard," a $100 million plan for an "integrated airspace, maritime, and border control regime" for the Caspian Sea area that would, of course, operate under U.S. oversight.[32] Initially, the United States gave Azerbaijan several refurbished patrol boats along with a maritime command-and-control center for monitoring traffic in the Caspian Sea.[33] The project was subsequently extended to Kazakhstan, after its top officials signed a "strategic partnership" agreement with Azerbaijan, making it eligible for additional U.S. arms aid.[34]

In a typical example of how swiftly the major contenders in this region have responded to one another's initiatives, in January 2006 Russia proposed its own version of the Caspian Guard—the Caspian Rapid-Deployment Force, or CASFOR. The Russian plan was unveiled during a visit by Defense Minister Ivanov to Baku, the Azerbaijani capital. CASFOR, he indicated, will be "a real-time interaction naval group" made up of forces from all five Caspian Sea states—Azerbaijan, Iran, Kazakhstan, Russia, and Turkmenistan—designed to combat drug trafficking, arms smuggling, and terrorism in the area.[35] Ivanov also offered modern Russian arms and military hardware to Azerbaijan in a further attempt to limit American influence.[36] Though unwilling to sacrifice his country's close ties to Washington, Azerbaijani president Ilham Aliyev was inclined, in the view of local analysts, to take the Russians up on at least some aspects of their multiplying offers in order to bolster his bargaining position.[37]

This three-way struggle for geopolitical advantage is militarizing the Caspian basin, inundating the region with advanced arms and an ever-growing corps of military advisers, instructors, technicians, and combat-support personnel. Although often touted as a boon to regional cooperation, these programs—no matter which outside power is sponsoring them—heighten traditional suspicions and rivalries that have long plagued the region. The Great Powers are not only adding tinder to possible future fires, but also increasing the risk that they will be caught in any conflagration.

A renewed arms competition—with equally dangerous implications—has also erupted in the Persian Gulf area. The region was a major cockpit of superpower rivalry during the Cold War era, with both the United States and the Soviet Union offering some of their most advanced munitions in an unceasing struggle to win or retain the loyalty of local powers.[38] After the collapse of the Soviet Union, however, Russian officials lost their appetite for such costly transactions (which were rarely repaid in full) and, with Iraq's defeat in the first Gulf War, one of their wealthiest clients. As a result, Russian military sales to the Gulf area declined significantly in the post–Cold War era, while the United States—which continued to enjoy the patronage of such well-heeled arms customers as Saudi Arabia, Kuwait, and the United Arab Emirates (UAE)—saw no noticeable decline in the level of its weapons transfers.[39]

The picture began to change again in the early years of the twenty-first century as Moscow aimed to reestablish its geopolitical presence in the Gulf, while Iran—awash with petrodollars and fearful of U.S. attack—sought an array of modern weapons and enhancements for previously acquired munitions. In 2005, the Russians agreed to supply the Iranians with TOR surface-to-air missile defense systems (equipped with SA-15 Gauntlet missiles) in a deal worth an estimated $700 million. At the same time, the Russians agreed to upgrade previously supplied Su-24, MiG-24, and MiG-29 aircraft and T-72 main battle tanks in the Iranian inventory. Since then, Moscow has explored other possible weapons sales, including S-300 antiaircraft missiles.[40]

Needless to say, Washington has viewed these sales not just as a challenge to its drive to isolate Iran but as a potential danger to the U.S. military, should hostilities between the two countries erupt. "We have serious concerns about Russian arms sales to states we feel countries should not be engaging, such as Iran," David Kramer, deputy assistant secretary of state for European and Eurasian affairs, told reporters before meeting with European Union officials in Brussels in

February 2007.[41] Despite Washington's disapproval, the Russians have steadfastly refused to suspend their arms sales to Iran. "We don't think Iran should feel itself encircled by enemies," Putin declared in February 2007 after the Iranians successfully tested the Russian-supplied TOR air-defense system. "The Iranian people and the Iranian leadership should feel that they have friends in the world."[42]

In response to the Russian-backed Iranian buildup, and eager to demonstrate its loyalty to long-term Persian Gulf allies, the United States in July 2007 announced a major arms package of its own. Said to be worth $20 billion or more, the package will include satellite-guided bomb kits, aircraft upgrades, and naval vessels for Saudi Arabia plus an array of modern weapons for fellow members of the Gulf Cooperation Council—Bahrain, Kuwait, Oman, Qatar, and the UAE.[43] In defending the proposed transfers (which have encountered some resistance in Congress on the grounds that they might someday be used against Israeli forces), the Bush administration argued that they were needed to counter the growing influence of Iran and other hostile forces in the region. Provision of these arms, Secretary of State Rice declared in July, would help "bolster forces of moderation and support a broader strategy to counter the negative influences of Al Qaeda, Hezbollah, Syria, and Iran."[44] President Bush reiterated this theme during a January 2008 visit to Saudi Arabia, where he announced the sale of 900 laser-guided bomb kits to that country.[45]

These transactions, even if only partially fulfilled, will place Iran at greater risk and so increase Tehran's inclination to acquire additional arms from Russia and possibly other suppliers, including China. The result, of course, will be the outbreak of a new arms race in the Gulf, with unforeseeable—but potentially catastrophic—consequences. To make matters worse, American leaders will no doubt blame the Russians for stoking Iran's military appetite, adding to the already high level of distrust between Washington and Moscow; if Beijing also steps up arms deliveries to Iran, Sino-American relations will suffer as well. Even if this pattern of polarization does not affect developments in the Gulf itself, it is likely to color Great Power relations in other parts of the world, adding to the risk of misunderstanding and miscalculation in times of crisis.

Gunboat Diplomacy

When powerful states wish to signal their determination to pursue particular vital interests against the wishes of weaker powers or deter a rival from overstepping certain boundaries, they often make a conspicuous show of deploying air, ground, or naval forces within shooting range of the recipient of the intended "message." These deployments are not normally meant to initiate hostilities—although they depend on that threat—but rather to suggest a capacity to employ overwhelming levels of force should a decision be made to do so. Because naval forces were widely employed by the major imperial powers to intimidate and subdue weaker states in Asia, Africa, and Latin America in preceding centuries, the phrase "gunboat diplomacy" still captures the essence of this phenomenon today, even though the conspicuous deployment of heavy bombers or Marine expeditionary forces may serve the same purpose.

The fact that gunboat diplomacy of the classic variety is still very much in vogue was plainly manifest in the spring and summer of 2007, when the Bush administration deployed two aircraft carriers in the Persian Gulf, along with dozens of other warships and hundreds of combat aircraft, in an undisguised attempt to intimidate Iran. The two carriers—the USS *John C. Stennis* and the USS *Nimitz*—conducted two major combat exercises off the coast of Iran (in full view of Iranian naval vessels) and repeatedly sailed through the Strait of Hormuz to demonstrate Washington's determination to control vital sea lanes in the area. Both ships also participated in combat-support operations in Iraq and Afghanistan, with the *Stennis* alone launching 7,900 air sorties and dropping nearly 90,000 pounds of bombs on the two countries.[46]

Photographs and videos of the May 2007 combined-carrier operations, held in conjunction with the USS *Bonhomme Richard* (a carrier-sized helicopter-assault ship), the USS *Antietam* cruiser, the missile-armed destroyers USS *O'Kane* and USS *Higgins,* and assorted amphibious-assault ships, show the most impressive concentration of naval firepower deployed in these waters since the onset of the Iraq invasion in March 2003.[47] Officially, this was just a training exercise, intended to demonstrate "the importance of the strike groups' ability to plan and conduct multi-task force operations as part of the U.S.'s long-standing commitment to maintaining maritime security and stability in the region."[48] But Vice President Cheney, who observed the maneuvers from the deck of the *Nimitz,* made it clear that this was no routine operation: "With two carrier strike groups in the Gulf, we're sending clear messages to friends and adversaries alike. We'll keep the sea lanes open. We'll stand with our friends in opposing extremism and strategic threats. . . . [And] we'll stand with others to prevent Iran from gaining nuclear weapons and dominating this region."[49]

The *Stennis* and *Nimitz* were later rotated out of the Persian Gulf, but the Bush administration continued to deploy at least one and often two carrier battle groups in the Gulf as a constant reminder of its capacity to launch air attacks against Iran at a moment's notice. These vessels have usually been accompanied, moreover, by helicopter-assault ships with the capacity to conduct hit-and-run Marine attacks on key Iranian military installations. Although these naval deployments are rarely reported in the American press, they are plainly visible to the Iranian air and naval contingents that track their every move—and so represent a form of constant psychological pressure on the Tehran government, adding teeth to the threats issued on a regular basis by Vice President Cheney, President Bush, and other senior administration figures.

Gunboats have also been the emissaries of intimidation in the East China Sea, along a disputed maritime border between China and Japan. Citing conflicting provisions of the U.N. Convention on the Law of the Sea, Beijing and Tokyo have proclaimed different offshore boundaries in this strategic maritime region. Japan insists that the common offshore border falls along the median line between the two countries; China opts for its outer continental shelf (which lies much closer to Japan than to China). Between the two competing lines, of course, lies an area claimed by both.

What makes this boundary dispute so significant is the presence of a large natural gas field—called Chunxiao by the Chinese and Shirakaba by the Japanese—extending from undisputed Chinese territory into the contested area. Beijing has pledged to refrain from extracting gas in the disputed zone pending resolution of the issue; however, it has insisted on its right to drill on the Chinese side of the Japanese-claimed median line, even though Tokyo responds that this will inevitably suck up gas from the disputed region. For its part, Tokyo claims the right to drill for gas in the contested zone, even though Beijing insists that the area is part of its own sovereign territory.

In 2004, with Chinese firms already probing for gas deposits in places adjacent to the median line, Japan commenced a survey of the area, insisting it was operating in its own national territory. Needless to say, this produced an angry reaction from Beijing and a demand

Disputed Boundaries in the East China Sea

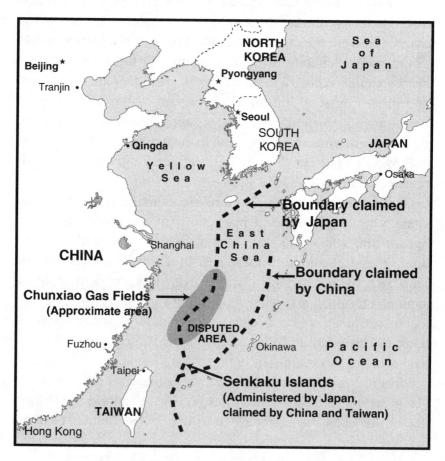

from Vice Foreign Minister Wang Yi to the Japanese ambassador to cease and desist. He specifically characterized the Japanese survey of the disputed zone as an infringement of China's "sovereignty"—a powerful signal indeed in the Asian historical context.[50] As everyone understood, he was suggesting that Japan was again invading Chinese territory, as it had done in the 1930s to devastating effect. When Tokyo refused to halt the survey, Beijing acted forcefully. In early November, it dispatched a submarine into waters claimed by Japan, prompting the Japan Maritime Self-Defense Force (JMSDF, Japan's navy) to go on full alert for the first time in five years.[51] The Chinese later apologized for the move, insisting it was an "accident," but the message was clear: Beijing was prepared to employ force if necessary to defend its claim to the contested area.[52]

Although subsequently several rounds of negotiations were held in an effort to resolve the boundary dispute, no substantive progress was achieved; in early 2005, the China National Offshore Oil Corporation began drilling in the Chunxiao field from a position just a mile or so away from the median line claimed by Japan. At about this time, protests broke out in Beijing and other Chinese cities against the publication in Japan of new history textbooks that downplayed Japanese atrocities in China during World War II. Soon thereafter, Tokyo announced that it would allow Japanese firms to apply for drilling rights in the contested zone, melding ancient grievances and recent ones.[53] In July 2005, Tokyo upped the ante once again by awarding drilling rights in the contested zone to Teikoku Oil. This prompted another sharp protest from Beijing: "If Japan persists in granting drilling rights to companies in disputed waters it will cause a serious infringement of China's sovereign right."[54] Far less diplomatic language was wielded in a commentary in the government-backed newspaper *China Daily*: "Giving Teikoku the go-ahead to test drill is a move that makes conflict between the two nations inevitable, though what form this clash will take is hard to tell."[55]

Both sides quickly removed any uncertainty as to what form their immediate responses would take. By early September 2005, patrol planes of the JMSDF had commenced regular flights over Chinese drilling rigs along the disputed median line where, before long, there was an unprecedented sight in these waters: the arrival of a Chinese naval squadron of five missile-armed destroyers and frigates.[56] Beijing was quick to acknowledge the warships' presence: "I can now confirm that in the East China Sea, a Chinese reserve vessel squadron has been established," Foreign Ministry spokesman Qin Gang announced on September 29, 2005.[57] Within days of their arrival, a gun turret on one of the Chinese ships was aimed at a circling Japanese patrol plane. No shots were actually fired, but an ominous precedent for a future confrontation had been set.[58]

Possibly chastened by this incident, Beijing and Tokyo agreed to undertake a new round of negotiations over the disputed boundary. These commenced in January 2006 and proceeded on an irregular basis, even as the Chinese continued to pump gas from rigs along the median line under the watchful eyes of Chinese naval forces and as the Japanese announced plans to expand their own maritime patrol capabilities.[59] Hopes for an early settlement were raised in October 2006, when Shinzo Abe replaced Junichiro Koizumi as prime minister and, in a state visit to China, pledged to invigorate the negotiations.[60] But Abe resigned in disgrace in September 2007 before any progress was made.[61] Although his successor, Yasuo Fukuda, is thought to be more conciliatory on matters involving China, the dispute remains unresolved and, with both sides building up their naval capabilities, additional instances of mutual gunboat diplomacy can likely be expected in the East China Sea.

Gunboat diplomacy has also occurred in waters of the Caspian Sea claimed by both Azerbaijan and Iran. Although three of the Caspian states—Russia, Azerbaijan, and Kazakhstan—have delineated their maritime boundaries in the Sea's northern section, Iran and Turkmenistan have not agreed on a legal regime that would determine boundaries in its southern reaches, with each asserting a claim to ownership of undersea reserves also claimed by Azerbaijan.

The Azerbaijanis, for their part, have proceeded to award production-sharing agreements to foreign energy firms to explore for and produce hydrocarbons in the disputed areas, prompting predictable protests from the other two claimants. In July 2001, Iran took its ire one step further when one of its warships approached an oil-exploration vessel in a field being developed by BP under a PSA granted by Azerbaijan and ordered it out of the area. The survey ship complied, but Azerbaijan reportedly responded by sending in a patrol boat of its own that chased off the Iranian vessel; warplanes from the two countries may also have been involved.[62] (The Azerbaijanis and Iranians provided conflicting accounts of what occurred.)

Though no further clashes have been reported in the area, American and Azerbaijani officials used this episode as a justification for creating the Caspian Guard and beefing up U.S. support for Azerbaijan's maritime patrol capabilities.[63] Meanwhile, the competitive Russian-sponsored CASFOR fleet in the Caspian is likely to include Iranian participation.[64] As in the East China Sea, the stage is being set for more menacing versions of gunboat diplomacy.

The deployment of ground forces and advanced military bases can sometimes have the same effect as traditional gunboat diplomacy—as can a refusal to remove them, despite an unambiguous commitment to do so. Particularly worrisome instances of such behavior in the early twenty-first century have been American and Russian troop deployments in the Caspian Sea basin, notably in Georgia and Kyrgyzstan. In no other obvious global flashpoint are forces of the major powers deployed in such close proximity, staring each other down.

Since the collapse of the Soviet Union, substantial Russian troop detachments have been stationed in the Republic of Georgia, a pro-Western nation that enjoys warm ties with Washington and would prefer to see all the Russians depart. Two of the four Russian contingents are stationed in rebellious, breakaway regions of Georgia, Abkhazia and South Ossetia. They are supposedly serving in a "peacekeeping" capacity, officially monitoring a cease-fire between separatist forces and Georgian government troops. However, Moscow can hardly claim to be neutral in these disputes: In November 2006, its officials gave tacit approval to declarations by Abkhazian and South Ossetian leaders of their intent to sever all ties with Georgia and amalgamate with Russia.[65] (Moscow reiterated its threat to amalgamate these territories in February 2008, as potential retaliation for the West's recognition of an independent Kosovo.) As for the other two detachments, they are at former Soviet bases that have never been abandoned, despite numerous promises. Moscow agreed in May 2005 to redeploy the two garrisons to Russia as part of a political accommodation with Tbilisi, but then suspended the move in September 2006 after Georgia arrested five Russian military officers as alleged spies.[66]

While these militarized maneuverings can be read as part of an ongoing effort to force Georgia's pro-Western leadership to pay greater deference to Moscow, they must also be viewed in light of Russia's larger geopolitical struggle with the United States over the flow of Caspian basin energy. Three of the four Russian contingents are located within a relatively short distance of the Baku-Tbilisi-Ceyhan (BTC) pipeline, the 1,100-mile conduit built with considerable American backing to transport Azerbaijani (and possibly Kazakh) oil from the Caspian Sea to the Mediterranean. As part of the $1 billion U.S. aid program for Georgia, the Department of Defense has deployed over 100 military instructors in Tbilisi to train Georgian troops in basic combat skills and help prepare them to assume responsibility for protecting the pipeline.[67] While relatively modest, the American military mission in Georgia represents a challenge to Russia and helps explain, in part, its reluctance to remove any of its own forces. So long as these detachments remain in place, Moscow retains an implied capacity to sever the BTC pipeline or otherwise frustrate U.S. strategic objectives in the region.

A similar set of motives seems to govern the emplacement of Russian and American military contingents in Kyrgyzstan. In this case, the United States was the first power to acquire a foothold in the country in the post-Soviet era. Shortly after 9/11, the Bush administration secured permission from Kyrgyz leaders to establish a logistics center at Manas International Airport, not far from the capital city of Bishkek; since then, Manas has served as a supply base for American and allied forces in Afghanistan.[68] The presence of a U.S. military facility in this former Soviet republic was a challenge evidently too great for Moscow to ignore, so the Russians responded by cajoling the Kyrgyz leadership into letting them acquire a military facility of their own. Under the auspices of the Collective Security Treaty Organization, Kyrgyzstan agreed in December 2002 to host a joint "rapid-reaction force" at the former Soviet base at Kant, some forty miles east of Bishkek. While some non-Russians have been incorporated into the force for form's sake, few observers see it as anything but an expression of Moscow's determination to counter Washington's influence.[69]

The geopolitical rivalry sparked by the establishment of a Russian base just a few dozen miles down the road from the American facility at Manas was only the beginning of this geopolitical jousting. In October 2003, the CSTO rapid-reaction force was fully deployed; since then, Russians leaders have applied increasing pressure on Kyrgyz leaders to evict the Americans. In July 2005, the Shanghai Cooperation Organization, of which Russia and Kyrgyzstan are members, called on the United States to vacate its military facilities in Central Asia, including that at Manas.[70] The Uzbeks, for their part, responded to this injunction by demanding an American withdrawal from Khanabad air base. In the end, the Kyrgyz leadership allowed the Americans to remain, but only after obtaining a much bigger rental fee for Manas, estimated at $150 million per year (seventy-five times what the United States had previously been paying).[71] Kyrgyz president Kurmanbek Bakiyev was then able to claim financial necessity in the face of Russian and Chinese pressure; even so, it is obvious that the American tenure at Manas is not likely to outlast the fighting in Afghanistan. Meanwhile, Moscow has proposed the establishment of a second Russian-staffed CSTO base in Kyrgyzstan.[72]

So, on all sides, the stakes are already sky-high. Neither Moscow nor Washington will voluntarily give ground on the basing issue in the Caspian Sea region, so American and Russian troop contingents are likely to remain in relatively close proximity in the political equivalent of an active earthquake zone. One great peril is that these contingents may find themselves on opposite sides of a developing civil war or ethnic conflict from which easy extrication proves impossible. It is in precisely such unpredictable circumstances that a process of unintended escalation can be triggered.

Proto-Blocs in Eurasia

Competitive arms deliveries and gunboat diplomacy are especially worrisome because they are associated with the emergence of incipient military alliances in Eurasia. These systems are not yet true military blocs like NATO or the former Warsaw Pact, but "proto-blocs" that are nonetheless taking on a decided geopolitical character, with a strong focus on the Persian Gulf, the Caspian Sea basin, and the western Pacific. While they serve a variety of functions, these proto-blocs have increasingly embraced "energy security"—vigorous efforts to ensure the safe and uninterrupted production, transportation, and allocation of needed energy supplies—as a key part of their identities.

Two proto-blocs have emerged in recent years. One, with a decidedly anti-American character, is composed of China, Russia, and the Central Asian members of the Shanghai Cooperation Organization; the other, with an anti-Chinese cast, centers around the United States and Japan, but includes Australia, South Korea, and several other states as supporting players. However rudimentary, these blocs heighten international polarization, potentially constraining the maneuverability of national leaders when a major crisis erupts.

Both of these proto-blocs developed around a core partnership of two key powers—China and Russia on one side, Japan and the United States on the other. Of the two, the U.S.-Japanese relationship is the stronger. While the United States and Japan have not as yet established an equivalent to the SCO, most countries allied with them in Asia enjoy formal security ties to the United States, house American bases, and have cooperated with the United States in past military engagements.

The Sino-Russian partnership, by contrast, has a decidedly convoluted history. The two communist powers were close allies in the early years of the Cold War, only to became the bitterest of adversaries in the late 1960s, when they clashed over ideological differences and fought in a series of large-scale border skirmishes. President Richard Nixon and his national security adviser, Henry Kissinger, sought to exploit this schism before the Vietnam War even ended, establishing diplomatic ties with Beijing and using the "China card" (as it was called at the time) in an attempt to isolate Moscow diplomatically and shift the "correlation of forces" in America's favor.

After the collapse of the USSR, the Russians and Chinese discovered that their fear of America's "sole superpower" status far outweighed their residual suspicion and so they began maneuvering toward a rapprochement.[73] China's eagerness to tap into Russia's vast energy reserves to supply its booming economy hastened this process. Following several preliminary meetings among senior officials, Presidents Jiang Zemin of China and Vladimir Putin of Russia signed a "treaty of friendship and cooperation" on July 16, 2001, pledging close collaboration in efforts to constrain American power in Eurasia.[74]

An early outcome of this restored partnership was an increase in Russian arms sales to China and an expansion of military links between the two countries. Since 2000, the Chinese have purchased billions of dollars' worth of advanced Russian weapons, including Su-27 fighter aircraft, Su-30 multirole combat planes, Sovremenny-class destroyers, Kilo-class submarines, and an array of modern missiles.[75] Although not as sophisticated as the most advanced munitions in the American and Japanese arsenals, these Russian arms are viewed by U.S. analysts as "enhancing [China's] military projection capabilities in Asia" and thus its "ability to influence events throughout the region."[76] In a further expression of Sino-Russian military cooperation, the two countries agreed in late 2004 to hold joint military exercises for the first time in fifty years. Dubbed "Peace Mission 2005," these maneuvers were conducted on China's Shandong Peninsula with some 10,000 Chinese and Russian military personnel participating.[77]

Two major concerns have dominated the attention of Chinese and Russian policymakers: growing American assertiveness in Eurasia, and China's growing needs for oil and natural gas. In the immediate aftermath of 9/11, Beijing and Moscow acceded to American requests for assistance in combating the Taliban in Afghanistan, raising no objection to the establishment of what were seen as temporary U.S. bases in Kyrgyzstan and Uzbekistan. Once it became apparent that the American military intended to remain in Central Asia, war on terror or no, Chinese and Russian leaders began to call for the withdrawal of American forces.[78] Although careful to avoid identifying the United States by name, they have endorsed a number of statements condemning any aggressive use of military power outside the bounds of international law. In the most remarkable expression of this outlook, Presidents Hu and

Putin signed a "Declaration on World Order in the 21st Century" in Moscow on July 1, 2005, in which they denounced a certain unnamed country for undermining world security by unabashedly pursuing its "aspirations for monopoly and domination in international affairs."[79]

Energy, regional security, and anti-Americanism are also the binding elements of the Shanghai Cooperation Organization, first convened by China in April 1996 as the "Shanghai Five," a coordinating group of diplomats from China, Russia, Kazakhstan, Kyrgyzstan, and Tajikistan aimed at resolving border disputes and promoting cooperation in the suppression of Islamic extremism and ethnic separatist movements.[80] Buoyed by its promising start, Beijing and Moscow began to promote a more ambitious agenda for the fledgling body. Under China's prodding, Uzbekistan was invited to join the group and, in June 2001, the original body was recast as the SCO and endowed with a small secretariat in Beijing.[81]

The organization continues to place heavy emphasis on counterinsurgency and antiterrorist activities. It has established a regional antiterrorism center in Bishkek, Kyrgyzstan, and conducted a number of joint counterterrorism exercises.[82] But it has also addressed larger issues of international security, notably by declaring its opposition to any use of force not sanctioned by the U.N. Security Council and condemning Washington's plans for the construction of a theater missile-defense system in the western Pacific.[83] As the organization has grown in self-confidence, its leaders have more assertively stressed their desire to exclude nonmembers from direct military involvement in the area—including that 2005 call for the United States to vacate its bases in Kyrgyzstan and Uzbekistan.[84]

Recently, the organization has taken on a more overtly military character. Following an SCO summit in Bishkek in August 2007, troops from all six member states took part in multinational combat exercises dubbed "Peace Mission 2007." Conducted in remote areas of both China and Russia, the exercise featured the participation of 6,000 soldiers (including 2,000 Russians and 1,700 Chinese) and was witnessed by top officials of all countries involved. In comments delivered at the summit, Presidents Putin and Hu emphasized the importance of relying on local powers to ensure regional security—and, by inference, to exclude outside powers like the United States. "The SCO nations have a clear understanding of the threats faced by the region and thus must ensure their security themselves," Hu declared.[85]

Energy cooperation is also a major focus. From public reports on its activities, it appears that the SCO serves as a forum in which national leaders can reach agreements on major energy deals and work out the logistical measures necessary for their implementation.[86] Given the organization's emphasis on regional security and the threat of extremist violence, it can be taken for granted that the defense and interior ministers of SCO member states are devoting greater attention to the protection of the oil and gas pipelines now beginning to stretch across the steppes of Central Asia.[87]

The Japanese-American Alliance

Security and energy considerations also drive the second proto-bloc in Eurasia, which has largely been fueled by concern over the rise of China and the possibility that its growing economic vigor may threaten the prosperity of older, less vibrant industrial powers.[88] In the security realm, there is an allied fear: that China's rapid growth in a world of intensified energy competition will impel China to enhance its military capabilities in major ways.[89]

Since the 1990s, American strategists have sought to counter China's rise and limit its regional influence. The original public blueprint for such a strategy of post–Cold War "containment" can be found in an article Condoleezza Rice wrote for the prestigious *Foreign Affairs* magazine in January 2000, just before she became George W. Bush's national security adviser. Claiming that Beijing seeks to "alter Asia's balance of power in its own favor," Rice affirmed that China must be viewed as a "strategic competitor," not a "strategic partner" (the descriptive term that the Clinton administration had been using). Given this assessment, she continued, "the United States must deepen its cooperation with Japan and South Korea and maintain its commitment to a robust military presence in the region." Moreover, "it should pay closer attention to India's role in the regional balance."[90]

By all accounts, Rice made the implementation of this blueprint her highest priority during the few months of her tenure as national security adviser that preceded the attacks of September 11, 2001. In particular, she (and Secretary of Defense Donald Rumsfeld) pressed forward with plans for the construction of a theater missile-defense system in Asia that would link advanced antimissile defense systems the Pentagon was planning to sell to Japan, South Korea, and Taiwan with America's own forces—a system officially intended to guard against future North Korean missiles but that was obviously meant for China as well.[91] Then came 9/11, and Rice's attention—like that of all senior officials—was largely directed to the president's Global War on Terror, the conflict in Afghanistan, and eventually the invasion and occupation of Iraq. Thoroughly distracted, the Bush administration initially found it expedient to dampen criticism of China and seek Beijing's help on its newly launched campaign against Islamic extremists in Central Asia and the Middle East.

By the beginning of 2005, despite the Iraq war's endless drain on the administration's attention, some attempt was being made to refocus on the priority of containing China. The first sign of this shift came in February, during a meeting of the U.S.-Japan Security Consultative Committee, a high-level body composed of senior officials from both countries. Those present, including Secretary of State Rice and Secretary of Defense Rumsfeld, endorsed a common document calling for enhanced military cooperation between the two countries— precisely the sort of move envisioned in Rice's 2000 blueprint.[92] This, alone, was enough to alarm the Chinese, but they were further incensed by the document's call for linked U.S.-Japanese efforts to "encourage the peaceful resolution of issues concerning the Taiwan straits through dialogue"—an implicit recognition of Taiwan's quasi-independent status and an attempt to involve Japan, Taiwan's previous colonial overlord, in the island's future. "[China] resolutely opposes the United States and Japan in issuing any bilateral document concerning China's Taiwan, which meddles in the internal affairs of China and hurts China's sovereignty," a senior Chinese official was quoted as saying.[93]

At its next meeting, in October 2005, the committee agreed to a further expansion of U.S.-Japanese military ties.[94] This would lead, on May 1, 2006, to the signing of a formal document incorporating these new measures, with Secretaries Rice and Rumsfeld again in attendance. The document, "U.S.-Japan Alliance: Transformation and Realignment for the Future," largely concerned the relocation of certain U.S. military facilities in Okinawa and elsewhere in Japan to the U.S.-controlled island of Guam or less populated sites within Japan itself—a move intended to quell domestic Japanese opposition to the presence of American forces. However, it also focused on increased binational cooperation in ballistic missile defense and combat-support activities.[95] Undergirding all this was a clear commitment for the United States and Japan to cooperate more effectively in addressing "situations in areas surrounding Japan." What exactly this meant was not spelled out in the public texts, but Chinese leaders surely concluded that the containment of China was the ultimate target of this collaboration.[96] These U.S.-Japanese agreements occurred, of course, against the backdrop of the Chinese navy's muscle flexing in disputed energy-rich areas of the East and South China Seas. In July 2005, moreover, the Department of Defense released its annual report on *The Military Power of the People's Republic of China*, noting that China's relentless pursuit of energy "played a role in increased Sino-Japanese tensions over the disputed East China Sea."[97]

Because Japan will continue to rely on the United States for nuclear defense, it will remain America's principal alliance partner in Asia. But Rice and her colleagues have worked to expand the U.S.-Japan core alliance outward in a broad arc surrounding China by incorporating other "friendly" powers.

At the northern end of this arc, U.S. strategists have been eager to expand the U.S.-Japanese partnership to include South Korea. In testimony before the Senate Armed Services Committee in March 2006, the head of the U.S. Pacific Command, Admiral William Fallon (later named head of the Central Command), noted that while he was working to strengthen America's bilateral military ties with Japan and South Korea, "We also hope to foster greater trilateral cooperation between the RoK [Republic of Korea], Japan, and the United States." Such cooperation was needed, he argued, to address a variety of regional threats, including North Korean weapons programs, terrorism, and China's military modernization.[98] Fallon and other U.S. officials know that the South Koreans are wary of close military association with Japan, given that country's brutal occupation of the Korean peninsula from 1905 to 1945; they nevertheless hope to promote such ties under the guise of "trilateralism," and by offering "incentives" like participation in U.S.-supplied advanced missile defense systems.

Looking southward along this arc, the administration has made a concerted effort to incorporate Australia into its developing proto-bloc, despite that country's increasingly close economic ties with China. During a March 2006 visit to Sydney for a "Trilateral Strategic Dialogue" involving the foreign ministers of the United States, Australia, and Japan, Secretary of State Rice warned of the danger posed by growing Chinese military capabilities. Before leaving for Australia, she told reporters that China's military buildup had become a "negative force" in the region and that the trilateral talks would concentrate on how best to address it.[99] While there, she invited Australia to join the other two countries in countering this peril. In February 2007, Vice President Cheney visited Tokyo and then Sydney for consultations[100]—and, two weeks later, Australian prime minister John Howard signed a joint security agreement with his Japanese counterpart, Shinzo Abe, at an elaborate ceremony in Tokyo.[101]

In its present form, the Australian-Japanese accord falls short of a mutual defense pact; it does not require each side to come to the other's assistance in the event of war (as does the U.S.-Japan Security Treaty). Nevertheless, it opened the way for joint military training, joint military exercises, the sharing of intelligence information, and other forms of militarized collaboration.[102] Both sides saw it as a move that would facilitate their integration into the proto-alliance being constructed by Washington.[103] "I think it's fair to say that Japan and the U.S. and Australia are the three great Pacific democracies and we look at these relationships on their own merit as well as looking at them in the context of the impact they have on the entire region," Howard said at the time.[104] But not all Australians appear to share his eagerness to participate in U.S.-led efforts to "contain" China: in November 2007 parliamentary elections, Howard lost his job to opposition leader Kevin Rudd, who promised to forge a more evenhanded stance in the region.

The Bush administration also attempted to enmesh Indonesia in these evolving security arrangements. Thus, on her 2006 trip to Australia, Secretary Rice stopped in Jakarta and proposed a "strategic partnership" between the United States and Indonesia. Praising Jakarta's efforts to modernize its armed forces—long condemned by human rights advocates for consistent patterns of abuse—Rice declared that "a reformed and effective Indonesian military is in the interest of everyone in this region, because threats to our common security have not disappeared."[105] Although she was vague as to the nature of such threats, observers assumed she was alluding to the rising power of China.[106] Many analysts believe that concern over China's growing power is also the catalyst for burgeoning U.S. military ties with Vietnam—once a major adversary of the United States, and later of China. During a June 2006 visit to Hanoi, Defense Secretary Rumsfeld met with senior Vietnamese military leaders and announced that the two countries had agreed to step up "exchanges at all levels of the military."[107]

Finally, there was the U.S. nuclear accord with India, which, if ratified by both countries, would allow for the transfer of U.S. nuclear technology and materials to India in return for its decision to open its civilian power reactors to international inspection. Although primarily focused on nuclear cooperation, the agreement was described by President Bush as part of a larger "strategic partnership" with India that would entail cooperation in many areas of mutual concern, including regional security and energy production.[108] Examine the Bush announcement closely, and it is hard not to be reminded of Rice's *Foreign Affairs* proposal for incorporating India into a broad anti-China alliance system.[109] Supporters of the nuclear pact in Washington have argued that it will bolster U.S.-Indian security ties and better position India to serve as a "counterweight" to China in the region.[110]

Despite these efforts, Australia, India, Indonesia, and Vietnam have not committed to joining the United States and Japan in an explicitly anti-Chinese alliance system—just as not all the members of the SCO have universally embraced an unambiguous anti-American posture. On the contrary, India and China have made vigorous efforts in recent years to bury their past conflicts and cooperate in the pursuit of foreign energy assets. A number of other states in these proto-blocs have exhibited considerable flexibility in maneuvering among the large, imposing powers. Nonetheless, the trend toward greater polarization in East and South Asia is clear, as the weaker states of Eurasia come under increasing pressure to align with one of the two incipient blocs.

The solidification of these systems would not automatically translate into an increased risk of war. All these efforts could produce an equilibrium of sorts, in which the strength of each side might mitigate against a crisis. History suggests, however, that opposing military alliances of this sort tend to aggravate tensions and suspicions, giving any minor incident that arises the potential to spark something far more dangerous.

Infernal Combustion

The accumulation of aggravations and resentments among the Great Powers stemming from the competitive pursuit of energy has not yet reached the point where a violent clash between any pair or group of them can be considered likely. However resentful the losers in recent energy contests—the Chinese in the Unocal affair or the British following Royal Dutch Shell's loss of its major stake in Sakhalin-2—none have displayed an inclination to alter the outcome through armed threat, no less combat. Nevertheless, the conflation of two key trends—the rise of energy nationalism and accumulating ill will between the Sino-Russian and U.S.-Japanese proto-blocs—should be taken as a dangerous sign for the future. Each of these phenomena may have its own roots, but the way they are beginning to intertwine in competitive struggles over prime energy-producing areas in the Caspian Sea basin, the Persian Gulf, and the East China Sea is ominous. Resource contests in these areas are increasingly being viewed not just through the lens of nationalism, but also as part of a deeper struggle over core geopolitical interests.

Finally, there is the zero-sum aspect of major energy disputes. Were the supply of vital resources considered infinite, it is unlikely that these areas of potential conflict would ever lead to a full-blown crisis ending in war. But global stockpiles of oil, natural gas, and uranium are almost certainly facing contraction in the long term. This is where the "edge of desperation" truly bears consideration: One can argue in the abstract that global energy supplies remain adequate for future needs, but if national leaders fear the loss of a major field to a rival state and are convinced that global energy supplies may be inadequate in a "tough oil" era, they may act irrationally and order a muscular show of force—setting in motion a chain of events whose ultimate course no one may be able to control.

The Cuban Missile Crisis of 1962, and other more recent events, have given national leaders some experience in managing such inherently perilous encounters. But no one in recent times has had to contend with a world of many aggressive powers competing for increasingly scarce and valuable resources on a global basis—often in regions that are inherently unstable and already on the edge of conflict. Preventing a complex struggle of this sort from erupting into unimaginable slaughter calls for cool heads at the best of times; doing so when conditions begin to deteriorate may exceed the capabilities of even the most lucid and accomplished leaders.

9

AVERTING CATASTROPHE

The danger that a minor clash over contested energy supplies might trigger an international conflagration is not the only risk we face. The proto-blocs now forming in Eurasia could, for instance, harden into rigid military alliances and spark a new Cold War, sucking up prodigious economic resources and precluding efforts to develop environmentally sensitive energy alternatives. Other possible perils include a global expansion of the power of the state (ostensibly in the pursuit of "energy security") to the detriment of democracy; severe economic trauma; and the acceleration of global climate change with its attendant disasters. The mounting probability of these events, singly and in catastrophic conjunction, argues for placing a high priority on efforts to address the global energy dilemma.

Although leaders of the two major proto-blocs—the United States, Russia, Japan, and China—insist on their commitment to friendly relations, all have engaged in deeply divisive acts over the past five years. We've already discussed the military steps taken by the different parties that have heightened polarization.[1] Inevitably, the intensified energy competition will aggravate the long-standing suspicions and hostilities that persist among these powers. China and Japan have a bitter history of rivalry and conflict, extending back to Japan's invasion and occupation of China in the 1930s; the United States and Russia emerged from a relentless nuclear arms race only in the early 1990s, and many senior leaders in both countries continue to view their counterparts through the hostile lens of the Cold War. Though each pair of states managed to forge generally positive relationships by the end of the last century, the era of good feeling is on the wane.

Of most immediate danger is the possibility that energy-seeking states, in order to establish or strengthen ties with major foreign oil suppliers, will increase the flow of arms and military assistance into areas of instability in Africa, the Middle East, and the Caspian basin. Deliveries of this sort were a cardinal feature of the original Cold War and are bound to factor prominently in any future energy-driven revival. Undoubtedly, such efforts would lead to increased levels of government repression, ethnic conflict, criminal violence, insurgency, and the risk of Great Power conflict.

A new Cold War atmosphere would continue the trend toward state supervision of all fields related to energy exploration, procurement, transportation, and distribution. Because energy and other raw materials are needed to sustain critical industries and the military establishment, scarcity might well legitimize greater state intervention in the name of national security or even national survival. The fact that oil is regarded as a "strategic commodity," essential for the operation of military forces, will justify government rationing and the diversion of available supplies from civilian to military use.

Finally, an increase in inter-bloc tensions will produce a sharp and sustained increase in military spending, draining funds from any national (or even international) effort to develop alternative energy systems. Many such alternatives have been identified and are being tested—though on a very modest scale—in university and corporate laboratories. But as of now none of these can be produced on an industrial scale, and so will not serve as a substitute for oil and natural gas when these materials become scarce.

By all accounts, trillions of dollars will have to be invested in new energy forms to make the transition from the existing energy infrastructure to one based on alternative fuels. A new Cold War, then, entailing trillions of dollars per decade in added military expenditure, would preclude any such investment and spell a global catastrophe—even if no conflicts resulted. In this context, recent government declarations are particularly alarming. The chairman of the Joint Chiefs of Staff, Admiral Mike Mullen, assured reporters at a Pentagon meeting in October 2007 that the United States will have to maintain military spending at historically high levels past the end of the Iraq war to sustain a robust American military presence in the Middle East and prepare for potential conflicts in Asia, Africa, and Latin America. "[A]s a country," he declared, "we're just going to have to devote more resources to national security in the world that we're living in right now."[2] In line with this prospect, President Bush in January 2008 announced the largest U.S. defense budget in real terms since World War II—$515 billion, not counting funds for operations in Iraq and Afghanistan.

Assuming we manage to escape the risks of a Great Power rivalry, we still face the pitfalls of resource scarcity and global warming. That petroleum, natural gas, and various other vital materials will become less abundant in the decades ahead has already been demonstrated. Perhaps serious conservation efforts will cut energy use significantly and other sources of energy will no doubt be harnessed to compensate for some of those disappearing stocks. But the world's economies are so totally dependent on oil, gas, and coal, and the development of alternative fuels is proceeding so slowly, that there is bound to be a period—probably extending from the second decade of this century to its midpoint—during which the mix of existing fuel sources and new materials will prove inadequate to satisfy global needs. This period is likely to cause economic hardship for all nations that do not possess abundant sources of energy or the means to procure what they require from those with a surplus to export.

The forms that such hardships take will, of course, vary. In general, states that rely on imported oil and gas will have to pay ever higher prices to acquire needed supplies. Those that are wealthy will become less so; those that are not will become truly impoverished. Because oil is critical to modern transportation, a significant contraction in supply—and the attendant increase in price—will ripple through the global economy, boosting the cost of everything from manufactured goods to foodstuffs, producing unrelieved misery for the poor, the elderly, and those on fixed incomes. For some—those unable to pay the higher prices of heating oil and food—the effects will be lethal.

Here, too, a likely result will be an increase in state oversight. At the very least, governments will come under immense pressure from domestic constituencies to satisfy energy demands by any means necessary. Meeting demand was, in fact, the stated objective of the National Energy Policy adopted by the Bush administration in May 2001—a time when the nation was already suffering from an "energy crisis" brought about by shortages of oil, natural gas, and electricity. To "ensure a steady supply of affordable energy for America's homes and businesses and industries"—the policy's ultimate goal—the president advocated the removal of existing restrictions on oil and gas drilling in environmentally sensitive areas, such as the Arctic National Wildlife Refuge; along with increased government subsidies for Big Oil, King Coal, and the nuclear power industry; intensified efforts to gain access to overseas oil and gas deposits; and greater reliance on arms transfers and military aid to cement U.S. ties with key suppliers abroad.[3]

The adoption of statist measures of this sort will occur at the expense of both corporate and societal autonomy. Greater governmental intervention in the procurement and distribution of oil and natural gas will usurp powers long enjoyed by the major energy firms (though it is worth recalling that, in many parts of the world, the state often played a key role in creating or nurturing giant firms such as BP, Total, and Eni, which are now mostly independent actors). Any increase in state oversight of energy affairs will undermine basic democratic rights and the prerogatives of local authorities. In general, the lower the level at which a decision is made about the design or location of a drilling rig, refinery, reactor, dam, or power plant, the greater the opportunity for public scrutiny of, and participation in, plans for such facilities; once control shifts to central state authorities, these opportunities largely disappear.

Even in the United States, where suspicion of and hostility toward federal authority remains strong, one can see a trend toward reduced local control over energy-related matters. A key turning point may have been the Energy Policy Act of 2005, which gave the Department of Energy increased authority over the siting of regasification facilities and interstate electric transmission lines—major installations whose construction can alter the character of a community and expose it to new hazards. Previously, control over the placement of such facilities was largely exercised by state, county, and municipal authorities; under the new law, these powers will be wielded by the Federal Energy Regulatory Commission. This may set a precedent for the granting of authority in such matters as the placement of nuclear power plants and oil refineries, all potentially contentious issues—especially if monopolized by unelected federal bureaucrats.

Overshadowing these concerns, however, is global climate change. The Intergovernmental Panel on Climate Change (IPCC), in a comprehensive 2007 report considered definitive by the international scientific community, asserted, "Warming of the climate system is unequivocal, as is now evident from observations of increases in global average air and ocean temperatures, widespread melting of snow and ice, and rising global average sea level."[4] The IPCC further concluded that human activity is largely responsible for the recent buildup of greenhouse gases in the atmosphere and that carbon dioxide—released in the burning of fossil fuels—"is the most important anthropogenic [human-induced] greenhouse gas."[5] Because carbon-based fuels—oil, natural gas, and coal—now provide about 85 percent of the world's primary energy supply (a percentage not expected to change appreciably for years or even decades to come), the climate change problem is at root an *energy* problem. Its solution will, accordingly, require a radical transformation in the way the human population obtains and uses energy supplies.

As a result of the IPCC's 2007 report and the award of the 2007 Nobel Peace Prize to both the IPCC and former Vice President Al Gore for their role in raising public awareness about climate change, the subject is finally on the agenda of national and international policymakers. But there is not, as yet, any sign that world leaders are prepared to undertake the mammoth and phenomenally expensive efforts needed to reverse the ever-growing greenhouse-gas buildup that threatens to produce a variety of catastrophic scenarios, ranging from extreme drought and rapid desertification of large swaths of the planet to rising sea levels and the inundation of coastal regions, home to a substantial proportion of humanity. At present rates of growth, international atmospheric emissions of carbon dioxide will jump from 27 billion metric tons in 2004 to 43 billion in 2030—a stunning, planet-roasting increase of 60 percent.⁶ While it is possible that future policy initiatives will alter these projections, any fundamental change would require a rapid acceleration in the commercialization of energy alternatives that are still largely in the laboratory stage of development.

What we are most likely to experience instead is the worst of both worlds: a continuing reliance on fossil fuels—with all the geopolitical consequences already described—and the accelerated buildup of greenhouse gases, leading to ever more severe climate-change disasters. Each of these scenarios will reinforce the other. Thus an increase in geopolitical tensions will discourage policymakers from diverting funds and attention to the development of costly, elaborate, and experimental new-energy fuels and systems. And the consequent ramping up of old-energy systems—in a context of friction and conflict among the greater and lesser powers—will pour more greenhouse gases into the atmosphere, further warming the planet.

To sum up, if global energy behavior continues along its current trajectory, the risk of crisis, economic trauma, and conflict on a staggering scale will increase. Even in the absence of war, most people in the world will experience a steady deterioration of conditions, especially as the more severe effects of resource scarcity and climate change kick in. Merely avoiding a military conflagration is not enough: Averting catastrophe requires efforts to demilitarize energy procurement policies and radically speed the development of climate-friendly alternatives.

At its core, this task requires repudiating the zero-sum, ultra-nationalistic impulses that threaten to dominate energy policy in most major industrial nations and replacing them with a collaborative approach to solving the world's energy challenges. So long as policymakers believe they can best advance vital national interests by using risky and provocative methods to procure valuable, if limited, oil and natural gas deposits abroad, the stage is set for unceasing competition and mutual suspicion; in such an atmosphere, no meaningful progress is likely to be made toward addressing the global warming problem.

Even the most enlightened of leaders rarely respond creatively to exhortations based solely on the avoidance of negative outcomes. Saying that we should jettison a zero-sum approach to avert various future dangers when a country needs more oil and gas *right now* is not likely to prove particularly effective. To gain traction, such appeals must be reinforced by the promise of tangible gains that outweigh any temporary inconveniences. Especially in the energy field, alternative strategies must offer credible solutions. To be more specific, international cooperation must yield not only a reduction in crisis and conflict, but also an increase in the availability of new-energy options that both supplant dwindling old-energy stockpiles and slow the accumulation of greenhouse gases in the atmosphere.

Devising a strategy of this sort must be a top priority for policymakers, scientists, energy experts, and ordinary citizens in every country on the planet. There are myriad possible ways nations and organizations can work together for the purpose of exploring new energy initiatives. But of all such conceivable partnerships, none is more important or pivotal than one between the United States and the People's Republic of China.

The United States and China: From Competition to Collaboration

Why start with the United States and China? Because, they are the world's top two consumers of energy. At present, they jointly account for 36 percent of international energy consumption; by 2030, their joint share will rise to 39 percent, or nearly two-fifths of the planet's total energy use. Clearly, any drive to alter global energy behavior will have to involve these two countries if it is to have any impact. The United States is the top consumer of oil, China of coal, and both nations are expected to retain those positions in the decades to come. Neither the United States nor China possesses adequate domestic supplies of petroleum; both will have to rely on coal to generate electricity; both will compete for foreign sources of oil; and both will be the leading emitters of carbon dioxide.[7] (See Table 9.1.)

The United States, of course, possesses the world's largest economy; China has the third or fourth largest at this point, but it is widely expected to overtake Japan and become number two in the decades ahead. Both also boast extensive scientific and engineering establishments capable of conducting large-scale research and development (R&D) on alternative energy systems. The United States is a leader of the mature industrial powers; China, of the newly industrialized ones—and so their collaborative efforts to develop new energy options might well inspire other nations to follow suit. This would be particularly important in India's case, since it trails Chinese economic development by a decade or so. A decision by China's leadership to engage in a radical energy transformation would encourage the Indians to follow a similar path; in the absence of such a signal, India could join the United States and China as a major consumer of coal—and, in consequence, as a major emitter of carbon dioxide.

Thus a Sino-American partnership aimed at developing climate-friendly alternative fuels should be the starting point for a sane energy policy. Forging such a partnership will require disavowal of the view that a conflict between the United States and China over foreign energy supplies is "inevitable"—a view widely held in Washington ever since the 2005 Unocal fracas. In fact, some policymakers have begun to suggest that the United States and China have more *in common* as energy consumers than as adversaries. "Though our economic circumstances are different," Sen. Joseph Lieberman, Independent from Connecticut, observed in 2005, "there is a very comparable reality here that both countries face, which is that each of our energy systems depends on a form of energy, oil, that neither nation has naturally in abundance." It follows, he argued, that "it is time the U.S. and China not only recognize the similarity of our oil dependency status, and the direction that competition may take us, but begin to talk more directly about this growing global competition for oil so that we can each develop national policies and cooperative international policies—even joint research and development projects—to cut our dependency on oil before the competition becomes truly hostile."[8]

Some Chinese officials have expressed similar views. Zhang Guobao, vice chairman of the National Development and Reform Commission (NDRC), said the United States and China "need to oppose the Cold War mentality" and work together in developing new oil

Table 9.1
CHINA AND THE UNITED STATES:
SELECTED ENERGY INFORMATION

		Actual (2004)	Percent of World Total	Projected (2030)	Percent of World Total
Gross Domestic Product (at market exchange rates, billion U.S. dollars)	United States	10,704	30.6	22,494	29.3
	China	1,707	4.9	8,752	11.4
	World	34,937	100.0	76,850	100.0
Total Energy Use (quadrillion BTUs)	United States	100.7	22.5	131.2	18.7
	China	59.6	13.3	145.4	20.7
	World	464.7	100.0	701.5	100.0
Liquids/Petroleum Consumption (million barrels per day)	United States	20.7	25.1	26.6	22.6
	China	6.4	7.8	15.7	13.4
	World	82.5	100.0	117.6	100.0
Liquids/Petroleum Production (million barrels per day)	United States	8.2	9.7	10.2	8.7
	China	3.8	4.5	4.9	4.2
	World	84.3	100.0	117.7	100.0
Natural Gas Consumption (trillion cubic feet)	United States	22.4	22.5	26.1	16.0
	China	1.4	1.4	7.0	4.3
	World	99.6	100.0	163.2	100.0
Coal Consumption (quadrillion BTUs)	United States	22.6	19.7	34.1	17.1
	China	41.1	35.9	95.2	47.8
	World	114.5	100.0	199.1	100.0
Nuclear Energy Consumption (billion kilowatt-hours)	United States	789	30.1	896	24.8
	China	48	1.8	329	9.0
	World	2619	100.0	3619	100.0
Carbon Dioxide Emissions (million metric tons)	United States	5923	22.0	7950	18.5
	China	4707	17.5	11,239	26.2
	World	26,922	100.0	42,880	100.0

Source: U.S. Department of Energy, *International Energy Outlook 2007.*

supplies to meet both countries' needs. Zhang's remarks were delivered at a September 2006 industry forum in Hangzhou attended by representatives of U.S. and Chinese energy firms, and preceded by several days a meeting between top energy officials of the two countries.[9]

The United States and China also have a common interest in tackling the global warming dilemma. Together, they are projected to account for a staggering 45 percent of worldwide carbon dioxide emissions by 2030—a truly terrifying prospect, given the grievous harm in the form of intense storms, floods, droughts, fires, and pestilence that climate change is likely to inflict on both countries. One can imagine the two countries making some progress on CO_2 emissions individually, but in an atmosphere of fierce energy competition and growing hostility, this is not likely to be a high national priority or receive anywhere near adequate levels of funding. Only by embracing the path of cooperation will it be possible to overcome the worst effects of climate change.

In advancing his vision of cooperation, Sen. Lieberman harked back to the original Cold War for a valuable lesson in Great Power politics. The energy race of today, he noted, bears considerable similarity to the nuclear arms race of that earlier period. And just as the arms race was ultimately slowed through arms-control talks between the nuclear rivals, so, too, can the oil race between Washington and Beijing be reined in and turned into a race toward cooperative energy projects.[10]

The Cold War–era arms control analogy, in fact, provides a concrete model for bringing Washington and Beijing together. At the start of the arms-control process, the United States and the Soviet Union were highly suspicious of each other. They nevertheless managed to develop negotiating forums and other mechanisms that allowed them, over time, to achieve tangible arms-control breakthroughs. A similar process should now be initiated in the energy field.

Perhaps the place to start would be with an annual U.S.-China Energy Summit presided over by the presidents of both countries and accorded the gravity given the U.S.-Soviet "summit" meetings held at the peak of the original Cold War, when the survival of both nations was thought to be at stake. The aim of these annual summits would be twofold: to eliminate areas of possible friction, such as disputes over

contested foreign oil and gas deposits; and to review and finalize proposals on the joint development of alternative, climate-friendly sources
of energy. The meetings should be accompanied by the creation of a
bilateral infrastructure—joint committees and working groups composed of government officials, scientists, and industry figures—to carry
on the process of cooperative engagement on a daily basis. The goal
would be to build trust quickly while demonstrating the viability of
genuine cooperation.

American and Chinese officials have, in fact, already taken the first
tentative steps in this direction. On May 23, 2004, Secretary of Energy
Spencer Abraham signed a Memorandum of Understanding with
Zhang Guobao of the NDRC for the establishment of a "U.S.-China
Energy Policy Dialogue" made up of midlevel officials from both
agencies. Its aim is to foster "discussions on a range of energy issues,
including energy policy-making, supply security, power sector reform,
energy efficiency, renewable energy, and energy technology options."[11]
At present, the officials involved have no authority to negotiate formal
agreements between the two countries, but the dialogue does provide a
forum in which government representatives from both sides can discuss solutions to shared problems—and which, in time, could provide
the foundation for more binding forms of collaboration.

The DoE-NDRC dialogue has also provided a model for other
Sino-American energy exchanges, including the U.S.-China Oil and
Gas Industry Forum, a periodic colloquium among industry and government officials from the two countries. Launched in 1998, it assumed real importance once the Memorandum of Understanding was
signed in 2004.[12] In yet another initiative, the top economic officials of
both countries agreed at the third session of the U.S.-China Strategic
Economic Dialogue, held at Xianghe, China, in December 2007, to establish a joint working group to develop a ten-year plan for cooperation in energy security, energy efficiency, and environmental
protection. "The issues of energy security and environmental sustain-
ability are vitally important to both of our nations," U.S. Treasury Secretary Henry M. Paulson, Jr., declared at the conclusion of the meeting.
"I find it an exciting prospect that we will set out to a long term and

strategic plan for working together toward progress in these important areas."[13]

The United States and China also cooperate, however minimally, in a number of multilateral energy endeavors, including the International Partnership for a Hydrogen Economy and the Asia-Pacific Partnership for Clean Development and Climate.[14] Quite apart from these modest official efforts, many U.S. corporations have established joint ventures with Chinese firms to explore advances in alternative fuels and automotive design.

Once a process of collaboration has taken hold, the ultimate goal of any Sino-American energy partnership must be to achieve demonstrable progress in reducing both countries' dependence on imported petroleum, developing climate-friendly alternatives, and spurring long-term economic growth. Many individual initiatives might contribute to these broad aims, but three key categories seem crucial: accelerating the development of petroleum alternatives, promoting a resource-efficient industrial transformation, and developing environmentally safe uses for coal.

Developing Petroleum Alternatives

In 2030, the United States and China will jointly consume an estimated 42 million barrels of oil per day, of which 27 million barrels, or 64 percent, will have to be imported.[15] Of all the tasks facing American and Chinese leaders in the energy field, procuring this quantity of imported petroleum will prove the most Herculean. Unfortunately, there is no obvious, cost-free way to eliminate the need for all this imported energy at the moment—no "magic bullet"—which means there is much work to be done by the two nations, individually and in concert. To reduce motor vehicle gasoline consumption, for instance, each country will have to impose strict fuel-efficiency standards in accordance with its own laws and regulations. However, when it comes to the development of *new* motor fuels—a gigantic endeavor, entailing immense expense and effort—cooperation will be a necessity. Such cooperation would also ensure the adoption of interchangeable standards for the production, transportation, distribution, and consumption of what could prove to be vast quantities of alternative fuels.

As the global supply of petroleum contracts, many substances will be considered as potential sources of liquid fuels. Those currently receiving the greatest attention are natural gas, coal, ethanol, biodiesel, and hydrogen. All deserve close examination—if not necessarily full-scale support—from American and Chinese authorities.

Natural gas, in liquid form, has certain attractions as a transportation fuel because its consumption releases less carbon dioxide than oil or coal, and it is relatively plentiful in some parts of the world. But China and the United States possess only limited natural gas reserves and so would once again face the prospect of competition over imports from unstable, potentially hostile areas of the planet. Hence, a gas-to-liquids program would not be an appropriate choice for Sino-American cooperation, although it might make sense for countries with an abundance of natural gas, such as Iran, Qatar, or Russia.

Ethanol, or grain alcohol, has long been viewed as a viable automotive fuel. Indeed, Henry Ford's earliest cars were powered by it, and his famous Model T was capable of using either ethanol or gasoline (or a combination of the two). Even today, most cars manufactured in the United States can operate on a fuel mixture containing up to 10 percent ethanol (E-10), while those manufactured with minor modifications ("flex fuel" vehicles) can use an 85 percent ethanol mix (E-85). With concern over oil dependency and global warming growing, the demand for ethanol has skyrocketed. However, most of America's ethanol is obtained through the fermentation of corn kernels, and this presents a whole new set of problems: No matter how productive, American cornfields are not capable of replacing even a small share of the nation's gasoline demand while also providing food for humans and feed for animals.[16] On top of this, America's existing, corn-based ethanol industry is itself a significant consumer of energy, in that huge amounts of oil and other fuels are used in sowing, spraying, harvesting, and transporting the crop and heating the corn mash as it is transformed into alcohol.[17] Clearly, any hope of relying on ethanol as an alternative to oil must rest on something other than the current method of producing it.

Ethanol manufacturers prefer to use corn kernels for fermentation because the microorganisms that feed on the sugary mash, releasing alcohol as a byproduct, find them easy to digest; they show little appetite for the thicker, cellulose-filled stalks of the plant. If, however, powerful enzymes can be developed that are capable of breaking the cellulose down and freeing the sugars within, it should be possible to employ the *entire* corn plant for ethanol, thus greatly increasing net output per acre and possibly avoiding a crisis in food production. These same techniques would also permit the use of other plants for this purpose, such as switchgrass, wheat straw, sugar cane (widely used as a feedstock for ethanol in Brazil), and miscanthus (a grass native to China); such plants can also be grown with less energy-intensive cultivation. Many experts now view the development of processes to produce "cellulosic ethanol" from corn stalks and other cellulose-rich plants as the most promising route to petroleum alternatives.[18] Efforts now under way in the United States to test various methods for the production of cellulosic ethanol on a pilot-plant basis might hold out particular promise as a vehicle for Sino-American cooperation.[19]

Ethanol is just one of a family of "biofuels," or liquid fuel alternatives made from organic matter. Also growing in popularity is biodiesel—diesel fuel made from soybeans, rapeseed, palm oil, jatropha, or other oil-rich crops.[20] A recent study by the U.S. National Academy of Sciences found that while conventionally manufactured ethanol provides only 25 percent more energy per gallon than was consumed in making it, soybean-based biodiesel generated 93 percent more energy.[21] Although interest in biodiesel is intensifying in both the United States and China, neither country has as yet invested significant funds or effort in moving the process along or proceeded far in plans to install new plant capacity—which, while disappointing, makes it a perfect opportunity for bilateral collaboration.[22]

Lastly, there is the potential use of hydrogen as an energy "carrier" in vehicles powered by electrochemical fuel cells. Hydrogen is not considered an energy source in and of itself because it does not exist in a pure state in nature but absorbs energy when being separated from other substances, like water or natural gas; this acquired energy can then be released in a fuel cell or similar device. The essential design of fuel cells has long been established, but designing and installing a national system for the production, distribution, and delivery of hydrogen fuel is proving another Herculean task.[23] In addition, the existing means of separating hydrogen from water or gas consumes considerable quantities of energy—and, depending on the method used, releases significant quantities of CO_2 as well. Accordingly, many doubts have been raised as to the suitability of hydrogen as an alternative to petroleum and other fossil fuels.[24]

Although this is not the place to evaluate the arguments for and against the large-scale development of hydrogen, its use—if produced in large enough volumes—would greatly reduce the emission of greenhouse gases while eliminating reliance on foreign sources of oil. On the other hand, since existing means of producing hydrogen consume too much energy to be efficient or effective, alternative methods would have to be developed. It now seems clear that considerably more research and testing is needed to establish whether hydrogen will ever prove amenable to full-scale commercial production. Because the United States and China would be among the principal beneficiaries of a fully developed "hydrogen economy," collaborative R&D of this sort should be a major part of any Sino-American energy partnership.[25]

A New Industrial Paradigm

Finding substitutes for petroleum—and other finite sources of energy—will be essential if the United States and China are to avert a potentially violent global struggle over dwindling reserves. But the ultimate objective of any collaboration cannot be merely to replace existing fuels (and other vital materials) with equal quantities of new ones; it must also devise new technologies and industrial processes that consume fewer resources while stimulating economic growth, improving human life, and protecting the global climate.

Some aspects of a new industrial strategy will arise naturally as a result of global economic pressures and the initiatives described above. For example, a spike in oil prices combined with the introduction of more fuel-efficient vehicles will combine to reduce worldwide petro-leum consumption. But many other innovations could emerge from a comprehensive strategy aimed at reducing the overall rate of resource extraction while keeping the Chinese and American economies hum-ming. Such a strategy should apply to the full range of industrial pro-cesses and transportation systems, and extend to the design of cities, office buildings, schools, hospitals, and other large facilities.

As growing scarcities generate higher prices, manufacturers and in-dividual consumers will be eager to adopt resource-sparing technolo-gies. Though energy-efficient equipment and materials might cost more to buy and install than existing models, they promise to yield substantial savings over the long run.[26] "Using energy more efficiently offers an economic bonanza," says Amory B. Lovins of the Rocky Mountain Institute (RMI), "because saving fossil fuel is a lot cheaper than buying it."[27] Lovins claims that the United States and China can substantially reduce their consumption of oil and other basic resources through practical, money-saving investments in advanced materials and efficiency.[28]

Renewable sources like wind and solar power have obvious advan-tages over fossil fuels, including the fact that they emit no greenhouse gases when consumed and face no risk of exhaustion, so long as the sun continues to shine and the earth revolves about its axis. Although wind and solar power are, at present, more costly than coal or natural gas in producing electricity, they will not be subjected to future taxes on carbon-releasing substances when—as is almost certain to be the case—such charges are imposed. The cost of renewables is also likely to fall as a result of continuing technological innovation. For example, a study published in *Scientific American* for January 2008 suggests that a massive array of photovoltaic panels in the American Southwest, when connected to new electrical infrastructure, could supply as much as 69 percent of the nation's electricity by 2050 at rates equivalent to today's costs for conventional power sources.[29]

Currently, considerable research and development on energy re-newables is under way in both the United States and China. For example, Google.com, the dominant Internet-search company, has announced plans to commit hundreds of millions of dollars to R&D on renewable sources of energy, and its philanthropic affiliate, Google .org, has promised to add to the largess.[30] The American and Chinese governments have also announced plans to increase their spending on renewable-energy research, awarding sizable grants to participating universities, research institutes, and private firms. Given the obvious attraction to both countries of increasing their reliance on these sources, any future collaboration between them should place particular emphasis on identifying and nurturing projects that would clearly benefit from cooperative effort.

In considering the alternatives to existing sources of energy, some experts and policymakers—including President Bush—have argued that nuclear power be considered a viable option because it produces no greenhouse-gas emissions. But nuclear power is not a renewable source of energy—it is fueled by nonrenewable uranium, a material that is likely to become increasingly scarce in coming decades and so trigger yet another geopolitical struggle among the Great Powers. It also produces radioactive wastes whose disposal, in ever-increasing quantities, will produce a mammoth environmental peril of its own. Some scientists believe that new nuclear technologies, such as the development of fusion reactors, will eliminate these obstacles, but pending evidence that such innovations are practical and affordable, nuclear power should not be a priority for U.S.-Chinese collaboration (though university-level research on fusion power could be).

A far more practical arena for future cooperation would be the development of super-efficient, lightweight motor vehicles. The United States is the world's number one market for automobiles, and China is now number two. If consumers in both countries continue to acquire cars, vans, and other vehicles like those now on the road, the implications in terms of global resource demand for both motor fuel and auto-body materials would be catastrophic. It is vital, then, that automotive engineers undertake the design of radically new types of vehicles that use fewer materials in their construction and consume little or no petroleum products. Technologies developed by the airline industry, including the use of carbon-composite materials and ultralight alloys, could be borrowed for this purpose.

Needless to say, these new materials are more costly than ordinary steel, but their employment would so reduce the weight of the car or van (and the size of the engine needed to propel it) that the resulting gain in fuel efficiency would far outweigh the higher price of materials over the lifetime of the vehicle. Combined with advanced "plug-in" hybrid engines (which can be recharged at night off residential electrical outlets, thus reducing gasoline usage) and vastly more powerful batteries, such cars would substantially reduce the demand for petroleum. Amory Lovins and his colleagues at RMI have designed one such ultralight vehicle, pictured in the September 2005 issue of *Scientific American*. The vehicle, designed to run on a hydrogen-powered fuel cell, would have a fuel economy equivalent to 114 miles per gallon of oil.[31]

Working together, American and Chinese officials could accelerate the shift toward a new industrial paradigm by supporting cooperative R&D on renewable energy and other resource-conserving technologies. Among the areas that call for particular attention (in addition to those already cited) are:

· Advanced photovoltaic cells and solar-collection technologies
· Advanced wind turbines and electrical distribution networks
· Energy-efficient factories and building design
· Advanced heating and cooling systems
· Energy-efficient computers and electronic devices
· Advanced construction materials research

One need not spell out all the specifics of these initiatives to make the point that the preeminent powers must move together toward a new industrial paradigm that posits economic growth while lowering the consumption of energy and other basic materials. As the world's two leading resource consumers, the United States and China must take the lead in devising such strategies—and should do so, wherever practical, in a collaborative manner. But the benefits of their collaboration should be shared with other resource-consuming nations. After all, the ultimate objective of this enterprise is to substantially slow the exhaustion of vital raw materials—not to create an exclusive Sino-American alt-energy club.

Climate-Friendly Coal

Any discussion of possible Sino-American cooperation in the energy field must inevitably circle back to the issue of coal, if for no other reason than that coal looms so large in the energy equations of both nations. According to the most recent DoE projections, the United States and China will jointly account for 65 percent of world coal consumption in 2030.[32] In fact, the International Energy Agency predicted in 2007 that the use of coal will actually *rise* in the decades ahead—reversing a long-term decline—as oil and natural gas become more scarce and their price increases.[33]

From an environmental perspective, any increase in coal consumption using existing methods of combustion will be catastrophic. Virtually every serious proposal for reduced greenhouse-gas emissions begins, therefore, with a plea for substantial reductions in coal consumption. Such pleas were included, for example, in recent reports from the Intergovernmental Panel on Climate Change and the International Energy Agency. A growing number of political figures in the United States—including all of the Democratic candidates for president in 2008—have spoken in similar terms.[34] But however eloquent and urgent their entreaties, these calls are unlikely to curb the appetite for coal in the United States and China so long as affordable alternatives are unavailable. Hence, developing such alternatives should be a top priority for any collaboration. At the same time, it is essential to do everything possible to ensure that whatever coal *is* consumed is done so in a climate-friendly way.

To make progress in this area, the two countries must make major investments in developing and installing the technology to strip coal of its impurities and burn it in such a manner that prevents the carbon content from combining with oxygen and escaping into the atmosphere. Two promising developments might address these challenges in whole or in part: the integrated gasification combined-cycle method of power generation (IGCC), and carbon capture and storage, also known as "carbon sequestration."

In conventional power plants, coal is ground into a powder and burned in a furnace to turn water into steam; the steam is then used to power a turbine-generator to make electricity while the coal exhaust (containing carbon dioxide, sulphur dioxide, nitrogen oxides, and smog-causing particulates) is expelled through a chimney. Scrubbers and filters in the exhaust stack can be used to reduce the release of CO_2 and other waste products, but their price rises in direct proportion to their efficiency—a powerful disincentive to cost-conscious utility companies.

Integrated gasification combined-cycle plants, although more expensive to install, have a double advantage over conventional plants: They simplify the task of removing impurities from the coal and boost electrical output per amount of fuel consumed. In an IGCC plant, the coal is crushed into a fine powder and mixed with steam and heated oxygen to produce a combustible mixture called "syngas" while toxic pollutants like sulphur and mercury are stripped away and disposed of. The syngas is fired in a turbine-generator to make electricity while the hot exhaust is used to heat water into steam, which powers a second set of turbines (hence, "combined-cycle"). At present, the technology for facilities of this type is still at an early stage of development, and so only a few small IGCC plants have been constructed. Significant additional investment and testing is needed to make such facilities the standard for future coal-powered plants.[35]

The widespread introduction of IGCC facilities alone would reduce carbon dioxide emissions when compared to existing coal-fired plants, but its true promise would be wasted if not wedded to another innovation—the sequestration of all excess carbon in secure underground storage sites, where it cannot escape into the atmosphere and contribute to global warming. As IGCC plants come on line, they must be equipped with devices to strip the excess carbon from the syngas and channel it into storage facilities for eventual burial in secure underground sites, such as exhausted oil fields or emptied coal mines. Only when the carbon is buried in this manner can coal be considered a safe or "clean" source of energy.[36]

A few final words on this: If the world ever does move closer to a hydrogen economy, coal gasification using the techniques employed in IGCC power plants could prove a safe and practical means of manufacturing hydrogen for fuel cells—if accompanied by carbon sequestration. Coal could, in fact, become a major source of hydrogen if processed in this manner, so long as there was no risk to the environment through the release of carbon dioxide and other waste products.

With sequestration, moreover, coal could also be a feedstock for diesel fuel and natural gas alternatives using the Fischer-Tropsch (F-T) chemical process developed by German scientists in the 1920s. A number of companies, both American and Chinese, are exploring updated versions of the F-T process to produce liquid fuels or syngas from coal— so this, too, appears a promising area for possible future collaboration.[37]

Other Collaborative Partnerships

Because China and the United States are the most obvious candidates for a constructive energy partnership, I have focused on the attractions of a Sino-American compact. But certainly other pairs or groups of competitors could also benefit from cooperation of this sort, particularly China and Japan. These two countries have already clashed over disputed natural gas supplies in the East China Sea and oil from Siberia and are likely to square off against each other again and again in the future unless their competition can be redirected into collaborative efforts.[38]

Many of the specific endeavors proposed for a possible U.S.-Chinese energy partnership would also make sense in a Sino-Japanese compact. For example, both countries would benefit from projects aimed at improving the fuel efficiency of motor vehicles and accelerating the development of petroleum alternatives; both could also make significant contributions to the emergence of a hydrogen economy, if obstacles to such a system can be overcome. In addition, there are some areas of collaboration particularly well suited to Sino-Japanese cooperation. These include the widespread introduction of high-speed "bullet" trains—a field in which Japan (but not the United States) has acquired considerable expertise, and from which China, with its vast distances, large population, and its need for an alternative to a car culture, could benefit.

Like the United States and China, Japan and China have begun to see the advantages of collaboration of this sort. During a four-day visit to Beijing in December 2007, his first after assuming office earlier in the year, Japanese prime minister Yasuo Fukuda emphasized the importance of working together to curb the buildup of greenhouse gases in the atmosphere. Although no specific agreements to this end were signed during Fukuda's visit, the two sides reportedly explored the potential for Japan to assist the Chinese in making their factories more energy-efficient and reducing their greenhouse-gas emissions.[39]

One can also imagine an array of similar agreements involving these countries plus India and the European Union. Even Russia, with its vast reserves of oil and natural gas, would gain from participation in partnerships of this sort. At present, Russia's energy infrastructure is largely composed of old-energy systems that are relatively inefficient in their consumption of primary fuels, especially coal and gas. Although Russia is currently enjoying high rates of economic growth, it risks the eventual depletion of its most valuable reserves of fuels if it continues to consume them in an inefficient manner (also contributing, of course, to greenhouse-gas accumulations). Because other countries are ahead in the development of new-energy systems, it makes sense for Russia to team up with one or more of its neighbors to make better use of its natural resource inheritance.

The New International Energy Order Revisited

Collaborative partnerships would fundamentally alter the power dynamics of the new international energy order and possibly create a new dynamic: As cooperating consumer states begin to decrease their dependence on the energy-surplus states, they will swing the balance of power back in their favor while reducing the overall risk of conflict. For the United States, this would have the added benefit of stemming the massive outflow of dollars to pay for imported oil and the risk that key sectors of the economy will be acquired by the sovereign-wealth funds of Middle Eastern petro-states.

Assuming that such a dynamic took hold, many of the more dangerous behaviors brought up in this book might be mitigated. For example, there would be less necessity to offer military rewards to secure access to overseas supplies of oil and gas. Once engaged in joint efforts to reduce their imports of oil, the United States and China would, in theory, have less reason—other foreign policy considerations aside—to compete in the provision of arms and military equipment to key suppliers in Africa, the Caspian Sea basin, and elsewhere.

Similarly, an energy partnership between China and Japan would render irrelevant their continuing dispute over the Chunxiao/Shirakaba natural gas field in the East China Sea. If the two were able to determine their common maritime boundary, they might even develop this undersea resource jointly, dividing the costs and sharing the benefits. A similar approach could be adopted in other unresolved maritime boundary disputes, such as that involving China and its neighbors with respect to the South China Sea (which is thought to harbor substantial reserves of oil and gas).[40]

Finally, the adoption of common energy strategies by China, Japan, Russia, and the United States would undercut the drive to establish new military alliances in Eurasia. Admittedly, these proto-blocs have other motivating impulses besides energy, but given the fact that energy security is cited as one of the major reasons for forming such alliances, the establishment of Sino-American and Sino-Japanese energy partnerships would eliminate a major rationale for their very formation.

In these and other ways, the risk of unintended escalation would gradually diminish. With the major powers connected to one another through a dense web of cooperative energy projects—all designed to enhance the vitality of their respective economies—they would be less inclined to view one another's overseas procurement activities as a threat to their own well-being. International competition for access to energy reserves would not simply disappear in this environment, but it would more closely resemble competition over other, commonplace commodities—and so lose its capacity to spark hostilities.

A lessening in international friction and conflict over contested sources of energy would also permit a gradual reduction in global military expenditures and thereby free up substantial funds for systematic efforts to tackle the threat of global warming. Indeed, this could well prove the most significant outcome of a shift from confrontation to cooperation. With the threat of a new Cold War receding and the need for competitive arms diplomacy eliminated, the major energy-seeking states would be able to redirect massive sums from military accounts to the climate-friendly initiatives described above.

Reduced spending on military activities and increased investment in energy alternatives would also unleash a wave of scientific and entrepreneurial innovation, generating the ideas, inventions, and production technologies that could lead us from the now-fading Petroleum Age to the new energy epoch that must follow. Many promising concepts are now being tested in university and corporate laboratories, but without a dramatic infusion of talent and capital even the most valuable could languish for years to come. With a new national commitment, however, the country's scientists and engineers will no doubt leap at the opportunity to turn their best ideas into reality. Whereas America's current reliance on imported oil contributes to the nation's economic enfeeblement, massive investment in energy innovation of this sort could spark an economic rebirth.

Make no mistake: Rising powers/shrinking planet is a dangerous formula. Addressing the interlocking challenges of resource competition, energy shortages, and climate change will be among the most difficult problems facing the human community. If we continue to extract and consume the planet's vital resources in the same improvident fashion as in the past, we will, sooner rather than later, transform the earth into a barely habitable scene of desolation. And if the leaders of today's Great Powers behave like those of previous epochs—relying on military instruments to achieve their primary objectives—we will witness unending crisis and conflict over what remains of value on our barren wasteland.

This can be avoided only by redirecting the competitive impulses now channeled into the hunt for vital resources into a cooperative effort to develop new sources of energy and climate-friendly industrial processes. If successful, a transition of this sort would allow the major energy-consuming nations—both new and old—to face the future with confidence that their basic needs will be met without recourse to war or unleashing environmental catastrophe. We must choose this course for the sake of all humanity's children.

NOTES

PROLOGUE: THE UNOCAL AFFAIR

1. David L. Goodstein, *Out of Gas* (New York: W. W. Norton, 2004), p. 15. For a similar analysis, see Kenneth Deffeyes, *Hubbert's Peak: The Impending World Oil Shortage* (Princeton: Princeton University Press, 2001); and Paul Roberts, *The End of Oil* (Boston: Houghton Mifflin, 2004).

2. "If you want to increase your reserves, you have to buy a company," observed Adam Sieminski, an energy analyst for Deutsche Bank. Quoted in Thaddeus Herrick, "Unocal Becomes a Hot Property," *Wall Street Journal*, June 27, 2005.

3. Unocal's global reserves are detailed in its 2004 Annual Report as incorporated in its Form 10-K submitted to the U.S. Securities and Exchange Commission on March 8, 2005, electronic document accessed at www .unocal.com on March 16, 2006. See also James F. Peltz, "Chinese Firm Is Said to Be Eyeing Unocal," *Los Angeles Times*, January 7, 2005; and Jad Mouwad, "Hints of Oil Industry Mergers to Come," *New York Times*, February 2, 2005.

4. Russell Gold, "In Deal for Unocal, Chevron Gambles on High Prices," *Wall Street Journal*, August 10, 2005.

5. Quoted in Gold, "In Deal for Unocal, Chevron Gambles on High Prices."

6. Edmund L. Andrews, "Capital Nearly Speechless on Big China Bid," *New York Times*, June 24, 2005. See also Neil King Jr., Greg Hitt, and Jeffrey Ball, "Oil Battle Sets Showdown Over China," *Wall Street Journal*, June 24, 2005.

7. For background on CNOOC, see Kate Linebaugh, et al., "After Earlier

Fumbles, Cnooc Uses Wall Street Tactics in Unocal Bid," *Wall Street Journal,* June 27, 2005; and Joseph Kahn, "A Deft Balance in Orchestrating China's Oil Offer," *New York Times,* July 7, 2005. In the discussion that follows, "CNOOC" will generally refer to CNOOC Ltd., the offshoot.

8. Quoted in David Barboza and Andrew Ross Sorkin, "Chinese Oil Giant in Takeover Bid for U.S. Company," *New York Times,* June 23, 2005.

9. Ibid. See also Paula Dittrick, "CNOOC Bid Raises Stakes in the Takeover of Unocal," *Oil and Gas Journal,* June 27, 2005, pp. 25–27; and Russell Gold, Matt Pottinger, and Dennis K. Berman, "China's Cnooc Lobs in Rival Bid to Acquire Unocal," *Wall Street Journal,* June 23, 2005.

10. See Russell Gold and Greg Hitt, "Chevron Labors to Derail Rival's Unocal Bid," *Wall Street Journal,* June 30, 2005; Steve Lohr, "The Big Tug of War Over Unocal," *New York Times,* July 6, 2005; and Jonathan Weisman, "In Washington, Chevron Works to Scuttle Chinese Bid," *Washington Post,* July 16, 2005. In 2007, the Federalist Group changed its name to Ogilvy Government Relations.

11. Lohr, "The Big Tug of War Over Unocal."

12. While there is no question that Chevron officials and their well-paid lobbyists did everything in their power to stoke the rising anti-Chinese sentiment in Washington, there were clearly many in the capital who were predisposed to counter CNOOC in order to curb China's growth and protect America's vital energy assets. "What we're seeing in Washington shows the hysteria about China," said William A. Reinsch, a former trade official in the Clinton administration. "It means that any deal like this is going to be debated in a red-hot rhetorical atmosphere." Quoted in Lohr, "The Big Tug of War Over Unocal."

13. Quoted in Brody Mullins and Dennis K. Berman, "Republicans Urge White House to Review Cnooc's Unocal Bid," *Wall Street Journal,* June 29, 2005.

14. House Resolution 344, June 30, 2005. For text and discussion, see *Congressional Record,* June 30, 2005, pp. H5570–77.

15. The body created for this purpose, the Committee on Foreign Investment in the United States (CFIUS), has rarely called for such action; only once, in its twenty-seven years of existence, has its call for blockage of a proposed investment been endorsed by the president. Nevertheless, CNOOC's opponents in Congress saw in this measure an opportunity to hobble and eventually kill the deal. For background, see Steve Lohr, "Unocal Bid Opens Up New Issues of Security," *New York Times,* July 13, 2005; and Jonathan Peterson, "Panel Has a Big Say in Foreign Purchases," *Los Angeles Times,* July 5, 2005. The Exon-Florio amendment was added to the Defense Production Act of 1950 as Section 721 by the Omnibus Trade and Competitiveness Act of 1988.

16. Prepared statement before the House Armed Services Committee, Hearing on the National Security Implications of the Possible Merger of the China National Offshore Oil Corporation with the Unocal Corporation, Washington, D.C., July 13, 2005, electronic document accessed at www. globalsecurity.org on October 31, 2007.

17. Even the advice of Alan Greenspan, the legendary chairman of the Federal Reserve Board, was ignored in this instance: "It is essential that we not put . . . our future at risk with a step back to protectionism," he testified on June 23, 2005. Quoted in King, Hitt, and Ball, "Oil Battle Sets Showdown Over China."

18. A *Wall Street Journal*/NBC poll taken in mid-July disclosed that 73 percent of Americans opposed the takeover of Unocal by a Chinese firm, further energizing the deal's critics in Congress. See Dennis K. Berman, Greg Hitt, and Matt Pottinger, "U.S. Public Is Hostile to Cnooc Bid," *Wall Street Journal*, July 14, 2005. See also Joel Havemann and Elizabeth Douglass, "Lawmakers Seek to Stop CNOOC Bid," *Los Angeles Times*, July 18, 2005.

19. Quoted in Edward Alden and Stephanie Kirchgaessner, "CNOOC Faces Wall of Opposition from U.S.," *Financial Times*, July 8, 2005.

20. In a harshly worded statement, the company denounced "the unprecedented political opposition" in the United States and a hostile "political environment" that made it "very difficult for us" to succeed in the bidding war. As quoted in Matt Pottinger, et al., "Cnooc Drops Offer for Unocal, Exposing U.S.-China Tensions," *Wall Street Journal*, August 3, 2005.

21. George W. Bush, Remarks at Capital City Partnership, St. Paul, Minn., May 17, 2001, electronic document accessed at www.whitehouse.gov on October 31, 2007.

CHAPTER 1: ALTERED STATES

1. George W. Bush, address at the Citadel, Charleston, S.C., September 23, 1999, electronic document accessed at www.citadel.edu on May 5, 2007.

2. See Deb Riechmann, "Bush Urges Saudis to Boost Oil Production," *Los Angeles Times*, April 25, 2005.

3. Richard G. Lugar, address at the Brookings Institution, Washington, D.C., March 13, 2005, electronic document accessed at lugar.senate.gov on March 14, 2006.

4. U.S. Department of Energy, Energy Information Administration (DoE/EIA), "U.S. Imports by Country of Origin," Total Crude Oil and Imports, as of July 26, 2007, electronic document accessed at www.eia.doe .gov on August 26, 2007.

5. DoE/EIA, *International Energy Outlook 2007* (Washington, D.C.: DoE/EIA, 2006), Table A1, p. 83. (Hereinafter cited as DoE/EIA, *IEO 2007*.)

6. Thomas D. Crowley, et al., *Transforming the Way the DoD Looks at Energy*, Report FT602T1, April 2007, LMI Government Consulting, pp. 2–6. See also Bryan Bender, "Pentagon Study Says Oil Reliance Strains Military," *Boston Globe*, May 1, 2007.

7. International Energy Agency (IEA), *World Energy Outlook 2007* (Paris: IEA, 2007), pp. 41, 43. (Hereinafter cited as IEA, *WEO 2007*.)

8. Data for 1990–2006 from BP, *Statistical Review of World Energy June 2007* (London: BP, 2007), p. 40; projection for 2030 from DoE/EIA, *IEO 2007*, Table A1, p. 83.

9. The author first laid out this argument in Michael Klare, "Entering the Tough Oil Era," TomDispatch.com, August 16, 2007, posted at www.tomdispatch.com/post/174829. See also Goodstein, *Out of Gas*.

10. DoE/EIA, *IEO 2007*, Table A2, p. 85.

11. For background on oil in its various forms (and the future supply thereof), see U.S. Government Accountability Office (GAO), *Crude Oil: Uncertainty About Future Oil Supply Makes It Important to Develop a Strategy for Addressing a Peak and Decline in Oil Production* (Washington, D.C.: GAO, February 2007). For further discussion, see Russell Gold and Ann Davis, "Oil Officials See Limit Looming on Production," *Wall Street Journal*, November 19, 2007.

12. For a discussion of "energy security" and a spectrum of views on its characteristics, see Jan H. Kalicki and David L. Goldwyn, eds., *Energy and Security* (Washington, D.C.: Woodrow Wilson Center Press, 2005). See also IEA, *WEO 2007*, pp. 159–90.

13. The author first laid out this argument in "Petro-Power and the Nuclear Renaissance: Two Faces of an Emerging Energo-fascism (Part 2)," TomDispatch.com, posted January 16, 2007, accessed at www.tomdispatch.com/post/157744.

14. Matthew Higgins, Thomas Klitgaard, and Robert Lerman, "Recycling Petrodollars," *Current Issues in Economics and Finance*, Federal Reserve Bank of New York, vol. 12, no. 9 (December 2006), p. 1.

15. See Guy Chazan, "Fueled by Oil Money, Russian Economy Soars," *Wall Street Journal*, March 13, 2007; Eric Dash, "Citi to Announce Big Cuts and New Investors," *New York Times*, January 15, 2008; and Steven R. Weisman, "Oil Producers See the World and Buy It Up," *New York Times*, November 28, 2007.

16. See Jeffrey Gettleman, "War in Sudan? Not Where the Oil Wealth Flows," *New York Times*, October 24, 2006.

17. For background and discussion, see James A. Baker III Institute for Public Policy (Baker Institute), "The Changing Role of National Oil Companies in

International Energy Markets," *Baker Institute Policy Report,* Rice University, March 2007; Robert Pirog, *The Role of National Oil Companies in the International Oil Market,* CRS Report for Congress (Washington, D.C.: Library of Congress, Congressional Research Service, August 21, 2007).

18. As the Congressional Research Service (CRS) reported in 2007, "[it is] not likely that the reserve positions of the companies will change in favor of the international oil companies in the future." Pirog, *The Role of National Oil Companies,* p. 4.

19. Ibid., pp. 5–7.

20. Baker Institute, "The Changing Role of National Oil Companies," p. 10.

21. On Venezuela, see, for example, David Luhnow and Peter Millard, "How Chávez Aims to Weaken U.S.," *Wall Street Journal,* May 1, 2007. On Russia, see chapter 4.

22. See DoE/EIA, "Venezuela," Country Analysis Brief, September 2006, electronic document accessed at www.eia.doe.gov on May 6, 2007.

23. For discussion, see Baker Institute, "The Changing Role of National Oil Companies," pp. 10–11. See also Peter Behr, "Energy Nationalism," *CG Global Researcher,* vol. 1, no. 7 (July 2007), pp. 151–80.

24. On Gazprom, see Marc Champion, "Russian Energy Grip Splits EU," *Wall Street Journal,* November 13, 2006; on Aramco-Sinopec, see "China, Saudi Arabia Strengthen Agreement on Refinery Ventures," *Wall Street Journal,* April 24, 2006.

25. For background and discussion, see Michael T. Klare, *Resource Wars: The New Landscape of Global Conflict* (New York: Metropolitan Books, 2001), pp. 81–108; and Klare, *Blood and Oil: The Dangers and Consequences of America's Growing Dependency on Imported Petroleum* (New York: Metropolitan Books, 2004), pp. 132–39.

26. See chapter 5.

27. For background on these developments, see Geoffrey Jones, *The State and the Emergence of the British Oil Industry* (London: MacMillan, 1981), pp. 129–76.

28. For an account of these developments, see Daniel Yergin, *The Prize: The Epic Quest for Oil, Money, and Power* (New York: Simon and Schuster, 1991), pp. 303–39.

29. For background and discussion, see ibid., pp. 389–560.

30. For background, see Klare, *Blood and Oil,* pp. 133–35, 137–38, 155, 170.

31. See chapter 4.

32. See Simon Romero and Clifford Krauss, "High Stakes: Chávez Plays the Oil Card," *New York Times,* April 10, 2007. For background on PdVSA, see

David R. Mares and Nelson Altamirano, *Venezuela's PdVSA and World Energy Markets* (Houston: James A. Baker III Institute for Public Policy, Rice University, 2007).

33. See, for example, Behr, "Energy Nationalism," p. 153.

34. The author first argued this point in "Resurgent Resource Nationalism at a Time of Mounting Energy Insufficiency," a working paper prepared for delivery at the Workshop on the Militarization of Energy Security convened by the Long-Range Assessment Unit of the National Intelligence Council at the Naval Postgraduate School, Monterey, Calif., November 30, 2006.

35. For background and discussion, see Klare, *Resource Wars*, pp. 173–82.

36. Flynt Leverett and Pierre Noël, "The New Axis of Oil," *National Interest* (Summer 2006), p. 63.

37. Prepared testimony of Mikkal E. Herberg, Hearing on Energy Trends in China and India: Implications for the United States, Senate Foreign Relations Committee (SFRC), July 26, 2005, electronic document accessed at foreign.senate.gov on March 30, 2006.

38. The author first made this argument in "Resurgent Resource Nationalism."

39. National Energy Policy Development Group (NEPDG), *National Energy Policy* (Washington, D.C.: NEPDG, May 17, 2001), chap. 8, pp. 4, 6. For a thorough analysis of the NEP, see Klare, *Blood and Oil*, pp. 56–73.

40. See Ilan Greenberg and Andrew E. Kramer, "Cheney, Visiting Kazakhstan, Wades into Energy Battle," *New York Times*, May 6, 2006.

41. For background, see Klare, *Blood and Oil*, pp. 99–105.

42. Agency for Natural Resources and Energy, "New National Energy Strategy," press release, May 31, 2006, electronic document accessed at www.meti.go.jp on July 8, 2006. The 15 percent figure for the current situation is from Masaki Hisane, "Japan's New Energy Strategy," *Asia Times*, January 13, 2006, electronic document accessed at www.japanfocus.org on January 24, 2006.

43. Masaki Hisane, "Japan's New Energy Strategy," *Asia Times*, January 13, 2006, electronic document accessed at www.japanfocus.org on January 24, 2006.

44. Teikoku Oil Company, "Information about Business Integration with INPEX," electronic document accessed at www.teikokuoil.co.jp on July 8, 2006.

45. See chapter 6.

46. Richard G. Lugar, address at the Brookings Institution, March 13, 2006.

47. *Congressional Record*, June 30, 2005, p. H5574. Representative Pombo lost his bid for reelection in the 2006 election cycle.

48. Schlesinger testimony, SFRC, November 16, 2005.

49. Crowley, et al., *Transforming the Way the DoD Looks at Energy*, pp. 2–9.

50. For discussion, see John D. McKinnon, John J. Fialka, and Yochi J. Dreazen, "Bush Says Plan Would Wean U.S. from Foreign Oil," *Wall Street Journal*, January 24, 2007; Fialka, "Energy Mandates Fuel a Rift," *Wall Street Journal*, January 26, 2007; and Greg Hitt, "Can Bush Reach Ethanol Goal with Proposed Spending Plan?" *Wall Street Journal*, February 7, 2007.

51. Schlesinger testimony, SFRC, November 16, 2005.

52. For background and discussion, see Klare, *Blood and Oil*, pp. 56–112. See also chapter 3.

53. See Keith Bradsher and Christopher Pala, "China Ups the Ante in Its Bid for Oil," *New York Times*, August 23, 2005.

54. Ben Dummett, "Chinese Firms to Pay $1.42 Billion for EnCana Oil Assets in Ecuador," *Wall Street Journal*, September 14, 2005.

55. As quoted in Keith Bradsher, "Alert to Gains by China, India Is Making Energy Deals," *New York Times*, January 17, 2005.

56. Ibid. See also Keith Bradsher, "2 Big Appetites Take Seats at the Oil Table," *New York Times*, February 18, 2005; and John Larkin, "Indian Firm Bids About $2 Billion for Nigerian Oil," *Wall Street Journal*, December 16, 2005.

57. See chapter 4 for more details.

58. See Andrew E. Kramer, "Kazakhs Suspend Permits for Oil Field," *New York Times*, August 28, 2007; Gabriel Kahn and Liam Moloney, "Kazakhs Ratchet Up Pressure on Eni Over Oil Field," *Wall Street Journal*, September 7, 2007; Guy Chazan, "Kazakh Official Urges Halt of Chevron Oil Project," *Wall Street Journal*, September 21, 2007; Chazan and Kahn, "Kazakhs Seek Bigger Slice," *Wall Street Journal*, October 23, 2007; and Chazan, "Kashagan Dispute Ends as State Doubles Stake," *Wall Street Journal*, January 14, 2008.

59. On China's role in arming the Sudanese military, see Human Rights Watch (HRW), *Sudan, Oil, and Human Rights* (New York and Washington, D.C.: HRW, 2003), pp. 478–86, 606–7.

60. As quoted in Andrew E. Kramer, "Russia Criticized for Withdrawing Sakhalin Oil Permit," *New York Times*, September 20, 2005.

CHAPTER 2: SEEKING MORE, FINDING LESS

1. DoE/EIA, *IEO 2007*, Table A1, p. 83.

2. Ibid., Table A2, p. 85.

3. Ibid.

4. Donald F. Fournier and Eileen T. Westervelt, *Energy Trends and Their*

Implications for U.S. Army Installation, ERDC/CERL TR-05-21 (Washington, D.C.: U.S. Army Corps of Engineers, Engineer Research and Development Center, Construction Engineering Research Laboratory, September 2005), p. iv.

5. The author first laid out this argument in Klare, "Entering the Tough Oil Era." For a similar analysis, see Gold and Davis, "Oil Officials See Limit Looming on Production."

6. Robert L. Hirsch, "The Inevitable Peaking of World Oil Production," *Bulletin* of the Atlantic Council of the United States, vol. 26, no. 3 (October 2005), p. 1.

7. DoE/EIA, *Annual Energy Review 2004,* Table 11, p. 317, electronic document accessed at www.eia.doe.gov on June 24, 2006. (Hereinafter cited as DoE/EIA, *AER 2004.*)

8. For a list of giant oil fields and their dates of discovery, see Matthew R. Simmons, *Twilight in the Desert* (Hoboken, N.J.: John Wiley, 2005), p. 373.

9. BP Amoco, *BP Amoco Statistical Review of World Energy June 2000* (London: BP Amoco, 2000), p. 4.

10. DoE/EIA, *International Energy Outlook 2003* (Washington, D.C.: DoE/EIA, 2003), Tables A4 and D1, pp. 185, 235. (Hereinafter cited as DoE/EIA, *IEO 2003.*)

11. For discussion of this controversy, see GAO, *Crude Oil,* pp. 12–26. See also Javier Blas, "World Will Face Oil Crunch 'in Five Years,' " *Financial Times,* July 10, 2007; Ed Crooks, "Total Chief Warns on Oil Output," *Financial Times,* November 1, 2007; and Gold and Davis, "Oil Officials See Limit Looming on Production."

12. See Mike Bahorich, "End of Oil? No, It's a New Day Dawning," *Oil & Gas Journal,* August 21, 2006, p. 30; and David Luhnow, "Mexico's Oil Output May Decline," *Wall Street Journal,* February 9, 2006.

13. See Gold and Davis, "Oil Officials See Limit Looming on Production."

14. DoE/EIA, *IEO 2007,* Table G1, p. 187.

15. Simmons, *Twilight in the Desert,* p. xv.

16. DoE/EIA, *International Energy Outlook 2004* (Washington, D.C.: DoE/EIA: 2004), p. 37. (Hereinafter cited as DoE/EIA, *IEO 2004.*) This was in reference to an article citing Simmons's assessment of Saudi capacity in Jeff Gerth, "Forecasts of Rising Oil Demand Challenges Tired Saudi Fields," *New York Times,* February 24, 2004.

17. DoE/EIA, *IEO 2004,* Table D1, p. 213; DoE/EIA, *International Energy Outlook 2005* (Washington, D.C.: DoE/EIA: 2005), Table E1, p. 157; (Hereinafter cited as DoE/EIA *IEO 2005.*) DoE/EIA, *International Energy*

Outlook 2006 (Washington, D.C.: DoE/EIA: 2006), Table E1, p. 155. (Hereinafter cited as DOE/EIA, *IEO 2006.*)

18. On Saudi preferences, see Bob Williams, "Saudi Oil Minister Al-Naimi Sees Kingdom Sustaining Oil Supply Linchpin Role for Decades," *Oil & Gas Journal,* April 5, 2004, pp. 18–24. On doubts as to their motives, see Jeff Gerth, "Doubts Raised on Saudi Vow for More Oil," *New York Times,* October 27, 2005; and Gerth, "Forecast of Rising Oil Demand Challenges Tired Saudi Fields."

19. See Bahorich, "End of Oil? No, It's a New Day Dawning," pp. 30–34. See also Jad Mouawad, "Oil Explorers Searching Ever More Remote Areas," *New York Times,* September 9, 2004; and Gold and Davis, "Oil Officials See Limit Looming on Production."

20. See Fournier and Westervelt, *Energy Trends and Their Implications for U.S. Army Installation,* fig. 3, p. 13. See also Kenneth S. Deffeyes, *Beyond Oil* (New York: Hill and Wang, 2003), pp. 47–51.

21. IEA, *WEO 2007,* p. 95 (in year-2006 dollars).

22. This version appeared in *The New Yorker,* October 31, 2005, p. 5.

23. As cited in Blas, "World Will Face Oil Crunch 'in Five Years.'"

24. See James Kanter, "Rise in World Oil Use and a Possible Shortage of Supplies Are Seen in Next 5 Years," *New York Times,* July 10, 2007. The report's findings were summarized in IEA, *WEO 2007,* pp. 83–85.

25. National Petroleum Council (NPC), *Facing the Hard Truths About Energy,* draft report (Washington, D.C.: NPC, July 18, 2007), p. 1. See also Jad Mouawad, "A Warning About Future of Energy," *New York Times,* July 19, 2007.

26. NPC, *Facing the Hard Truths About Energy,* p. 26.

27. Julian Darley, *High Noon for Natural Gas* (White River Junction, Vt.: Chelsea Green, 2004), pp. 57–58.

28. For an assessment of these sources, see Deffeyes, *Beyond Oil,* pp. 99–123. See also GAO, *Crude Oil,* pp. 18–21, 52–55.

29. As cited in Crooks, "Total Chief Warns on Oil Output."

30. For discussion, see GAO, *Crude Oil,* pp. 49–61; Mouawad, "Oil Explorers Searching Ever More Remote Areas"; Jad Mouawad, "A Quest for Energy in the Globe's Remote Places," *New York Times,* October 9, 2007; and Clifford Krauss, et al., "As Polar Ice Turns to Water, Dreams of Treasure Abound," *New York Times,* October 10, 2005.

31. DoE/EIA, "Natural Gas," from *IEO 2005,* July 2005, electronic document accessed at www.eia.doe.gov/oiaf/ieo/nat_gas.html on June 1, 2006.

32. BP, *Statistical Review of World Energy June 2007,* p. 27.

33. DoE/EIA, *IEO 2006*, Table A2, pp. 134–36.

34. DoE/EIA, *IEO 2007*, Table A6, p. 89.

35. For further discussion of Europe's and Asia's demands for energy, see "Natural Gas," from DoE/EIA, *IEO 2005*.

36. DoE/EIA, *IEO 2007*, Table A6, p. 89.

37. Ibid.

38. For background on these supplies, see Deffeyes, *Beyond Oil*, pp. 66–76.

39. BP, *Statistical Review of World Energy June 2007*, p. 22.

40. As cited in Darley, *High Noon for Natural Gas*, pp. 91–92.

41. Asher Imam, Richard A. Startzman, and Maria A. Barrufet, "Multicyclic Hubbert Model Shows Global Conventional Gas Output Peaking in 2019," *Oil & Gas Journal*, August 16, 2004, pp. 20–28.

42. This study, conducted by former Total geologist Jean Laherrère, is summarized in Bob Williams, "Debate Grows Over U.S. Gas Supply Crisis as Harbinger of Global Gas Production Peak," *Oil & Gas Journal*, July 21, 2003, p. 21. This article also examines other estimates of peak gas production.

43. For discussion of this point, see Goodstein, *Out of Gas*, pp. 23–33.

44. BP, *Statistical Review of World Energy June 2006*, p. 22.

45. For discussion of the impediments to reliance on LNG, see Darley, *High Noon for Natural Gas*, pp. 55–67.

46. For an assessment of global gas reserves by region, see ibid., pp. 94–120.

47. See Sam Fletcher, "Analysts See Problems for North American Gas Market," *Oil & Gas Journal*, February 7, 2005, pp. 30–31; Phyllis Martin, "EIA: LNG Will Supply More Than 20% of U.S. Gas by 2025," *Oil & Gas Journal*, March 28, 2005, pp. 60–64; Simon Romero, "Demand for Natural Gas Brings Big Import Plans, and Objections," *New York Times*, June 15, 2005; and Jad Mouawad, "Wary of Protests, Exxon Plans Natural Gas Terminal in the Atlantic," *New York Times*, December 12, 2007.

48. For discussion of this point, see Neela Banerjee, "Natural Gas Seems Headed the Way of Oil: More Demand, Less Supply, Higher Cost," *New York Times*, August 30, 2004.

49. For details, see chapter 4.

50. See Bhushan Bahree, Russell Gold, and Gregory L. White, "Gas Cartel Gains Traction with Alliance Set to Meet," *Wall Street Journal*, April 5, 2007; and Ayesha Daya and James Herron, "Gas Exporters to Study Cartel," *Wall Street Journal*, April 10, 2007.

51. As quoted in Daya and Herron, "Gas Exporters to Study Cartel."

52. For discussion, see Daniel Dombey, Neil Buckley, and Carola Hoyos,

"Nato Fears Russian Plans for 'Gas Opec,'" *Financial Times,* November 14, 2006; and David Wood, "Could a Future Gas OPEC Shape LNG Import Plans?" *Oil & Gas Journal,* May 28, 2007, pp. 22–34.

53. George W. Bush, Remarks at Capital City Partnership.

54. For an analysis of the 2005 bill, see Mark Holt and Carol Glover, *Energy Policy Act of 2005: Summary and Analysis of Enacted Provisions,* CRS Report to Congress (Washington, D.C.: Library of Congress, Congressional Research Service, March 8, 2006).

55. DoE/EIA, *IEO 2007,* Table A7, p. 90.

56. For background and discussion, see Elizabeth C. Economy, "The Great Leap Backward?" *Foreign Affairs,* September/October 2007, pp. 38–60. See also Keith Bradsher, "China's Green Energy Gap," *New York Times,* October 24, 2007.

57. If all come on line, nuclear-generated electricity in China will rise from 48 billion kilowatt-hours in 2004 to 329 billion in 2030, a 585 percent increase. DoE/EIA, *IEO 2007,* Table A8, p. 91. See also DoE/EIA, "China," Country Analysis Brief, August 2006, electronic document accessed at www.eia.doe.gov on August 31, 2007.

58. For a comparison of "old energy" and "new energy" systems, see Jeffrey Ball, "Handicapping the Environmental Gold Rush," *Wall Street Journal,* October 29, 2007.

59. BP, *Statistical Review of World Energy June 2007,* p. 32.

60. See Edmund L. Andrews, "Lawmakers Push for Big Subsidies for Coal Process," *New York Times,* May 29, 2007; Simon Romero, "Fuel of the Future? Some Say Coal," *New York Times,* November 20, 2004.

61. BP, *Statistical Review of World Energy June 2007,* p. 35.

62. For analysis of future demand, see DoE/EIA, "Coal," from *IEO 2005,* July 2005, electronic document accessed at www.eia.doe.gov/oiaf/ieo/coal.html on June 1, 2006. See also IEA, *WEO 2007,* pp. 126–28, 334–43, 503–10.

63. Energy Watch Group (EWG), *Coal: Resources and Future Production* (Ottobrunn, Germany: EWG, March 28, 2007), p. 4.

64. Ibid., p. 7.

65. See Kirk Johnson, "Facing the Multiple Risks of Newer, Deeper Mines," *New York Times,* August 16, 2007.

66. As paraphrased in Johnson, "Facing the Multiple Risks of Newer, Deeper Mines."

67. John M. Broder, "Rule to Expand Mountaintop Coal Mining," *New York Times,* August 23, 2007.

68. See John J. Fialka, "Nuclear Power Revival Could Encounter Hurdles,"

Wall Street Journal, December 5, 2006; and Susan Moran and Anne Raup, "A Rush for Uranium," *New York Times,* March 28, 2007.

69. The long-term demand for uranium is provided in DoE/EIA, "World Annual Uranium Requirement Projections by Region and Country, Reference Case, 2000–2020," electronic document accessed at www.eia .doe.gov/cneaf/nuclear/page/forecast/annura.html on June 5, 2006. The number of reactors is from DoE/EIA, "Electricity," from *IEO 2005,* July 2005, electronic document accessed at www.eia.doe.gov/oiaf/ieo/ electricity.html on June 8, 2006. The major producers of uranium are provided in Commodity Research Bureau (CRB), *The CRB Commodity Yearbook 2005* (Hoboken, N.J.: John Wiley, 2005), p. 293. The estimate of years remaining from existing supplies is from Fournier and Westervelt, *Energy Trends and Their Implications for U.S. Army Installation,* p. 28.

70. For discussion of this point, see Lizette Alvarez, "Finland Rekindles Interest in Nuclear Power," *New York Times,* December 12, 2005; Alan Cowell, "British Review of Energy to Include Atomic Power," *New York Times,* November 30, 2005; and Mark Henderson, "New Generation of Nuclear Reactors Promises 'Greener and Safer' Energy," *The Times* (London), January 11, 2008.

71. See John J. Fialka, "Bush Tries to Jump-Start Nuclear Power," *Wall Street Journal,* January 26, 2006; and Matthew Wald, "Uncertainty Surrounds Plans for New Nuclear Reactors," *New York Times,* June 4, 2006.

72. Rebecca Smith, "Power Producers Rush to Secure Nuclear Sites," *Wall Street Journal,* January 29, 2007. See also David Whitford, "Going Nuclear," *Fortune,* August 6, 2007, pp. 42–54.

73. Deutsche Bank, *Commodities Outlook 2006* (London: Deutsche Bank, January 13, 2006), p. 38. See also Chris Buckley, "Chance to Revive Sales Draws Nuclear Industry to China," *New York Times,* March 10, 2004.

74. Deutsche Bank, *Commodities Outlook 2006,* p. 38.

75. Tim Johnson, "Australia Signs a Sensitive Uranium Agreement with China," *San Jose Mercury News,* April 3, 2006.

76. See Jane Perlez, "Australia to Sell Uranium to China for Energy," *New York Times,* April 3, 2006; and Andrew McGregor, "Mining for Energy: China's Relations with Niger," China Brief, Jamestown Foundation, October 4, 2007, electronic document accessed at www.jamestown.org on October 4, 2007.

77. DoE/EIA, "Russia," Country Analysis Brief, January 2006, electronic document accessed at www.eia.doe.gov/emeu/cabs/russia.html on June 8, 2006.

78. Sergei Blagov, "Russia Eyes Central Asia Uranium Deposits," *Eurasia Daily Monitor,* June 6, 2006, electronic document accessed at www .jamestown.org on June 7, 2006.

79. See Fialka, "Nuclear Power Revival Could Encounter Hurdles."

80. On the risks associated with Japan's breeder program, see Shinichi Ogawa and Michael Schiffer, "Japan's Plutonium Reprocessing Dilemma," *Arms Control Today,* October 2005, pp. 20–24. On India's breeder reactor project, see Wade Boese, "Nuclear Deal Center Stage for U.S., China," *Arms Control Today,* March 2006, pp. 40–45.

81. Data for 2005 from USGS, *Minerals Yearbook 2005,* vol. 1, chap. 5 ("Aluminum"), Table 12; chap. 40 ("Iron Ore"), Table 1; chap. 21 ("Copper"), Table 22. Data for 1995 from 1995 edition.

82. See Clifford Krauss, "Commodities' Relentless Surge," *New York Times,* January 15, 2008.

83. Deutsche Bank, *Commodities Outlook 2006,* p. 7.

84. The global inventory of major minerals and international consumption rates are provided in CRB, *The CRB Commodity Yearbook* (annual).

85. Patrick Barta, "With Easy Nickel Fading Fast, Miners Go After the Tough Stuff," *Wall Street Journal,* July 12, 2006. See also Barta, "Miners' Daunting Task: Digging in Risky Zones," *Wall Street Journal,* May 31, 2007.

86. John Noble Wilford, "In a Ruined Copper Works, Evidence That Bolsters a Doubted Biblical Tale," *New York Times,* June 13, 2006.

87. For analysis and data on world copper consumption, see USGS, *Minerals Yearbook 2005,* vol. 1, chap. 21 ("Copper").

88. Deutsche Bank, *Commodities Outlook 2006,* fig. 4, p. 29.

89. Patrick Barta, "A Red-Hot Desire for Copper," *Wall Street Journal,* March 16, 2006.

90. "Many analysts believe the country is approaching its peak as old mines are depleted and mineral grades decline." Barta, "A Red-Hot Desire for Copper."

91. Barta, "A Red-Hot Desire for Copper."

92. On the Ivanhoe project, see "Oyu Tolgoi (Turquoise Hill)," electronic document accessed at www.ivanhoe-mines.com on June 15, 2006. On the Congo project, see Barta, "Miners' Daunting Task: Digging in Risky Zones."

93. Deutsche Bank, *Commodities Outlook 2006,* fig. 4, p. 29.

94. For background on these minerals and their industrial applications, see the respective entries in CRB, *The CRB Commodity Yearbook 2007* (and earlier editions).

95. Deutsche Bank, *Commodities Outlook 2006,* fig. 3, p. 29.

96. "[Because] Japan is a country lacking in minerals and depends on imports from overseas for the majority of these resources," a government Web site

explains, Tokyo "implements various measures to ensure the stable supply of mineral resources from overseas." Agency for Natural Resources and Energy, "Mineral Resources Indispensable to Our Lives and Industry," electronic document accessed at www.enecho.meti.go.jp on June 16, 2006.

97. John C. Wu, "Japan," USGS *Minerals Yearbook 2004*, vol. 3, chap. 12, pp. 1–2.

98. "Zimbabwe Signs China Energy Deal," BBC World News, June 12, 2006, electronic document accessed at www.bbc.co.uk on June 12, 2006. See also "Zim, Chinese Firms Seal Power Deal," *Sunday Times*, South Africa, June 12, 2006, electronic document accessed at www.sundaytimes.co.za on June 16, 2006.

99. See William Wallis, "China to Invest $5bn in Congo," *Financial Times*, September 19, 2007; William Wallis and Rebecca Bream, "Chinese Deal with Congo Prompts Concern," *Financial Times*, September 20, 2007.

100. As quoted in Jon Boone and Geoff Dyer, "Chinese Group Wins $3bn Rights to Afghan Copper," *Financial Times*, November 21, 2007.

101. Ron Synovitz, "Afghanistan: China's Winning Bid for Copper Rights Includes Power Plant, Railroad," Radio Free Europe/Radio Liberty, electronic document accessed at www. rferl.org on December 24, 2007.

102. For a summary of the most recent scientific findings on the likely effects of global climate change, see Intergovernmental Panel on Climate Change, "Summary for Policymakers," Report of Working Group I, Climate Change 2007, Fourth Assessment Report of the Intergovernmental Panel on Climate Change, electronic document accessed at www.ipcc.ch on August 26, 2007. (Hereinafter cited as IPCC, "Summary for Policymakers, 2007.")

103. IPCC, "Summary for Policymakers, 2007."

104. See Jad Mouawad, "No Quick Fix for Gulf Oil Operations," *New York Times*, August 31, 2005. See also Bob Tippee, "Previews of 2006 Reflect New Variable: Hurricanes," *Oil & Gas Journal*, January 2, 2006, pp. 20–28.

105. See Krauss, et al., "As Polar Ice Turns to Water, Dreams of Treasure Abound."

106. See Patrick Barta, "Crop Prices Soar, Pushing Up Cost of Food Globally," *Wall Street Journal*, April 9, 2007; Prasenjit Bhattacharya, "Ethanol Could Fuel Rise in Corn," *Wall Street Journal*, January 16, 2007; Lauren Etter, Julie Jargon, and Conor Dougherty, "Ethanol Push Adds to Forces Lifting Food Costs," *Wall Street Journal*, April 16, 2007; and C. Ford Runge and Benjamin Senauer, "How Biofuels Could Starve the Poor," *Foreign Affairs*, vol. 86, no. 3 (May–June 2007), pp. 41–53.

107. For discussion, see GAO, *Crude Oil*, pp. 29–30. See also Greg Hitt, "Can Bush Reach Ethanol Goal with Proposed Spending Plan?" *Wall Street Journal*, February 7, 2007; Matthew L. Wald and Alexei Barrionuevo, "Chasing a Dream Made of Weeds," *New York Times*, April 17, 2007.

108. For an assessment of the impact of global warming on human communities, see Intergovernmental Panel on Climate Change (IPCC), *Climate Change 2007: Impacts, Adaptation and Vulnerability*, Report of Working Group II of the Fourth Assessment Report of the IPCC (Cambridge: Cambridge University Press, 2007).

CHAPTER 3: THE "CHINDIA" CHALLENGE

1. IEA, *WEO 2007*, pp. 41, 43.

2. Soong Ch'ing-ling (Song Qingling), "Shanghai's New Day Has Dawned," May 26, 1950, as cited in John Gittings, *The Changing Face of China* (Oxford: Oxford University Press, 2005), p. 22.

3. For background on this period, see Gittings, *The Changing Face of China*, pp. 42–90.

4. For background on these developments, see ibid., pp. 90–99.

5. Deng Xiaoping, statement of September 2, 1986, as cited in ibid., p. 103.

6. For background on this period, see Gittings, *The Changing Face of China*, pp. 98–118, 208–22.

7. Ibid., p. 101.

8. World Bank Group (WBG), World Development Indicators, electronic data accessed at web.worldbank.org on October 23, 2007.

9. See James J. Areddy, "China Revises Economic Data Sharply Upward," *Wall Street Journal*, December 10, 2005; David Barboza and Daniel Altman, "That Blur? It's China, Moving Up in the Pack," *New York Times*, December 21, 2005; Keith Bradsher, "China Reports Another Year of Strong (or Even Better) Growth," *New York Times*, January 26, 2006; and Marcus Walker and Andrew Batson, "China's GDP Poised to Top Germany's as Power Shift Speeds Up," *Wall Street Journal*, July 16, 2007.

10. Quoted in "CPC Sets Blueprint for Next Five Years," Xinhua News Agency, October 12, 2005, electronic document accessed at service.china.org.cn on February 20, 2006.

11. United Nations, Department of Economic and Social Affairs, Statistics Division, *Statistical Yearbook 2002–2004* (New York: United Nations, 2005), pp. 476, 479, 505. On automobiles, see Keith Bradsher, "G.M. to Speed Up Expansion in China," *New York Times*, June 8, 2004.

12. One fifty-three-year-old woman interviewed by Keith Bradsher of the *New York Times* in Zhanjiang said that for the first half of her life, the only electrical appliance in her home was a single electric lightbulb; in 1984, however, she purchased a black-and-white television set, and in 1988 a refrigerator; by 2003 she owned an air conditioner, two color televisions, an electric rice cooker, a radio, and numerous light fixtures. Keith Bradsher, "China's

Boom Adds to Global Warming Problem," *New York Times,* October 22, 2003.

13. See David Barboza, "China Builds Its Dreams and Some Fear a Bubble," *New York Times,* October 18, 2005; and Howard W. French, "A City's Traffic Plans Are Snarled by China's Car Culture," *New York Times,* July 12, 2005.

14. To slow the migration to coastal cities and boost income in central and western China, the government has championed the development of selected interior cities. One of the principal beneficiaries of this drive is Chongqing, located 1,500 miles up the Yangtze River from Shanghai. Once a minor provincial center far removed from the hustle and bustle of eastern China, Chongqing is now a thriving metropolis of 12 million people with two airports (one under construction), numerous freeways, railways, and a port that can accommodate large ocean-going cargo ships (which are able to reach the city courtesy of the new Three Gorges Dam and associated locks, located 360 miles downstream). To propel Chongqing's growth, Beijing is spending $33 billion on 105 major infrastructure projects, including eight highways, a monorail network, new bridges across the Yangtze, a container port, and a second airport terminal; another $200 billion in investment is expected from the private sector. See Howard W. French, "Big, Gritty Chongqing, City of 12 Million, Is China's Model for the Future," *New York Times,* June 1, 2007; and Richard Tomlinson, "The New Wild West," *Fortune,* October 4, 2004, pp. 200–10.

15. As quoted in Erik Eckholm, "China's Car Shoppers Prepare for a Great Drive Forward," *New York Times,* October 7, 2001.

16. See Gordon Fairclough and Shai Oster, "As China's Auto Market Booms, Leaders Clash Over Heavy Toll," *Wall Street Journal,* June 13, 2006. The projections for 2030 are from IEA, *WEO 2007,* pp. 44, 298–303.

17. See "The Fast and the Furious," *The Economist,* November 25, 2006, pp. 63–64; Fairclough and Oster, "As China's Auto Market Booms, Leaders Clash Over Heavy Toll"; and Keith Bradsher, "G.M. Plans Shift to Small Cars for the Emerging World," *New York Times,* November 29, 2006.

18. Fairclough and Oster, "As China's Auto Market Booms, Leaders Clash Over Heavy Toll."

19. USGS, *Minerals Yearbook 2005,* vol. 1, chap. 5 ("Aluminum"), Table 16; chap. 38 ("Iron and Steel"), Table 11; and chap. 22 ("Copper"), electronic document accessed at www.usgs.gov on September 8, 2007. Data for prior years from earlier editions. (A metric ton is equal to 1000 kilograms or approximately 1.1 American tons.)

20. DoE/EIA, *IEO 2007,* Table A1, p. 83.

21. BP, *BP Statistical Review of World Energy June 2007,* p. 11 (and earlier editions).

22. DoE/EIA, *IEO 2007*, Tables A1 and A5, pp. 83 and 88.

23. For a comprehensive assessment of China's energy requirements and capabilities, see IEA, *WEO 2007*, pp. 243–421. On China's oil import requirements in 2030, see the gap between domestic production and consumption in DoE/EIA, *IEO 2007*, Tables A5 and G1, pp. 88, 187. On China's coal imports, see Richard McGregor, "Coal Imports Become China's Burning Issue," *Financial Times*, April 24, 2007.

24. IEA, *WEO 2007*, p. 45.

25. See Eric Watkins, "China, Kazakhstan Sign Oil Pipeline Agreement," *Oil & Gas Journal Online*, June 3, 2003, electronic document accessed at www.ogjonline.com on June 5, 2003.

26. For background, see DoE, *Energy Policy Act of 2005, Section 1837: National Security Review of International Energy Requirements*, prepared in accordance with Section 1837 of the Energy Policy Act of 2005 (Washington, D.C.: DoE, February 2006), pp. 11–12. (Hereinafter cited as DoE, *EPA-05 Energy Report*.) See also "Energy: Continuous Struggle with Shortage," Xinhua News Agency, October 3, 2005, electronic document accessed at service.china.org.cn on February 20, 2006; and IEA, *WEO 2007*, pp. 268–71.

27. For background on China's energy behavior and policies, see DoE/EIA, "China" 2006; IEA, *WEO 2007*, pp. 271–82.

28. DoE/EIA, *IEO 2006*, Table E1, p. 155.

29. For analysis of China's foreign energy policies, see DoE, *EPA-05 Energy Report*, pp. 16–32; Philip Andrews-Speed, Xuanli Liao, and Roland Dannreuther, *The Strategic Implications of China's Energy Needs*, Adelphi Paper no. 346 (Oxford: Oxford University Press and International Institute of Strategic Studies, 2002); Erica Strecker Downs, *China's Quest for Energy Security* (Santa Monica: RAND Corporation, 2000); and Kenneth Lieberthal and Mikkal Herberg, "China's Search for Energy Security: Implications for U.S. Policy," *NBR Analysis*, National Bureau of Asian Research, April 2006, pp. 5–42.

30. DoE, *EPA-05 Energy Report*, p. 22.

31. See chapters 3 and 5.

32. For discussion, see DoE, *EPA-05 Energy Report*, pp. 14–15, 31–32. See also Gittings, *Changing Face of China*, pp. 101–18.

33. For background and discussion, see DoE, *EPA-05 Energy Report*, pp. 33–34.

34. Flynt Leverett and Jeffrey Bader, "Managing China-U.S. Energy Competition in the Middle East," *Washington Quarterly*, Winter 2005–06, p. 191.

35. "China, Russia Ink Major Gas Deal," BBC World News, March 21, 2006, electronic document accessed at www.bbb.co.uk on March 21, 2006.

36. DoE/EIA, "Venezuela" 2006.

37. See Economy, "The Great Leap Backward?"; and James Kahn and Jim Yardley, "As China Roars, Pollution Reaches Deadly Extremes," *New York Times*, August 26, 2007.

38. For background, see Sanjaya Baru and C. Rammanohar Reddy, "Economy," in "India" entry in *South Asia 2005*, 2nd ed. (London: Europa Publications, 2005), pp. 174–85.

39. For background, see B. H. Farmer, "India," in *South Asia 2005*, pp. 163–68.

40. WBG, "Key Development Data and Statistics," electronic document accessed at web.worldbank.org on April 28, 2006.

41. For discussion, see Clay Chandler, "India's Bumpy Ride," *Fortune*, October 31, 2005, pp. 135–48. On the continuing divide between rich and poor, see Peter Wonacott, "Gandhi Influence Raises Doubt About India's Growth Strategy," *Wall Street Journal*, May 23, 2006.

42. See Keith Bradsher, "A Younger India Is Flexing Its Industrial Brawn," *New York Times*, September 1, 2006; Henry Chu, "A Tale of a Rising Tiger Chasing a Soaring Dragon," *Los Angeles Times*, May 1, 2006; Anand Giridharadas, "India, Known for Outsourcing, Expands in Industry," *New York Times*, May 19, 2006; and Peter Wonacott and P. R. Venkat, "India's Economic Growth Keeps Pace with China," *Wall Street Journal*, June 1, 2006.

43. Giridharadas, "India, Known for Outsourcing, Expands in Industry."

44. Ibid. See also Saritha Rai, "I.B.M. Will Triple Investment in India in Next Three Years," *New York Times*, June 7, 2006; and Heather Timmons, "G.M. Says It Will Make More Vehicles and Buy More Parts in India," *New York Times*, April 18, 2007.

45. As quoted in Giridharadas, "India, Known for Outsourcing, Expands in Industry."

46. Amy Waldman, "In Today's India, Status Comes with Four Wheels," *New York Times*, December 5, 2005.

47. See Heather Timmons, "In India, a $2,500 Pace Car," *New York Times*, October 12, 2007. Projection for 2030 from IEA, *WEO 2007*, p. 122.

48. Amy Waldman, "Mile by Mile, India Paves a Smoother Road to Its Future," *New York Times*, December 4, 2005.

49. DoE/EIA, *IEO 2007*, Table A1, p. 83. For background on India's energy requirements and capabilities, see IEA, *WEO 2007*, pp. 425–587.

50. DoE/EIA, *IEO 2007*, Tables A5 and A6, pp. 88, 89.

51. USGS, *Minerals Yearbook 2005*, vol. 1, chap. 21 ("Copper"), Table 22, and chap. 38 ("Iron and Steel"), Table 11, electronic document accessed at www.usgs.gov on September 8, 2007. Data for prior years from earlier editions.

52. Patrick Barta, "India Isn't Devouring Commodities—Yet," *Wall Street Journal*, January 9, 2006.

53. As quoted in Bradsher, "Alert to Gains by China, India Is Making Energy Deals." For background on India's energy policies, see IEA, *WEO 2007,* pp. 450–62.

54. As quoted in Eric Bellman, "Indian Oil Firms Scour Globe," *Wall Street Journal,* June 18, 2004.

55. See Bellman, "Indian Oil Firms Scour Globe"; Bradsher, "Alert to Gains by China, India Is Making Energy Deals"; and Andrew Browne et al., "Asian Rivals Put Pressure on Western Energy Giants," *Wall Street Journal,* January 10, 2005.

56. See John Larkin, "Iran, India Reach Accord on Work on Gas Deposits," *Wall Street Journal,* November 3, 2004; and DoE/EIA, "Venezuela" 2006.

57. See John Larkin, "India Urges Buying of Global Oil Assets," *Wall Street Journal,* August 25, 2005.

58. As quoted in John Larkin, "India and China Forge an Energy Tie," *Wall Street Journal,* August 18, 2005.

59. See Tamsin Carlisle, "India, China Win on Venture's Bid for Syria Oil Stake," *Wall Street Journal,* December 21, 2005; and Shai Oster and John Larkin, "China and India Jointly Pursue Syrian Oil Assets," *Wall Street Journal,* December 12, 2005.

60. See "Take Your Partners," *The Economist,* January 21, 2006, p. 59; and Richard McGregor, Jo Johnson, and Carola Hoyos, "China and India Forge Alliance on Oil," *Financial Times,* January 13, 2006.

61. For discussion of the attractions of and obstacles to greater Indo-Chinese economic cooperation, see Deutsche Bank, *India as a Global Power?* (Frankfurt: DB Research, December 16, 2005).

62. See Somini Sengupta and Howard W. French, "India and China Are Poised to Share a Defining Moment," *New York Times,* April 10, 2005; and Himangshu Watts, "India, China Agree to Cooperate on Energy Security," Reuters, April 11, 2005, electronic document accessed at www.reuters.com on April 12, 2005.

63. See Henry Chu, "India and China Agree There's Room for Two Giants," *Los Angeles Times,* November 22, 2006; and Saritha Rai, "India and China Work on Building Trust," *New York Times,* November 22, 2006.

64. As quoted in Jawed Naqvi, "China, India to Forge N-Cooperation," *Dawn* (Pakistan), November 22, 2006, electronic document accessed at www .dawn.com on November 22, 2006.

65. "China, India Sign Wide-Ranging Joint Declaration," *People's Daily Online,* November 22, 2006, electronic document accessed at english.people.com.cn on November 22, 2006.

66. As quoted in Jim Yardley, "Indian Leader in China Urges Closer Ties," *New York Times,* January 16, 2008.

67. See Randeep Ramesh, "Chindia, Where the World's Workshop Meets Its Office," *Guardian,* September 30, 2005, electronic document accessed at www.guardian.co.uk on December 5, 2005.

68. See chapter 7.

69. Joseph E. Lin, "China and India to Conduct First-Ever Joint Army Exercises," *China Brief,* June 13, 2007, electronic document accessed at www.jamestown.org on July 27, 2007.

70. Martin Wolf, "The World Begins to Feel the Dragon's Breath on Its Back," *Financial Times,* December 14, 2005.

71. Andrew Browne et al., "Asian Rivals Put Pressure on Western Energy Giants," *Wall Street Journal,* January 10, 2005.

72. National Intelligence Council (NIC), *Mapping the Global Future,* Report of the National Intelligence Council's 2020 Project (Washington, D.C.: U.S. Government Printing Office, December 2004), p. 62.

73. As quoted in Michael A. Fletcher, "Saudis Have No Easy Fix for Oil," Raleigh-Durham *News and Observer,* April 26, 2005.

74. As quoted in Tabassum Zakaria, "Bush-Saudi Talks Focus on Long-Range Oil Plan," Reuters, April 25, 2005, electronic document accessed at www.reuters.com on April 25, 2005.

75. As quoted in Riechmann, "Bush Urges Saudis to Boost Oil Production."

76. As quoted in Andrew Tully, "Bush, Saudi Prince to Meet to Discuss Oil, Mideast Politics," Radio Free Europe/Radio Liberty, April 25, 2005, electronic document accessed at www.rferl.org on May 15, 2006.

77. See, for example, the photograph accompanying Richard W. Stevenson, "Bush and Saudi Meet at Ranch to Discuss Oil," *New York Times,* April 26, 2005.

78. The Saudi plan "can't help but have a positive downward effect on prices and deal with some of the volatility in the market by assuring people that supply will be available as the economies grow," Hadley declared. As quoted in Stevenson, "Bush and Saudi Meet at Ranch to Discuss Oil."

79. See, for example, John D. McKinnon, "Saudis Give Bush Little Relief on Oil," *Wall Street Journal,* April 26, 2005.

80. As quoted in Steven Lee Myers, "As Economic Worries Grow, Bush Prods Saudi Arabia on High Oil Prices," *New York Times,* January 16, 2008.

CHAPTER 4: AN ENERGY JUGGERNAUGHT

1. As cited in *Financial Times,* May 8, 2006.

2. BP Amoco, *Statistical Review of World Energy June 2000* (London: BP Amoco, 2000), pp. 7, 22, 32.

3. Ibid., p. 8.

4. DoE/EIA, *IEO 2007,* Table G1, p. 187.

5. Chazan, "Fueled by Oil Money, Russian Economy Soars."

6. As cited in Steven Lee Myers, "Putin's Assertive Diplomacy Is Seldom Challenged," *New York Times,* December 27, 2006.

7. International Energy Agency (IEA), *World Energy Outlook 2004* (Paris: IEA, 2004), p. 284.

8. For a profile of the Russian energy industry, see ibid., pp. 283–328.

9. BP, *Statistical Review of World Energy June 2007,* pp. 8, 11.

10. Ibid., pp. 24, 27.

11. DoE/EIA, "Russia," Country Analysis Brief, April 2007, electronic document accessed at www.eia.doe.gov on April 24, 2006.

12. For a profile of seven leading oligarchs, see Erin E. Arvedlund, "The World; Money, if Not Power," *New York Times,* November 9, 2003. For discussion of their role in Russian politics, see Stephen Lee Myers, "Big Business Plays Largest Role in Current Russian Vote," *New York Times*, December 2, 2003.

13. My portrait of Putin is much influenced by the analysis provided by Martha Brill Olcott in *The Energy Dimension in Russian Global Strategy* (Houston: Rice University, James A. Baker III Institute for Public Policy, October 2004). See also Arkady Ostrovsky, "Energy of the State: How Gazprom Acts as Lever in Putin's Power Play," *The Economist,* March 14, 2006.

14. For background and discussion, see Olcott, *The Energy Dimension in Russian Global Strategy,* pp. 15–23.

15. Ibid., p. 17. Olcott, who first drew public attention to this document, suggests that it was not uncommon for senior political figures like Putin to enlist others to help write their dissertations and published summaries like this. "[But] whether or not Putin wrote it himself," she observes, "he obviously authorized its publication in his name and so subscribed to its contents. He endorsed its contents with knowledge of his political future."

16. As cited in ibid., pp. 17, 18.

17. As cited in ibid., p. 19.

18. Ibid.

19. As cited in ibid., pp. 19–20.

20. See Sabrina Tavernise and Timothy L. O'Brien, "Russian Tycoon Moves into Politics and Then Jail," *New York Times,* November 10, 2003.

21. See Olcott, *The Energy Dimension in Russian Global Strategy,* pp. 5–10, 13–14; Tavernise and O'Brien, "Russian Tycoon Moves into Politics and Then Jail"; Steven Lee Myers and Erin E. Arvedlund, "Moscow Freezes in

Stock of Oil Producer," *New York Times*, October 31, 2003; Timothy L. O'Brien and Arvedlund, "Putin vs. the Jailed Tycoon: Defining Russia's New Rules," *New York Times*, January 2, 2004; Timothy L. O'Brien, "The Capitalist in the Cage," *New York Times*, June 20, 2004.

22. See Seth Mydans and Erin E. Arvedlund, "Police in Russia Seize Oil Tycoon," *New York Times*, October 26, 2003; Steven Lee Myers, "Hints in Russia of Crisis Over Tycoon's Case," *New York Times*, October 30, 2003; and Arvedlund and Sabrina Tavernise, "Billionaires Aren't Targets, Putin Tells Russian Group," *New York Times*, November 15, 2003. For an editorial comment on the case, accusing Putin of involvement, see "Putin's Old-Style K.G.B. Tactics," *New York Times*, October 29, 2003.

23. Erin E. Arvedlund, "Russian Court Refreezes Shares of Yukos Unit," *New York Times*, August 10, 2004.

24. See Erin E. Arvedlund and Steven Lee Myers, "An All-but-Unknown Bidder Wins a Rich Russian Oil Stake," *New York Times*, December 20, 2005.

25. Gregory L. White and Matt Pottinger, "Rosneft Takes Over Key Unit of Yukos," *Wall Street Journal*, January 3, 2005. See also Steven Lee Myers and Andrew E. Kramer, "From Ashes of Yukos, New Russian Oil Giant Emerges," *New York Times*, March 27, 2007.

26. See Arkady Ostrovsky, "Energy of the State: How Gazprom Acts as Lever in Putin's Power Play," *Financial Times*, March 14, 2006. See also DoE/EIA, "Russia" 2007.

27. See Paula Dittrick, "Gazprom to Sell Additional Stake to Russian Government," *Oil & Gas Journal*, June 27, 2005, pp. 27–28; and Ostrovsky, "Energy of the State."

28. As quoted in Ostrovsky, "Energy of the State."

29. Gregory L. White, "Kremlin Gobbles Up Sibneft," *Wall Street Journal*, September 29, 2005. See also Kim Murphy, "As Gazprom Grows, So Does Russia's Sway," *Los Angeles Times*, October 16, 2005.

30. See "Oil's Well That Ends Well," *The Economist*, October 1, 2005, pp. 57–58; "Gazprom to Buy Controlling Stake in Sibneft," *Oil & Gas Journal*, October 10, 2005, p. 35; and White, "Kremlin Gobbles Up Sibneft."

31. DoE/EIA, "Sakhalin Island," Country Analysis Brief, April 2007, electronic document accessed at www.eia.doe.gov on April 23, 2006.

32. Ibid.

33. Ibid. See also Andrew E. Kramer, "Russians Buy Control of Oil Field," *New York Times*, December 22, 2006.

34. See Andrew E. Kramer, "A Mix of Oil and Environmentalism," *New York Times*, October 6, 2006.

35. Eric Watkins, "Russia Files Suit to Suspend Sakhalin-2 Project," *Oil & Gas*

Journal Online, electronic document accessed at www.ogjonline.com on September 6, 2006.

36. Greg Walters, "Russia Cancels Shell Permit, May Seek Better Deal," *Wall Street Journal,* September 19, 2006.

37. "We continue to believe that the aim of this campaign is to force the foreign companies to accept Russian state companies as equal or even majority partners in their projects," Rory MacFarquhar of Goldman Sachs's Moscow office observed at the time. As quoted in Kramer, "A Mix of Oil and Environmentalism." See also Kramer, "Russia Criticized for Withdrawing Sakhalin Oil Permit."

38. As cited in Eric Watkins, "Russia Moves to Suspend Sakhalin-2 Development Project," *Oil & Gas Journal,* October 2, 2006, pp. 25, 28.

39. As quoted in Eric Watkins, "Several Sakhalin-2 Pipeline Work Sections Halted," *Oil & Gas Journal Online,* electronic document accessed at www.ogjonline.com on October 25, 2006.

40. Eric Watkins, "Sakhalin-2 Water-Use Licenses Suspended," *Oil & Gas Journal Online,* electronic document accessed at www.ogjonline.com on December 8, 2006.

41. Andrew E. Kramer, "Russians Buy Control of an Oil Field," *New York Times,* December 22, 2006.

42. Ibid.

43. DoE/EIA, "Sakhalin Island" 2007.

44. "The basic point of the Sakhalin-2 is that major international oil companies will not be allowed to have majority control of any substantial or strategic assets in the Russian Federation," explained Alex Turkeltaub and Stephen Bailey of Frontier Strategy Group, a risk consultancy, in *Oil & Gas Journal.* They may be allowed to hold minority status when deemed convenient to Moscow, but otherwise will be excluded altogether. Alex Turkeltaub and Stephen Bailey, "Sakhalin-2 Deal Will Alter Business Climate, Markets," *Oil & Gas Journal,* January 15, 2007, pp. 34–35.

45. DoE/EIA, "Russia" 2007; Andrew E. Kramer, "Gazprom Intends to Develop Huge Gas Field on Its Own," *New York Times,* October 10, 2006.

46. Judy Clark and Nina Rach, "Gazprom to Develop Shtokman Alone, Pipe Gas to Europe," *Oil & Gas Journal,* October 16, 2006, pp. 20–24.

47. See Guy Chazan and David Gauthier-Villars, "Total Settles for Less, Wins Russia Project," *Wall Street Journal,* July 13, 2007; and Andrew E. Kramer, "French Oil Giant Agrees to Work on Russian Natural Gas Project," *New York Times,* July 13, 2007.

48. See Guy Chazan and Gregory L. White, "BP Set to Leave Russia Gas Project," *Wall Street Journal,* June 22, 2007; Benoit Faucon and Geoffrey Smith, "BP Unveils New Russia Deal as Gazprom Buys Venture Stake," *Wall*

Street Journal, June 23–24, 2007; and Andrew E. Kramer, "Moscow Presses BP to Sell a Big Gas Field to Gazprom," *New York Times,* June 23, 2007.

49. As quoted in Kramer, "Russia Criticized for Withdrawing Sakhalin Oil Permit."

50. See Sabrina Tavernise and Birgit Brauer, "Russia Becoming an Oil Ally," *New York Times,* October 19, 2001. The appeal of Russia as an alternative to the Middle East is also highlighted in the *National Energy Policy* of May 17, 2001. See NEPDG, *National Energy Policy 2001,* chap. 8, pp. 13–14.

51. Office of the Press Secretary, White House, "Press Conference by President Bush and Russian Federation President Putin," Brdo Castle, Brdo Pri Kranju, Slovenia, June 16, 2001, electronic document accessed at www .whitehouse.gov on September 9, 2007.

52. Office of the Press Secretary, White House, "President Bush, President Putin Announce New Energy Dialogue," May 24, 2002, electronic document accessed at www.whitehouse.gov on February 7, 2006.

53. Baker Institute, "U.S. Russia Commercial Energy Summit," *Baker Institute Study,* Rice University, February 2003.

54. Ibid.

55. As quoted in ibid., p. 3.

56. Office of the Press Secretary, White House, "Joint Statement by President Bush and President Putin on U.S.-Russian Energy Cooperation," February 24, 2005, electronic document accessed at www.whitehouse.gov on January 12, 2007.

57. For prepared statements of administration witnesses at the hearing, held on September 27, 2005, visit www.foreign.senate.gov/hearings/2005/ hrg050927p.html.

58. See Arvedlund, "U.S. Seeks Pacts with Russia to Raise Natural Gas Exports"; and Clark and Rach, "Gazprom to Develop Shtokman Alone, Pipe Gas to Europe."

59. Office of the Press Secretary, White House, "Vice President's Remarks at the 2006 Vilnius Conference," May 4, 2006, electronic document accessed at www.whitehouse.gov on September 5, 2006.

60. See Sheryl Gay Stolberg, "Chastising Putin, Bush Says Russia Derails Reform," *New York Times,* June 6, 2007.

61. See, for example, Thom Shanker, "Russian Criticizes U.S. Plan for Missile Defense System," *New York Times,* February 10, 2007; Andrew E. Kramer and Thom Shanker, "Russia Suspends Arms Agreement Over U.S. Shield," *New York Times,* July 15, 2007; Kramer, "Recalling Cold War, Russia Resumes Long-Range Sorties," *New York Times,* August 18, 2007; and

Thom Shanker and Steven Lee Myers, "Stark Differences on Arms Threaten U.S. Russia Talks," *New York Times,* October 10, 2007.

62. Ministry of Foreign Affairs of Japan, "Japan-Russia Action Plan," January 10, 2003, electronic document accessed at www.mofa.go.jp on July 12, 2006.

63. Ministry of Foreign Affairs of the People's Republic of China, "China and Russia Finalize Petroleum and Natural Gas Cooperation," September 24, 2004, electronic document accessed at www.fmprc.gov.cn on July 12, 2006.

64. See Martin Fackler, "Japan May Win Siberian Pipeline Deal," *Wall Street Journal,* December 1, 2004.

65. This argument was reportedly made by Japanese diplomats during a visit by Koizumi to Russia's Far East in January 2003. See James Brooke, "Koizumi Visits Energy-Rich Russian Region, Seeking Oil," *New York Times,* January 13, 2003.

66. See James Brooke, "A New Turn for Siberian Pipeline," *New York Times,* January 21, 2005; and Eric Watkins, "Japan, Russia Start Talks on Oil Pipeline Details," *Oil & Gas Journal,* January 24, 2005, pp. 26–28.

67. Watkins, "Japan, Russia Start Talks on Oil Pipeline Details," p. 26.

68. As cited in David Holley, "Russia, China Team Up to Assail U.S. Foreign Policy," *Los Angeles Times,* July 2, 2005.

69. See DoE/EIA, "Russia" 2006; "Work Planned on First Part of Taishet-Nakhodka Line," *Oil & Gas Journal,* June 13, 2005, pp. 32–33; and Eric Watkins, "Japan, Russia Agree to Two-Stage Pipeline to Pacific," *Oil & Gas Journal,* November 28, 2005, pp. 24–25.

70. See David Pilling and Isabel Gorst, "Tokyo Threat to Withdraw from $11 Bn Oil Pipeline," *Financial Times,* April 30–May 1, 2005.

71. "Roundup: Koizumi, Putin Fail to Solve Islands Dispute Issue," Xinhua News Agency, November 22, 2005, electronic document accessed at english.people.com.cn on July 12, 2006.

72. Ministry of Foreign Affairs of Japan, "Press Conference 22 November 2005," electronic document accessed at www.mofa.go.jp on July 12, 2006.

73. As cited in Shai Oster and Gregory L. White, "Beijing and Moscow Agree to Widen Energy Ties," *Wall Street Journal,* March 22, 2006.

74. See Andrew E. Kramer, "Russia's Energy Roadshow Is Taken for a Spin in China," March 22, 2006.

75. DoE/EIA, "Russia" 2007. See also Eric Watkins, "ESPO Pipeline Project on Track, Energy Minister Says," *Oil & Gas Journal Online,* July 10, 2007, electronic document accessed at www.ogjonline.com on July 13, 2007.

76. For background and discussion, see Nikolai Sokov, "The Ukrainian Gas

Crisis Revisited," *Current History,* October 2006, pp. 348–51; and Marc Campion and Guy Chazan, "Russia's Gas Diplomacy Fuels Realignment of Former Soviet Bloc," *Wall Street Journal,* January 30, 2006.

77. For background on these developments, see Sokov, "Ukrainian Gas Crisis Revisited," pp. 348–49. See also Andrew E. Kramer, "Russia Cuts Off Gas to Ukraine in Cost Dispute," *New York Times,* January 2, 2006; Kramer, "Russia Restores Most of Gas Cut to Ukraine Line," *New York Times,* January 3, 2006; and Kramer, "Ukraine Concedes It Took Gas from Pipeline but Says It Had the Contractual Right," *New York Times,* January 4, 2006.

78. For background on these developments, see Neil Buckley and Arkady Ostrovsky, "Russia Ready to Cut Off Belarus and Georgia Gas," *Financial Times,* December 14, 2006; and Buckley, "Putin Turns on Close Ally with a Double Energy Blow," *Financial Times,* December 14, 2006.

79. Arkady Ostrovsky, "Georgia Agrees to Gazprom Price," *Financial Times,* December 23–24, 2006; and Alan Cullison, "Belarus Yields to Russia," *Wall Street Journal,* January 2, 2007.

80. See Andrew E. Kramer, "Resolving a Supply Dispute, Armenia to Buy Russian Gas," *New York Times,* April 7, 2006.

81. Gregory L. White, "Gazprom Extends Its Reach in Europe," *Wall Street Journal,* June 23, 2006.

82. "Eni, Gazprom Sign Energy Deal," *International Herald Tribune,* November 14, 2006.

83. Quoted in White, "Gazprom Extends Its Reach in Europe."

84. For discussion, see Champion, "Russian Energy Grip Splits EU."

85. Cullison, "Belarus Yields to Russia."

86. Andrew E. Kramer, "New Pipeline Will Bypass the Bosporus but Involve Russia," *New York Times,* March 16, 2007; and Judy Dempsey, "Russia Signs Deal for Gas Pipeline Along Caspian Sea," *New York Times,* December 21, 2007.

87. Vladimir Socor, "Gazprom Achieves an Anschluss of Austria," *Eurasia Daily Monitor,* May 29, 2007, electronic document accessed at www.jamestown.org on May 30, 2007.

88. Theodor Troev and Ed Crooks, "Bulgaria Backs Putin's Plans for Gas Pipeline to Rival EU's," *Financial Times,* January 19–20, 2008.

89. See Ilan Greenberg, "Russia Will Get Control of Central Asian Gas Pipeline," *New York Times,* May 13, 2007; and Judy Dempsey, "Russia Signs Deal for Gas Pipeline Along Caspian Sea," *New York Times,* December 21, 2007.

90. C. J. Chivers, "Eyeing Future Wealth, Russians Plant the Flag on the Arctic Seabed, Below the Polar Cap," *New York Times,* August 3, 2007.

91. As quoted in C. J. Chivers, "President Putin Talkes of the Future Under Premier Putin," *New York Times*, February 15, 2008.

CHAPTER 5: DRAINING THE CASPIAN

1. DoE/EIA, "Caspian Sea," Country Analysis Brief, January 2007, electronic document accessed at www.eia.doe.gov on January 3, 2007.

2. DoE/EIA, *IEO 2007*, Table G1, p. 187.

3. For background, see DoE/EIA, "Caspian Sea" 2007; Rosemarie Forsythe, *The Politics of Oil in the Caucasus and Central Asia*, Adelphi Paper no. 300 (Oxford: Oxford University Press and International Institute for Strategic Studies, 1996); Klare, *Resource Wars*, pp. 81–108; and Julia Nanay, "Russia and the Caspian Sea Region," in Kalicki and Goldwyn, *Energy and Security*, pp. 127–47.

4. For background on this period, see Yergin, *The Prize*, pp. 58–72, 132–33, 182–83.

5. See ibid., pp. 334–39.

6. Guy Chazan, "From Boom to Bust and Back," *Wall Street Journal*, November 29, 2005.

7. BP Amoco, *Statistical Review of World Energy June 2000*, p. 7.

8. U.S. Department of State, *Caspian Region Energy Development Report*, Report to the House International Relations Committee Pursuant to H.R. 3610, April 15, 1997, p. 1.

9. Thus, in a July 1997 speech on U.S. interests in the Caspian, Deputy Secretary of State Strobe Talbott declared that "it would matter profoundly to the United States" if U.S. energy firms were denied access to "an area that sits on as much as 200 billion barrels of oil." Talbott, "A Farewell to Flashman: American Policy in the Caucasus and Central Asia," address delivered at the Johns Hopkins School of Advanced International Studies, Washington, D.C., July 21, 1997, electronic document accessed at www .state.gov on August 14, 1997.

10. DoE/EIA, "Caspian Sea Region," Country Analysis Brief, June 2000, electronic document accessed at www.eia.doe.gov on July 12, 2000.

11. DoE/EIA, "Caspian Sea," Country Analysis Brief, September 2005, electronic document accessed at www.eia.doe.gov on May 18, 2006.

12. DoE/EIA, "Caspian Sea" 2007. Additional data from DoE/EIA, *IEO 2007*, Table G1, p. 187.

13. BP, *Statistical Review of World Energy June 2007*, p. 22.

14. For discussion of the Caspian's potential as a natural gas supplier, see DoE/EIA, "Caspian Sea" 2007.

15. Ibid.

16. DoE/EIA, "Azerbaijan," Country Analysis Brief, August 2006, electronic document accessed at www.eia.doe.gov on August 11, 2006. For background on the ACG project, see Forsythe, *The Politics of Oil in the Caucasus and Central Asia,* pp. 39–41.

17. DoE/EIA, "Kazakhstan," Country Analysis Brief, October 2006, electronic document accessed at www.eia.doe.gov on August 8, 2006.

18. Ibid.

19. Ibid. See also Mark J. Kaiser and Allan G. Pulsipher, "Kazakhstan's Outlook 1—High Costs, Uncertainty Challenge Operators in Promising Kazakhstan," *Oil & Gas Journal,* July 3, 2006, pp. 39–44.

20. DoE/EIA, "Kazakhstan" 2006.

21. See also Kaiser and Pulsipher, "Kazakhstan's Outlook 1," pp. 43–44.

22. DoE/EIA, "Kazakhstan" 2006.

23. See Kramer, "Kazakhs Suspend Permits for Oil Field"; Guy Chazan, "Kazakh Official Urges Halt of Chevron Oil Project," *Wall Street Journal,* September 21, 2007; Andrew E. Kramer, "Report Stirs Concern Kazakh Oil Deal May Be Scuttled," *New York Times,* January 12, 2008; and Kramer, "Capitalizing on Oil's Rise, Kazakhstan Expands Stake in Huge Offshore Project."

24. DoE/EIA, "Caspian Sea" 2007.

25. Ibid.

26. For background on the Tengiz deal, see Forsythe, *The Politics of Oil in the Caucasus and Central Asia,* pp. 37–39; and Dan Morgan and David B. Ottaway, "Vast Kazakh Field Stirs U.S.-Russian Rivalry," *Washington Post,* October 6, 1998.

27. Chevron currently owns 50 percent of the Tengiz field; Exxon Mobil owns another 25 percent; KazMunaiGaz, 20 percent; and LukArco, 5 percent. DoE/EIA, "Kazakhstan" 2006.

28. Forsythe, *Politics of Oil in the Caucasus and Central Asia,* p. 38.

29. For a thorough airing of U.S. policy during the Clinton period, see U.S. Congress, Senate, Committee on Foreign Relations, Subcommittee on International Economic Policy (SFRC/SIEP), *U.S. Economic and Strategic Interests in the Caspian Sea Region,* Hearing, 105th Congress, 1st Session, October 23, 1997 (Washington, D.C.: U.S. Government Printing Office, 1998). For discussion, see Klare, *Resource Wars,* pp. 80–108; and Nanay, "Russia and the Caspian Sea Region," pp. 127–30, 133–34.

30. Office of the Press Secretary, White House, "Visit of President Heydar Aliyev of Azerbaijan," August 1, 1997, electronic document accessed at www.whitehouse.gov on March 2, 1998.

31. On the Clinton administration's role, see Forsythe, *The Politics of Oil in the Caucasus and Central Asia,* pp. 18–19.

32. SFRC/SIEP, *U.S. Economic and Strategic Interests in the Caspian Sea Region,* p. 16.

33. For background on U.S. economic aid, see Jim Nichol, *Central Asia: Regional Developments and Implications for U.S. Interests,* CRS Issue Brief for Congress (Washington, D.C.: U.S. Library of Congress, Congressional Research Service, March 29, 2006), pp. 14–15. For background on military aid, see Richard Giragosian, "The Strategic Central Asian Arena," *China and Eurasia Forum Quarterly,* vol. 4, no. 1 (2006), pp. 140–44; and Klare, *Resource Wars,* pp. 1–7, 95–97.

34. For background, see Forsythe, *The Politics of Oil in the Caucasus and Central Asia,* pp. 17–21; and Klare, *Resource Wars,* pp. 88–92, 100–104.

35. As quoted in Stephen Kinzer, "On Piping Out Caspian Oil, U.S. Insists the Cheaper, Shorter Way Isn't Better," *New York Times,* November 8, 1998.

36. NEPDG, *National Energy Policy,* chap. 8, pp. 12–13. For background, see Klare, *Blood and Oil,* pp. 56–73.

37. For background, see Giragosian, "The Strategic Central Asian Arena," pp. 144–45.

38. For background on these developments, see Tavernise and Brauer, "Russia Becoming an Oil Ally."

39. For discussion, see Klare, *Blood and Oil,* pp. 146–79. See also Bay Fang, "The Great Energy Game," *U.S. News & World Report,* September 3, 2006, electronic document accessed at www.usnews.com on January 3, 2007.

40. For discussion, see Steve Mufson, "U.S. Seeks Ways to Route Natural Gas Around Russia," *Washington Post,* July 11, 2006.

41. Statement of Karen Harbert, SFRC/SIEP, Washington, D.C., September 27, 2005 (photo-copy).

42. See C. J. Chivers, "U.S. Courting a Somewhat Skittish Friend in Central Asia," *New York Times,* June 21, 2007; and Eric Watkins, "US's Rice, UK Officials Seek Turkmen Oil, Gas," *Oil & Gas Journal Online,* September 21, 2007, electronic document accessed at www.ogjonline.com on September 24, 2007.

43. See Greenberg and Kramer, "Cheney, Visiting Kazakhstan, Wades into Energy Battle."

44. See Guy Dinmore and Isabel Gorst, "Bush Seeks to Seal Strategic Link as Kazakh President Visits Washington," *Financial Times,* September 29, 2006; James Gerstenzang, "Bush Hails 'Free' Kazakhstan," *Los Angeles Times,* September 30, 2006; and Sheryl Gay Stolberg, "Bush and Kazakh Leader Play Up Partnership," *New York Times,* September 30, 2006.

45. The author first provided this perspective on the Caspian in Klare, *Blood and Oil*, pp. 146–79. For a more recent assessment, see Klare, "The Tripolar Chessboard," TomDispatch.com, June 15, 2006, electronic document posted at www.tomdispatch.com/post/92161. For parallel perspectives, see Fang, "The Great Energy Game"; and Greenberg and Kramer, "Cheney, Visiting Kazakhstan, Wades into Energy Battle."

46. Andrei Y. Urnov, "Russian and Caspian Energy Prospects," address at Central Asia-Caucasus Institute, Johns Hopkins University, Washington, D.C., May 17, 2000, electronic document accessed at www.cacianalyst.org on August 7, 2000.

47. For example, Russia is believed to have played a covert role in the ouster of Abulfaz Elchibey, the pro-Western president of Azerbaijan who was deposed by a coup d'etat in June 1993. See Forsythe, *The Politics of Oil in the Caucasus and Central Asia*, pp. 13–15.

48. See ibid., p. 16.

49. For background and discussion, see ibid., pp. 29-31; and Klare, *Resource Wars*, pp. 98–100.

50. DoE/EIA, "Caspian Sea" 2005.

51. Andrew E. Kramer and Heather Timmons, "Lukoil Reports a Big Find in the Caspian Sea," *New York Times*, January 26, 2006.

52. Eric Watkins, "Nazarbayev: CPC Line Capacity to be Doubled," *Oil & Gas Journal Online*, electronic document accessed at www.ogjonline.com on April 19, 2006.

53. See Gregory L. White and Alan Cullison, "Russia Firms Up Grip on Fuel Supply," *Wall Street Journal*, September 6, 2006.

54. Vladimir Socor, "Kazakhstan's Growing Gas Exports to Go Russia's Way," *Eurasia Daily Monitor*, May 17, 2007, electronic document accessed at www.jamestown.org on May 25, 2007.

55. See Ilan Greenberg, "Russia Will Get Central Asian Gas Pipeline," *New York Times*, May 13, 2007; Vladimir Socor, "Russia Surging Farther Ahead in Race for Central Asian Gas," *Eurasia Daily Monitor*, May 16, 2007, electronic document accessed at www.jamestown.org on May 25, 2007; and Dempsey, "Russia Signs Deal for Gas Pipeline Along Caspian Sea."

56. Socor, "Russia Surging Farther Ahead in Race for Central Asian Gas."

57. Several factors seemed to account for Moscow's success in gaining control over the flow of Caspian gas, including the fact that virtually all existing conduits are already linked to the Gazprom system, which means that, in many new Russian-backed projects, there's no need to start from scratch (with all the added expenses this entails), and that the rulers of these countries are generally more comfortable dealing with familiar, like-minded

autocrats in Moscow than with Western diplomats and entrepreneurs, with all their (sometimes self-interested) demands for "transparency." For discussion, see Vladimir Socor, "Central Asia–Europe Energy Projects: Itemizing What Went Wrong," *Eurasia Daily Monitor,* May 31, 2007, electronic document accessed at www.jamestown.org on June 7, 2007.

58. Sergei Blagov, "Russia Eyes Central Asia Uranium Deposits," *Eurasia Daily Monitor,* June 6, 2006, electronic document accessed at www .jamestown.org on June 7, 2006.

59. Marat Yermukanov, "Kazakhstan Uses Energy Deals with Russia in 'Constructive Dialogue' with Europe," *Eurasia Daily Monitor,* May 14, 2007, electronic document accessed at www.jamestown.org on May 14, 2007.

60. Although Russia has an overall surplus of coal, Kazakh coal is imported into southern Russia for producing electricity. See DoE/EIA, "Kazakhstan" 2006

61. See, for example, John C. K. Daly, "Turkmenistan Back in Former USSR's Orbit," *Eurasia Daily Monitor,* June 8, 2007, electronic document accessed at www.jamestown.org on June 29, 2007; Vladimir Socor, "Moscow Pressuring Kazakhstan to Frustrate Western Energy Transport Projects," *Eurasia Daily Monitor,* April 5, 2007, electronic document accessed at www.jamestown .org on April 5, 2007; and Roger McDermott, "Putin Seeks Closer Ties with Turkmenistan," *Eurasia Daily Monitor,* February 20, 2007, electronic document accessed at www.jamestown.org on February 20, 2007.

62. The author first described this three-way "dance" in Klare, *Blood and Oil,* pp. 146–79. For additional background and analysis, see Bates Gill and Matthew Oresman, *China's New Journey to the West* (Washington, D.C.: Center for Strategic and International Studies, 2003); Giragosian, "The Strategic Central Asian Arena," pp. 133–53; Andrew Neff, "Central Asian Oil and Gas, Part 1: China Competing with Russia for Central Asian Investments," *Oil & Gas Journal,* March 6, 2006, pp. 41–46, Part 2: "Russian-Chinese Competition May Marginalize U.S., European Influence," March 13, 2006, pp. 39–42; and Martha Brill Olcott, "The Great Powers in Central Asia," *Current History,* October 2005, pp. 331–35.

63. For background on China's strategic interests in Central Asia, see Gill and Oresman, *China's New Journey to the West,* pp. 13–21.

64. On the evolution of the SCO, see ibid., pp. 5–12.

65. On the origins and aims of the "Go West" strategy, see Stephen Blank, "China's Emerging Energy Nexus with Central Asia," *China Brief,* July 19, 2006, electronic document accessed at www.jamestown.org on July 26, 2006.

66. For discussion, see Gill and Oresman, *China's New Journey to the West,* pp. 22–30.

67. Downs, *China's Quest for Energy Security,* pp. 25, 47.

68. For further discussion of this point, see Andrews-Speed, et al., *The Strategic Implications of China's Energy Needs.*

69. For background and discussion, see Andrews-Speed, et al. *The Strategic Implications of China's Energy Needs,* pp. 58–61; Gill and Oresman, *China's New Journey to the West,* pp. 24–26, 30–31; Neff, "China Competing with Russia for Central Asian Investments," pp. 41–46.

70. As quoted in Eric Watkins, "China, Kazakhstan Sign Oil Pipeline Agreement," *Oil & Gas Journal Online,* June 3, 2003, electronic document accessed at www.ogjonline.com on June 5, 2003.

71. DoE/EIA, "Kazakhstan" 2006.

72. See Lina Saigol and Dan Roberts, "Partners Move to Block Chinese," *Financial Times,* May 10–11, 2003.

73. See Bradsher and Pala, "China Ups the Ante in Its Bid for Oil"; Enid Tsui, "Expensive Offer with an Eye to Kazakhstan's Wealth in Reserve," *Financial Times,* August 23, 2005.

74. Jason Singer, "CNPC's Kazakh Oil Deal Advances," *Wall Street Journal,* October 17, 2005.

75. "China, Kazakhstan Form Energy Alliance," *Oil & Gas Journal,* July 18, 2005, p. 5.

76. See Isabel Gorst, "Kazakhstan and China Sign Oil and Gas Pipelines Agreement," *Financial Times,* August 20, 2007; Neff, "China Competing with Russia for Central Asian Investments," p. 46.

77. For an account of the Andizhan crackdown, see C. J. Chivers, "Tales of Uzbek Violence Suggest Larger Tragedy," *New York Times,* May 19, 2005. For more detailed testimony, see Human Rights Watch (HRW), *"Bullets Were Falling Like Rain": The Andijan Massacre, May 13, 2005* (New York: HRW, June 2005).

78. As quoted in Andrew Yeh and Guy Dinmore, "China Agrees to $600m Uzbek Oil Deal," *Financial Times,* May 20, 2005. For more on this deal, see Neff, "Russian-Chinese Competition May Marginalize U.S., European Influence," p. 39.

79. Stephen Blank, "Turkmenistan Completes China's Triple Play in Energy," *China Brief,* May 10, 2006, electronic document accessed at www.jamestown.org on May 12, 2006.

80. See Guy Chazan, "Turkmenistan's Energy Rush," *Wall Street Journal,* August 31, 2007.

81. Neff, "China Competing with Russia for Central Asian Investments," p. 46.

82. See Martha Brill Olcott, testimony before the U.S.-China Economic and Security Review Commission, Washington, D.C., August 4, 2006, electronic document accessed at www.uscc.gov on August 7, 2006.

83. For speculation on this point, see foreword by Zbigniew Brzezinski to Gill and Oresman, *China's New Journey to the West,* pp. v–vi. See also Ariel Cohen, "The Dragon Looks West: China and the Shanghai Cooperation Organization," statement before the U.S.-China Economic and Security Review Commission, Washington, D.C., August 4, 2006, electronic document accessed at www.uscc.gov on August 7, 2006; and Martha Brill Olcott, "The Great Powers in Central Asia," *Current History,* October 2005, pp. 331–35.

84. DoE/EIA, "Azerbaijan," 2006; DoE/EIA, "Caspian Sea," 2005.

85. DoE/EIA, "Kazakhstan," 2005.

86. "KNOC to Acquire Stake in Kazakh Oil Field," *Oil & Gas Journal Online,* November 6, 2006, electronic document accessed at www.ogjonline.com on November 8, 2006.

87. Vladimir Socor, "Constanta-Trieste Pipeline Proposal for Kazakhstan's Oil," *Eurasia Daily Monitor,* August 3, 2006, electronic document accessed at www.jamestown.org on August 7, 2006.

88. "Five Countries Sign Key Pipeline Deal at Vilnius Summit," Radio Free Europe/Radio Liberty, October 11, 2007, electronic document accessed at www.rferl.org on October 12, 2007.

89. See Stefan Wagstyl, "EU Blessing for 3,300km Gas Pipeline," *Financial Times,* June 27, 2006; "Nabucco Pipeline Project Can Diversify Europe's Gas Supplies," *Eurasia Daily Monitor,* June 30, 2006, electronic document accessed at www.jamestown.org on July 6, 2006; and Vladimir Socor, "Nabucco Gas Pipeline Project Is Back on Track," *Eurasia Daily Monitor,* September 19, 2007, electronic document accessed at www.jamestown .org on October 4, 2007.

90. See "White Stream: Additional Outlet Proposed for Caspian Gas to Europe," *Eurasia Daily Monitor,* October 12, 2007, electronic document accessed at www.jamestown.org on October 15, 2007.

91. See Scott Baldauf, "Afghan Gas Pipeline Nears Reality," *Christian Science Monitor,* February 15, 2006.

92. Matt Pottinger, Guy Chazan, and John Larkin, "Pursuit of Oil Firm Stokes Rivalry of Asian Giants," *Wall Street Journal,* August 23, 2005.

93. Shirish Nadkarni, "OVL, GAIL to Explore Off Azerbaijan," *Oil & Gas Journal Online,* June 21, 2005, electronic document accessed at www .ogjonline.com on June 29, 2005.

94. Chazan, "From Boom to Bust and Back."

95. Testimony of Edward Chow, SFRC/SIEP, *U.S. Energy Security: Russia and the Caspian,* p. 45.

96. For background, see DoE/EIA, "Azerbaijan" 2006.

97. Chazan, "From Boom to Bust and Back."

98. See ibid.; and C. J. Chivers, "Monitors Report Fraud in Azerbaijan Parliamentary Vote," *New York Times,* November 8, 2005.

99. As quoted in Chazan, "From Boom to Bust and Back."

100. See Andrew W. Kramer, "Mix of Nepotism and Nationalism Rules Kazakhstan Oil Industry," *New York Times,* December 23, 2005.

101. Mark J. Kaiser and Allan G. Pulsipher, "Kazakhstan's Outlook—3, Business Environment Still Seen as Risky in Kazakhstan," *Oil & Gas Journal,* July 17, 2006, p. 36.

102. For background on political conditions and the human rights situation in Central Asia, see Jim Nichol, *Central Asia: Regional Developments and Implications for U.S. Interests,* CRS Issue Brief for Congress (Washington, D.C.: U.S. Library of Congress, Congressional Research Service, March 29, 2006), pp. 4–10.

103. As noted by Edward Chow in his 2003 testimony before the Senate Foreign Relations Committee, "these unfortunate, but often repeated, developments associated with sudden oil income have in the past led to political instability, for example, in Latin America and West Africa." Testimony of Edward Chow, SFRC/SIEP, *U.S. Energy Security: Russia and the Caspian,* p. 45. For further discussion of this point, see Nanay, "Russia and the Caspian Sea Region," pp. 130–34.

104. See Nichol, *Central Asia: Regional Developments and Implications for U.S. Interests,* pp. 4–7.

105. "A number of years ago, most of us in industry were shocked to find a State Department report to Congress [see note 8 above] discussing the possibility of close to 200 billion barrels of crude oil reserves in the Caspian at a time when industry estimates were, at best, 10 percent of that level," Edward Chow told the Senate Foreign Relations Committee in 2003. "In the global context, the Caspian represents another North Sea or Alaska. It is significant, but even full development will not represent a fundamental shift in oil market dynamics or the world supply picture." Testimony of Edward Chow, SFRC/SIEP, *U.S. Energy Security: Russia and the Caspian,* p. 44.

106. Nanay, "Russia and the Caspian Sea Region," fig. 5.2, p. 141.

107. See Testimony of Edward Chow, SFRC/SIEP, *U.S. Energy Security: Russia and the Caspian,* p. 45; and Nanay, "Russia and the Caspian Sea Region," pp. 141–43.

CHAPTER 6: THE GLOBAL ASSAULT ON AFRICA'S VITAL RESOURCES

1. The author and a colleague, Daniel Volman, first advanced this argument in "The African 'Oil Rush' and American National Security," a paper

delivered at the African Studies Association, Washington, D.C., November 18, 2005. The paper was later published in modified form as Michael Klare and Daniel Volman, "The African 'Oil Rush' and U.S. National Security," *Third World Quarterly*, vol. 27, no. 4 (2006), pp. 609–28. See also Carola Hoyos, "Continent All Set to Balance Power," *Financial Times*, March 1, 2006.

2. For discussion, see Ian Gary and Terry Lynn Karl, *Bottom of the Barrel: Africa's Oil Boom and the Poor* (Baltimore: Catholic Relief Services, 2003).

3. Judy Clark, "Libya Awards 15 Exploration Blocks in Licensing Round," *Oil & Gas Journal*, February 7, 2005, pp. 35–37; and Clark, "Asian, European Firms Dominate Libya's Round 2," *Oil & Gas Journal*, October 24, 2005, pp. 39–44.

4. For discussion of Africa's allure, see Mohamed Barkindo and Ivan Sandrea, "Undiscovered Oil Potential Still Large Off West Africa," *Oil & Gas Journal*, January 8, 2007, pp. 30–34; and Barkindo and Sandrea, "West Africa Second Only to Russia in non-OPEC Supply Contribution," *Oil & Gas Journal*, January 15, 2007, pp. 43–47.

5. Testimony of John R. Brodman, U.S. Congress, Senate, Committee on Foreign Relations, Subcommittee on International Economic Policy, Export, and Trade Promotion, *The Gulf of Guinea and U.S. Strategic Energy Policy*, Hearing, 108th Cong., 2nd Sess., July 15, 2004, p. 12. (Hereinafter cited as SFRC, *Gulf of Guinea*.)

6. The author first advanced this argument in Klare and Volman, "The African 'Oil Rush' and U.S. National Security."

7. Quoted in Mike Crawley, "With Mideast Uncertainty, U.S. Turns to Africa for Oil," *Christian Science Monitor*, May 23, 2003.

8. For background and discussion, see Paul M. Lubeck, Michael J. Watts, and Ronnie Lipschutz, "Convergent Interests: U.S. Energy Security and the 'Securing' of Nigerian Democracy," *International Policy Report*, Center for International Policy, February 2007.

9. Quoted in Charles Cobb Jr., "Larger U.S. Troop Presence May Be Needed in Africa, Says NATO Commander," All Africa, May 2, 2003, electronic document accessed at www.allafrica.com on May 18, 2003.

10. David Stout, "U.S. to Create a Single Command for Military Operations in Africa," *New York Times*, February 7, 2007.

11. For background on the formation of AFRICOM, see Lauren Ploch, *Africa Command: U.S. Strategic Interests and the Role of the U.S. Military in Africa*, CRS Report for Congress (Washington. D.C.: Library of Congress, Congressional Research Service, December 7, 2007).

12. For background and discussion, see Joshua Eisenman and Joshua Kurlantzick, "China's Africa Strategy," *Current History*, May 2006, pp. 219–24.

13. See Joseph Kahn, "China Courts Africa, Angling for Strategic Gains," *New York Times,* November 3, 2006; and Alex Vines, "China in Africa: A Mixed Blessing?" *Current History,* May 2007, pp. 213–19.

14. On Hu's trip, see Robyn Dixon, "On His Africa Tour, Hu Is All Business," *Los Angeles Times,* February 7, 2007; and Wenran Jiang, "Hu's Safari: China's Emerging Strategic Partnerships in Africa," *China Brief,* Jamestown Foundation, February 21, 2007, electronic document accessed at www.jamestown.org on December 12, 2007.

15. See Susan Perke, "Resources, Security, and Influence: The Role of the Military in China's Africa Strategy," *China Brief,* Jamestown Foundation, May 30, 2007, electronic document accessed at www.jamestown.org on December 12, 2007.

16. For discussion, see Gary and Karl, *Bottom of the Barrel.*

17. BP, *Statistical Review of World Energy June 2007,* pp. 6, 22.

18. DoE/EIA, *IEO 2007,* Table G1, p. 187.

19. For background, see DoE/EIA, "Algeria," Country Analysis Brief, February 2006, electronic document accessed at www.eia.doe.gov on September 19, 2006.

20. For background, see DoE/EIA, "Libya," Country Analysis Brief, March 2006, electronic document accessed at www.eia.doe.gov on April 12, 2006.

21. On the fighting in the south, see HRW, *Sudan, Oil, and Human Rights.* On the violence in Darfur, see HRW, *Entrenching Impunity: Government Responsibility for International Crimes in Darfur* (New York and Washington: HRW, 2005).

22. For background, see DoE/EIA, "Sudan," Country Analysis Brief, April 2007, electronic document accessed at www.eia.doe.gov on April 23, 2007.

23. For background, see DoE/EIA, "Nigeria," Country Analysis Brief, April 2007, electronic document accessed at www.eia.doe.gov on April 23, 2007. See also DoE/EIA, "Angola," Country Analysis Brief, January 2007, electronic document accessed at www.eia.doe.gov on March 20, 2007.

24. For background on the conflict in the Niger Delta region, see Okey Ibeanu and Robin Luckham, "Nigeria: Political Violence, Governance and Corporate Responsibility in a Petro-State," in Mary Kaldor, Terry Lynn Karl, and Yahia Said, eds., *Oil Wars* (London and Ann Arbor, Mich.: Pluto Press, 2007), pp. 41–99. See also Lubeck, Watts, and Lipschutz, "Convergent Interests," pp. 5–10; John Donnelly, "Burdens of Oil Weigh Heavily on Nigerians," *Boston Globe,* October 3, 2005; and Lydia Polgreen, "Blood Flows with Oil in Poor Nigerian Villages," *New York Times,* January 1, 2006.

25. See DoE/EIA, "Nigeria" 2007; Thomas Catan, Dino Mahtani, and Jimmy Burns, "The Warriors of Warri: How Oil in Nigeria Is Under Siege," *Financial Times,* April 7, 2006; Jad Mouawad, "Growing Unrest Posing a Threat to Nigerian Oil," *New York Times,* April 21, 2007; Lydia Polgreen, "Armed Group Shuts Down Part of Nigeria's Oil Output," *New York Times,* February 25, 2006; and Spencer Schwartz, "Nigeria's Strife Forces Shell to Cut Outlay," *Wall Street Journal,* June 15, 2007.

26. See Chip Cummins, "Nigeria's Election Heightens Oil Worries," *Wall Street Journal,* April 11, 2007; and Dino Mahtani, "Besieged Oil Industry Has Little Hope Nigerian Elections Will Bring Relief," *Financial Times,* April 20, 2007.

27. Jad Mouawad, "Nowadays, Angola Is Oil's Topic A," *New York Times,* March 20, 2007. See also DoE/EIA, "Angola" 2007.

28. See Gary and Karl, *Bottom of the Barrel,* pp. 31–33; Sharon LaFraniere, "As Angola Rebuilds, Most Find Their Poverty Persists," *New York Times,* October 14, 2007; and Ken Silverstein, "Gusher to a Few, Trickle to the Rest," *Los Angeles Times,* May 13, 2004.

29. DoE/EIA, "Nigeria" 2007.

30. See Gettleman, "War in Sudan? Not Where the Oil Wealth Flows."

31. "Africa already plays an important role in world oil markets," U.S. Secretary of Energy Samuel Bodman told the Africa Oil and Gas Forum in December 2005. And, with continuing exploration and investment, "Africa will likely be the source of significant additional supplies over the next twenty years." U.S. Department of Energy Office of Public Affairs, Remarks of Samuel Bodman before the Africa Oil and Gas Forum, December 1, 2005, electronic document accessed at www.energy.gov on October 1, 2006.

32. Testimony of David L. Goldwyn, SFRC, *Gulf of Guinea,* p. 30.

33. Total is an amalgam of several French firms, including Elf Aquitaine, which in turn incorporated two companies set up by the French government to explore for oil in Africa, the Bureau de Recherches Pétroliers and Régie Autonome des Pétroles. See Yergin, *The Prize,* pp. 525–27. See also Anne-Sylvanine Chassany, "Total Taps Africa's Oil Reserves in Bid to Outdo Rivals' Growth," *Wall Street Journal,* May 22, 2007.

34. Total, *Total in 2005,* electronic document accessed at www.total.com on September 29, 2006.

35. On Congo's oil prospects, see DoE/EIA, "Congo-Brazzaville," Country Analysis Brief, May 2006, electronic document accessed at www.eia.doe.gov on September 29, 2006. For background on Total's political ties with the ruling faction in Congo, see Gary and Karl, *Bottom of the Barrel,* pp. 34–38.

36. DoE/EIA, "Angola" 2007; DoE/EIA, "Nigeria" 2007.

37. See DoE/EIA, "Nigeria" 2007; "Nigerian Militants Assault Oil Industry, Abducting 9 Foreigners," *New York Times,* February 19, 2006; Polgreen, "Armed Group Shuts Down Part of Nigeria's Oil Output"; Benoit Faucon, "Shell's Nigeria Field Remains Offline," *Wall Street Journal,* January 3, 2007; Mouawad, "Growing Unrest Posing a Threat to Nigerian Oil"; and Schwartz, "Nigeria's Strife Forces Shell to Cut Outlay."

38. DoE/EIA, "Algeria" 2006.

39. Rebecca Bream and Ben Hall, "BP in $900m Gas Exploration Deal with Libya," *Financial Times,* May 30, 2007.

40. DoE/EIA, "Angola" 2007.

41. DoE/EIA, "Libya," Country Analysis Brief, July 2007, electronic document accessed at www.eia.doe.gov on July 24, 2007. See also Gabriel Kahn, "Eni Bolsters Libya Ties as Rivals Circle," *Wall Street Journal,* October 17, 2007.

42. DoE/EIA, "Angola" 2007; DoE/EIA, "Nigeria" 2007.

43. Testimony and Prepared Statement of J. Robinson West, in U.S. Congress, Senate, Committee on Foreign Relations, Subcommittee on International Economic Policy, Export and Trade Promotion, *U.S. Energy Security: West Africa and Latin America,* Hearing, 108th Cong., 1st Sess., October 21, 2003, pp. 43, 48. (Hereinafter cited as SFRC, *West Africa and Latin America.*)

44. For discussion, see Deutch and Schlesinger, *National Security Consequences of U.S. Oil Dependency,* p. 30; Klare and Volman, "The African 'Oil Rush' and U.S. National Security"; and Lubeck, Watts, and Lipschutz, "Convergent Interests."

45. NEPDG, *National Energy Policy,* chap. 8, p. 11.

46. Statement before the House Committee on International Relations, Washington, D.C., June 20, 2002, electronic document accessed at www .energy.gov on December 7, 2003.

47. Testimony of John R. Brodman, SFRC, *Gulf of Guinea,* p. 21.

48. Testimony of Deputy Assistant Secretary of State Paul Simons, SFRC, *Gulf of Guinea,* p. 6.

49. Testimony of John R. Brodman, SFRC, *West Africa and Latin America,* p. 6.

50. For discussion of these efforts, see Ploch, *Africa Command,* pp. 17–22. See also Klare and Volman, "The African 'Oil Rush' and U.S. National Security"; and Lubeck, Watts, and Lipschutz, "Convergent Interests."

51. See Ploch, *Africa Command.*

52. Greg Jaffe, "In Massive Shift, U.S. Is Planning to Cut Size of Military in Germany," *Wall Street Journal,* June 10, 2003.

53. Jeffrey Ball, "Angola Possesses a Prize as Exxon, Rivals Stalk Oil," *Wall Street Journal,* December 5, 2005.

54. DoE/EIA, "Angola" 2007. See also "Kizomba B Attains Production Capacity Early," *Oil & Gas Journal,* October 10, 2005, pp. 44–50.

55. Ball, "Angola Possesses a Prize as Exxon, Rivals Stalk Oil."

56. For background on the corrosive impact of oil income on Angola's poor and war-devastated economy, see Silverstein, "Gusher to a Few, Trickle to the Rest."

57. DoE/EIA, "Nigeria" 2007.

58. DoE/EIA, "Equatorial Guinea," Country Analysis Brief, May 2006, electronic document accessed at www.eia.doe.gov on May 9, 2006.

59. DoE/EIA, "Chad and Cameroon," Country Analysis Brief, December 2005, electronic document accessed at www.eia.doe.gov on October 1, 2006.

60. For background, see the testimony before U.S. Congress, House, Committee on International Relations, Subcommittee on Africa, *The Chad-Cameroon Pipeline: A New Model for Natural Resource Development,* Hearing, 107th Cong., 2nd Sess., April 18, 2002 (Washington, D.C.: U.S. Government Printing Office, 2002). See also Peter Rosenblum, "Pipeline Politics in Chad," *Current History,* May 2000, pp. 195–99. On more recent developments, see Raymond Thibodeaux, "Anger Rises in Oil-Rich Chad as Funds Don't Aid Poor," *Boston Globe,* April 30, 2006.

61. See, for example, "Esso Adds Fields as Chad's Oil Output Lags Expected Level," *Oil & Gas Journal,* September 4, 2006, pp. 58–59; and Ball, "Angola Possesses a Prize as Exxon, Rivals Stalk Oil."

62. DoE/EIA, "Angola" 2007.

63. DoE/EIA, "Nigeria" 2007. See also Spencer Schwartz and Chip Cummins, "Chevron Move Hurts Oil Markets, Nigeria," *Wall Street Journal,* May 12–13, 2007.

64. DoE/EIA, "Equatorial Guinea" 2006.

65. DoE/EIA, "Algeria" 2006.

66. See James F. Peltz, "Oil Firms Eager to Turn the Tap Back on in Libya," *Los Angeles Times,* December 6, 2004.

67. DoE/EIA, "Libya" 2006. See also Jeffrey Ball, "U.S. Oil Firms Reach Deal with Libya," *Wall Street Journal,* December 30, 2005; and Steven R. Weisman, "U.S. Lifts Trade Embargo on Libya in Return for Promise on Arms," *New York Times,* September 21, 2004.

68. See Neela Banerjee, "Libya to Open 8 Oil Projects to Bidders," *New York Times,* May 5, 2004; and Carola Hoyos, "Libya 'Will Need $30bn Investment' to Expand Oil Sector," *Financial Times,* March 31, 2004.

69. DoE/EIA, "Libya" 2006.

70. Russell Gold, "Exxon Signs Exploration Pact with Libya," *Wall Street Journal,* November 21, 2007.

71. For background and discussion, see DoE, *EPA-05 Energy Report,* pp. 23–29. See also David White, "China's Quest for Commodities Leads to Africa," *Financial Times,* June 20, 2006.

72. For background and discussion, see Michael T. Klare, "Fueling the Dragon: China's Strategic Energy Dilemma," *Current History* (April 2006), pp. 180–85; and Klare and Volman, "The African 'Oil Rush' and U.S. National Security."

73. For background and discussion, see Eisenman and Kurlantzick, "China's Africa Strategy."

74. For background and discussion, see testimony delivered at U.S. Congress, House, Committee on International Relations, Subcommittee on Africa, Global Human Rights and International Operations, *China's Influence in Africa,* Hearing, 109th Cong., 1st Sess., July 25, 2005. (Hereinafter cited as HCIR, *China's Influence in Africa.*) See also Vines, "China in Africa."

75. See Jiang, "Hu's Safari: China's Emerging Strategic Partnerships in Africa," p. 5; and Vines, "China in Africa," p. 213.

76. Joseph Kahn, "China Courts Africa, Angling for Strategic Gains," *New York Times,* November 3, 2006.

77. Address by Hu Jintao at the Opening Ceremony of the Beijing Summit of the Forum on China-Africa Cooperation, November 4, 2006, Foreign Ministry of the People's Republic of China, electronic document accessed at www.fmprc.gov.cn/eng on December 3, 2006.

78. See Richard McGregor, "Sino-African Summit Ends with Aid Pledges and Swipe at Critics," *Financial Times,* November 6, 2006. See also Eisenman and Kurlantzick, "China's Africa Strategy."

79. For discussion, see Jiang, "Hu's Safari: China's Emerging Strategic Partnerships in Africa," pp. 5–7; Craig Timberg, "In Africa, China Trade Brings Growth, Unease," *Washington Post,* June 13, 2006; Yaroslav Trofimov, "In Africa, China's Expansion Begins to Stir Resentment," *Wall Street Journal,* February 2, 2007; and Michael Wines, "China's Influence in Africa Arouses Some Resistance," *New York Times,* February 10, 2007.

80. DoE/EIA, "Sudan" 2007. See also see HRW, *Entrenching Impunity: Government Responsibility for International Crimes in Darfur;* and Samantha Power, "Dying in Darfur," *The New Yorker,* August 30, 2004, pp. 56–73.

81. DoE/EIA, "Sudan," Country Analysis Brief, December 2001, electronic document accessed at www.doe.eia.gov on October 21, 2002.

82. DoE/EIA, "Sudan" 2007.

83. Ministry of Foreign Affairs of the People's Republic of China, "Hu Jintao

Meets with Sudanese President Bashir," Jakarta, Indonesia, April 23, 2005, electronic document accessed at www.fmprc.gov.cn/eng on October 4, 2006.

84. For discussion of these points, see HCIR, *China's Influence in Africa*, esp. pp. 22, 24–26. See also Eisenman and Kurlantzick, "China's Africa Strategy," pp. 220, 223.

85. For a thorough exposition of these charges, see HRW, *Sudan, Oil, and Human Rights*.

86. See Eric Reeves, Prepared Statement, in U.S.-China Economic and Security Review Commission (USCC), *China's Role in the World: Is China a Responsible Stakeholder?* Hearing, 109th Cong., 2nd Sess., August 3, 2006, electronic document accessed at www.uscc.gov on May 12, 2007.

87. See Eric Watkins, "Sudanese Government Dismisses Threats on Oil Fields," *Oil & Gas Journal Online*, October 29, 2007, electronic document accessed at www.ogjonline.com on October 30, 2007; and Watkins, "China Calls for Oil Worker Safety in Sudan, Ethiopia," *Oil & Gas Journal Online*, electronic document accessed at www.ogjonline.com on December 21, 2007.

88. Ball, "Angola Possesses a Prize." See also DoE/EIA, "Angola" 2007.

89. DoE, *EPA-05 Energy Report*, p. 25.

90. DoE/EIA, "Nigeria" 2007.

91. On the 2005 meeting, see Kevin C. Hall, "Global Race Is On to Snag Oil Supplies," *Seattle Times*, May 1, 2005.

92. Ministry of Foreign Affairs of the People's Republic of China, "Hu Jintao Talks with Nigerian President Obasanjo," April 27, 2006, electronic document accessed at www.fmprc.gov.cn/eng on October 7, 2006.

93. See Dino Mahtani and David White, "China in $4bn Move to Gain Foothold in Nigerian Oilfields," *Financial Times*, April 27, 2006.

94. David Barboza, "Chinese Energy Giant to Buy Stake in Nigerian Oil Field," *New York Times*, January 10, 2006.

95. "This transaction," said chief executive Fu Chengyu, "is perfectly aligned with CNOOC's long-term strategy of achieving growth through the exploration and development of offshore fields and achieving geographic diversification of the company's portfolio." As quoted in Barboza, "Chinese Energy Giant to Buy Stake in Nigerian Oil Field."

96. See Benoit Faucon, "Cnooc Shows Interest in Shell Nigerian Holdings," *Wall Street Journal*, November 23, 2007.

97. DoE/EIA, "Algeria" 2006; DoE/EIA, "Libya" 2006; and DoE/EIA, "Equatorial Guinea" 2006. On Chad, see Eric Watkins, "Chad, CNPC Unit to Build Refinery Near N'Djamena," *Oil & Gas Journal Online*, October 9,

2007, electronic document accessed at www.ogjonline.com on October 10, 2007.

98. Quoted in Vines, "China in Africa," p. 218.

99. Jeffrey Gettleman, "Rebels Storm a Chinese-Run Oil Field in Ethiopia, Killing 70," *New York Times,* April 25, 2007.

100. See Watkins, "China Calls for Oil Worker Safety in Sudan, Ethiopia."

101. Pui-Kwan Tse, "The Mineral Industry of China," in *USGS, Minerals Survey Yearbook 2004,* vol. 3, chap. 8, p. 6.

102. See Wallis, "China to Invest $5bn in Congo"; and Wallis and Bream, "Chinese Deal with Congo Prompts Concern."

103. Abdoulaye Massalatchie, "Niger Rebels Free Chinese Hostage in Uranium Firm," Reuters, July 10, 2007, electronic document accessed at www .alternet.org on October 7, 2007. For background on uranium mining in Niger and the rebel struggle there, see Andrew McGregor, "Niger's Uranium Industry Threatened by Rebels," *Terrorism Focus,* July 31, 2007, electronic document accessed at www.jamestown.org on October 7, 2007.

104. See, for example, statement of Rep. Christopher H. Smith (R-N.J.), HCIR, *China's Influence in Africa,* pp. 1–4. See also Jiang, "Hu's Safari: China's Emerging Strategic Partnerships in Africa"; and Eisenman and Kurlantzick, "China's Africa Strategy," pp. 222–23.

105. See Trofimov, "In Africa, China's Expansion Begins to Stir Resentment."

106. See, for example, testimony of Allan Thornton, president, Environmental Investigation Agency, HCIR, *China's Influence in Africa,* pp. 60–70.

107. Statement of Rep. Christopher H. Smith (R-N.J.), HCIR, *China's Influence in Africa,* pp. 1–2.

108. Testimony of Commissioner Carolyn Bartholomew, HCIR, *China's Influence in Africa,* p. 45.

109. "There is a concern that actions by Chinese companies to acquire energy assets will 'remove' energy resources from the competitive market, which, according to some, has the effect of constricting supply and thereby raising world prices. However, because China can be expected to consume the vast majority of any resources it does acquire, the effects of these purchases should be economically neutral. Even if China's equity oil investments 'remove' assets from the global market, in the sense that they are not subsequently available for resale, these actions merely displace what the Chinese would have otherwise bought on the open market." DoE, *EPA-05 Energy Report,* p. 3.

110. U.S.-China Economic and Security Review Commission, *2006 Report to Congress,* 109th Cong., 2nd Sess., November 2006 (Washington, D.C.: U.S. Government Printing Office, 2006), pp. 95–96.

111. U.S. Department of Defense, Office of the Secretary of Defense (DoD/OSD), *Military Power of the People's Republic of China 2006*, Annual Report to Congress (Washington, D.C.: DoD/OSD, 2006), p. 1.

112. This from a senior Pentagon official quoted in Dixon, "On His Africa Tour, Hu Is All Business."

113. See Dixon, "On His Africa Tour, Hu Is All Business."

114. For background, see Klare, *Blood and Oil*, p. 116.

115. For discussion, see Gary and Karl, *Bottom of the Barrel;* Norimitsu Onishi and Neela Banerjee, "Chad's Wait for Its Oil Riches May Be Long," *New York Times*, May 16, 2000; and Silverstein, "Gusher to a Few, Trickle to the Rest."

116. DoE/EIA, "Angola," Country Analysis Brief, January 2006, electronic document accessed at www.eia.doe.gov on March 20, 2006. See also Gary and Karl, *Bottom of the Barrel*, pp. 31–33.

117. See LaFraniere, "As Angola Rebuilds, Most Find Their Poverty Persists"; and Silverstein, "Gusher to a Few, Trickle to the Rest." For background and details, see Global Witness, *Time for Transparency: Coming Clean on Oil, Mining, and Gas Revenues* (London: Global Witness, 2004), pp. 40–59; and Global Witness, *All the Presidents' Men: The Devastating Story of Oil and Banking in Angola's Privatised War* (London: Global Witness, 2002).

118. As cited in Silverstein, "Gusher to a Few, Trickle to the Rest."

119. For background and discussion, see Gary and Karl, *Bottom of the Barrel*, pp. 25–28; and Ibeanu and Luckham, "Nigeria: Political Violence, Governance, and Corporate Responsibility in a Petro-State." See also Polgreen, "Blood Flows with Oil in Poor Nigerian Villages."

120. As quoted in Polgreen, "Blood Flows with Oil in Poor Nigerian Villages."

121. DoE/EIA, "Chad and Cameroon," Country Analysis Brief, December 2003, electronic document accessed at www.eia.doe.gov on August 10, 2004.

122. See Somini Sengupta, "Greasing the Engines of Change in Chad," *New York Times*, February 18, 2004.

CHAPTER 7: ENCROACHING ON AN "AMERICAN LAKE"

1. The author first argued for the centrality of the Gulf in U.S. foreign policy in Klare, *Resource Wars*, pp. 51–80, and returned to it in *Blood and Oil*, pp. 26–55 and 74–112. For summaries of U.S. policy in the Persian Gulf area by other analysts, see Zalmay Khalilzad, "The United States and the Persian Gulf: Preventing Regional Hegemony," *Survival*, vol. 37, no. 2 (Summer 1995), pp. 95–120; and Kenneth M. Pollack, "Securing the

Gulf," *Foreign Affairs,* July–August 2003, pp. 2–16. On the characterization of the Gulf as an "American lake," see Gregory F. Gause, *Oil Monarchies: Domestic and Security Challenges in the Arab Gulf States* (New York: Council on Foreign Relations Press, 1994), p. 175.

2. BP, *Statistical Review of World Energy June 2007,* p. 6.

3. Consider, for example, the extent of U.S. corporate participation in the energy industries of Saudi Arabia and Qatar. See Doe/EIA, "Saudi Arabia," Country Analysis Brief, February 2007, electronic document accessed at www.eia.doe.gov on February 6, 2007. See also DoE/EIA, "Qatar," Country Analysis Brief, May 2007, electronic document accessed at www.eia.doe.gov on October 8, 2007.

4. Jimmy Carter, State of the Union Address, January 23, 1980, electronic document accessed at www.jimmycarterlibrary.org on March 31, 2007. For background, see Michael A. Palmer, *Guardians of the Gulf* (New York: Free Press, 1992), pp. 101–11.

5. U.S. Congress, Senate, Committee on Armed Services, *Crisis in the Persian Gulf Region: U.S. Policy Options and Implications,* Hearings, 101st Cong., 2nd Sess., September 11, 1990, pp. 10–11. (Hereinafter cited as SCAS, *Crisis in the Persian Gulf Region.*)

6. For background on these developments, see Lawrence Freedman and Efraim Karsh, *The Gulf Conflict 1990–1991* (Princeton, N.J.: Princeton University Press, 1993), pp. 410–27.

7. For discussion, see Seymour Hersh, "The Debate Within," *The New Yorker,* March 11, 2002, pp. 34–39; and Bob Woodward, *Bush at War* (New York: Simon and Schuster, 2002).

8. Dick Cheney, Remarks at Veterans of Foreign Wars Convention, Nashville, Tenn., August 26, 2002, electronic document accessed at www.whitehouse.gov on December 12, 2007.

9. For background on the secret White House planning for the invasion, see Mark Danner, *The Secret Way to War* (New York: New York Review of Books, 2006).

10. "Address by the President to the Nation on the Way Forward in Iraq," White House, September 13, 2007, electronic document accessed at www.whitehouse.gov on October 10, 2007.

11. Both Senators Hillary Clinton and Barack Obama have called for a permanent U.S. military presence in the Persian Gulf area to ensure the stability of the region and, implicitly or explicitly, the safe flow of oil. See, for example, Michael R. Gordon and Patrick Healy, "Clinton Says Some G.I.'s in Iraq Would Stay if She Took Office," *New York Times,* March 15, 2007; Jeff Zeleny, "Obama, in Foreign Policy Speech, Urges U.S. Leadership," *New York Times,* April 24, 2007.

12. The author first recounted this history in Klare, *Blood and Oil*, pp. 27–37. In developing this narrative, I relied in particular on three useful sources: David S. Painter, *Oil and the American Century* (Baltimore: Johns Hopkins University Press, 1986); Palmer, *Guardians of the Gulf*; and Michael B. Stoff, *Oil, War, and American Security* (New Haven, Conn.: Yale University Press, 1980).

13. For background on these developments, see Stoff, *Oil, War, and American Security*, pp. 18–21, 35–39, 48–51, 57–70; and Yergin, *The Prize*, pp. 204–5, 298–301.

14. For background on these developments, see Stoff, *Oil, War, and American Security*, pp. 70–87; and Yergin, *The Prize*, pp. 396–99.

15. Painter, *Oil and the American Century*, p. 1. See also Stoff, *Oil, War, and American Security*, pp. 178–208.

16. For background on this encounter, see Aaron Dean Miller, *Search for Security* (Chapel Hill: University of North Carolina Press, 1980), pp. 128–31.

17. Thus, when asked to justify the decision to deploy troops in Saudi Arabia after the August 1990 Iraqi invasion of Kuwait, then Secretary of Defense Dick Cheney told the Senate Armed Services Committee, "Our strategic interests in the Persian Gulf region . . . hark back with respect to Saudi Arabia to 1945, when President Franklin Delano Roosevelt met with King Abdul Aziz on the USS *Quincy*, toward the end of World War II, and affirmed at that time that the United States had a lasting and a continuing interest in the security of the kingdom." SCAS, *Crisis in the Persian Gulf Region*, p. 10.

18. For background on the creation of Aramco, see Simmons, *Twilight in the Desert*, pp. 23–41; and Yergin, *The Prize*, pp. 410–19.

19. For background on these developments, see Palmer, *Guardians of the Gulf*, pp. 27–29, 46–50.

20. See Yergin, *The Prize*, pp. 391–99.

21. Ibid., pp. 450–70. See also Stephen Kinzer, *All the Shah's Men* (Hoboken, N.J.: John Wiley, 2003).

22. For background on these developments, see Michael T. Klare, *American Arms Supermarket* (Austin: University of Texas Press, 1985), pp. 108–26; and Palmer, *Guardians of the Gulf*, pp. 52–99.

23. On the formulation of this policy, see Klare, *Blood and Oil*, pp. 45–46; and Palmer, *Guardians of the Gulf*, pp. 103–11.

24. As indicated by Kenneth M. Pollack, former head of Persian Gulf Affairs at the National Security Council, "America's primary interest in the Persian Gulf lies in ensuring the free and stable flow of oil from the region to the world at large." Pollack, "Securing the Gulf," p. 3.

25. In September 2006, the U.S. special inspector general for Iraq reconstruction, Stuart W. Bowen Jr., reported that Iraq lost an estimated $16
billion in potential oil export revenue from January 2004 to March 2006
because of insurgent attacks, criminal activity, and aging and poorly
maintained infrastructure. See Nick Snow, "U.S. Estimates Iraq Lost $16
Billion in Oil Revenues," *Oil & Gas Journal,* October 9, 2006, pp. 28–29.

26. In August 2004, for example, Ambassador John Negroponte, then the top
U.S. official in Iraq, announced plans to reduce funding on water, electricity, and sewer projects by $2.25 billion and use the funds released in
this manner for increased infrastructure security and oil-industry reha-
bilitation. See David S. Cloud and Greg Jaffe, "U.S. Diplomat Wants More
Funds for Iraqi Security," *Wall Street Journal,* August 30, 2004.

27. Chip Cummins, "U.S. Digs In to Guard Iraq Oil Exports," *Wall Street
Journal,* November 12, 2007.

28. On the Pentagon's plans to retain permanent bases in Iraq, see Tom
Engelhardt, "Can You Say 'Permanent Bases'? *The Nation,* March 27,
2006, pp. 28–29; Bradley Graham, "Commanders Plan Eventual
Consolidation of U.S. Bases in Iraq," *Washington Post,* May 22, 2005; and
Peter Spiegel, "Bush's Requests for Iraqi Base Funding Make Some Wary
of Extended Stay," March 24, 2006.

29. Neil MacFarquhar, "After Attack, Company's Staff Plans to Leave Saudi
Arabia," *New York Times,* May 3, 2004.

30. Neil MacFarquhar, "Saudi Military Storms Complex to Free Hostages,"
New York Times, May 31, 2004; and Hugh Pope and Chip Cummins,
"Saudis Suffer Fresh Terrorist Attack," *Wall Street Journal,* May 31, 2004.

31. See Bhushan Bahree and Chip Cummins, "Thwarted Attack at Saudi
Facility Stirs Energy Fears," *Wall Street Journal,* February 25–26, 2006.

32. See Andrew England, "Saudis Set Up Force to Guard Oil Plants," *Financial
Times,* August 27, 2007; and Rasheed Abou-Alsamh, "Saudis Arrest 208 in
a Sweep to Head off Terrorist Attacks," *New York Times,* November 29,
2007.

33. For background, see Klare, *American Arms Supermarket,* pp. 108–26.

34. For an assessment of U.S. concerns regarding Iran, see Kenneth Katzman,
Iran: U.S. Concerns and Policy Responses, CRS Report for Congress
(Washington, D.C.: Library of Congress, Congressional Research Service,
September 25, 2007). See also Paul Richter and Peter Spiegel, "Wider Ira-
nian Threat Seen," *Los Angeles Times,* October 31, 2007.

35. See, for example, Helene Cooper, "Rice Plays Down Hawkish Talk About
Iran," *New York Times,* June 2, 2007.

36. As quoted in Sheryl Gay Stolberg, "Cheney, Like President, Has a Warning
for Iran," *New York Times,* October 22, 2007.

37. See Seymour Hersh, "Shifting Targets," *The New Yorker,* October 1, 2007, electronic document accessed at www.newyorker.com on October 1, 2007; and Hersh, "The Iran Plans," *The New Yorker,* April 17, 2006, electronic document accessed at www.newyorker.com on October 18, 2007.

38. As quoted in John B. McKinnon and Yochi J. Dreazen, "Bush Warns Iran Not to Attack U.S. Ships," *Wall Street Journal,* January 10, 2008. For coverage of the incident, see Thom Shanker and Brian Knowlton, "Iranian Boats Confront U.S. in Persian Gulf," *New York Times,* January 8, 2008; Sheryl Gay Stolberg and Thom Shanker, "Bush Castigates Iran, Calling Naval Confrontation 'Provocative Act,'" *New York Times,* January 9, 2008; and Nazila Fathi, "Iran Accuses U.S. of Faking Video of Boat Showdown in Gulf," *New York Times,* January 10, 2008.

39. NEPDG, *National Energy Policy,* chap. 8, p. 6.

40. Ibid., p. 5.

41. DoE/EIA, "Saudi Arabia," Country Analysis Brief, August 2005, electronic document accessed at www.eia.doe.gov on October 21, 2006; and DoE/EIA, "Saudi Arabia" 2007.

42. DoE/EIA, "Kuwait," Country Analysis Brief, November 2006, electronic document accessed at www.eia.doe.gov on November 6, 2006.

43. DoE/EIA, "Qatar" 2007. On the Shah project, see Russell Gold and Oliver Klaus, "Conoco Leads Pack for Shah Project," *Wall Street Journal* (European edition), January 11–13, 2008.

44. For background on these efforts, see Robert Dreyfuss, "Tinker, Banker, Neocon, Spy," *American Prospect,* November 18, 2002, electronic document accessed at www.prospect.org on November 18, 2002; Dan Morgan and David B. Ottaway, "In Iraq War Scenario, Oil Is Key," *Washington Post,* September 15, 2002; and David Reiff, "Blueprint for a Mess," *New York Times Magazine,* November 2, 2003, pp. 31–33.

45. Quoted in Morgan and Ottaway, "In Iraq War Scenario, Oil Is Key."

46. For background and discussion, see Blanchard, *Iraq: Oil and Gas Legislation,* pp. 1–9, 14–15.

47. Ibid., pp. 12–13. On Iraq's "prequalification" process, see Eric Watkins, "Iraq Starts Licensing Round Prequalification Process," *Oil & Gas Journal Online,* electronic document accessed at www.ogjonline.com on January 4, 2008.

48. On the presence of American firms in Iran during the reign of the shah, see Yergin, *The Prize,* pp. 470–72, 475–78, 533–35.

49. Andrews-Speed, et al., *The Strategic Implications of China's Energy Needs,* p. 65.

50. For background and discussion, see ibid., pp. 65–67.

51. Ibid., p. 66.

52. Ibid.

53. DoE, *EPA-O5 Energy Report*, p. 22.

54. Andrews-Speed, et al., *The Strategic Implications of China's Energy Needs*, pp. 66–67. See also Downs, *China's Quest for Energy Security*, p. 18.

55. See DoE/EIA, "Iraq," Country Analysis Brief, June 2006, electronic document accessed at www.eia.doe.gov on June 29, 2006; and "China and Iraq Plan to Resurrect Oil-Field Deal Set in Hussein Era," *Wall Street Journal*, October 30, 2006.

56. "Iraq to Boost Oil Output, Develop Al Ahdab Field," *Oil & Gas Journal*, November 20, 2006, p. 5. See also Shai Oster, "Iraq to Seek Chinese Help to Reinvigorate Oil Industry," *Wall Street Journal*, June 20, 2007.

57. DoE/EIA, "Iran," Country Analysis Brief, May 2002, electronic document accessed at www.eia.doe.gov on May 31, 2002.

58. DoE/EIA, "Iran," Country Analysis Brief, August 2006, electronic document accessed at www.eia.doe.gov on October 28, 2006.

59. DoE/EIA, "Iran" 2006; Peter S. Goodman, "China Rushes Toward Oil Pact with Iran," *Washington Post*, February 18, 2006; Matt Pottinger, "China and Iran Near Agreement on Huge Oil Pact," *Wall Street Journal*, November 1, 2004; "Iran, China Strike Energy Deal," Associated Press, September 14, 2007, electronic document accessed at www.businessweek.com on October 8, 2007; and "China's Sinopec Signs Iran Pact, Veering from the Wishes of U.S.," *Wall Street Journal*, December 10, 2007.

60. Andrews-Speed, et al., *The Strategic Implications of China's Energy Needs*, p. 66.

61. "Memorandum of Understanding on Petroleum Cooperation between the Government of the People's Republic of China and the Government of the Kingdom of Saudi Arabia," electronic document accessed at www.fmprc.gov.cn/eng on October 28, 2006.

62. DoE/EIA, "Saudi Arabia" 2005.

63. Ibid.

64. Ministry of Foreign Affairs of the People's Republic of China, "Premier Wen Jiabao Meets with Saudi Arabian King Abdullah," January 24, 2006, electronic document accessed at www.fmprc.gov.cn/eng on February 6, 2006.

65. Ministry of Foreign Affairs of the People's Republic of China, "President Hu Jintao Holds Talks with Saudi Arabian King Abdullah," April 23, 2006, electronic document accessed at www.fmprc.gov.cn/eng on May 2, 2006.

66. See Eric Watkins, "Saudis, Chinese Agree to Landmark Accord," *Oil & Gas Journal,* February 6, 2006, pp. 35–36.

67. See Neil King Jr., Jay Solomon, and Jason Dean, "Hu Assures U.S. of Cooperation, but Gaps Remain," *Wall Street Journal,* April 21, 2006.

68. See Hassan M. Fattah, "Avoiding Political Talk, Saudis and Chinese Build Trade," *New York Times,* April 23, 2006; and "China, Saudi Arabia Strengthen Agreement on Refinery Ventures," *Wall Street Journal,* April 24, 2006.

69. See "China, Saudi Arabia Strengthen Agreement on Refinery Ventures"; and "Chinese President in Saudi Visit," BBC News, April 22, 2006, electronic document accessed at www.bbc.co.uk on April 22, 2006.

70. For background on this transaction, see Richard Fieldhouse, "China's Role in Proliferation," *Transnational Law and Contemporary Problems* (University of Iowa College of Law), vol. 2, no. 2 (Fall 1992), pp. 550–52.

71. For background on the Silkworm and its acquisition by the Iranians, see Anthony H. Cordesman and Abraham R. Wagner, *The Lessons of Modern War,* vol. 2, *The Iran-Iraq War* (Boulder, Colo.: Westview Press, 1990), pp. 274–77.

72. For a description of this incident, see ibid., pp. 329–30.

73. Shirley A. Kan, *China and Proliferation of Weapons of Mass Destruction and Missiles: Policy Issues* (Washington, D.C.: Library of Congress, Congressional Research Service, May 9, 2007), p. 16. (Hereinafter cited as Kan, *China and Proliferation of WMD.*)

74. As quoted in Ibid., p. 16.

75. John Pomfret, "Cohen Hails Achievements in China Visit," *Washington Post,* January 20, 1998.

76. See Kan, *China and Proliferation of WMD,* p. 17; and John Mintz, "Tracking Arms: A Study in Smoke," *Washington Post,* April 3, 1999.

77. See Kan, *China and Proliferation of WMD,* pp. 13–16.

78. See Jay Solomon, "U.S. Sanctions 4 Chinese Firms for Aiding Iran," *Wall Street Journal,* June 14, 2006; and David E. Sanger, "U.S. to Punish 9 Companies Said to Help Iran on Arms," *New York Times,* December 28, 2005. For a complete list of the sanctioned firms, see Kan, *China and Proliferation of WMD,* table 1, pp. 49–55.

79. "President Hu Jintao Holds Talks with Saudi Arabian King Abdullah," April 23, 2006.

80. As quoted in Fattah, "Avoiding Political Talk, Saudis and Chinese Build Trade."

81. Figure is for 2006. BP, *Statistical Review of World Energy June 2007,* p. 20.

82. DoE/EIA, "Kuwait" 2006.

83. Inpex Corporation, "Our Business: Projects: Middle East," electronic document accessed at www.inpex.co.jp on July 20, 2006.

84. See Michiyo Nakamoto, Mariko Sanchanta, and Guy Dinmore, "Japan Signs Oilfield Development Deal with Iran," *Financial Times,* February 18, 2004; and "Defying U.S., Japan Signs Oil Deal with Iran," *New York Times.* See also Inpex Corporation, "Our Business: Projects: Middle East."

85. See Bruce Wallace, "Japan Is in a Quandary Over Iran Nuclear Crisis," *Los Angeles Times,* February 2, 2006; and Elaine Lies, "U.S. Asks Japan to Stop Iran Oil Development," Reuters, March 23, 2006, electronic document accessed at www.japanfocus.org on March 29, 2006.

86. Yuka Hayashi, "Japan Hits Big Setbacks in Push to Expand Its Access to Energy," *Wall Street Journal,* October 25, 2006.

87. Ministry of Foreign Affairs of Japan, "Towards the Building of Strategic and Multi-Layered Partnership between Japan and the Kingdom of Saudi Arabia," April 6, 2006, electronic document accessed at www.mofa.go.jp on July 20, 2006.

88. As quoted in David Pilling, "Japan's Middle East Rhetoric Masks Energy Policy Failure," *Financial Times,* May 1, 2007.

89. David Pilling, "Japan to Give $1bn in Loans for Gulf Oil Supply," *Financial Times,* April 30, 2007.

90. See Hector Foster, "Japan Seeks Oil Security in Iraq, Indonesia after Iran Setback," Bloomberg.com, October 27, 2006, electronic document accessed at www.bloomberg.com on October 29, 2006; and Hisane Masaki, "Goodbye Iran, Hello Iraq: Japan's and China's Oil Prospects in the Balance," original from *Asia Times,* posted at Japan Focus on November 13, 2006, electronic document accessed at www.japanfocus.org on November 20, 2006.

91. As quoted in Foster, "Japan Seeks Oil Security in Iraq."

92. John Larkin, "Iran, India Reach Accord to Work on Gas Deposits," *Wall Street Journal,* November 3, 2004.

93. Shirish Nadkarni, "IOC Gets Block in Iran's North Pars Field," *Oil & Gas Journal Online,* June 14, 2005, electronic document accessed at www.ogjonline.com on June 14, 2005.

94. For background on this endeavor, see DoE/EIA, "Iran" 2006.

95. As quoted in David J. Lynch, "India Unlikely to Drop Pipeline Deal with Iran," USAToday.com, March 16, 2005, electronic document accessed at www.usatoday.com on March 16, 2005. See also Jau Solomon, "Rice Airs Concern Over Gas Pipeline from Iran to India," *Wall Street Journal,* March 17, 2005.

96. As quoted in Lynch, "India Unlikely to Drop Pipeline Deal with Iran."

97. Elisabeth Bumiller and Somini Sengupta, "Bush and India Reach Pact That Allows Nuclear Sales," *New York Times,* March 3, 2006. For background on the accord, see K. Alan Kronstadt, *India-U.S. Relations* (Washington, D.C.: Library of Congress, Congressional Research Service, June 26, 2007), pp. 18–24.

98. Office of the Press Secretary, White House, "Fact Sheet: United States and India: Strategic Partnership," March 2, 2006, electronic document accessed at www.whitehouse.gov on March 12, 2006.

99. See Kronstadt, *India-U.S. Relations,* pp. 21–24. See also "The Sound of One Hand Clapping," *The Economist,* July 22, 2006, pp. 41–42.

100. See Eric Watkins, "India, Saudi Arabia Sign Energy Pact," *Oil & Gas Journal Online,* January 30, 2006, electronic document accessed at www.ogjonline.com on January 30, 2006.

101. IEA, *World Energy Outlook 2001,* p. 107.

102. Vladimir Socor, "Lukoil Seeking Return to Iraq with Russian Government Support," *Eurasian Daily Monitor,* August 10, 2007, electronic document accessed at www.jamestown.org on October 4, 2007.

103. Andrew E. Kramer, "Iraq, with U.S. Support, Voids a Russian Oil Contract," *New York Times,* November 4, 2007.

104. As quoted in Thom Shanker and Mark Landler, "Putin Says U.S. Is Undermining Global Stability," *New York Times,* February 11, 2007. See also Thomas E. Ricks and Craig Whitlock, "Putin Hits U.S. Over Unilateral Approach," *Washington Post,* February 11, 2007.

105. "Russian President Putin's Historic Visit Boosts Moscow-Riyadh Ties," Saudi-U.S. Relations Information Service, February 12, 2007, electronic document accessed at www.saudi-us-relations.org on June 24, 2007.

106. As quoted in Andrew Hammond, "Putin, Saudi King Meet in Landmark Visit," *Boston Globe,* February 12, 2007.

107. "Russia, Saudi Arabia Energy Partners, Not Rivals—Putin," Novosti News Agency, February 12, 2007, electronic document accessed at en.rian.ru on June 24, 2007.

108. Ibid. See also Victor Yasmann, "Russia: Putin Uses Gulf Trip to Boost Russian Role in Arab World," Radio Free Europe/Radio Liberty, February 13, 2007, electronic document accessed at www.rferl.org on June 24, 2007.

109. As quoted in Hassan M. Fattah, "Putin Visits Qatar for Talks on Natural Gas and Trade," *New York Times,* February 13, 2007.

110. See Neil Buckley and Andrew England, "Putin Visits Qatar Amid Talk of 'Gas Opec,'" *Financial Times,* February 13, 2007.

111. Quoted in Fattah, "Putin Visits Qatar for Talks on Natural Gas and Trade."

112. See Vladimir Socor, "Caspian Summit Balances Interests and Differences," *Eurasian Daily Monitor,* October 17, 2007, electronic document accessed at www.jamestown.org on October 18, 2007. See also Steven Lee Myers, "Pact with Iran on Gas Sales Is Possible, Putin Says," *New York Times,* February 2, 2007.

113. As quoted in Nazila Fathi and C. J. Chivers, "Putin Says Caspian Area Is Off-Limits to Attacks," *New York Times,* October 17, 2006. See also Socor, "Caspian Summit Balances Interests and Differences."

114. See Nazila Fathi, "Putin Is Said to Offer Idea on Standoff Over Iran," *New York Times,* October 18, 2007.

115. Hassan M. Fattah, "U.S. Iraq Role Is Called Illegal by Saudi King," *New York Times,* March 29, 2007.

CHAPTER 8: CROSSING A THRESHOLD

1. For background on U.S. arms sales to Saudi Arabia, see Klare, *American Arms Supermarket,* pp. 127–55; and David E. Long, *The United States and Saudi Arabia* (Boulder, Colo.: Westview Press, 1985), pp. 33–50.

2. The author first examined this point in Klare, *Blood and Oil,* pp, 146–79.

3. For statistical data and analysis, see U.S. Arms Control and Disarmament Agency (ACDA), *World Military Expenditures and Arms Transfers 1995* (Washington, D.C.: ACDA, 1996).

4. For background and discussion, see HRW, *Sudan, Oil, and Human Rights;* Peter S. Goodman, "China Invests Heavily in Sudan's Oil Industry," *Washington Post,* December 23, 2004; and DoE/EIA, "Sudan," Country Analysis Brief, November 2000, electronic document accessed at www.eia .doe.gov on November 11, 2000.

5. For reactions in Washington, see the testimony in HIRC, *China's Influence in Africa.* See also Charles W. Corey, "Africa of Key Strategic Importance to U.S., World, Scholar Says," USInfo, March 8, 2006, electronic document accessed at usinfo.state.gov on December 17, 2006.

6. HIRC, *China's Influence in Africa,* p. 28.

7. On the importance of Nigeria to U.S. energy policy, see the testimony of Deputy Assistant Secretary of State Paul Simons in SFRC, *Gulf of Guinea and U.S. Strategic Energy Policy,* pp. 3–6; also testimony of J. Stephen Morrison of the Center for Strategic and International Studies in the same document, pp. 39, 43–45.

8. U.S. Department of State (DoS), *Congressional Budget Justification for Foreign Operations,* Fiscal Year (FY) 2007 (Washington, D.C.: DoS, 2006), p. 307.

9. The $30 million includes Foreign Military Sales Financing, International Military Education and Training grants, narcotics and law enforcement assistance, Emergency Support Funds, and commercial and Pentagon-managed arms transfers. Ibid., pp. 307–9, 589, 628. Due to a Congressional impasse on foreign aid funding for FY 2007, the *Congressional Budget Justification* for FY 2008 did not include updated information for FY 2007, but included a $5 million request for security aid in FY 2008.

10. On indirect sources of military aid to Nigeria, see Klare and Volman, "The African 'Oil Rush' and U.S. National Security." For background on these programs, see Ploch, *Africa Command,* pp. 17–22.

11. Dino Mahtani, "Nigeria Shifts to China Arms," *Financial Times,* February 28, 2006.

12. See Ruby Rabiu, "China Donates $3m Military Equipment to Nigeria," *Daily Trust* (Abuja), October 20, 2005, electronic document accessed at www.dailytrust.com/archives on December 16, 2006. See also "Nigeria to Mass-Produce Nigerian Version of AK-47 Rifles," Xinhua News Service, October 2, 2006, electronic document accessed at english.people.com.cn on December 15, 2006.

13. For background on Chinese arms transfers to Africa, see Amnesty International, "People's Republic of China: Sustaining Conflict and Human Rights Abuses, the Flow of Arms Accelerates," June 11, 2006, electronic document accessed at www.amnesty.org on December 15, 2006. See also David H. Shinn, "Africa and China's Activism," paper presented at National Defense University Pacific Symposium: China's Global Activism, Washington, D.C., June 20, 2006.

14. See DoS, *Congressional Budget Justification for Foreign Operations,* FY 2007 (Washington, D.C.: DoS, 2006), pp. 213–14, 628–29.

15. On U.S. training programs, see Klare and Volman, "The African 'Oil Rush' and U.S. National Security." On Chinese programs, see Susan Puska, "Resources, Security, and Influence: The Role of the Military in China's Africa Strategy," *China Brief,* Jamestown Foundation, May 30, 2007, electronic document accessed at www.jamestown.org on December 12, 2007; and Shinn, "Africa and China's Activism."

16. The author first discussed these developments in Klare, *Blood and Oil,* pp. 152–79.

17. For background and discussion, see Giragosian, "The Strategic Central Asian Arena."

18. Linda D. Kozaryn, "U.S., Kazakhstan Increase Military Ties," Armed Forces Information Service News, November 26, 1997, electronic document accessed at www.defenselink.mil on December 16, 2006.

19. For background, see Klare, *Resource Wars,* pp. 1–2, 95–97.

20. DoS, *Congressional Budget Justification for Foreign Operations,* FY 2006 (Washington, D.C.: DoS, 2005), p. 304. See also Nichol, *Central Asia: Regional Developments and Implications for U.S. Interests,* p. 11.

21. DoS, *Congressional Budget Justification for Foreign Operations,* FY 2007, pp. 501, 591, 631.

22. See Nichol, *Central Asia: Regional Developments and Implications for U.S. Interests,* pp. 3–4; and Vladimir Socor, "CIS Collective Security Treaty Organization Holds Summit," *Eurasia Daily Monitor,* June 24, 2005, electronic document accessed at www.jamestown.org on December 17, 2005.

23. See Roger McDermott, "Nazarbayev's Caspian Security Deals: What Can Moscow Offer?" *Eurasia Daily Monitor,* June 27, 2006, electronic document accessed at www.jamestown.org on December 17, 2006.

24. Yuriy Chernogayev, "Uzbeks Will Take Up Russian Guns to Rebuff Islamist Offensive," *Kommersant* (Moscow), March 2, 2001, from translation in Foreign Broadcast Information Service.

25. Gill and Oresman, *China's New Journey to the West,* p. 20.

26. For background, see Klare, *Resource Wars,* pp. 95–97; and Klare, *Blood and Oil,* 135–39.

27. DoS, *Congressional Budget Justification for Foreign Operations,* FY 2006, pp. 375–76, 407–8, 520, 555–56.

28. See "Military Deal with Moscow Bolsters Leader of Uzbekistan," *Financial Times,* November 15, 2005; and Nichol, *Central Asia: Regional Developments and Implications for U.S. Interests,* pp. 4, 7. See also Sergei Blagov, "Russia Seeks Closer Military Links with Uzbekistan," and Roger N. McDermott, "Karimov Prioritizes Russian Armaments," both in *Eurasia Daily Monitor,* September 25, 2006, electronic document accessed at www.jamestown.org on September 25, 2006.

29. As quoted in Sergei Blagov, "Moscow Beefs Up Security Ties with Kyrgyzstan," *Eurasia Daily Monitor,* October 13, 2006, electronic document accessed at www.jamestown.org on October 13, 2006.

30. Ibid.

31. DoS, *Congressional Budget Justification for Foreign Operations,* FY 2007, pp. 394–95, 591, 630.

32. Nichol, *Central Asia: Regional Developments and Implications for U.S. Interests,* p. 11. The $100 million figure is from Global Security, "Caspian Guard," electronic document accessed at www.globalsecurity.org on December 17, 2006.

33. See "U.S. Working to Boost Sea Forces in Oil-Rich Caspian: Envoy," Caucaz.com, November 22, 2005, electronic document accessed at www

.caucaz.com on December 18, 2006; and "USA Plans to Expand Military Presence in Azerbaijan Close to Iran," *Alexander's Gas & Oil Connection,* May 10, 2005, electronic document accessed at www.gasandoil.com on December 18, 2006.

34. Roger McDermott, "Kazakhstan's Parliament Ratifies Strategic Partnership with Azerbaijan," *Eurasia Daily Monitor,* July 5, 2006, electronic document accessed at www.jamestown.org on December 17, 2006.

35. Rovshan Ismayilov, "Azerbaijan Ponders Russian Caspian Defense Initiative," Eurasianet.org, February 1, 2006, electronic document accessed at www.eurasianet.org on December 18, 2006.

36. Fariz Ismailzade, "U.S., Russian Defense Leaders Court Baku with Incentive Offers," *Eurasia Daily Monitor,* January 27, 2006, electronic document accessed at www.jamestown.org on December 18, 2006.

37. Ismayilov, "Azerbaijan Ponders Russian Caspian Defense Initiative."

38. For background and discussion, see Klare, *American Arms Supermarket,* esp. pp. 127–62, 204–33.

39. For data on U.S. and Russian arms transfers to the region, see Richard F. Grimmett, *Conventional Arms Transfers to Developing Nations, 1998–2005,* CRS Report for Congress (Washington, D.C.: Library of Congress, Congressional Research Service, October 23, 2006).

40. Ibid., pp. 9–10. See also Lionel Beehner, "Russia-Iran Arms Sales," Council on Foreign Relations Backgrounder, November 1, 2006, electronic document accessed at www.cfr.org on June 24, 2007.

41. David Brunnstrom, "U.S. Concerned by Russian Arms Sales to Iran, Syria," Reuters, March 21, 2007, electronic document accessed at www.reuters.com on June 24, 2007. See also Gregory L. White and Neil King Jr., "Russian Deals in Middle East Snarl U.S. Strategy on Iran," *Wall Street Journal,* February 28, 2007.

42. As quoted in White and King, "Russian Deals in Middle East Snarl U.S. Strategy on Iran."

43. See David S. Cloud, "U.S. Set to Offer Huge Arms Deal to Saudi Arabia," *New York Times,* July 28, 2007; Mark Mazzetti and Helene Cooper, "U.S. Arms Plan for Mideast Aims to Counter Iranian Power," *New York Times,* July 31, 2007; and Jim Wolf, "U.S. Readies Arms Sales to Saudis and Gulf Arabs," *Washington Post,* November 15, 2007.

44. As quoted in Wolf, "U.S. Readies Arms Sales to Saudis and Gulf Arabs."

45. David Gollust, "U.S. to Sell Precision-Guided Bombs to Saudi Arabia," Voice of America News, January 14, 2008, electronic document accessed at voanews.com on January 15, 2008.

46. See William Cole, "Stennis Pulls In for a Visit," *Honolulu Advertiser,* August 21, 2007; and U.S. Naval Forces Central Command, "Stennis, Nimitz, and Bonhomme Richard Enter the Arabian Gulf," May 23, 2007, electronic document accessed at www.cusnc.navy.mil on October 21, 2007.

47. See photographs attached to U.S. Naval Forces Central Command, "Stennis, Nimitz, and Bonhomme Richard Enter the Arabian Gulf."

48. U.S. Naval Forces Central Command, "Stennis, Nimitz, and Bonhomme Richard Enter the Arabian Gulf."

49. As quoted in David E. Sanger, "Cheney on Carrier, Warns Iran to Keep Sea Lanes Open," *New York Times,* May 12, 2007.

50. As cited in "China Condemns Japanese Survey," BBC News, July 8, 2004, electronic document accessed at news.bbc.co.uk on July 10, 2006.

51. The assertion that Beijing deliberately sent the submarine into Japanese waters to signal Tokyo over the territorial dispute is the author's alone; Japanese authorities did not formally take this position, although they protested the action vigorously. See "Japan Protests to China over Sub," BBC News, November 12, 2004, electronic document accessed at news.bbc.co.uk on July 10, 2006.

52. See Mure Dickie and David Pilling, "Tensions Ease as China Admits Its Submarine Entered Japanese Waters," *Financial Times,* November 17, 2004.

53. "Japan Risks China Anger over Gas," BBC News, April 13, 2005, electronic document accessed at news.bbc.co.uk on July 10, 2006.

54. As cited in "Japan Stokes China Sea Dispute," BBC News, July 14, 2005, electronic document accessed at news.bbc.co.uk on July 10, 2006.

55. "Japan's Dangerous Move in E. China Sea," *China Daily,* July 18, 2005, electronic document accessed at www.china.org.cn on July 10, 2006.

56. Norimitsu Onishi and Howard W. French, "Japan's Rivalry with China Is Stirring a Crowded Sea," *New York Times,* September 11, 2005.

57. As quoted in "China Confirms Sending Warships to E. China Sea," *Oil & Gas Journal,* October 10, 2005, p. 5.

58. "Oil and Gas in Troubled Waters," *The Economist,* October 2005, pp. 52–53.

59. See "China Taps Field for Natural Gas in Disputed Area," *Wall Street Journal,* April 6, 2006; and Masaki Hisane, "Japan's New Energy Strategy," *Asia Times,* January 13, 2006, electronic document accessed at www.japanfocus.org on January 24, 2006.

60. Joseph Kahn, "China and Japan Take Steps to Mend Fences," *New York Times,* October 9, 2006.

61. See Eric Watkins, "China, Japan Postpone Dispute Resolution Talks," *Oil & Gas Journal,* October 1, 2007, p. 26.

62. "Iran Is Accused of Threatening Research Vessel in Caspian Sea," *New York Times,* July 25, 2001.

63. See DoS, *Congressional Budget Justification for Foreign Operations,* FY 2005 (Washington, D.C.: DoS, 2004), p. 346; Global Security, "Caspian Guard."

64. Ismayilov, "Azerbaijan Ponders Russian Caspian Defense Initiative."

65. Vladimir Socor, "Moscow Hosts Three Secessionist Leaders," *Eurasia Daily Monitor,* November 20, 2006, electronic document accessed at www .jamestown.org on November 20, 2006.

66. David Holley, "Russia Puts Base Closures on Ice," *Los Angeles Times,* October 1, 2006.

67. DoS, "U.S. Assistance to Georgia—Fiscal Year 2005," July 29, 2005, electronic document accessed at www.state.gov on December 21, 2006. See also "Azerbaijan, Georgia Address Security Threats to BTC Pipeline," *Oil and Gas Journal Online,* January 23, 2003, electronic document accessed at www.ogj.pennnet.com on January 24, 2003.

68. See Edmund L. Andrews, "A Bustling U.S. Air Base Materializes in the Mud," *New York Times,* April 27, 2002.

69. See David Holley, "Russia Opens a New Base," *Los Angeles Times,* October 24, 2003; and Steven Lee Myers, "Russia to Deploy Air Squadron in Kyrgyzstan, Where U.S. Has Base," *New York Times,* December 4, 2002.

70. C. J. Chivers, "Central Asians Call on U.S. to Set a Timetable for Closing Bases," *New York Times,* July 6, 2005.

71. See Stephen Blank, "Beyond Afghanistan: The Future of American Bases in Central Asia," Central Asia–Caucasus Institute Analysts, July 26, 2006, electronic document accessed at www.cacianalyst.org on August 17, 2006; Joel Brinkley, "Rice Reaches Pact on Keeping Central Asia Base," *New York Times,* October 12, 2005; and Steven R. Weisman and Thom Shanker, "Uzbeks Order U.S. from Base in Refugee Rift," *New York Times,* July 31, 2005.

72. Vladimir Socor, "CIS Collective Security Treaty Organization Holds Summit," *Eurasia Daily Monitor,* June 24, 2005, electronic document accessed at www.jamestown.org on December 18, 2006.

73. See Craig S. Smith, "Putin Visits China in Hope of Strengthening a Strategic Axis," *New York Times,* July 18, 2000; John Pomfret, "Beijing and Moscow to Sign Pact," *Washington Post,* January 13, 2001; Erik Eckholm, "Power of U.S. Draws China and Russia to Amity Pact," *New York Times,* January 14, 2001; and Andrew Higgins, "Russia, China Show Old-Time Solidarity," *Wall Street Journal,* June 15, 2001.

74. Patrick E. Tyler, "Russia and China Sign 'Friendship' Pact," *New York Times,* July 17, 2001.

75. Grimmett, *Conventional Arms Transfers to Developing Nations, 1998–2005*, p. 10.

76. Ibid.

77. Mure Dickie, "Beijing and Moscow Hope Joint Exercise Will Strengthen Ties," *Financial Times*, August 3, 2005.

78. For background on these developments, see Klare, *Blood and Oil*, pp. 146–79.

79. As cited in David Holley, "Russia, China Team Up to Assail U.S. Foreign Policy," *Los Angeles Times*, July 2, 2005.

80. Gill and Oresman, *China's New Journey to the West*, pp. 5–6.

81. Ibid., pp. 7–8.

82. Ibid., pp. 8–10, 19–20. See also David Stern, "Beijing and Kyrgyzstan Hold Anti-Terror Exercise," *Financial Times*, October 15, 2002.

83. Gill and Oresman, *China's New Journey to the West*, pp. 6–7.

84. Chivers, "Central Asians Call on U.S. to Set a Timetable for Closing Bases." See also Lionel Beechner, "The Rise of the Shanghai Cooperation Organization," Backgrounder, Council on Foreign Relations, June 12, 2006, electronic document accessed at www.cfr.org on December 3, 2006.

85. As quoted in Fred Attewill, "Russia-China War Games Send Message to U.S," *Guardian*, August 17, 2007, electronic document accessed at www.guardian.co.uk on August 17, 2007. See also Isabell Gorst and Richard McGregor, "Russia Adds Muscle to Central Asian Summit," *Financial Times*, August 15, 2007.

86. Indeed, such cooperation was cited as a major objective in the "Declaration on Establishment of Shanghai Cooperation Organization," signed in Shanghai on June 15, 2001, and figures in other official documents. For texts of basic SCO documents and a chronology of its activities, visit the SCO homepage at www.sectsco.org. See also "Suppression, China, Oil," *The Economist*, July 9, 2005, pp. 35–36.

87. For a tally of these encounters, see "Chronology of Main Events" posted at the SCO homepage, www.sectsco.org. For discussion, see Ariel Cohen, "The Dragon Looks West: China and the Shanghai Cooperation Organization," testimony before the U.S.-China Economic and Security Commission, Washington, D.C., August 3, 2006, electronic document accessed at www.uscc.gov on August 7, 2006.

88. For a scholarly expression of this concern, see John J. Mearsheimer, "China's Unpeaceful Rise," *Current History*, April 2006, pp. 160–62.

89. This view is most vividly expressed in the Pentagon's annual assessment of Chinese military power. For example, the 2006 report indicated,

"China's dependence on imported energy and raw materials continues to grow. . . . PRC strategists have discussed the vulnerability of China's access to international waters. Evidence suggests that China is investing in maritime surface and sub-surface weapons systems that could serve as the basis for a force capable of power projection to secure vital sea lanes of communication and/or key geostrategic terrain." DoD, *Military Power of the People's Republic of China 2006,* p. 1.

90. Condoleezza Rice, "Promoting the National Interest," *Foreign Affairs,* vol. 79, no. 1 (January/February 2000), p. 56.

91. See Douglas Jehl and David E. Sanger, "New to Job, Rice Focused on More Traditional Threats," *New York Times,* April 5, 2004.

92. DoS "Joint Statement of the U.S.-Japan Security Consultative Committee," Washington, D.C., February 19, 2005, electronic document accessed at www.state.gov on December 10, 2006.

93. Jim Yardley and Keith Bradsher, "China Accuses U.S. and Japan of Interfering on Taiwan," *New York Times,* February 11, 2005.

94. DoS, "Rumsfeld Hosts U.S.-Japan Security Consultative Committee," Washington, D.C., October 29, 2005, electronic document accessed at www.state.gov on December 9, 2006. See also Thom Shanker, "U.S. to Reduce Troops in Japan and Strengthen Military Ties," *New York Times,* October 30, 2005.

95. DoS, "United States-Japan Roadmap for Realignment Implementation," Washington, D.C., May 1, 2006, electronic document accessed at www .state.gov on December 9, 2006.

96. For background and discussion, see Emma Chanlett-Avery, Mark E. Manyin, and William H. Cooper, *Japan-U.S. Relations: Issues for Congress* (Washington, D.C.: Library of Congress, Congressional Research Service, October 5, 2006), p. 9.

97. DoD, *The Military Power of the People's Republic of China,* Annual Report to Congress (Washington, D.C.: DoD, 2005), p. 2.

98. "U.S.-Japan-South Korea Military Coordination Targets China, North Korea," Kyodo News Agency, as published in *Japan Times,* March 9, 2006, electronic document accessed at www.japanfocus.org on March 21, 2006.

99. The Chinese buildup, she explained, was "concerning for those of us that had a responsibility for defending the peace in the Asia Pacific region, of which I would count all three." As quoted in Sundeep Tucker, "Hawkish Comments on China Give Rice Visit to Australia Added Edge," *Financial Times,* March 16, 2006.

100. See Dennis Shanahan, "Pacific Allies Aim to Include India in Security

Pact," *The Australian,* March 15, 2007, electronic document accessed at www.news.com.au on March 15, 2007.

101. "Australia and Japan Sign Agreement on Security," Associated Press, March 13, 2007, electronic document accessed at www.iht.com on March 14, 2007; and Isabel Reynolds, "Japan and Australia Sign Landmark Defense Pact," Reuters, March 13, 2007, electronic document accessed at uk.reuters.com on March 14, 2007.

102. See "Australia and Japan Make Security Commitment," *Sydney Morning Herald,* March 13, 2007, electronic document accessed at www.smh.com .au on March 14, 2007; and Reynolds, "Japan and Australia Sign Landmark Defense Pact."

103. For discussion, see Peter Alford, "Japan-Australia Cement Military and Economic Ties," *The Australian,* February 5, 2007, as posted at Japan Focus, electronic document accessed at www.japanfocus.com on February 13, 2007. See also Shanahan, "Pacific Allies Aim to Include India in Security Pact"; and Greg Sheridan, "Truth Crucial to Regional Security," *The Australian,* March 15, 2007, electronic document accessed at www.theaustralian.news.com.au on March 14, 2007.

104. As quoted in Keiichi Yamamura and Stuart Biggs, "Japan's Abe, Australia's Howard Sign Security Accord," Bloomberg.com, March 13, 2007, electronic document accessed at www.bloomberg.com on March 14, 2007.

105. As quoted in Steven Weisman, "Rice, in Indonesia, Supports Renewed Military Assistance," *New York Times,* March 15, 2006.

106. Ibid. See also Jane Perlez, "China's Role Emerges as Major Issue for Southeast Asia," *New York Times,* March 14, 2006.

107. As quoted in Michael Gordon, "Rumsfeld, Visiting Vietnam, Seals Accord to Deepen Military Cooperation," *New York Times,* June 6, 2006.

108. Office of the Press Secretary, White House, "U.S.-India Joint Statement," March 2, 2006, electronic document accessed at www.whitehouse.gov on March 12, 2006.

109. Vice President Cheney is also reported to have raised the possibility of including India in an expanded U.S.-Japanese-Australian alliance during his meetings with Prime Ministers Shinzo Abe and John Howard during his trip to Asia in February 2007. See Shanahan, "Pacific Allies Aim to Include India in Security Pact."

110. See, for example, Steven R. Weisman, "Rice Seeks Backing for Nuclear Deal for India," *New York Times,* April 6, 2006.

CHAPTER 9: AVERTING CATASTROPHE

1. To these, we should add the Bush administration's decision to deploy a battery of ballistic missile interceptors in Poland, a move supposedly intended to deflect future Iranian missiles aimed at Europe but viewed in Moscow as a first step in plans to incapacitate Russia's own ballistic missile deterrent. The Russians, in turn, have threatened to withdraw from the Conventional Forces in Europe Treaty—a landmark agreement that helped bring about the end of the original Cold War—and have embarked on other provocative counteractions, including the resumption of patrols by nuclear-armed bombers beyond Russian borders. See C. J. Chivers and Mark Landler, "Putin to Suspend Pact with NATO," *New York Times*, April 27, 21007; Gregory L. White, "Putin Threatens West Over Plan to Deter Missiles," *Wall Street Journal*, June 4, 2007; Thom Shanker, "U.S. to Keep Europe as Site for Deterrent to Missiles," *New York Times*, June 15, 2007; Kramer and Shanker, "Russia Suspends Arms Agreement Over U.S. Shield"; and Kramer, "Recalling Cold War, Russia Resumes Long-Range Sorties."

2. "Interview with New Chairman of the Joint Chiefs of Staff," *New York Times*, October 22, 2007, electronic document accessed at www.nytimes .com on October 26, 2007.

3. The basic tenets of the National Energy Policy (including Bush's supporting comments) are laid out in NEPDG, *National Energy Policy*, pp. vii–xv. For background and discussion, see Klare, *Blood and Oil*, pp. 56–73.

4. IPCC, "Summary for Policymakers," p. 5.

5. Ibid., p. 2.

6. DoE/EIA, *IEO 2007*, Table A10, p. 93.

7. DoE/EIA, *IEO 2007*, Tables A1, A5, A7, pp. 83, 88, 90.

8. Remarks of Sen. Joseph Lieberman to Council on Foreign Relations: "China/US Energy Policies: A Choice of Cooperation or Collision," Council on Foreign Relations, Washington, D.C., December 2, 2005, electronic document accessed at lieberman.senate.gov on December 5, 2005.

9. Shai Oster, "Chinese Official Calls on U.S. to Jointly Develop Oil Fields," *Wall Street Journal*, September 12, 2006.

10. "The U.S.-China energy engagement that I foresee could be, in one sense, the 21st century version of what arms-control negotiations with the Soviet Union were in the last century." Remarks of Sen. Lieberman to Council on Foreign Relations.

11. DoE, Office of Public Affairs, "Secretary of Energy Abraham Signs Agreement

with China's National Development and Reform Commission," May 13, 2004, electronic document accessed at www.doe.gov on January 12, 2007.

12. U.S. Energy Association, "Seventh U.S.-China Oil and Gas Industry Forum," Hangzhou City, China, September 11–12, 2006, electronic document accessed at www.usea.org on January 12, 2007.

13. Transcript of U.S. Delegation Press Conference, Third Meeting of the U.S.-China Strategic Economic Dialogue, Xianghe, China, December 13, 2007, electronic document accessed at www.treasury.gov on December 22, 2007. See also Ariana Eunjong Cha, "U.S., China Sign 10-year Agreement to Work Together on Environment," *Washington Post*, December 13, 2007.

14. Statement of Katharine A. Fredriksen before the U.S.-China Economic and Security Review Commission, "China's Role in the World: Is China a Responsible Stakeholder?" August 4, 2006, electronic document accessed at www.policy.energy.gov on January 12, 2007.

15. DoE/EIA, *IEO 2007*, Tables A5 and G1, pp. 88 and 187.

16. According to one estimate, even if all of the corn harvested in the United States was used to make ethanol, the resulting liquid would replace less than 12 percent of America's daily gasoline intake—and cause the U.S. food industry to collapse. See Alexei Barrionuevo, "It's Corn vs. Soybeans in a Biofuels Debate," *New York Times*, July 13, 2006; and Barrionuevo, "Rise in Ethanol Raises Concerns About Corn as Food," *New York Times*, January 5, 2007.

17. For discussion, see Lauren Etter, "Can Ethanol Solve the Nation's Energy Problems?" *Wall Street Journal*, June 17–18, 2006; and Etter, "Ethanol Craze Cools as Doubts Multiply," *Wall Street Journal*, November 28, 2007.

18. See Patrick Barta, "Jatropha Plant Gains Steam In Global Race for Biofuels," *Wall Street Journal*, August 24, 2007; John J. Fialka and Scott Kilman, "Big Players Join Race to Put Farm Waste into Your Gas Tank," *Wall Street Journal*, June 29, 2006; Andrew Pollack, "Redesigning Crops to Harvest Fuel," *New York Times*, September 8, 2006; and Matthew J. Wald and Alexei Barrionuevo, "Chasing a Dream Made of Weeds," *New York Times*, April 17, 2007.

19. In June 2007, the Department of Energy announced three grants of $125 million each to consortia of universities, national laboratories and private firms to develop pilot plants for the production of cellulosic ethanol. See Matthew Wald, "U.S. Is Creating 3 Centers for Research on Biofuels," *New York Times*, June 26, 2007. See also Angel White, "DOE Hopes for Cellulosic Ethanol Plant by 2012," *Oil & Gas Journal*, October 23, 2006, p. 30.

20. See Karen Lundegarrd, "The Other Alternative," *Wall Street Journal*, April 17, 2006.

21. Barrionuevo, "It's Corn vs. Soybeans in a Biofuels Debate."

22. On U.S. interest, see, for example, Monica Davey, "Governor Plans an Energy Shift for Illinois," *New York Times,* August 22, 2006; Susan Moran, "Biodiesel Comes of Age as Demand Rises," *New York Times,* September 12, 2006; and Ray Rivera, "Biodiesel Makers See Opening in City's Green Plans," *New York Times,* May 28, 2007. On China, see Eric Watkins, "UK Firm to Build Biodiesel Plant in China," *Oil & Gas Journal Online,* June 18, 2007, electronic document accessed at www.ogjonline.com on June 21, 2007.

23. Essentially, a fuel containing hydrogen is brought in contact with a negative electrode (anode) that blocks the passage of electrons, channeling them instead into a circuit that can be used to power an electrical motor; meanwhile, the anode allows protons from the hydrogen fuel to migrate through an electrolyte to a positive electrode (cathode), where they combine with the returning electrons and oxygen from the air to produce water as the sole waste product. See A. John Appleby, "The Electrochemical Engine for Vehicles," *Scientific American,* July 1999, pp. 74–86; and Lawrence D. Burns, J. Byron McCormick, and Christopher E. Borroni-Bird, "Vehicle of Change," *Scientific American,* October 2002, pp. 64–72.

24. See Steven Ashley, "On the Road to Fuel-Cell Cars," *Scientific American,* March 2005, pp. 62–69; Jeffrey Ball, "Hydrogen Fuel May Be Clean but Getting It Here Looks Messy," *Wall Street Journal,* March 7, 2003; and Matthew L. Wald, "Questions About a Hydrogen Economy," *Scientific American,* May 2004, pp. 66–73.

25. For discussion of hydrogen's promise and drawbacks, see Deffeyes, *Beyond Oil,* pp. 152–66; Jeremy Rifkin, *The Hydrogen Economy* (New York: Penguin, 2003); and Paul Roberts, *The End of Oil* (Boston: Houghton Mifflin, 2004), pp. 66–90. See also "Steps Toward a Hydrogen Economy," illustrated chart attached to Burns, McCormick, and Borroni-Bird, "Vehicle of Change," p. 70.

26. For discussion, see Marc Gunther, "Taking on the Energy Crunch," *Fortune,* February 7, 2005, pp. 97–104.

27. Amory B. Lovins, "More Profit with Less Carbon," *Scientific American,* September 2005, p. 74.

28. Ibid., pp. 74–83.

29. For discussion, see Lovins, "More Profit with Less Carbon," pp. 80–81; and Nicholas Varchaver, "How to Kick the Oil Habit," *Fortune,* August 23, 2004, p. 114. The ambitious solar project is described in Ken Zweibel, James Manson, and Vasilis Fthenak is "A Solar Grand Plan," *Scientific American,* January 2008, electronic document accessed at www.sciam.com on January 22, 2008.

30. Brad Stone, "A Subsidiary Charts Google's Next Frontier: Renewable Energy," *New York Times,* November 28, 2007.

31. See Lovins, "More Profit with Less Carbon," pp. 78–79, 81. See also Amory B. Lovins, et al., *Winning the Oil Endgame* (Snowmass, Colo.: Rocky Mountain Institute, 2004).

32. DoE/EIA, *IEO 2007,* Table A7 and A10, pp. 88, 93.

33. See Uchenna Izundu, "IEA Warns of Coal's Comeback in Energy Mix by 2030," *Oil & Gas Journal Online,* November 7, 2007, electronic document accessed at www.ogjonline.com on November 8, 2007.

34. For an assessment of the candidates' views on energy options, including coal, see Edmund L. Andrews, "Candidates Offer Different Views on Energy Policy," *New York Times,* November 28, 2007.

35. See S. Julio Friedman and Thomas Homer-Dixon, "Out of the Energy Box," *Foreign Affairs,* vol. 83, no. 6 (November–December 2004), pp. 71–82; and Cogeneration Technologies, "Integrated Gasification Combined Cycle," electronic document accessed at www.cogeneration.net on January 21, 2007.

36. For discussion of such techniques, see Dave Ball, Neeraj Gupta, and Bernhard Metzger, "Energy Industry Examining CO_2 Sequestration Options," *Oil & Gas Journal,* May 14, 2007, pp. 20–27.

37. On the F-T process, see Deffeyes, *Beyond Oil,* p. 85. On modern applications, see Matthew Wald, "Both Promise and Problems for New Tigers in Your Tank" *New York Times,* October 26, 2005; and Richard McGregor, "China Looks at a $24bn Coal-to-Oil Plan as Beijing Bets on Oil Price Staying High," *Financial Times,* September 27, 2005.

38. Recognizing the danger of a Sino-Japanese clash over energy, Minxin Pei and Michael Swaine of the Carnegie Endowment for International Peace have proposed an arrangement of exactly this sort. One way to reverse the downward slide in their relations, Pei and Swaine suggested, is for Beijing and Tokyo to forge a "regional energy consortium" with other Asian consumers and then "use their collective bargaining power to mutual advantage" in price negotiations with foreign energy suppliers. A Sino-Japanese energy partnership would be further bolstered by the prospect that Japan—"as the world's most efficient energy user"—could help China upgrade its own notoriously inefficient energy systems. Minxin Pei and Michael Swaine, "Simmering Fire in Asia: Averting Sino-Japanese Strategic Conflict," *Policy Brief,* no. 44, November 2005, Carnegie Endowment for International Peace, Washington, D.C., p. 7.

39. Joseph Kahn, "Japan Aims to Enlist China in Fight Against Global Warming," *New York Times,* December 29, 2007.

40. For background on this dispute, see Klare, *Resource Wars,* pp. 109–37.

ACKNOWLEDGMENTS

Those who know me well, know that I have labored long and hard to bring this book to fruition. To many who watched me work, it must have appeared that was essentially a solitary task, best performed in isolation from the rest of the world. But while it's true that I sometimes needed to hole myself up in my remote little study to pound out the paragraphs, I could never have completed this without the support, assistance, and encouragement of many individuals. This is where I get to acknowledge and thank all those wonderful people!

My first expression of gratitude goes to the two people most instrumental in bringing this book to press: my publisher, Sara Bershtel of Metropolitan Books, and my editor, Tom Engelhardt. I have had the great privilege and pleasure of working with both for many years now, and I couldn't have chosen a better team of colleagues. Sara provided crucial backing for this project at every stage of the process, and I am deeply grateful for her unwavering support and encouragement. Tom was my choice for editor from the start, and I am so glad that we were finally able to make it happen. Both provided crucial advice on everything from the overall structure of the book to chapter titles and word choices, and so in many ways their instincts and insights are reflected in the pages of this volume; to the degree that this is so, it a measure of the high esteem in which I hold them.

I also wish to thank all of the other people at Henry Holt and Metropolitan Books who worked with Sara Bershtel in bringing this book to press—some known to me, some not. Special thanks first to Megan Quirk, Sara's assistant, who helped in so many important ways. Among Sara's colleagues at Holt whom I've come to know, and wish to acknowledge, are Riva Hocherman, Richard Rhorer from marketing, my publicist Kate Pruss Pinnick, and finally, Kathy Andre, who always has a smile waiting for me. There are many others I've seen in the hallways who in some key way will contribute to the success of this book whom I *don't* know, but I'm well aware of your contribution, and I thank you.

Many other individuals played an important role in enabling me to write this book by helping with research, providing documents or information, or suggesting ways of framing certain points. Special thanks are due to Daniel Volman, for assistance on the chapter on Africa. Daniel has an encyclopedic knowledge of developments in Africa and was very gracious in making all that available to me when I set out to examine the competition for Africa's energy resources. Thanks also to Ed Connelly for feeding me with a constant stream of clippings, reports, and commentaries on the global struggle over oil assets—many have proved exceedingly valuable. I also benefited from two online journals published by good friends and colleagues: Japan Focus (www.japanfocus.org), published by Mark Selden; and TomDispatch (www.tomdispatch.com), published by Tom Engelhardt. I derived many valuable insights from articles that first appeared on these sites. I also wish to acknowledge two good friends, Jerry Epstein and Laura Reed of the University of Massachusetts at Amherst, who often listened patiently as I laid out the core concepts of this book and provided me with both encouragement and valuable feedback.

In my dedication, I thank the students at Hampshire College and the other members of the Five College consortium—Amherst College, Mount Holyoke College, Smith College, and the University of Massachusetts at Amherst. For the past three years, I have been teaching courses on "global resource politics" and "Asian security affairs" at these wonderful institutions, and have had the opportunity to test out my ideas in front of bright, interested, and engaged undergraduates. It can be hard to convey what a thrill (and a trial) it is to have your concepts tested in this way—to receive both affirmation when your ideas seem to make sense to inherently skeptical young adults, and discouragement, in the form of frowns and sharp questions when they don't. But I do want to say that this book has benefited immeasurably from this experience, and I am deeply grateful to all of the students who participated in these courses or who otherwise contributed in one way or another to the success of this book.

Finally, and most importantly, I want to acknowledge the loving support and encouragement of my partner, Andrea Ayvazian, and our son, Sasha Klare-Ayvazian. Even when I was by myself working in that little study in the back of our house, I was aware of their love and solidarity—and without it, I couldn't have persevered. As Sasha has gotten older (he's now a sophomore at Oberlin College), I've also benefited from our conversations over the state of the world, and *his* feedback on my ideas. I thank you both from the bottom of my heart.

INDEX

ABOUT THE AUTHOR

MICHAEL T. KLARE is the author of thirteen books, including *Blood and Oil* and *Resource Wars*. A contributor to *Harper's, Foreign Affairs,* and the *Los Angeles Times,* he is the defense correspondent for *The Nation* and the director of the Five College Program in Peace and World Security Studies at Hampshire College in Amherst.